Enlightened Duality

Essays on Art, Beauty, Life and Reality As It Is

Enlightened Duality

Essays on Art, Beauty, Life and Reality As It Is

Lee Lozowick

and

M. Young

Hohm Press
Prescott, Arizona

Cover art: "Madanagopala" by Nara Allsop
Cover design: Zachary Parker, Kadak Graphics, Prescott, Arizona
Layout and design: Becky Fulker, Kubera Book Design, Prescott, Arizona

Library of Congress Cataloging-in-Publication Data

Lozowick, Lee, 1943-
  Enlightened duality : essays on art, beauty, life and reality as it is / Lee Lozowick and M. Young.
    p. cm.
  ISBN 978-1-935387-02-2 (trade paper : alk. paper)
  1. Spiritual life--Hohm Community. I. Young, M. (Mary) II. Title.
  BP605.H58L687 2009
  299'.93--dc22
                            2009009158

HOHM PRESS
P.O. Box 2501
Prescott, AZ 86302
800-381-2700
www.hohmpress.com

This book was printed in the U.S.A. on acid-free paper using soy ink.

For Yogi Ramsuratkumar,
who demonstrated Enlightened Duality
in every fiber of His being
and continues to in every moment,
though His body is no more.

Diacritical marks on Sanskrit terms appearing in the text have been omitted for the sake of simplicity.

Contents

Foreword

*G*ood morning. Or afternoon or evening. The book which, or is it "that," you now hold in your hands, or hand as the case may be, is ostensibly about me—well, at least it has many essays of mine featured—and so when the author asked me if I would write a preface, after some deliberation, but not too, too much, I decided that I would put pen to paper and see what came out. So far, this is it. And being the intrepid trooper that I am, I am continuing, which continuation will inevitably lead to what follows.

I am continually pleased by the revelatory little facets that God has been so gracious to use me as a vehicle to reveal—pleased, that is, when I forget that it is God who is generating this current and, for a moment, actually imagine that it is me, well, "Meeeee," ta da! And one of the little phrases that most pleases me in such moments is "Enlightened Duality." The context and content of this little, and very significant, phrase is well considered in this book, and I would like to add that it is a crucial definition of Truth, of Reality, without which (and it is not "that") our attempts to finally and definitively grasp the answers to our primal questions must be frustrated. So I am very please that, at last—at last meaning that I have been requesting a book on "Enlightened Duality" for several, or at least a couple of years now—this consideration is now extant and has found its way into your hands, whoever you are. I sincerely hope that you, "dear reader," as M. Young is fond of addressing you in her text, are willing to deeply consider, wrestle with if you will, the exposition of this subject, "Enlightened Duality." I would like, if possible, before

I die, death being a cheap and easy way to say pass into another life cycle, albeit of very different form, have been convinced that my life's work, described in many such catch phrases as "Enlightened Duality"—a few examples being "Spiritual Slavery," "Draw no conclusions mind," and "be that which nothing can take root in," all of which are discussed in greater depth within the main text of this book—has not fallen on deaf ears or closed hearts. So I do, very sincerely, wish for this little bit of literature to find its way into your, dear reader, struggle and help, even in some small way, to ease that struggle a bit. I wish to be of service. And having said that, I understand, as fully as I can at this point, that my style is not for everyone, even if my teaching, the truth, is (for everyone). So when I am being put-offish, a highly developed skill of mine, if I do say so my double-Scorpio self, I do so, always, with a bit of trepidation and a tear almost in my eye, as I don't want to miss the possibility that one of the "put-offs" might just be the one whom could be most deeply moved, touched, by the very arrows that my style keeps from hitting their mark, their target in those individuals. Ah well, so be it, if it must which seems like it must as that is what is, at the moment. In any case, read on if you can and profit, please. I bow to you, adventurers and explorers, all.

Jai Guru,
Lee Lozowick
December 12, 2008
Prescott, Arizona

Preface

Twenty years ago in India, an elderly gentleman—a devotee of Lee Lozowick's Guru—said to me: "Why speak of such things like detachment? I am equally and deeply attached to everything—I feel such an affection for all things, and experiences, whether joyful or sorrow filled." Such must be the blessings of Yogi Ramsurat Kumar, for those very words that so impressed me all those years ago I find repeated by Lee in this wonderfully honest and invigorating book. "I am totally attached to Reality" says Lee—and, as it should be in the spiritual path, this extremely readable publication delivers the central thrust of importance to seekers everywhere: it is not answers that we should seek, for enlightenment, even if such a thing exists, is not a question. It is Reality that we should pursue—at the expense of our expectations, false perceptions and self images that we create.

Lee's discourses interspersed with Mary Young's inquisitive and informative essays form a perfect right brain–left brain balance. The tone of utter devotion is ever present, Lee's to Yogi Ramsurat, and Mary's to Lee. The tone of devotion that is frequently found in this book is a type that has not been popularized in the West: it is the devotion of the most excruciating type, the mood of separation, the mood of the broken heart, that forever keeps our mind, heart and attention gripped to the object of our devotion. There is an utter surrender that is required to navigate such a state, and such teachings are rare. As each decade progresses and the maturity of the seekers in the West evolves, the urgency for getting to the heart of the matter of seeking to live in Reality, and not bound by our illusions, grows more and more prevalent. This book can certainly be considered such an upgrade. It is filled with honesty, piercing insight and encouragement, and is a testament to the sincerity and total commitment of its authors.

Eddie Stern
Co-publisher, *Namarupa Magazine*

Foreword

by Robert Frager

I love the wonderful interplay of alternate chapters written by teacher and student in this book. They act as two mirrors reflecting each other, deepening potent images. Each provides different perspectives on varied topics and reflects some of the deeper aspects of the other. Looking at a mirror reflected in another mirror leads to an infinite recurrence, which isn't a bad thing. It might even have something to do with enlightened duality.

I'm writing this foreword mainly from the perspective of a Sufi teacher, a sister tradition to the Bauls. The position of Sufi teacher is a formal role and not necessarily anything more.

One day Rumi and his teacher Shams were sitting over tea and one of Rumi's dervishes ran up, dusty and exhausted, having travelled hundreds of miles to see Rumi. He fell to his knees, kissed Rumi's hand, and exclaimed, "Master, the sheikh you sent to us has passed away. Please send us another sheikh." Rumi laughed and said to Shams, "I'm glad he asked for a sheikh. If he asked for a dervish either you or I would have had to go!"

Like Lee I often get irritated, or worse, at those so-called teachers of nondualism who confuse Reality and reality. As the great Zen master Dogen once wrote, "The real and the ideal are like a box and its lid, like two arrows that meet and collide in mid-air." Focusing solely on either one and ignoring the other only leads to more delusion, not to mention confusion. And, as Dogen pointed out, you really can't have one without the other. Without the bottom of the box there *is* no lid; what was once a lid is just a useless piece of wood or metal.

As far as I'm concerned the most appropriate response to someone who claims, "Nothing is real. It's all a dream" is to smack them in the head. If they become upset you can remind them that if nothing is real they have nothing to be upset about.

My first spiritual teacher, Paramahansa Yogananda, wrote, "Yes, life is only a dream. But if someone hits your dream head with a dream two-by-four, you will have a dream headache. And unless you wake up, that headache will persist." Yogananda also wrote about a saint whose arm was cut off by mistake by an overzealous policeman who mistook him for a dangerous criminal. The saint pressed his arm back into his shoulder and continued on his way. I'd love to see any of those clever nondualists cut off a finger and then reattach it. Then I'd take them much more seriously.

My Sufi teachers have explained the veils of ignorance discussed by Lee are both real and illusory at the same time. They often quoted a famous *hadith qudsi,* an extra-Koranic revelation in which God says, "There are 70,000 veils between you and Me, but there are no veils between Me and you." For us the veils seem real, for God they are not. (By the way, in Arabic 70,000 means uncountable. In English the equivalent would be, "There are millions of veils." That's a lot of illusion!)

I love Lee's term "Spiritual Slavery." Muhammad (peace and blessings upon him) is traditionally referred to as a "slave and a Messenger of God." The Prophet is considered a perfect human being so how can we begin to follow his example? It's easy to say "Spiritual Slave." But it's incredibly hard to become one.

Some Sufi teachers say a dervish should give up all self-will and become like a corpse in the hands of the corpse-washer. But we can't even let someone lift our arm without either resisting or "helping." Entering the state of Spiritual Slavery is as great a transformation as the metamorphosis of a caterpillar into a butterfly. It's a long, tough road and it requires unbelievable patience and perseverance. This kind of patience is illustrated in an old Turkish Sufi saying, "The Path is like chewing an iron peanut." This book provides an authentic taste of that peanut.

I've learned a lot about love from my Sufi teachers. For the Bauls human love leads to divine love and my teachers have said the same. But how can we turn human love to divine love? Most of us can't even manage human love. Unfortunately, we generally refuse to understand how incapable of love we are.

As a psychologist (which I am in another life), I'm convinced that Freud emphasized the wrong Greek myths. We are not so much plagued by the sexual issues of Oedipus or Elektra as by the egotism of Narcissus. To make a long myth short, Narcissus was a gorgeous Greek youth. Almost everyone fell in love with him, but he turned them all down and eventually was cursed by the goddess Nemesis (someone you really don't want to upset). She cursed Narcissus to fall in love with himself since he refused to love anyone else. The next day Narcissus saw his reflection in a pond and became so entranced with his image that he couldn't stop staring. He ended up starving to death by the side of the pond.

Of course Narcissus didn't really fall in love with himself, but with his image. This is one of our greatest challenges—to stop our self absorption and become capable of love. A teacher serves as a model of someone who is capable of love. A teacher is also someone who tries to kick us out of our self-absorbed trance so we have a chance at becoming mature human beings. (The alternative is to starve to death emotionally and spiritually.) This book provides a rich and nuanced picture of a real teacher and how he lives in the real (dualistic) world.

Lee's comment on the essence of Buddhism is wonderfully illuminating. He writes, "Pain is inevitable, but suffering is optional." I can't tell you how much nonsense I've read over many years, nonsense that distorts this simple, basic truth of Buddhism. I love Lee's comment, and I certainly intend to steal it when I teach. And I can't think of a higher complement than that.

There are many other priceless nuggets in this book. I hope you enjoy turning them up as much as I have.

Robert Frager
March 25, 2009

Acknowledgments

I first heard my teacher, Lee Lozowick, use the term, "Enlightened Duality," almost twenty years ago. This phrase, in its simplicity and directness, spoke to a very deep instinct in me at the time. Finally, years later, this project came up. Like so many tasks the guru gives, this book has offered me the opportunity to move into a deeper practice of the teaching that Lee has given.

Initially I planned a book of essays taken from Lee's discourses, which I would edit and introduce with a brief commentary. As other projects were finished and the time drew near to focus my attention on this task, I mentioned to Lee in the spring of 2008 that I needed more material for the book—that was when he changed the game plan. "I don't want more transcripts. *Most of the book*," he emphasized, eyeing me in a way that seemed to somehow size up the irony of the situation, "should be written by *you*." My face must have registered the shock I felt, since I had been so sure this project would be a fairly simple process of editing and co-ordinating material from Lee's talks into essays.

My mind made a quick search of my current resources for such a task: How to venture into such a vast terrain? To compound it all, when would I write this book? I travel a lot. Out of the last twelve months, I had been on the road with my teacher for about six of those, mostly in France and Europe, but also in India—Gujarat and Bengal. Once again I was poised at the doorway of departure into the world of travel-as-sadhana on my teacher's caravan.

Still not sure how to proceed, I accompanied Lee and some of his students in May 2008 to Montana just before embarking on a long summer in Europe. We were there for a two-week visit at Trimurti, the ashram of Lee's student, Purna Steinitz, where Lee was recording his third solo CD, "Tongue of Poison, Soul of Love." I realized that this interlude would offer some quiet time to begin the writing; in fact, it had the potential to be more like a retreat than most of my travels. And so, I sat down to write on a spring morning in Montana, knowing that the book would have to be finished in about ten months.

I was spurred on by a burning desire to do justice to the depth and richness of the teaching and practice that Lee has given to his students and the inspiration that he so fully provides by virtue of his life. I have personally found great value in receiving the teaching from both teachers and students of many traditions, and so it was my wish to open a small window, in these commentaries on Lee's teaching, through which a reader from any Path might take heart, find succor and a living, breathing, real-life spiritual practice—not some fantasy or self-righteous, white-washed, holier-than-thou message we've all heard far too many times.

In order to write on this rather daunting subject, I had to go into my own practice and witness there. What became obvious right away was that the secrets of Enlightened Duality do not yield themselves to the practitioner who does not cultivate an active and conscious reliance upon the nondual—the truth of unity. The fast road to the nondual vision of life is to embrace impermanence in a direct way. It's very easy to talk about impermanence—to mouth truisms like, "all things pass" or "this too shall pass" or speak euphemistically about the cycles of life. To cultivate an in-the-moment practice of conscious relationship with impermanence is a lot more gritty and bloody. It involves grief and loss and walking a razor's edge which demands that we drop the cast iron shackles of attachment and identification.

Like the burning grounds of Varanasi or Tarapith, courting impermanence forces one to take death as an advisor, as Don Juan

Matus[1] put it, which leads inexorably to facing death (especially of one's self and one's loved ones) and the inherent emptiness of phenomena. The grip of primal passions can tear our lives to shreds; under the spell of ferocious identification with these forces, we are compelled to face our own helplessness. Again and again we must make the journey to the charnel ground within ourselves, where we look into the emptiness of the void—the subject of one of the essays herein.

Making the decision to write from within daily life was a big relief, because it is in the creative heat of everyday life that something *interesting* can happen; if we are receptive, our practice will yield the secrets of a passionate, full-on engagement with the multi-dimensional spectrum of Life. In a practice that is founded upon the potentials of Enlightened Duality, everything is grist for the mill; this is true of any genuine spiritual Path, because the more authentic and true our practice is, the more human we become: the more clarity we have about our strengths and weaknesses, the more compassion we have. Although a strictly intellectual consideration of Enlightened Duality could be useful in many ways, I have held to the possibility that the writing could transmit something of the living teaching and the real practice. This was a far brighter star to guide my boat across the uncharted waters of this project.

In the early summer 2008 during our ashram celebration of Guru Purnima, Lee gave a talk, which he began by reading a quote from author Tom Robbins. In closing, I would like to share that quote, for it gave me tremendous inspiration and a jolt of energy to proceed on this project:

> *There is evidence that the honoree [Leonard Cohen]*
> *might be privy to the secret of the universe, which, in*

---

[1]   Don Juan Matus is the central character of Carlos Castaneda's books, beginning with *The Teachings of Don Juan: A Yaqui Way of Knowledge.*

case you're wondering, is simply this: everything is connected. Everything. Many, if not most, of the links are difficult to determine. The instrument, the apparatus, the focused ray, that can uncover and illuminate those connections is language. And just as a sudden infatuation often will light up a person's biochemical sky more pyrotechnically than any deep, abiding attachment, so an unlikely, unexpected burst of linguistic imagination will usually reveal greater truths than the most exacting scholarship. In fact, the poetic image may be the only device remotely capable of dissecting romantic desire, let alone disclosing the hidden, mystical essence of the material world.[2]

This project has engaged me quite passionately in the desire to discover "the hidden, mystical essence of the material world," for the very idea of such a possibility is rooted in the precept of Enlightened Duality. Robbins' insight into the power of the word accurately describes the prime reason I have included a number of Lee's poems to his master, Yogi Ramsuratkumar, as the ground of inspiration for deeper consideration of the teaching.

I would particularly like to acknowledge the important contribution of the teachings of Arnaud Desjardins and his guru, Swami Prajnanpad, Chögyam Trungpa Rinpoche and G.I. Gurdjieff, all of whom are referenced liberally in this work. A note of thanks is due also to Robert Svoboda, Robert Beer, Tom Robbins, and *Namarupa* magazine, who are quoted in these essays. Many thanks are due to Nara Allsop for his painting, "Madana Gopala," which appears on the cover, and for his line drawings—"Kiriti Mukha," "Gandharva,"

---

[2] Tom Robbins, "Leonard Cohen," *Wild Ducks Flying Backward: The Short Writing of Tom Robbins*, pages 78–79.

and "Flower"—which appear throughout the text. I would also like to thank those who transcribed many of Lee's talks and worked on this manuscript in various capacities—particularly Becky Fulker, Nachama Greenwald and Paula Zuccarello.

Above all, my deepest gratitude belongs rightfully to my guru, Lee Lozowick, for the opportunity to write about his teaching and his life, and for all that he has given, and for the possibility of radical transformation in his company.

M. Young
December 21, 2008

Introduction

The purpose of these essays is to present the teachings of American Baul master Lee Lozowick on Enlightened Duality in a different way than they have been previously offered. At the same time, we have engaged a subject of such infinite potentials that mere definition or academic wrangling is inadequate. What we have are a series of essays that explore the terrain of our theme in a highly nonlinear fashion, offering an unfinished and sometimes cryptic map which points toward practice on the spiritual Path within daily life. It is very much like taking a large, multifaceted jewel and looking at it from many different directions: each facet reflects its own specific hue, brilliance, clarity or opaque quality.

When we read Lee's spoken words, which have been rendered into the essays that follow, we are given the opportunity to extract his teachings on Enlightened Duality that are often concealed within a dharma teaching or obscured by virtue of provocation or sheer ordinariness in the teacher's presentation. When we hear the dharma, we are given a view of what is possible in spiritual practice: to live firmly rooted in an integrated awareness of the nondual nature of reality, and from this place, to enter into a conscious relationship with the Immanent Divine manifested in the play of opposites, or the dual nature of the phenomenal world in which we find ourselves.

The Baul tradition calls this *sahaj samadhi*: an "open-eyed" ecstasy of unitive awareness that endures, even while living in ordinary ways. Unlike classical *advaita* teachings, Lee asserts that unity is the law *and* that distinctions, which we experience as the manifest world, are Real. The paradox (if there is one) is that distinctions are real, but they are real when perceived through the seamless circle of no distinctions. Many of us have experienced this perception of Reality as it is, but rare and precious is the abiding, direct knowledge of this realization, in which the individual lives in a state of union with the Divine while remaining easefully, naturally, functionally in relationship with the world of appearances: *sahaj samadhi.*

Therefore, the highest aim of spiritual practice is to integrate mystical experience and insights into nonduality into ordinary life. Most of us will agree that the greatest challenge in this regard is found in human relationships. Because the digestion and integration of spiritual principles and mystical ascent into the whirl of everyday life and relationships is so difficult to achieve, the experience of the practitioner who is living the Path on a day-to-day basis becomes a rich field of work. For this reason, the practitioner's perspective, found in these essays, may be of value to anyone journeying on the spiritual Path in a particular tradition.

One of the themes of these essays is a consideration of the pitfalls of contemporary spirituality. As a field of human endeavor, spirituality is not separate from secular life and bears the same degradations of aggression and narcissism, sometimes obviously and sometimes in ways that are subtle but devastating to an authentic life. While we wait breathlessly for an ecological disaster that looms over us like an apocalyptic shadow, the assault on nature by science and technology—ruthlessly wielded worldwide by corporations and governments devoid of conscience—continues unabated. Masses of people are spellbound by glamorous appearances and cheap eroticism. We relentlessly pursue anything that distracts us from the deeper mysteries of the self, holding out the false hope that we might escape death and avoid a taste of the unknown at any cost.

A particularly dangerous complexity has taken over our lives. If humanity is going to survive on this planet, we must return to the simplicity and wisdom of the *sahajiya* (natural) way. The only lasting and true solution is a return to the dharma, and yet, ancient traditions all over the world have suffered under the onslaught of scientific materialism and globalization, falling prey to the marketing mentality that profits so fantastically from passing fads. Sacred mantras, yoga and meditation techniques are sold like cheap wine and fast food on the internet, while false teachers and teachings proliferate along with the fear of cults that taints the public mind.

Because of these many factors, traditional teachers and practitioners are concerned with the purity and preservation of pristine teachings; some, like Lee Lozowick, are speaking out in an attempt to educate seekers in the importance of making distinctions as to what is true and what is hype on the spiritual Path. Perhaps most unsatisfying are the popular, fast-spreading teachings of nondualism—referred to in this book as *neo-advaita,* in order to make an important distinction between these teachings and the respected, time-honored teachings of classical Advaita Vedanta. Teachers who advocate nondual philosophy too often hold out false promises of a fast and easy enlightenment—and therefore a certain relief from suffering—but at the same time leave us adrift in the tumultuous ocean of the world without a life raft, without skillful means (to use a Buddhist term), and without the unerring instinctual wisdom of the heart.

The failure of neo-advaita and other contemporary nondualistic teachings that are not rooted in the wisdom of tradition is perhaps most poignant and tragic in the world of human relationship. Our intimate and familial relationships reflect the state of the world: highly unstable, with little or no foundation of a deeper context that engenders trust, commitment, or the nobility of sacrifice for the other, postmodern relationships are riddled with the illusion of separation, the desire for power, manipulation and domination. We have lost sight of the sacred, of the dharma or cosmic law that says we are in fact one and can live as an interdependent, interconnected whole. However, to overlay a strict teaching of nonduality on the troubled lives of our contemporary times without offering practical help for navigating the dualistic world of daily life is a certain suicide of the soul—a declaration that will be explored in depth in the pages to come.

There is a great deal of practical wisdom to be found here for one who yearns for a path through life that is transforming and yet honors the innate dignity and potential of the human incarnation. Many people today feel a deep pain of loss of the sacred—that which is universally and eternally true. Paradoxically enough, as strange as it may seem in these times in which complexity reigns supreme, it is toward simplification (a road rarely taken these days) that we must turn, toward the easeful, natural way of the innate non-separative self that is offered in this book. The Bauls of Bengal, an eclectic, predominantly Hindu sect that we will hear a lot more about in the coming pages, call this the *sajah manush*—the natural human being who lives from the foundation of Organic Innocence, to use one of Lee's teaching phrases that will become very familiar in the essays that follow.

And so, here is the offering of Lee's teachings juxtaposed with one student's reflections, reveries and research, both academe and experiential, that came and went in the ongoing impermanence of all things which arise and subside. The text unfolds in many directions, moods and pathways that reveal the intention of the message as a whole; at the same time, each essay has its own integrity and stands on its own authority. It is my sincere prayer that this book will bring the reader enjoyment, insight, useful inspiration, sanctuary in the storm, and maybe even some humorous moments, to enhance and nourish your practice and your Path. May you take courage from knowing that others walk beside you.

And finally, the only true way to embark is by offering all praise and gratitude to the lineage gurus, Papa Ramdas, Yogi Ramsuratkumar and his spiritual son, Lee Lozowick, who are the Sun and Moon of my heart. Anything of value in this effort is due to their blessings; that which is in error is solely my own. Jai Guru!

M. Young
March 21, 2009
Prescott, Arizona

Nondualism and the Spiritual Path

Lee Lozowick

I have tremendous difficulty with people who use ultimate truths—like the truth of nondualism—out of context, in circumstances in which those ultimate truths can do damage. In very simplistic terms, nondualism means that there is nothing that is independent of anything else; everything is continuously arising and subsiding, sustained and connected to every other thing that is continuously arising, being sustained and disappearing. If we have an organic or tacit understanding of nondualism, then we live based on this viewpoint. If you understand that no thing is independent, then every thought, every breath, every emotion, every action, every gesture is a continuous part of your adherence in and demonstration of Reality. This is not an intellectual understanding to be discussed with articulate and powerful language but a literal life foundation, rock solid and reliable, that we stand on relative to everything that we do. Reality is continuous; to live on any other basis—no matter how articulately we can consider nondualism—is to be a hypocrite.

Reality is not chaotic in the way that we understand chaos. Reality is not random. It is not paradoxical in the way that we might be confused by things that don't make sense to our linear mind. Reality is absolutely and fundamentally lawful in every moment, under every circumstance, in every time and every place—meaning not just on Earth among the human race, but everywhere there is life and everywhere there isn't life as well. Reality functions according to the laws of relationships within the spontaneous and natural arising of all things. G.I. Gurdjieff, the Russian mystic who lived in France much of his life, said that everything is living. Everything is alive, even things that we might consider to be inorganic, like stones and metal, planets, the moon and the sun.

In Tibetan Buddhism there are three vehicles: Hinayana, Mahayana and Vajrayana. In the Nyingma lineage, the highest tantric practice of Vajrayana is *dzogchen*; in the Kagyu lineage the ultimate practice of Vajrayana is *mahamudra*. I resonate more to the Kagyu lineage and mahamudra than to dzogchen, but when you're practicing life being Real as it is, how much difference between them can there be? Even though we call one dzogchen and one mahamudra, ultimately they are the same thing.

The Tibetan Buddhists say that essentially all things are empty; however, things arise in their essential emptiness. The arising of those things generates other arisings, and those arisings generate other arisings, and that is how we have what we call a world, a solar system, and a universe. There is a continually ongoing process of "codependent origination," as the Buddhists say, meaning that all things work—or arise—in concert with all other things.

Ultimately everything functions cyclically; things arise in patterns, even if we don't understand the pattern. In the Hindu trinity, there are three primary deities: Brahma, Vishnu and Shiva. Brahma represents creation, Vishnu represents maintaining and sustaining, and Shiva represents dissolution. Obviously, everyone is born, lives and grows—some of us in happier states of mind than others, some of us healthier than others, some of us more creatively than others. Nonetheless, here we are; we are born, we live, and eventually we die. Everything arises, is sustained, and subsides, so that one of the laws of Reality is that things function cyclically. Sooner or later everything returns.

In spite of the fact that everything functions lawfully—things arise, are sustained, and subside—everything is essentially empty, which means that no thing has more essential thingness than anything else. When we're talking about essential thingness, every *thing* is exactly the same. However, if you are in the business of real estate, and one piece of property is two hundred thousand pounds and the other piece of property is four hundred thousand pounds, and you're going to get a commission based on how much the client spends, obviously you would rather make the commission on a four-hundred-thousand-pound piece of property. If you are an ashram renunciate, wouldn't you rather give your favorite charity the profit on the four-hundred-thousand-pound property? Of course you would.

In ordinary circumstances we can recognize that there are distinctions to be made in the world of things, and rightly so, even by virtue of talent or by virtue of flair. In the world of things, every beat-up old Ford is not a Z4 BMW. And yet, in spiritual magazines there are people who nobody ever heard of making statements on nonduality such as: there is no difference between murder and serving another. Under certain circumstances, yes, all things are essentially empty. This is a universal truth. However, to apply universal truths in a world of neurosis and illusion and suffering and confusion and doubt is *criminal*, in my view of things.

The *neo-advaita* spiritual scene in the world today stems from Nisargadatta Maharaj and Ramana Maharshi, both of whom are probably turning over in their graves because of what it has become. I recently read a manuscript in which the author advances a criticism towards the vast majority of those who are teaching nonduality, which is that these teachers take everything away, but they don't put anything in its place. Egos are knocked down and people's minds are blown, but there is no consideration of living life. In neo-advaita teachings they say, "Nothing is real, it's all a dream, nothing exists." Yes, that is part of the formula, but it's not the whole formula. If somebody gets only that part of the formula, it can be profoundly disorienting. If someone realizes that life is meaningless, and they don't have a stable base upon which to continue to live, serve, and love, then it can create psychosis instead of bliss. I think that is a very healthy criticism.

U.G. Krishnamurti was a fascinating and very useful character who died earlier this year.[1] My one hesitancy about his work was that he was absolutely brilliant at crushing *everything*, but he left nothing for anyone to stand on—not even nothing, that's the point. In the context of the great traditions, if everything is taken away, but what is left is the Void of God—the emptiness of the Universe—that is not nothing. Many neo-advaita teachers only know Advaita Vedanta to some degree; they are all very intelligent, so they put the rest together mentally, but because they haven't found the answer experientially, they can't offer the complete realization.

It is unquestionably true that the essential condition or state of existence is nondual. All things are essentially empty, and existence as we know it (and as we don't know it) is, as a condition of being, nondual. This is unarguable. If you study the scriptures in any tradition, and if you dig deeply enough into the esoteric mysticism of any tradition—Christianity, Judaism, Buddhism, Sufism, Hinduism, shamanism—you will find the same ultimate truth: the essential

---

[1]   U.G. Krishnamurti died in 2007.

nature of all things is emptiness. On the ultimate level the essential equity of all things is just that—equitable.

In the essential, ultimate nature of things, everything is exactly equal. Sex with a goose and sex with the most charming, beautiful, responsible, loving partner of your own species is the same. The most beautiful diamond or ruby is no different from an ordinary rock. Diamonds are very common these days, so let's use an example of something that's not so common: rubies, emeralds, and sapphires of perfect, true color are extremely rare, because most stones are colored by gem experts using chemicals or heat. In the ultimate sense of things, a rare, perfect emerald or sapphire is not different than some piece of granite or cement you find on the highway. But you and I would have to be blithering idiots to believe that, at the level of distinction, at the level of personal experience, there is no difference between a perfect ruby and a piece of cement; no difference between a loving partner who respected you as a human being, who is affectionate and tender, patient and understanding, and a raging bitch—man or woman, because men can certainly be bitches.

At the essential level of things, yes, everything is *shunyata*—empty, pure, pristine, perfect, flawless, without definition. One cannot editorialize or define or discuss or philosophize relative to the perfect, essential emptiness of all things created and all things uncreated—and, that's not the end of the story. In the Heart Sutra, one of the most sublime Buddhist texts, there is a small formula, hidden in one of the lines of poetry: "Form is emptiness, emptiness is form." "Form is emptiness" is easy to get, but that is not the whole formula. If you do not integrate the second half of the formula, which is "Emptiness is form," into perfect nondual essential relationship with the first part of the formula, "Form is emptiness," then you get stuck spinning your wheels, and, particularly if you are a teacher, you become the blind leading the blind, generating lots of questionable karma.

You and I suffer; not only do we suffer like animals who have nervous systems suffer, we suffer far beyond the way an animal could possibly suffer, because we have, as Gurdjieff said, three brains. We suffer in profoundly more dynamic ways than any other life form on this planet because we are three-brained beings—the only three-brained beings that exist in organic form on the face of this planet.[2] If our health is good and we are financially secure, and we have great children and a loving partner and wonderful parents and everything is fine, we will still suffer because other people suffer. When you read in the newspaper about an earthquake somewhere, and all the children whose parents have been killed and the homes that have been destroyed, even if you have the emotions of a stone, something in you resonates and suffers for the tremendous heartbreak, pain, and struggle of other human beings.

Yes, form is emptiness, and that's an easy part of the formula to get, because we suffer. This form suffers. This form is undeniably, even shockingly, fragile. It can be snuffed out instantly—anywhere, at any time. Even though you might fight the notion that you are going to die someday, this body is tentative. When Shakyamuni Buddha said, "All life is suffering," that is what he was talking about. He didn't mean that there was no beauty in the world, no satisfaction, no love, no tenderness or kindness and compassion; he meant that inevitably we must go down, disintegrate, die, along with all our greatest glories. For most of us, first the teeth go, then the nails, then the skin, then the hearing, and then the eyes. Most of us are not going out like the characters in "300," the movie. You and I are not Spartans! We are not going to get up and say to our team in the office, or wherever we work, with great zeal and enthusiasm, "Tonight, we die!"

"Form is emptiness" is an easy part of the formula to get, because this body is form. All of us have met with various disappointments in our lives: somebody we love has died unexpectedly, or we've tripped and fallen and hurt ourselves or broken a bone, or caught some virus.

---

[2]   A definition of Gurdjieff's teaching on the three brains or three centers in the human being appears on page 17.

Very recently, a week ago, the child of a friend of mine died. This is something you can live with and you can deal with, but you never get over it. Never. Maybe we've experienced something like that, and we know the reality that the physical world and this body is form, and form is essentially empty. Somewhere in us we know that this body is never going to "win." Of course, we win some money, we win some good health, we win some love, we win some beauty, we win many wonderful things—but ultimately this body is not going to win. Yes, we have our triumphs, we win many battles, but we're not going to win the war.

In a very real sense, my Work is to educate people about the pathologies of the Path, because every positive spiritual truism has a pathology. That is very important to understand: Every positive, hopeful inspiration has a pathological potential, including the experiential realization of "Form is emptiness," because if you stop there and do not go on, you have made a tragic error. Sooner or later only one of two things can happen: you get stuck in the realization of "form is emptiness" and animate its pathology; or, you get shot out of "form is emptiness" into the experiential domain of "emptiness is form."

Every positive, inspirational revelation has a pathological potential; that is a very important piece of information if you want to progress on the Path, because every step in that progression has a pathological potential. If you are not aware of that pathological potential, the probability of falling into the pathological side rather than into the other side of realization is extremely high, whether you're a teacher, a student or just a regular human being walking down the street, trying to support your family and love your kids and your partner. So, one of my functions is as an educator. It's very important to me that, as an educator, I'm able to communicate what it is that I have to educate people about, and that's what we're talking about tonight. We're talking about Ultimate Reality—the truth of nonduality—and the essential emptiness of all things, and we're also talking about the absolutely true reality of thingness, of distinction, of what I call Enlightened Duality.

If you had a Picasso hanging on your wall, and some scribbles that your cousin gave you, would you give the Picasso away if it was worth three million pounds? Maybe, but not without having a very clear distinction about what you were doing, because you know that even though essentially those two things are equal, in the reality of distinctions, those two things are not equal.

One of Werner Erhard's sayings is: "Reality is hard and persistent and will knock you on your ass every time." He didn't say, "Illusion is hard and persistent," he said "Reality," with a capital R. That means Reality will not stop and cannot be stopped. "Reality is hard and persistent and will knock you on your ass every time," is street language for "Reality will cut you down to size," every time. We are human; we have been born, and we have grown; we are being sustained to various degrees of effectiveness and efficiency, and we will also dissolve. The essential you will not dissolve; the you that is empty and continuous with all of Reality will not be dissolved—that part of you has never been born, is not being maintained, and will never die. Death happens in the domain of distinctions, which is the domain of Reality, and Reality will knock you on your ass, every time—without exception.

As an educator it's important for me to communicate information and be understood. I want that information to be used, not just written down in a notebook and put in some biography of Lee Lozowick, the western Baul master, someday after I die. For that information to be used, I have to communicate lucidly on more than one level, because verbal communication is only one aspect of communication—it's a superficial level of communication that hits the mind, is co-opted by the mind, and then the mind locks it away. The mind says, "Got it," and that's the end. You have to be able to unlock the mind, so that information is able to reach the organs and the cells and the nervous system and the muscles.

You may know from doing body work—bioenergetics, Rolfing, or the Alexander Technique—that you can't easily get to the information that is stored in the muscles, because the mind has stored it in a filing system and does not let any other part of the body have it. The essential you has to learn how to unlock the mind so that the information the mind is storing can be accessed by the part of your system that needs that information at any given time—muscles, bones, organs, blood, cells, brain and subtle bodies. In fact, the subtle bodies are more important than the physical body. The mind takes information that your subtle bodies need and does not allow you to use that information.

So, you have to understand that part of accessing this information is realizing that every spiritual event has a pathological potential, and if you know that, the saying is: "Forewarned is forearmed." Then when you advance on the Path and you're exhilarated by your breakthrough, that little voice can say to you, "Beware, because this event has a pathological side. Do not fall into that trap." If that little voice is articulate enough and communicative enough, then you will not fall into the pathology. If the little voice is not strong enough, the probability of becoming pathological is very high. If you do not bring the formula of the Heart Sutra—"Form is emptiness, emptiness is form"—into its sublime perfection of completeness in the context of the essential nondualism of Reality, then you cannot progress on the Path beyond the pivot point: the tangent between "Form is emptiness" and "Emptiness is form."

London
June, 2007

Enlightened Duality

M. Young

*E*nlightened Duality is a teaching that provides us with the practical means and wisdom to navigate through daily life with respect and innate regard for the sacred nature of the world. When recently asked the direct question, "What is Enlightened Duality," Lee answered, "Enlightened Duality is the Reality of existence; we can rest in it as a *perception*." He went on to say, "Enlightened Duality is Reality as it is." Enlightened Duality can be found in the teachings of countless numbers of realizers and expounders of dharma: Ramakrishna, Vallabhacharya, Chaitanya and the great bhakti traditions. As we will explore in the essays that follow, insights into Enlightened Duality can be discovered in ancient scriptures, in prose elucidations of dharma, and especially in poetry. Aspects of Enlightened Duality are particularly well-covered in the vast plethora of tantric Hindu, Sufi and Vajrayana Buddhist literature. Lee often uses the language and terms of Vajrayana Buddhist dharma teachings in his presentations, because of his great love of Buddhism, which has an elegance and straightforward simplicity that is most efficacious and useful.

There is a definite kinship between the Buddhist Heart Sutra— form is emptiness; emptiness is form—and Lee's teaching, which is nondual at its core. At the same time, Lee's teaching of Enlightened Duality is unique; it encapsulates the whole formula of the Heart Sutra and goes beyond, into the unabashed theism that is true of the lineage of Lee's guru, Yogi Ramsuratkumar, and his guru, Swami Ramdas. It is the fevered dulcet tone of loving God that is the crucial difference between *dzogchen* or *mahamudra*, which is at the heart of Vajrayana tantric practice, and Path of Enlightened Duality. Lee's teaching transmits a particular flavor—a certain sweet *rasa* that can be savored—that imbues the Path of Enlightened Duality with a strong thread of bhakti found in the passion and certainty of the Bauls for the relationship with the living Lord—the personal Beloved. Because of this, the tenet of Grace is placed in a central position throughout these pages, sounding a clear note that clearly reflects the living embodiment of Yogi Ramsuratkumar.

In the Hindu classic, *Tripura Rahasya: The Secret of the Supreme Goddess*, we find even the fierce, nondual, ascetic yogin Dattatreya making the following declaration of Grace and the importance of worshipping the Supreme Goddess, Tripura Sundari, to Parasurama:

> *"Listen! Rama, I am now telling you the secret of accomplishment. Of all the requisites for wisdom, Divine Grace is the most important. He who has entirely surrendered himself to the Goddess is sure to gain wisdom readily. Rama! This is the best of all the methods."*[1]

Dattatreya goes on to tell Parasurama, "Therefore bhakti yoga is the best of all and excels all else." He explains further that those *jnana* practitioners—those who seek liberation through knowledge alone—find themselves in the "state of perfection" of *sahaj samadhi* only when they are calm or composed in their investigation into the nature

---

[1]   *Tripura Rahasya: The Secret of the Supreme Goddess*, translated by Swami Sri Ramananda Saraswathi, pages 158–159.

of Reality. At other times, they are subject to "interludes of imperfection," even though they also experience interludes of wholeness.[2]

Anyone who practices honestly on the spiritual path knows quite well what is meant by "interludes of imperfection" that can be particularly troubling after an experience of a profound inner resting in Reality as it is. When focused attention and conscience are brought to this friction of opposites within, it is called *sadhana*, or, as Lee often prefers, "the Work," to borrow a term from the Russian mystic, G.I. Gurdjieff. In sadhana, the tension between these experiences of clarity and illusion sometimes becomes so extreme that the inner war must be directly addressed and confronted if we are to progress in any satisfactory way upon the Path.

Indeed, war is everywhere we look. Our whole planet is at war, from the U.S. and Iraq to Africa, Burma, Tibet and China, to the war against nature waged by the technocrats who rule. If we are honest, we know there is a war going on within ourselves. Our inner state is a mirror of the outer world: the "yes" versus the "no" of confusion, doubt, and gnawing insecurity; the growing dread in the world around us; the vacillation we experience daily over whether or not to sacrifice personal comforts and ideas of a private happiness for the good of another. We are at war within and we are also at war with those around us: we fight, argue, and compete for dominance and control. We are often irritated or at odds with those who directly oppose us or who have gotten under our skin, even when—in the face of global suffering—our petty struggles are glaringly revealed as paltry, selfish self-obsessions.

Life is so distracting and seductive that we forget who we are on a moment-to-moment basis. As Dattatreya explains, "Pure Intelligence illumining has cast a veil of ignorance of Her own over all. Her true nature is evident only after removing this veil by discrimination."[3]

---

[2]   Ibid, page 160.
[3]   Ibid, page 158.

One moment we are alert, present, compassionate and in relationship with others and our environment, then—despite our most profound insights into the oneness of all Life—the very next moment some random catalyst may cast us head long into a bout of greed, lust, anger, jealous rage or resentment. One moment there is harmony and a sense of rightness from the ground to the sky, a gentle relaxation of the primal knots within, and the next moment the basic psychological disease of our times has taken over and we are lost in the illusion of separation, armed to the teeth and defended against Reality as it is.

Nonetheless, moments of real insight arrive when we least expect them, but they are easy to miss because psychological defense mechanisms buffer us from the experience of Reality as it is. Those mechanisms have many different forms and manifestations; for example, just as we can have denial about inner darkness, we can also have denial about inner light—and both must be made conscious. When we begin to take responsibility for the totality of who we are, both bright and dark, then it becomes a lot less likely that we will make decisions based on childish reactions driven by our basic psychological strategy.

Sadhana, in which we are making both bright and dark conscious, is an ongoing gesture of gratitude for the gift of incarnation. The more awareness we have accumulated on the Path, the more we come to inhere in the intrinsic dignity and intrinsic nobility that is actually who we are as beings of basic goodness, or Organic Innocence.[4] We can begin to trust our wise instincts and impulses because we have

---

[4]   The phrase "intrinsic dignity and intrinsic nobility" is quoted from the teaching of Swami Prajnanpad, introduced in the West by Arnaud Desjardins; "basic goodness" is quoted from the teachings of Chögyam Trungpa Rinpoche; these two teaching precepts are highly complementary and are often used interdependently in this book with Lee's phrase, "Organic Innocence."

Jeremy Hayward provides a succinct definition of Chögyam Trungpa Rinpoche's teaching on basic goodness. The tenet of basic goodness pervades the Shambhala teachings given by Trungpa Rinpoche and refers to the tacit, basic

greater internal unity as a foundation from which acceptance, trust, compassion and service may arise. This is the natural function of the native self; it is the formative stage of the wise sage who will come to flower in the ripening and fruition of karmas.

Again and again we must turn toward the teaching and the company of the wise. When we encounter a living teacher and a living dharma, we can feel a resonance in the cells of the wise body. A living truth is revealing, healing, deeply satisfying, sometimes provocative or profoundly unsettling. It may shake the ground beneath our feet, in fact, and yet the nature of Reality is ultimately graceful. The living teaching and the teacher transmit Grace—which catalyzes a process of healing and harmonizing. Spiritual healing is basically what the Path is about.

It is possible to taste, feel, know and directly experience the truth of Enlightened Duality. It is an experience that is known with the intelligence of the heart, which informs the entire body and is not limited to the physical heart itself. It is possible and even likely that we are often having experiences of this awakened state, but we are not noticing it. We are too distracted, seduced, and fascinated with

---

awareness of human nature which is underlying all preconditioned concepts, judgments, ideas, or cultural attitudes and norms that have indoctrinated our worldview, including what we consider to be good or bad. Awareness is basically pure before this overlay: "This unconditioned aspect is equivalent, in Shambhala terms, to the basic nature that is pointed to in Buddhism by the terms emptiness and luminosity/joy." It is from this basic, pure ground of awareness that we may act as human beings with kindness and compassion, and from which we may create cultures and societies that nurture and empower the expression of this underlying truth of human nature. *Warrior-King of Shambhala: Remembering Chögyam Trungpa,* page 177.

arising phenomena to notice our own underlying state of being. The primary aim of spiritual practice is to come to abide or inhere consciously in this state of Realness.

In sadhana, there are moments all along the way that offer a glimpse of Enlightened Duality. These moments are extraordinarily feeding to the soul. They are food, nurturance of a very profound kind. We can profit greatly on the Path if we become aware of these moments when egoic concerns of survival, control, power, and dominance are swept away—melted into the shadows as if they never existed at all. We are delivered of our ordinary burdens in what Lee calls a "free moment," in which we are resting in the disposition of enlightenment, and we can say with complete sincerity, "This is Real." There is a naked experience of whatever is arising, which may be full of feeling—from joy to sorrow—or completely empty, void-like, and yet ecstatic: as the Buddhists say, emptiness and bliss. When these states arise, it is a moment of Assertion—a dharma term given by Lee that we will explore in some depth because it is central to any consideration of Enlightened Duality.

Lee has instructed his students that one may enter into the perception of Enlightened Duality by means of spiritual practice: specifically, Assertion, Enquiry,[5] and the practice of kindness, generosity and compassion, which the Buddhists call cultivating skillful means. These are practices that, when engaged over time, move one into an awareness of the world in which opposites are objectified. Assertion in particular is considered to be the fundamental declaration of Reality as it is. Any approach to the Path of Enlightened Duality must begin

---

[5]   Enquiry is one of the three core practices given by Lee to his students. Enquiry uses the phrase "Who am I kidding?" to investigate the nature of experience as it is arising in any given phenomenon as thought, feeling, emotion, mental or physical perception. The aim is to arrive at a penetrating insight into Reality as it is. The other two core practices are Assertion and the Heart Breath.

with this instruction to consider what Lee calls Assertion, which is best characterized by the statement, "Just This."

Just This is a practical way of articulating the moment of Assertion, while at the same time it is not Assertion per se nor is it a mantra or phrase to repeat as a form of practice. Assertion is an inner condition; it is an entirely interior state of being, of Enlightened Duality. Similar to *mahamudra* and *dzogchen* in Vajrayana Buddhism, Assertion is the beginning, middle and end of the Path, and that which we return to again and again. It is the spontaneous, radical insight into the nature of Reality.

In Assertion we consider the declarations "Just This" and "This is Real," which describe Enlightened Duality. Just This is a statement that asserts the perfection, completeness, fullness and emptiness of what is in any particular moment. When a moment arises in which we are aware of the fundamental truth of Reality, the egoic fixation relaxes and the being is naturally awake. Arnaud Desjardins describes this state with the phrase, "What is, as it is, here and now."

Just This is fortuitous in its simplicity; it articulates everything as an all-embracing, open-ended statement. As an Assertion of nonduality, it affirms the oneness as well as the emptiness of all phenomena; as an Assertion of Enlightened Duality, it affirms the fullness and potent distinct realness of every aspect and element of life. Assertion is the declaration that this moment now is complete and true.

Assertion is best understood placed within the holistic matrix of core teachings given by Lee, which will be explored throughout this book, including: Spiritual Slavery; Enlightened Duality; Organic Innocence; the Primacy of Natural Ecstasy; the Great Process of Divine Evolution. The totality of the teaching cannot be compartmentalized or divided up; it is holistic, a fabric of interconnected, interdependent truths that, woven together, form the whole. How can we separate the sun from the stars? Nothing is separate, and at times, the unified field of Reality comes profoundly into focus, as it does in the specific teachings of any authentic path. In pondering and living these teachings, one revelation leads to another.

Lee's original proclamation of Spiritual Slavery literally erupted after the awakening event that catalyzed his teaching work in 1975.[6] For the past twenty years, Lee has consistently refused to call this event "enlightenment." He prefers to speak of "a shift of context" which rendered him into a state of Spiritual Slavery—a term that contains the seed, flower and fruit of realized nonduality and Enlightened Duality. Nonduality is implicit in this term because Spiritual Slavery describes a *sunya*, a divine emptiness, which is filled and moved solely by Divine Will as It moves in the Great Process of Divine Evolution—another phrase used by Lee since the early years of his teaching. The very implication of movement, fullness and action necessitates duality—a dualism that springs out of unity. A Spiritual Slave is a slave precisely because of a perfect unity with the Divine as It manifests through the Will of God.

The statement "The body knows," which refers to Organic Innocence, is of great importance to the practice of Assertion and the perception of Enlightened Duality, for the fruition of practice is only possible through full embodiment. We are meant to be embodied beings—spirit in matter. Until we have passed beyond the veil of bodily death, we perceive Reality through the precious vehicle of the human body, with all of its potential for transformation of being. Enlightened Duality is therefore also very closely related with Organic Innocence and the Primacy of Natural Ecstasy, which describe embodiment, incarnation or spirit in matter.

What does the body know? Everything. It is the body that recognizes the innate truth of Enlightened Duality. It is of vital importance

---

6   An exploration of Lee's teaching on Spiritual Slavery is provided in Appendix I.

that practice be brought into the body, which is Organic Innocence. The body is capable of the most profound Assertion and the revelation of Reality; the body is the accurate arbiter of what is true or false in ordinary daily events. Tribal and indigenous people the world over know the certainty of these fundamental truths; great sacred cultures have risen based on the truth that the body knows. This is a secret that is not so secret at all—in fact, it is so obvious that one wonders why we would even need to consider it at all.

But, we must urgently ponder these principles, because the more we become star-struck by science, progress, technology and tools of the mind, the more we are separated from the profound instinctual wisdom of the body itself. We are so enthralled by technology that the human race is fast losing all relationship to the natural world and therefore to the solar system and cosmos. Spiritual practitioners are no different than anyone else in this regard: cell phones, computers, the unwise use of the internet, and technological gadgets rule our lives while the technology of agribusiness and use of fossil fuels are destroying the ecology of Earth. Too often we are more interested in these deadly seductions and distractions than in the life of the body, which weeps for its exile from earth, air, fire and water—from sun, moon, sunset, sunrise, winter, fall, summer and spring.

To enter into the perception of Enlightened Duality, we must return to the truth that is native to bodily life. Living fully within our bodies will lead us, sooner or later, back into *relationship* with the Earth, with plants, minerals and animals, with human beings, with the vast array of Creation, and with the Divine. In the amazing gift of Enlightened Duality, we discover what it means to be real.

"Life is real only then, when 'I am'." This is the title of a book written by G.I. Gurdjieff, the Russian mystic who developed what he called "The Fourth Way" of spiritual development.[7] Every great system of spiritual evolution has a teaching—a dharma—and a method or series of techniques or yogas, practiced within the context of an intentional life, whose aim is the realization of the "I am" that exists prior to all conditioning, birth, death and appearances of change and impermanence. When we practice Assertion, we are affirming the existence of this "I am," the *atman* or primordial self, as well as its unity with all life, which is a realization of nonduality. "Life is real only then, when 'I am'" is a succinct statement of Enlightened Duality, in which spiritual evolution moves into a mystery that brings the dance of opposites—which we call Life—out of veiled illusion and into the strong radiance of Reality.

To realize this requires some work. Gurdjieff states unequivocally that we only become an individual—a unique expression of the Divine—when we have become real through the process of inner unification. Eastern scripture and philosophy refer to the falling away of false identifications and *kleshas* (afflictions) which reveals the atman, the eternal self, shining at the center of awareness. Classic *advaita* teachings state that there is no distinction between one self, or atman, and any other self or aspect of existence.

From the perspective of Enlightened Duality, while it is undeniably true that there is only One—we are continuous in our intercon-

---

7   Very simplistically, in Gurdjieff's method of self-development, the "I am" is cultivated through an arduous process of self-observation and the integration of the many disparate "I's" that make up the human personality into a single, unified "I." When one begins to function as an integrated individual, an "I am," the three centers of thinking, feeling and moving—what he called the "three brains of a three-brained being"—begin to work together as a harmonious whole. Furthermore, Gurdjieff says this individual self must be built through extreme super effort. When the unified "I" has been forged, life becomes Real.

nected sameness—and there is only God, we are also created beings gifted by the act of Creation. Each one of us is unique: not special, not better or worse than others, merely unique. It is simple but not as easy as it sounds because, although we are each unique, we exist as that unique awareness when our innate blueprint of being is brought to life through a journey of becoming—whether that journey is called "super efforts" or "yoga" or "spiritual practice" or sadhana or "bringing Woman to Life," to use a phrase from E.J. Gold.

When the false selves fall away and the "I am" is stripped bare of modifications, embellishments, conditioned responses and needs and hopes to survive bodily death, then Reality informs perception of its immanent and impermanent truth. There, in the apex of a mystery, our essential emptiness and essential fullness is revealed. From that inexplicable potential, something real may arise within the world of form. The self that perceives at this moment of awareness is the same as every other self, and yet it can be experienced as a unique "I" that perceives an Enlightened Duality, in which arises the endless potentials of subtle and gross forms. In the Hindu tradition, the one who is living in the condition of liberation from the veils of illusion is called *jivanmukta*—a being (*jivan*) who is liberated (*mukta*). It is a word that hints toward the potential for a unique individuality that may exist beyond the realization of the nondual atman. These are considerations that we will return to in much greater depth in proceeding essays.

The realized self is the awakened experience of *what is*. Lee asserts that Enlightened Duality is a state of consciousness—a field of experience or point of view—in which the impermanent, ephemeral, passing and essentially empty condition of dualistic arising is objectively real in the moment. It is realer than real. Enlightened Duality only happens in the present moment—now. The mind cannot dally in the past or project toward the future and at the same time have the direct experience of Enlightened Duality. As Lee often says, mind cannot wrap itself around this as an idea; only the body can embrace and embody this potential. Of course, this is rhetorical until we are taken by the exquisite and raw experience of realness in the world of forms, until we have a direct knowledge, an epiphany of Realness—a moment that is penetrating, so hot and bright, or piercingly sweet, rare or full of sorrow, in which clarity is the quality of seeing and feeling in a brilliant view of our own experience.

One Gold Coin

Lee Lozowick

*A*n ultimate truism would be: The world is perfect as it is. Everything is just as it should be. A pathological relationship to that truism would be to shrug our shoulders and say, "I guess there's nothing I can do," which is like lying down and letting Reality roll all over us. What is, is, as it is, here and now, and every gesture we make is an action, so we can't *not* act. To be passive in the face of need is a pathological act.

Yes, duality is an illusion, and whoever doesn't know that it is an illusion is living in their reality, their truth. If we can help relieve their suffering in the world of their truth, we have done a very great thing. We don't have to make distinctions such as: Is this act helping God or not helping God? Is this an absolute act or a relative act? Attempting to make those distinctions is a waste of time and energy. Everyone who has been on the receiving end of an act of kindness, generosity, affection or love knows what it feels like to be *touched* by human goodness. Even if the actor is not enlightened, even if the actor is not acting for the right reason, even if the actor has selfish motives, when the act itself helps relieve suffering, God bless it.

Someone who is ignorant can be related with in his or her ignorance. If someone is identified with duality, to walk up to them and say, "Your suffering is an illusion, man. It's only your mind—get over it," is absolutely ridiculous. Some of you have probably tried that with your partners. How far has it gotten you, especially if they are not on the Path? "Honey, you don't need to suffer like that. You are creating all of this." If you tell someone who is identified with what they're creating that their creation is unnecessary, of course they're going to be a bit aggressive.

So, we search for the clarity of wisdom and knowledge of Reality. When we discover the truth, it seems so complete, so final, that we don't understand that there is more—not more quantitatively, but more qualitatively. The view can be: I'm struggling with practice and I'm working with these ideas *and* serving wherever I can, however I can, even though in the world of illusion, progress and change are illusions. That is what Jesus meant when he said, "Render unto God what is God's and render unto Caesar what is Caesar's."

In the Bible, Jesus and his disciples went into Jerusalem. In those days they had to pay a tax to get into the city. (These days to get into the city, you only have to pay a small part of your sanity!) So, they went to the city, and when the tax collector asked for money, the disciples of Jesus were righteously outraged: "This is the Messiah! The Messiah doesn't pay tax! C'mon man! This is God on earth!" The disciples started to get a little riled up, and they wanted to beat up the tax collector, but Jesus stopped them. They wanted to do something in the moment without any idea of the severity of the consequences, which is something disciples often do.

When he said, "Render unto Caesar what is Caesar's, and render unto God what is God's," Jesus was making a teaching on multiple levels. He was saying, "This guy doesn't know who I am. This guy is just the tax collector. He's just doing his job; give the guy a break.

Relax, guys." In those days, on one side of the coin of the realm there was a picture of Caesar, and on the other side of the coin there was some kind of statement about the all-knowing perfection of God or something like that. In the end, the disciples of Jesus gave the tax collector a gold coin.

Obviously if Mary had been there she would have slapped some sense into those guys! But she was back at the camp cooking for everybody, because all the disciples were too proud to cook. They had to walk by Jesus' side: "Grrr! . . . *Our* master. The Messiah! The King of the Jews!" The disciples were too stupid to know the politics of their times—they were dealing with the Romans for Chrissake! Did they think these Romans were going to understand what "King" means in the spiritual sense? When Herod called Jesus "King of the Jews"—sarcastically—he knew he had to kill him. Herod, as selfish and eccentric as he was, was not stupid enough to think that he was bigger and stronger than the Romans. Like many politicians today, for Herod it was a choice between giving up Jesus or losing his job—except that politicians today are afraid of corporations, not the Romans. No politician is going to lose his job for mere ethics!

Jesus was not insecure, unlike me, who's insecure and feels he's got to explain everything. He offered his students and disciples parables, and he didn't *explain* them. He let them figure them out for themselves, and those who actually figured out what Jesus was really teaching were the genuine Christians; the ones who didn't figure it out created the Church. It's that simple. "Render unto Caesar what is Caesar's" is a very important teaching; there is no paradox in it whatsoever. There is *one* coin—that's the esoteric teaching. There are not two coins; there is only one coin, and it is a gold coin, with Caesar on one side and God on the other. Therein is the entire teaching of duality and nonduality, of unicity and multiplicity, in one parable.

If we're thinking about God as the Absolute, it is useful not to super-impose human qualities and characteristics on our concept. When Yogi Ramsuratkumar called God "Father," which he did all the time, it was a manner of speech. He wasn't under any illusion that God as Absolute is in any way anthropomorphic. Even to say that God is all-merciful and all-loving is a manner of speech, because for God to be merciful and loving, for God to have qualities, God has to be a *thing*, and God isn't a thing.

When we superimpose even the most majestic human qualities on God, we might be confusing an issue that we're attempting to clarify, like in Judeo-Christianity, "the God of our fathers," or "the God of punishment." We read the story of Job, and it's very confus-ing. A lot of people think, "How could God, who is all-loving and all-merciful, do such a thing?" That is the God of our fathers—the patriarchal, punishing, judging being. God is not a being. Whenever we are seriously talking about God—not just having a conversation and using manners of speech for the convenience of conversation—we try not to give qualities to That which is not an object, even if the qualities are sublime, like mercy and compassion.

Yogi Ramsuratkumar often spoke of God as "Father in Heaven." He was educated in a Christian school, as were most educated Indians of his age. He couldn't be bothered with articulations; all conversa-tion was peripheral to what was actually going on, which was his transmission of Reality. His use of the phrase "Father in Heaven" was not a literal definition of God, as if God were something or some-one, or masculine or parental or anything like that. It is a conve-nience—a convention—and that's all. The Absolute has no children; the Absolute is absolute!

You cannot understand the relative if you distinguish the relative from the Absolute. As long as we are even unconsciously creating division, we cannot resolve what, to the divided mind, is an irre-solvable paradox. There are answers to your questions, and they are clear, but they cannot be translated into a linear dialogue. The only answer to such questions is to *be* that which we want to define in language, in which case the language we are using to solve the problem becomes meaningless.

Here is an example: We are always asking questions about the suffering in the world. Yes, there is great suffering in the world, and we want to somehow justify or make sense of it. There is no need to justify or resolve it; it is only the mind that needs justification and resolve. There is suffering in the world, and we don't need to split philosophical hairs to find some resolve for that. We just need to accept that it is true. At the level of the Absolute, is there a divine intention behind suffering? No, there is no divine intention, because the Absolute is not a "thing" that has intention. The only reasonable question is, "Can I do something about suffering? Can I relieve some of the suffering in the world?"

We may ask, "What about love?" Look at Nature. We might think when we look at animal mothers and their babies that they love their babies, but they don't love their babies. Animals don't think like that. It's pure instinct—survival of the species. Listen: Love is a great concept. I love the idea of love. It is very consoling. It's sweet, it's tender, it's beautiful, it's heartwarming, it's nurturing. It's everything good and beautiful. I recommend relaxing, because if you pursue love to its ultimate end on the Path, you are going to find out there is no such thing as love, and we don't need to do that. We are human, so let us keep at least one illusion, and let it be love, but, from the platform of the Absolute, love has no reality.

Unless, of course, you are able *to live* from the position of the Absolute; then everything in the relative takes on some reality—love, suffering and all the rest. So, instead of pursuing our philosophical questions, which can only lead to frustration or disillusionment, more suffering and more heartbreak which you cannot resolve through any mental exercise, no matter how smart you are—put your attention on the Absolute, because energy follows attention. When we find ourselves in a position of the Absolute, then the answers to our questions become clear, but we realize that those answers are nothing that possibly could have been answered on the level of rational conversation. So, leave us this one comforting illusion of love, please! It's such a wonderful one. And, when we have transcended our identification with the relative through identification with the Absolute, there is no problem, no question, and the answers are clear.

Hauteville, France
July 2007

Heart on Fire: The Bauls of Bengal

M. Young

Walking across the tarmac at the Kolkata airport in late December, 2007, my senses were inundated by the thick, haunting atmosphere—a collision between the cool misty morning air and a heavy pall of gray smog. On the way into the city, we passed dust-laden tropical canopy and glistening pools, where people squatted with bronze pots at the edge of the tank to get water or wash clothes. Having just arrived from the urban conflagrations of Mumbai, Varodara and Ahmedabad, I was feeling acutely sensitive to the decline of sacred culture and natural environments that is evident in the cities of India today. To my Western sensibility, it seemed improbable that this water, littered with refuse and darkly glowering, could be fit for any use. For the Bengalis, it is still sacred.

Even with the ubiquitous influence of Western techno-culture, Kolkata is a place of ancient rhythms and flows. The first strong impression was that this is Kali's playground; Kolkata is a city in which the *ista devata* is alive and thriving, where shrines to Kali Ma adorn every other street corner. There she resides in ecstatic four-armed form with lolling tongue and primordial eyes, beautifully adorned and freshly garlanded with marigolds and red hibiscus flowers; ghee lamps burn brightly at her feet in the smoky, soot-blackened air while people hurry past, wrapped in shawls against the chilly night air.

In Kolkata, you would do well to pay your respects to the Mother Goddess as soon as you arrive, and indeed, Kalighat was calling me. Kali's influence brings the transient nature of all things into sharp focus on the streets where life unfolds, where her images remind us that this fragile existence—miraculous in its exquisite beauty but also raw and cruel—is ephemeral.

After making *yatra* (pilgrimage) to Dakshineswar and Kalighat, Kolkata's most ancient Kali temple,[1] I turned to the primary mission of this sojourn into West Bengal: encounters with the Bauls.

I was traveling in Bengal with Lee and his blues band, Shri, who were being hosted by Purna Das Baul for a two-week tour. Shri was bringing traditional American blues and rock & roll to Bengali audi-

---

[1]   Dakshineswar is the Kali temple built in 1847 by Rani Rasmani, a wealthy, liberal woman of influence. Sri Paramahamsa Ramakrishna served there as priest, tending the presiding Kali deity at Dakshineswar and living on the temple grounds for over thirty years, until his death. Kalighat is one of fifty-two *shakti pithas* in India—the sites where parts of Sati's body fell to earth during Shiva's dance of grief. Fifty-one of these pithas are marked by temples, such as Kalighat. The legend of the shakti pithas has its origins in the *Rig Veda* (X, 61, 5–7) and was further elucidated in the Puranas. In the most popular version Sati was the daughter of Daksa Prajapati and the wife of Siva. Daksa was celebrating a great sacrifice to which neither Siva or Sati was invited. Sati was greatly insulted and went to her father's sacrifice uninvited, where she threw herself into the fire and perished. When the news of Sati's death reached Siva, he became furious and hastened to the scene with his many attendants. Enraged and grief-stricken, Shiva destroyed Daksa's sacrifice, extracted Sati from the fire, then left to wander over the earth in a mad dance with her dead body over his shoulder. His rage was threatening the balance of the three worlds, therefore the gods became concerned. Vishnu stepped in and threw his discus, Sudershan chakra, at Shiva, striking Sati and chopping her body into many pieces that then fell to earth. The places where pieces of Sati's body fell to earth are said to have become pithas—holy seats, altars or abodes of the Mother Goddess, where she dwells with a form of her husband Shiva.

ences in ten concerts in the Kolkata area, some in conjunction with Purna Das and his son, Dibyendu Das. Along the way we found ourselves connecting with Bauls from places as diverse as the vast, teeming city of Kolkata to rural West Bengal and Shanti Niketan in Birbhum. Wherever Baul musicians gathered to play their songs and dance there was a sense of freedom and elation, and yet, as Lee commented, "If there is no yoga, there is no Baul."

The Bauls are an excellent entry point into any consideration of Enlightened Duality, because their philosophy and sadhana is a natural expression of that perspective. This book, in fact, would not be complete without a rousing and passionate consideration of the Bauls, particularly in light of the fact that Lee considers his teaching, sadhana and way of life to be the Baul way as it has arisen in the Western world.

Because of their freedom-loving lifestyle, use of intoxicants, humanitarian idealism and penchant for music and dance, Bauls are sometimes referred to as the "hippies" of West Bengal. While it is true that Bauls are poets, singers, dancers, mystics and mavericks, most of all they are *sadhakas* who encode their way of spiritual development not in books and texts but in poetry, song and dance. They often disagree with each other on important aspects of practice, dharma or spiritual clan, although there are a few things they seem to agree on, such as radical reliance on the guru and *deha-tattva*, or the truth in the body. Iconoclastic and revolutionary in many ways, their path is called *ulta*: going against the common flow of society. Their nonconformist message of reclaiming the natural wisdom of the body has tremendous relevance to the great issues of our postmodern times, in which we live as if we are separate from nature—a belief that effectively severs us from direct knowledge of Reality as it is. As Osho Rajneesh once said:

In the beginning the whole humanity must have been like the Bauls. Even now you can watch it: every child is born a Baul, then later on he is corrupted. Every child is again born as madly in love with life, but we cultivate him, we prune him, we don't allow him spontaneity of being. We condition him, give him a certain character . . . . To be a Baul nothing is needed. In fact, the moment you need nothing, you become a Baul. The moment you are unburdened and you don't possess anything, any past, you are a Baul . . . . Nobody creates [the Bauls]; they happen. They are a part of nature.[2]

Those who are called "Bauls" are part of a unique, syncretistic path that centers around esoteric practices including classic tantric yogas of breath and sex and a very earthy brand of mysticism. Bauls have been wandering the villages of rural Bengal and Bihar for over five hundred years, bringing inspiration and joy to the often besieged lives of common people through their ecstatic song and dance. The word "Baul" in Bengali has been said to derive from the Sanskrit, *vatula*, meaning mad, affected by the wind. Baul practice involves taming the inner "winds" of the body, but the depth to which Bauls engage life in the raw, free from the veils of conditioned social proprieties, and relationship with the Beloved or ista devata—through relationship between man and woman and within the human body itself—yields a state of divine madness. One who has attained this coveted madness is called *khepa*.

The Bauls are synthesizers par excellence. They have a strong connection with the Sufi fakirs of West Bengal, particularly in their search for the Beloved, which the Baul poets often refer to in *sandhya-bhasa*, or highly symbolic twilight language, as "the Man of the Heart," or "the unknown bird," or simply as Lord Krishna, sometimes

---

[2]   Bhagwan Shri Rajneesh, *The Beloved, Volume I*, pages 282 and 285.

symbolized by the full moon. Scholars often claim that the Baul path is a blend of tantric Sahajiya practice (both Buddhist and Vaishnava) and devotional Vaishnava Hinduism, but the Bauls themselves are unwilling to be defined. They remain free to use the imagery of Krishna, Radha, Kali, Shiva and any other iconography that inhabits the poetic flight of their imaginations. The true Baul is a skillful yogi who engages a profound *sadhana* and Elysian inner life expressed in his or her music, poetry and dance.

The Baul message of the divinity within the human being— *manur manus* or "the Man of the Heart" discovered through the *sahaja* (easy, natural) way—has brought inspiration and a healing balm to ordinary people who face a mighty struggle in life's many vicissitudes. The Baul way offers an accessible path to liberation to the many who feel the weight of stultifying religious and caste hierarchies. Rebels and often outcasts, the Bauls shun caste distinctions and the dogmatic creeds and formal rituals of conventional Hindu religion, which they call *anuman*, "hearsay," "hypothesis" or "secondhand gossip." Instead, they seek *bartaman*—a direct experience of the divinity that resides within the human body. In the bartaman way, there is no need for the intervention of brahmin priests and complex rituals; bartaman is intricately linked to the inherence in the *sahaj manush*, or natural man, or *aadhar manush*, the essential man, in which the sadhaka realizes his or her innate capacity to experience God, both formless and in form.

After Rabindranath Tagore popularized the Bauls in the early part of the twentieth century, they began to capture the attention of musicologists and ethnographers, not only among scholars of both East and West, but in artistic circles as well. In the late sixties Albert Grossman introduced Bob Dylan to Purna Das Baul, which marked the beginning of numerous Bauls making their way into the West to perform before audiences in America and Europe. This kind of attention on indigenous music and musicians has resulted in the same kind of change that has occurred all over the world, where Western values and technologies have compromised or destroyed the integrity of traditional cultures and environments. Friend of such luminaries as Dylan and the Rolling Stones, Purna Das Baul—son of the great Baul yogi, Naboni Das—has become well-known by some and loved as the wise elder "Baul Samraj," or king of the Bauls. Purna Das is an inspired singer and accomplished yogi in his own right, but unfortunately, today many who don the iconographic garb—ochre dhotis, patchwork robes, long hair tied up in topknots then wrapped turban-style—and play the *ektaras, anandalaharis* and *duggis* of the Bauls are merely ambitious entertainers.

The original songs of great poets such as Lalan and many other composers continue to transmit the Baul spirit whether the performer falls into the camp of entertainer or yogi. Still, I find the entertainment performances vastly different than the extraordinary moods and ambiance that rises from the heart of the true Baul who sings and dances with a heart on fire. These authentic performances carry a mysterious transformational power: their music combs our minds free of tangles and grit, making way for an ecstatic communion to arise between musicians and listeners. Parvathy Baul wrote of the *bhava*, or divine mood, created through Baul music:

> *The voice of the Baul is "one flow" of song alone, with the Bhāva. When a performer handles two musical instruments, sings the poetry and dances at the same time, she/he has to let the song flow. Thus, a Baul makes an uninterrupted meditative journey through each song. The Bhāva and Rasa which flow through the song is only from the "seeing" in the Baul's song. That is why the people of Bengal love to listen to the singing, even if the singer's voice sometimes seems to go out of the pitch, or it cracks with the overflow of Bhāva.* [3]

---

[3]   Parvathy Baul. *Song of the Great Soul*, pages 21–22.

I first met Sanatan Das Thakur Baul in 1991, when he came with his sons, Bishwanath and Basudev, to perform on tour in the American Southwest for six weeks as the guests of Lee Lozowick. In between public concerts, the Bauls gave frequent spontaneous Baul *gan*— unpremeditated musical improvisations of bhava and *rasa* performed on bare ground under trees and sky on the ashram or in private living rooms. Sanatan was a formidable spiritual elder and fierce yogi—he was stern but compassionate, wholly committed to sadhana.

Almost twenty years later, in December 2007, Sanatan Das Baul and his entire family drove from their remote ashram in rural West Bengal to visit with Lee in Kolkata. Sanatan Das also brought his "spiritual daughter" and disciple, Parvathy Baul, to this reunion, during which we were treated to two days of Baul gan in the home of friends. Sanatan Das graciously agreed to an informal interview during this time.

"What is a Baul?" I asked.

"Baul is to know yourself. To know, to search, 'Who am I?' In Sanskrit, *atma tattva*. This doctrine: to know this body as a temple. To know all the bodies," Sanatan Das replied. With Parvathy Baul translating his Bengali into English, he continued, "This body is given by God. Like people have fields and they grow crops, and with those things that can be grown from those fields, they feed themselves and others. This body is also like that field."

Just then Bishwanath suggested that it was time to sing and dance—a hint that this was the best way to answer my question. Within moment, we had the opportunity to participate in the best kind of Baul gan—performed in an intimate environment— beginning with an invocational mantra and the traditional Baul salutation, "Jai guru!" Incense was lit and a large, two-headed drum appeared in Basudev's hands as if by magic. Parvathy brought an ektara—a simple instrument made with a calabash for a base and bamboo strips to hold up its one string—out of a cloth bag while Bishwanath got out the *kartals* (hand cymbals), handed them to his oldest son, then got out his own anandalahari—a kind of handmade plucking drum that is unique to Baul music. Its name, anandalahari, means "waves of bliss" in Sanskrit—an apt description of its effect upon the listener.

"Khyapa Re ...." Bishwanath's voice rang out in song as he raised his arm toward the sky invoking khepa, the one who is divinely mad. Then he began to dance, turning his body in a circle with delicate, small steps that fell in an exquisite pattern on the heavy cotton rug. With the simplest instruments and dance, rich polyrhythms and evocative melodies, we were enveloped in sound; ease and harmony flooded our road-weary bodies as we were carried along on the wave of song, awash in *ananda bhava*. The song unfolded as a sensual weave of rhythm and melody rooted in the body, the earth, sun, moon and that stars that drew the listeners into its bhava. Bishwanath began to bounce gently up and down, connecting heaven and earth.

The mood Bishwanath had invoked lingered as he sat down and Parvathy Baul translated, "Oh my heart, it goes to the city of *ananda*. If you want to see that *rupa*, that form, that beauty, there is no day or night. There is a full moon there, and it brightens the room. *Bindu!* It is surrounded by the bindu. It's beyond comparison. It is intense, and also very magical, like the Moon. The fine path of *sushumna* lights; you pierce the lotus, the middle path, and reach the higher place. The essential man hides there, in *triveni*, the meeting place. He is the essence of everything, he is the truth, and he is the one who never perishes. You enjoy it, you play there, and you find the Man of the Heart there. That is ananda."

Later Sanatan Das said, "We dance and sing to become egoless. We dance and jump to lose our egos. Hari flows downwards; Radha flows upwards. That's why we leap with joy, because it's the upward flow of Radha." Playing nothing but a simple, small drum called a *dubki*, Sanatan Das got up to sing and dance. His drum seemed to be at the center of the Universe. He looked directly into our eyes as he sang, and the language difference was not a barrier to the communion that flowed between us.

Afterward, Parvathy Baul stood up and strapped a duggi, or small round drum, on her hip. With ektara in hand, she threw her head back and let out a first note—a clear, honey-sweet wail. She was bending notes as deftly as Mahalia Jackson—and indeed, Baul music shares a kinship of the spirit with traditional African American blues and gospel.

"*Manipura* …!" she sang, and with a symbolic gesture she began to turn in a circle with flowing steps, the movements full of dignity and intrinsic grace. There was nothing suggestive or wanton about her dance; instead it was an objective communication of beauty, devotion and longing brought forth in praise of divinity seated in the body.

When Parvathy's song was over, she began to translate the poetry of Sanatan Das' song. "Baba's song was about rasa sadhana, male/female practice. Shiva has three daughters: Ganga, Kali and Durga. These are in the body, and we also find three different colors in a woman's body, in the river in the body. Every month the tide flows. When the woman gets awakened, for three days she plays in three colors—white, red and black. It's not easy to explain what is a woman, what the goddess is. Maybe Shiva knows. The Lord of all worlds, beings, he keeps one woman in his heart, one on top of his head and one by his side. In this life, when I die, in the next life I want to be a woman, and I will swim in the ocean of love and know the ocean of love."

The lyrics referred to the radical Baul practice of the "Four Moons"—the esoteric use of menstrual blood, semen, urine and feces. Much conjecture has been projected upon these "secret practices," considered heretical and "unclean" by orthodox Hindus. This kind of metaphorical reference to the Four Moons practice is about as specific as the Bauls usually get on this subject.

Sanatan Das and his clan are country Bauls. Despite performance tours in Europe, the UK and US, Sanatan Das and his family still live at Jagabandhu Ashram in rural West Bengal—a traditional cluster of handmade mud-brick huts with thatched palm roofs and dirt floors set amidst rice fields, skirted by thick networks of banyan trees and jungle growth. They are earthy, simple people of natural beauty. They glow with essential realness and embody the *sahaj* ideal. Their clothes are well-worn, faded, and obviously washed many times, but they carry the unmistakable power that clothes take on when worn many times in sacred spaces of one kind or another. There was nothing artificial about these Bauls and because of that, through their song and dance, they touched the truly essential within us. After three weeks of grueling travel, we were feeling rejuvenated; the music had infused us with energy and inspiration.

The next day we had a whole afternoon and evening with this Baul clan. As Parvathy told stories of her apprenticeship with Sanatan Das, who is now in his mid-eighties, his watchful gaze did not miss anything that was going on in the room around him. He had the childlike grace of the very old and very wise. At one point I asked him, "What is the most important practice of the Bauls?"

Sanatan Das replied: "Finally, there is only *Nama*.[4] Name. In the beginning, you are like all the other people, feeding yourself and your

---

4   Sanatan Das uses the word nama in its transcendent meaning: the divine name or Name of God as formula encapsulating Supreme Reality. Nama lies behind all appearances; nama is at work everywhere, permeating all of reality.

desires. Over time, your needs become smaller and smaller. You can sit in one place and everything comes to you. In the final stage, you realize oneness with the master. You find your master in yourself.

"Finally, it is a very lonely path; the guru may instruct you in a specific practice to do in solitude. After many years of rigorous practice, the student may realize the truth in the master's words. The student will realize that the master is not a common worldly man—he is the Beloved. You think of your guru as your God; to offer service to the guru is equal to offering service to God. You cannot see God, so God said, 'I will visit you in the form of your master.' Believe in what the guru says. Remain constant. Do not defy the guru. Nama. There is something beyond, when you reach this place of supreme joy, you find the master and you become one with the master. So, finally, the Name. Nama. Only a few people find it."

Bishwanath and Basudev were poised for the songs to begin; they quickly distributed small percussion instruments around to everyone and invited us to play along. With the ektara held to his ear and the dubki at his side, Bishwanath began to whirl. "Jai Guru!" he exclaimed joyfully. Within seconds we were transported by the storm of sound that came from the amazing anandalahari and drums—simple, handmade instruments of the earth.

After a rousing Krishna chant with everyone in the room up and dancing, we sang "Anonde Bawlo, Jai Guru Jai"—a song in praise of the guru and the *parampara* (lineage). The room and its occupants were suffused with brightness and joy; the rhythms and their potent soaring voices, the elegance of their dance, was the nama and rupa of which the Bauls had spoken, and they had transported us into it.

The next day we went to a local *mela* where we had been invited by Sandip Samaddar, a young Bengali who is part of a non-profit organization called Marfat that had sponsored the Kolkata Baul-Fakir Utsab for the past two years. This year the Utsab was held in a tiny park in the heart of Kolkata; it was billed as "a festival of wandering minstrels," where Hindu Bauls and Muslim Fakirs (sometimes called Auls) gathered to play handmade acoustic instruments and celebrate the spirit of their music.

We made our way past a large white canvas tent in a small park-like area with a few scattered trees, down the street and up stone stairs into a makeshift structure built on a flat porch on the side of a building. This "room" was loosely thrown together with canvas and plastic tarps stretched across bark-covered wooden poles and bamboo lashed together with rope. The floor, covered with scattered straw, reeds and cotton rugs, was littered with cigarette butts, ashes and bits of trash. The smell of marijuana and hashish drifted on the air, mingling with the heavy scent of tobacco. In the center of the space five musicians were playing.

As I sat down I noticed a very slight, thin man stretched out directly behind me. He was lying on his back on top of a helter-skelter collection of bamboo mats, cotton rugs and dirty blankets, with his feet pointed toward the musicians and his head near the canvas wall. He appeared to be asleep. Just beside him was a crude set-up for making tea. A duggi and anandalahari hung from the wooden supports near his head. He was bare-chested, wearing a dhoti of sadhu orange or ochre typical of the traditional Baul way of dress. An ektara lay nearby. He looked like a wanderer—a beggar, dust-stained from hard living.

I turned and faced the musicians who were playing now in the center of the tent. One was playing a *dotara*, a five-stringed lute, with passion and dexterity, and the music was working its magic. The small hand drums popped with exclamations of sound in rhythmic counterpoint to the deeper steady beats of the large double-headed drum. The song ended, and the singer relaxed into back-up mode with his dotara as the *sarinda* (a handmade violin-like instrument) player took over with a new song in which "Jai guru jai …" was the hearty refrain. One song flowed into the next until it seemed we were floating along on a river of music.

The man who had been lying on the floor behind me started speaking in English. Shifting positions, I turned to face him with notebook and pen in hand. The yogi was sitting up. His thin chest was bare except for a necklace of stone beads and a *rudraksh mala*. His cotton dhoti looked like it had seen some miles. His teeth were darkly stained brown from consuming chai and inhaling various kinds of smoke, I imagined. Despite his ragged appearance, he was by far the brightest light among the characters in this room. He gave me a brilliant smile and immediately started talking in broken but clear English.

Introducing himself simply as "Khepa," he said, "I am Baul Hindu."

"Baul Hindu!" He re-stated, pointing to himself and then toward the circle of musicians. "Those guys are all 'Muslim caste.' You know—Muslim?" Yes, I said, beginning to take notes.

"Yesterday I came here. I had no sleep day and night. I was traveling. I came here and made tea and drank it to wake up. This place is very much alcohol, drinking people. Nighttime comes, people no step right or left, just fall down on floor. And physical fight sometimes. Yesterday night, one a.m., a big fight and too much bad boola boola. All alcohol, all drunk. I drink only tea—they are drinking alcohol and smoking ganja. They drink too much."

He pointed proudly to his instruments and said, "Anandalahari," and then "ektara." He was smiling and talking fast as I scribbled in my notebook.

"Do you play those? Those are your instruments?" I asked.

He answered, "I play. I play those. I travel, I travel all over, Europe, many places. My name is Khepa. See? Here is my passport. You see, all places I have gone."

His passport appeared from somewhere; he opened it, then put it in my hand. In the space that said "Name" the single word, "Khepa" was typed. There were stamps from many countries, and the passport was weathered and old.

"I have a big problem," he continued in a friendly way, as if he has known me for a long time. I thought about how the Bauls consider the human being to be divine, so that, for the Baul, there are no strangers. It's a mark of the Baul version of the bodhisattva ideal that approaches life with this kind of universal acceptance of others. "I am not so good." He continued, referring to his health.

He went on to say that he had been sick for a long time. He had walked a very long way, cold and hungry, to an ashram. Somewhere along the way, he contracted typhoid, but he had no money for medicine. He lamented how expensive medicine had become in Bengal. Even five years ago, he said, people could afford medicine. But now, poor people are sick and they have no medicine.

He spoke about his extensive travels in the West and other details of his life, placing particular emphasis on the fact that his mother was a Khepa Baul, his grandmother was Baul, and all the rest of his family were Bauls.

The music started up again. A woman in a red and yellow sari had come in a few minutes earlier; now she joined the circle of musicians and was playing the kartals with skilled ease. A twelve-year-old girl, obviously her daughter, sat beside her. Khepa joined the musicians, and I couldn't help but notice the radiant smile that passed between him and the woman as the song began and the unique sounds of his anandalahari claimed the space. Immediately, I felt the mood brighten as they began to jam. Smoke floated on random sunbeams, so rare with the constant blanket of smog in Kolkata. The music was inducing a deep happiness that flowed through my veins. Another musician arrived to join the group and they flowed into a new melody that resounded with names of Krishna: "Madhava, Keshava!"

Walking out to the main tent with two friends, I spoke there with Sandip, one of the organizers who had invited us to the Utsab, mentioning that I would like to interview the man named Khepa. Sandip became enthusiastic. "Oh, that is Gour Khepa!" he said. "He is a very well-known Baul, one of the true Bauls, a real practitioner. He had a *huge* experience! He traveled a lot, all over Europe with Paban Das Baul, Purna Das Baul and Shubal, who took the Baul music out to the world. Gour Khepa is an amazing musician. Gour Khepa is *mad*—completely mad! That's why he is Khepa."

Back in the small tent moments later, I asked Gour Khepa if he was amenable to an interview. He immediately answered yes, but he put one condition on it. "*No money!* No money—I not business. Just talk," Gour Khepa stated emphatically.

Khepa picked up his instruments and a small bundle. Without any further ado, walking very fast, he led the way back over to the big tent, where he jumped up on the low plywood stage and sat in the middle of a big blue cotton rug that had just been placed there. Lee sat beside Gour Khepa while several other Westerners from his group gathered around along with Sandip, who was translating, and a few other Bengalis.

Many of Gour Khepa's comments were enigmatic or cryptic because he was speaking in the symbolic language that is typical of Bauls when they talk about dharma and practice. He began by saying that the time would come when the rhythm of the breath would stop, and he would be going to the graveyard.

"I am still alive," he said with a big smile, "so better you take my interview now—better you hear my words directly than when I am dead from someone else!" He laughed gleefully.

"What does it mean to be a Baul?" I asked.

Gour Khepa answered in Bengali. Sandip translated, "Baul is not a word. Baul is a sense. Baul is to control the air within the ida, pingala and shushumna."

Gour Khepa said, "Yoga. Baul yoga. *This* is Baul. *This* is Baul!" His knees struck the ground forcefully as he went into one hatha yoga *asana* after another. "*This* is Baul. I don't want to talk. It is better that I show you." He moved his body into another *asana*.

Khepa spoke again in Bengali and Sandip translated, "What we get from our sadhana, we try to teach the same thing to other people through our music."

"Baul sadhana!" Gour Khepa said with a broad smile, his charming sense of humor captivating us as he went into another *asana*. He struck me as one of the most joyful persons I'd ever seen. Coming out of the posture to take a seat, he continued in English, "Blah blah, no good. Many people blah, blah, blah, blah. No good! Sadhana no blah blah!" He smiled and laughed again, "Sadhana is sadhana! Again, and *again!*"

He paused for a moment as we took this in, then he said, "I am not eating for the last seven days and not eating again for seven days. Only milk and medicine. Problem something, now very good." He was quick to explain to us that he eats very little. "I don't like heavy food. Heavy food, no good. Light food, very good. Like milk, ghee, subji, potatoes, things like that. I am giving up eating rice."

Gour Khepa continued to make a trenchant point about those who were dressing up like Bauls but don't follow the lifestyle. "They are facing terrible problems in their lives," he said. This poignant criticism of the growing trend of entertainers who don the traditional Baul dress as a costume without actually doing the sadhana was a theme he had begun earlier, when I'd first talked with him in the smaller tent. It was clearly a big concern for him, as was Bauls with cell phones—symbolic of an inauthentic life and lack of practice. Khepa said that he had given his cell phone away. He passionately lamented the negative influences of the "modern world" that has impinged so completely upon his world.

Looking at Gour Khepa, I asked, "You do puja every day to your ista devata?"

Gour Khepa answered in English, "I worship my Self, my *brahmacharya*.[5] *This* is my worship," he said, touching his chest. This brought on another penetrating reproach of *puja* as business—the money-making activity of so many priests.

"I have no money puja," he stated. "This is my upper-stair puja. Like flowers are used in puja, every laughing face is like a flower for me," he said with a disarming smile. "That is what I use for my puja." Continuing in English, he said, "Outside puja, business puja. Inside puja—upper stairs, no downstairs." He told us that it was very important to be careful what we put in our two mouths (mouth and genitals). Then he chidingly poked fun at "business pujas," corporate business people and those who have no real feeling, who give large amounts of money to make big buildings and big temples.

He reiterated, "This is not my worship. This is not my puja."

"Would you say some more about the inner puja, the brahmacharya?" I ventured.

"One outside, one inside," he answered in English. "Grandfather, grandmother, mother…" He changed back to Bengali. Sandip said, "One worship is worshipping the Self, and one is like worshipping the parents, grandparents and worshipping the truth also."

I asked him about his guru, Horipada Goshai, who is still alive but very old, in his nineties. Khepa explained that his first gurus were his mother and father. His second guru was Shashan Bashgiri, and his last guru was Horipada Goshai. When we are born, he said, we

---

[5]   Brahmacharya, which often refers to celibacy, in this context refers holistically to a life that is defined by relationship with the Divine, including general conduct, spiritual discipline, daily relationships and the refining and garnering of bodily energies, including sexual energy, toward the aim of a divine alchemy.

have "everything" locked away in *manipura chakra*. "What I have here is a key," he said, "is Krishna, is a Krishna." I heard the word "khepi"—the feminine form of the word "khepa"—in the stream of Bengali that was rapidly tumbling out of Gour Khepa, which was translated by Sandip: "He says, 'My Khepi is like a partner, a thief who came to steal all my things I have inside.' "

Gour Khepa said in perfect English, "My Khepi, partner. Wife. Durga Dasi. She stole the key. She opened the manipura and stole everything." His smiling face was animated and triumphant. He said, "Khepi. Durga Dasi. Durga Dasi!" He continued in Bengali.

Sandip translated, "That's why we need the guru, to keep this thing intact, in the same place, to lock it again. The guru locks it again."

Gour Khepa found this absolutely delightful, and in between his joyous laughter and chuckles, he said, "Partner. Wife. Durga Dasi. Khepi is a *thief*!" He smiled broadly, enjoying the metaphor and interplay. "Durga Dasi terrorist! Smuggler!" He laughed some more. As Gour Khepa explained further in Bengali, Sandip relayed, "He is saying that the Khepi is like a terrorist who came to steal all his things, and the guru is the key to hold it, to lock it again." One of the Bengali men standing behind Gour Khepa commented, "It's a very deep philosophy."

Sandip said, "He says if the Khepi doesn't steal the soul…they can live together. If they know the trick—both of them—they can live together for a long time. But if they don't know the trick, one of them will have a lot of problems, and one of them will die or something. If both of them know the trick, they will have a saint's life."

Making sure we had understood correctly, Gour Khepa broke in again in English, saying, "If they do the same sadhana. *Same sadhana*. Same stay. If one stay and other one down, this is no good. The same completely—then they can stay together. *Together*," he emphasized. He said that one other very important sadhana for them was to serve people who are in their sphere of life, then he added, speaking of Durga Dasi, "She's a mother."

We soon learned that she was the woman in the red and yellow sari. When I asked if Durga Dasi would come and talk with us, Gour Khepa said yes with obvious enthusiasm, and immediately several people ran to get her. I remembered watching Gour Khepa and Khepi play music together earlier in the smaller tent.

While we waited, Sandip explained that Gour Khepa has a very big life traveling and playing music. Like many if not most Bauls, he has a penchant for intoxicants. "He doesn't have much discipline, because he's a completely *crazy* person. If he wanted to, he would travel a lot. You heard the name of Paban? In the seventies, Gour Khepa and Paban Das had many gigs in Europe. All the money Gour Khepa gave away. I saw him—he gives things to everyone. He doesn't want anything. He is still alive because of Khepi, because he drinks a lot, because he is something *crazy*! She keeps him really strong because he's completely crazy, and he's been drinking the last couple of weeks."

Later I discovered that Gour Khepa is considered one of the last of the older generation of Bauls, and although he has traveled extensively, he lives in a very modest, one-story house in Bolpur, near Shanti Niketan. Turning away from the glitz and glamour of fame and fortune, like Sanatan Das, he continues to live a simple, earthy life. At the Kenduli mela a few years ago, he and Durga Dasi avoided the crowds and high-profile *akhras*,[6] set up camp in a bamboo grove and cooked over an open fire for the visitors and students who came around them.

Gour Khepa was talking rapidly in Bengali. Sandip continued, "He is saying the last few weeks he has been drinking, but he is saying, 'I'm giving up drinking, I'm giving it up!'"

---

6   Akhra is the Baul term for ashram.

When Durga Dasi arrived a few minutes later, Gour Khepa spoke in English, saying, "This is my wife. This is my Khepi. She is my nitric acid. I am not silver, I am *gold*. This is nitric acid. I am gold. I am gold, no silver. I am not silver. I am pure gold. This is nitric acid. You understand?"

At first I was confused by this, but Lee interjected, "Nitric acid is the chemical used to test gold to see if it is real."

Gour Khepa seemed anxious to get across to us that this idea is found in the Bible and Koran as well as in the Puranas. It was not his idea, he said, but it was his scripture, his dharma.

Indeed, their way of life seemed to be working very well for this Baul couple, whose committed relationship has endured for twenty-five years. They told me that they met at the Kali (Kamakhya) temple, a famed shakti pitha in Assam, and decided to stay together; now they have a twelve-year-old daughter named Loki, who joined them a few minutes later.

"Khepi, what is the best way to serve Khepa? What is the best way for a woman to serve her partner?" I asked.

Durga Dasi responded in Bengali, then Gour Khepa and the other men intervened, talking with excitement. They seemed to be considering what she had said. While they discussed this passionately among themselves, she was calm and radiant. The debate was still going on when I interjected.

"What does Khepi say? What it is for a woman to serve?" I asked Sandip, who translated this directly to Khepi. She answered, turning to Gour Khepa again, who talked very fast in Bengali for what seemed like a long time.

"They are saying they live together," Sandip said, "so the best way is to help each other emotionally and physically. She is saying, 'I go to people, I beg and I cook. I try to help Khepa with whatever I have.'"

Fixing me with a strong look, Gour Khepa said in English, "She *stay*. She is not leaving me. *Very* important." His communication implied that this was not an easy choice at times, as Khepa has had a wild life with many excesses. But, it seemed that Khepi had a depth of character as a *sadhika* that kept her beside Khepa, no matter how difficult it may have been. It was clear that Durga Dasi was able to provide a kind of sanctuary for Gour Khepa that is found very rarely in today's Western relationships.

That Khepi placed a premium importance upon the fact that she begged as an aspect of her relationship with Gour Khepa placed her in a very traditional, old-time stream of Baul sadhana, as begging is an essential element of Baul life and practice. Traditionally, the wandering Bauls would enter a village and sing and dance, uplifting the hearts of people with their teachings that convey the divine potential in all human beings. Then they would beg for their dinner, a kind of begging considered a sacred act called *madhukari*.

Gour Khepa continued, "It's a very happy day. It's a really good day for me that I can talk and give information." He smiled. Speaking about his relationship with Khepi, he used an earthy metaphor, saying, "She is the land, and I am the farmer!" When Sandip translated this in English, Gour Khepa started laughing ecstatically. Khepi's broad smile and twinkling eyes said that she was enjoying the metaphors as well.

Khepi's presence brought an important new element into our exchange. For many years researchers have been uncertain about the role that women play among the Bauls. Some have asserted that women do not engage sadhana at all but are servants and exchangeable sexual partners to the men who perform sadhana—conclusions drawn largely because Baul women would not talk, or confide, in researchers who came among them. Without question, traditional female Bauls face many hardships, but Gour Khepa and Durga Dasi were painting a much bigger picture; their message was a fresh wind blowing in the oppressive gloom of projections made by scholars and anthropologists. Sitting before us was a woman of impressive presence—a woman immersed in sadhana, who exemplified the Baul ideal. Exuding equanimity and wisdom, Durga Dasi's eyes radiated a depth of maturity and sparkled with a quick sense of humor. I remembered a quote from Parvathy Baul's book, in which she speaks about the life of the female Baul:

> *Struggling hard, the female Baul attains the qualities of extraordinary compassion and stability of heart; so they can smile even at obstacles. As one [Baul poet] has aptly put it:*

> > *Oh Beloved!*
> > *Burn me*
> > *Burn me hopelessly*
> > *Burn the incense of my heart*
> > *For the incense*
> > *Does not give out its perfume*
> > *Until it is burned* [7]

"Who is ista devata for Durga Dasi?" I asked, looking at Khepi. Without hesitation, Durga Dasi looked at Khepa and gestured toward him, saying, "For me, my Khepa."

Gour Khepa gave us another one of his jubilant smiles and said, "Once you feel the real relating, it will *change* you inside." The beauty, simplicity and power of this quintessential Baul understanding of the alchemy of woman and man in relationship, alive in the potentials of an Enlightened Duality, was made all the more poignant by the music that drifted on the air as soaring melodic voices, drums and ektaras deepened the communion that we had entered into together. Time seemed to flow past us like warm honey.

After a few moments Gour Khepa explained further, then Sandip translated: "He is saying the reason why she sees him and considers him as God is because on the opposite, he also considers her as god-

---

[7]   Parvathy Baul. *Song of the Great Soul,* page 24.

dess, and they worship each other. He said, 'We are like the father and mother of Jesus. We see each other like this. I was alone, and I found a partner. We found each other, and we have an understanding and balance, and that is why we are so happy.'"

Gour Khepa generously gave us a particular glimpse into the sadhana of relationship between women and men in the Baul way. This exchange contained many key principles of the quintessential Baul message: Sadhana is about practice in the body, not about intellectualizing the dharma. "No blah blah."

Radha and Krishna are found within in the individual, and the quickest way to discover and cultivate this innate potential is in and through relationship. For man, woman is the key to this relationship, as Gour Khepa gives his Khepi the highest compliment: she is the one who determines whether or not he is "gold." And most importantly, the fruition of relationship sadhana is found in the fact of their mutual adoration of each other as ista devata, because the nature of the human being is ultimately Divine.

"They worship each other," Sandip translated, and Gour Khepa concluded, "That is why we are so happy." The truth of this declaration was transmitted to the Westerners who sat beside them, asking questions and listening to their answers: it came across loud and clear in their radiant, shining eyes, the exuberant joy communicated through their bodies, the freedom that is inherent in the total simplicity of their way of life. It was the inspiring key note of their message; it was the melody and rhythm of their song.

The Only Grace is Loving God

Lee Lozowick

*A*bout twenty-five years ago I wrote a book, *The Only Grace is Loving God,* and to this day people ask me what it means. I don't know, because I wrote it in a very unusual state of inspiration. I love the book, but the best part of that inspiration is lost to publication. At the beginning of this phase, when the mood of *The Only Grace* was arising, I was so inspired that I realized the complete absurdity of recording or reproducing anything, because every transmission is here, now, immediate, and either we get it or we don't. This phase only lasted for a few months; during that time I had all the tape recorders turned off, and I asked people not to take notes.

For two months I was giving the most eloquent, brilliant discourses of my life. The people who were there, of course, have that somewhere in their bodies—which was the point. Then I decided to write it down, but that was on the tail end of the inspiration. What is in *The Only Grace is Loving God* are the remnants of what really could have been something; it's still fantastic, so imagine what was coming in the original inspiration.[1]

When people ask me about my book, *The Only Grace is Loving God*, I tell them that it doesn't *explain* anything. *The Only Grace* has no answers; it leaves everything completely confusing. If you read the book, you will see there is no way to love God. You either do or you don't, and there's nothing you can do about it. However, assuming that you still have some small remnant of relationship to ordinary love, there is a possibility.

How does one discover not only the equality of all beings but equanimity in all things? You don't discover that by dividing and dividing and dividing. The more one divides, the more one is still lost in this and that, good and bad, yes and no—lost in the tension between things instead of the continuity of all things. Assuming that many of us might feel that we love God in some way—whatever we think God is: nature or humanity or the guru or the Path—how do we embrace and deepen and express that love? We deepen love for God by unifying, not dividing. We unify things instead of separating things. When we separate things, then we love the things that we're resonant with and we don't love the things that we're irritated or annoyed by. When we unify things, there is a possibility.

There's a saying: "I love humanity. It's people I can't stand." Often we feel that we're in love with Creation, and yet in the immediate sense of things, we're always losing our temper and being irritated. It can be some driver who cuts us off, or somebody who makes an appointment but doesn't show up and doesn't call to tell us they're not going to show up. It could be one of our children who promises to clean their room and then doesn't, and we walk in and there are live things growing under the bed. Have you ever had that hap-

---

[1] A consideration of Lee's teaching, The Only Grace is Loving God, appears in Appendix II on page 533.

pen? You walk in your kid's room, and you look under the bed, and something's growing there! You say, "What is that? Oh, it used to be a sandwich!" You walk in the room and suddenly your foot is stuck to the ground. You look down, and there's a pool of solidified Coca-Cola! Ah, kids—they're great! I personally am in favor of cleaning up after your kids, and not jumping on their shoulders and bitching at them all the time.

If we realize, let's say, that animals are ultimately as divine as human beings, it helps us develop a different relationship to animals. It doesn't mean we will never kill a mosquito or eat meat again, because animals have a different function than human beings. We might still eat meat, but we would have a different relationship to animals. In Native American and many other tribal cultures, which are actively meat-eating cultures, hunting is always associated with prayer and gratitude: gratitude to life for providing animals to feed the tribe, and prayer to and for the animal for taking its life; prayer to the babies of the animal for taking its life. Even though they kill animals for sustenance, they have a sacred relationship to the whole process of birth, life and death—which is unifying. We usually don't even think in those terms.

The way to encourage active participation in life with love is to look at Life with unicity, not division, division, division. How do you do that? You see the divinity in everything. The chemistry isn't the same, the form isn't the same, the taste isn't the same, the smell isn't the same, the function isn't the same, *and* somehow, miraculously, everything is divine. There is nothing that is separate from the ultimate Divine, whatever That is—and we don't have to know what It is. When we cultivate that vision of unicity, of oneness rather than division, then the automatic result is a deepening and a wisening of love.

We had a soirée the other night at the apartment of Arnaud and Veronique Desjardins at Hauteville. I showed up with the few people who were traveling with me, and then more people started coming in, mostly Arnaud's senior students. As people came in, the room got brighter and brighter until the space was shining like a million blazing suns, as they say in the *Upanishads*. Usually I don't feel things like this, because I'm very cynical, but I was in a good mood, and Arnaud was serving some of his special elixir. I was feeling, perceiving as a tactile perception, a brightness in the room. It was like *soma* then, but it's bittersweet now, because people are people; even great people are people. The next morning I was reflecting on the evening before and thinking about the law: the whole is always greater than the sum of its parts. Remembering who was in the room the night before, I was struck by how true it is that the whole is always greater than the sum of its parts. I think about this with my own students a lot: when I'm not here to monitor their representations of the teaching, it could be much better than it is now, or it could be confusing.

My master was very popular during the last few years of his lifetime. A lot of his strongest devotees are, in their own right, very powerful people who are highly educated, very wealthy, and politically and socially influential. While he was alive there was a lot of political strategizing going on—it was very Machiavellian, actually—but he held it all together. There was a certain willingness to work together for him. He was the focus. When he died things really fell apart. Of course, there is still a lot of good work being done on a gross physical level; there are clinics and orphanages and other philanthropic work being developed in his name; people are creating groups to chant his name. At the same time, the whole is greater than the sum of its parts.

I see the same thing in the Gurdjieff tradition. When Gurdjieff was alive there were very strong factions, and there was internal warfare, but somehow they were kept together under Gurdjieff's influence. There may have been all kinds of animosities, but there was also a whole. When he died, the bond of the whole weakened and went in different directions. There is some tremendous warfare—which is not too strong a word for it—that is actively going on, which is one of the not-so-nice consequences of his passing.

I was reflecting on all this and thinking that with my own work, certainly the discourses of those two months—when the mood of *The Only Grace is Loving God* was present—are in my student's bodies. One of the things that strikes me ongoingly is how people who seem to be incompetent and problematic can be amazingly brilliant when the demand is pertinent enough. For example, occasionally people will want to come to our ashram at the end of their lives. When somebody is dying, particularly of a debilitating disease, we always have twenty-four-hour-a-day care available for them. Some of the people who provide that care show up brilliantly—and, by a superficial estimate, I would have never thought they could bring integrity and compassion and reliable service to a task like that. I have faith, although it is tentative yet, that my students are going to show up like that after I'm gone; they will realize that the whole is greater than the sum of its parts, and the things that worry me now will not be an issue at all.

When we study a piece of writing like *The Only Grace is Loving God*, one of the things that we don't want to overlook is that the consideration of Loving God depends upon and cannot be separated from a tacit knowledge of and inherence in nonduality. Of course we have very real concerns in the real world: We have the desire for some kind of personal fulfillment, whether professional or artistic or relational; we may have some inner mystic urges that we are driven to fulfill; we have concerns of health and well-being—physical as well as mental and emotional—and we have considerations not only of our own suffering but of the suffering of the world.

A lot of these things are real in the world that we inhabit and at the same time their reality is based on our identification with illusion. It's not that these things are not real; they are as real as anything can be. It's that our relationship to them has a certain unreality, and without bringing that relationship into the clarity of truth, we never get to actually experience "what is, as it is, here and now," to use the language of Arnaud Desjardins and his guru, Swami Prajnanpad. We experience what we imagine is here and now, which may not be so bad relative to most people's perception of things—*and*, it's not the teaching that we have committed our lives to realizing and living. Realizing the teaching doesn't just depend upon coming to a point at which we are able to respond to the various up and downs in our lives with some degree of equanimity, or at which we have a striking ability to articulate the teaching accurately—that is true of many people on the Path. Realizing the teaching means that we actually pierce—finally and eternally *pierce*—the knot of separation.

Over the years I've used the expression Enlightened Duality, which captures what my teaching work is. We often come to understand or interpret that phrase as dualistic enlightenment, which is an understandable interpretation but completely an affectation of our illusory dualistic context. Enlightened Duality is actually the right vision of all of existence from the context of enlightenment—just the opposite, as you can see, of how enlightenment is most commonly understood. Instead of our movement towards and in the world being based on truth, it is based on illusion; it can look exactly the same on the surface, but it's not the same. It's not the same to the Universe, it's not the same to the Work, and it's not the same to Reality—and, as long as it's not the same, we have work to do.

The Work does not have to do with coming to terms with our psychology, although managing our minds and developing kindness, compassion and generosity is something that we work with.

If we have not pierced the central knot of illusion, which we call the illusion of separation, then we have failed to realize the essential emptiness of all things. We are identified with some thing. Of course in the world of duality there are things that demand that we identify with them: love for our partners, our children, our friends, our need to be respected, acknowledged and recognized—a need that has made fools out of greater men and women than you and I!

I just finished an unusual manuscript on the nondualistic teachings of Advaita Vedanta. It points out the error in the assumptions of the *neo-advaita* teachers who are giving *satsang*, using examples of some contemporary nondualist teachers. The error of their teaching is an error of misunderstanding, not an error of skill. The author says that Advaita Vedanta is not about knowledge, because there is nothing to know; it is about removing the veils of ignorance that keep us from knowing there is nothing to know.

The foundation of our illusions is very strong. You could easily build a substantial monument on the foundation of your illusions; even if what you build is a life of happiness, satisfaction, confidence and productivity, none of that is the aim of Advaita Vedanta. The aim of true nondual teaching is to slowly build a foundation upon which the teaching can stand, because it does take time—it cannot happen too quickly without creating psychosis. If you look at the major realizers in India—like Anandamayi Ma, Ramana Maharshi and the contemporary Amritananda Mayi—their families all thought they were insane when they began to manifest their teaching work. They did not see them as enlightened beings. Ramana Maharshi's shift of context was instantaneous; any therapist or psychiatrist who observed his behavior over the next several years would have considered him totally insane.

One of the dangers of the new *advaita* movement lies in kicking people's foundation out from under them without replacing that foundation with something real. The author of the manuscript gives several examples of suicide attempts by people attempting to live in a nondual realization that—without a foundation—became a kind of nihilism. Advaita Vedanta is designed to be communicated slowly, so as layers of illusion are peeled away, there is strength that replaces those illusions.

Essential teaching always falls to the nondual reality of existence because "what is, is, as it is here and now." The teachings are meant to be read and studied, so that as people come to a profound understanding of the teaching, they also provide a support system, which is an intellectual understanding of relativity. In the Zen tradition, in the very beginning the students sees, "There are the mountain and the trees." At a certain point of transition in practice the student sees, "There are no mountain and no trees." When the teaching and the practice matures, the student realizes, "There are the mountain and the trees." Once again there are the mountain and the trees, but as they *actually are*—not as they are in the student's imagination full of projection, assumption and expectation. It is a very real work of removing the veils of ignorance rather than building or accumulating something. Even if we could call that the earning of merit or good karma or work points, we are working on removing the veils to find Reality. Without a support system—the Buddha, the dharma, the sangha and the guru—then living in and on the basis of the truth that we have discovered is unlikely if not impossible.

Discovering the source is not so difficult; staying there is the trick. One would think that if one saw the truth, it would be so obvious that it would be easy to stay there. What would be the difficulty? Most people who have been on the Path have seen the truth but are not staying there, even if they imagine they are. With luck or hard work, they may have realized that it's not as easy as it might seem at first comprehension, because it means not identifying with the things that reinforce our most treasured illusions, which is different than just giving up sex, money, fame, or art.

So, it's becoming harder and harder for me to be enthusiastic about the relative teaching. I'm becoming more and more impatient. I see small signs of recognition, glimmers—like being on time. There's a difficult one! I keep telling the people who travel with me in the van that if we get invaded, I'm not waiting. I'm going to be running, and people are going to either be at my heels or dead! You wouldn't believe how slow people are getting out of the van. If I can be a little cruel, they are the Jews who thought they were German first and Jewish second: they all end up dead Jews, not living Germans. It's important not to be naïve about Reality.

One may think it's an insignificant thing not to take time seriously, because we all know in the ultimate Reality of things, time is an illusion, so why should we take it seriously? When we think time is just an illusion, then we can amble along. We can be caterpillars instead of butterflies. We can stop every once in while and nibble on some particularly good-looking weeds, until we progress—until we grow ourselves up and cage ourselves in a prison of our own making. In the meantime, we need to act *as if* we are butterflies, as if we had one day to live, and in that one day we had to do it all—fly and be beautiful, pick up a little nectar and lays some eggs, until one day, then that's it. Poof! One day we're standing on a leaf after our day of exuberance and the next thing we know we're dead, slowly falling off the leaf to the ground as the wind blows, because we have no flutter left, and here we are, gone from a butterfly to a flutterby.

France
Summer 2007

Nama and Rupa

M. Young

"Everyone should read these poems every day," Yogi Ramsuratkumar said to the nine American students with Lee who were visiting him in Tiruvannamalai in 1993. We had spent many hours sitting on the concrete floor of an enclosed porch with Yogi Ramsuratkumar and a handful of his Indian devotees, chanting his name in between readings of Lee's poems.

While we chanted or listened to the poems, a long line of people stood in the sun on the street outside the high wall that surrounded the Sudama House, where Yogi Ramsuratkumar lived for the last six years of his life. High tropical trees—palm, mango, amla and punnai trees—lined the street, and everyone sought any available patch of shade while they waited for the master's *darshan*. Random dogs, cows and beggars wandered by, while sadhus sat quietly on the side of the dirt lane to absorb the blessings of the beggar saint. Yogi Ramsuratkumar invited devotees into the house in small groups of three or four at a time, where they sat with him and his American guests while the poetry readings went on for hours.

When we first arrived in India that year, we watched as Lee received boxes of a small paperback book titled, *Poems of a Broken Heart*. Lee handed a copy to each one of us, while we listened in amazement as Rangarajan explained that Yogi Ramsuratkumar had asked his Indian devotees to publish Lee's poems to his master. No one knew that Lee had been writing poetry to Yogi Ramsuratkumar over the years. Holding the brand-new book in our hands, we were filled with wonder; a new world had just opened up before our eyes.

"Read that poem again," Yogi Ramsuratkumar would say at the end of a poem, or simply, "Again." Ma Devaki read the poems with great sensitivity and feeling, evoking a powerful mood that impressed the poems upon our senses even more deeply. The old beggar saint sat regally in his "rags" before us, eyes often brimming with tears as he listened to the poems. With Lee sitting at his left side, Yogi Ramsuratkumar cupped cigarettes between his palms and smoked while he gazed at Lee from time to time. He often reached out to take Lee's hand in his own, stroking his arm lovingly while the words of the poems resounded among us.

Years later, Lee's poetry has become a central communication of the teaching. Following Yogi Ramsuratkumar's instruction, many of Lee's students read one or more of the poems as a way of greeting the day each morning. When time allows, it is always auspicious to sink more deeply into them. One poem is better than none, but several poems, even ten or twenty, are a more satisfying meal, as the *bhavas* of the poems themselves begin to work their magic—the magic of the word. They waft from the page as the "sweetness that flows so freely from that Name," as the poet says, seep through the hardened shell of the heart to soften and moisten, while at the same time they warm and enkindle. It is the water and fire, the alchemy of these poems that is so efficacious: three poems and there is a gentle flow; twenty poems and there is fire.

Oh Lion of Faith,
    Yogi Ramsuratkumar —
You ask those of us who approach You
    the ones irrational enough to seek Surrender,
to have Faith, absolute Faith,
    in Your Name.
Your son chants to You and for You,
    endlessly on all levels possible.
Yogi Ramsuratkumar, Yogi Ramsuratkumar —
    what a Name for God!
Who would have thought such sweetness
    would flow so freely from that Name?
But lee must tell you this,
    oh Tiger in Rags:
to have Faith in Your Name
    is to have Faith in Your Form,
for God is not defined
    by distinctions, but by Unity.
For God, Name is Form,
    Form is Name — all is One.
Scold Your Heretic son
    if You will Father,
as he surrenders Faithfully to Your Name,
    even if You pretend to disapprove.
If Your Father in Heaven
    didn't want Your devotees
to adore Your Form
    and long to kiss Your Feet,
then why did He make You so irresistibly Beautiful?
    Answer that if You dare, oh dirty Sinner.[1]

---

[1]   Lee Lozowick, *Death of a Dishonest Man*, May 29, 1995.

After reading this poem perhaps a hundred times or more over the years, today it struck me anew, as these poems will often do. The crystalline rays of its transmission unleashed a flood of memories and revealed another view of Enlightened Duality—a transmission that occurs frequently in Lee's poetry to Yogi Ramsuratkumar. It was this phrase that started the reflection: "To have Faith in Your Name is to have Faith in Your Form, for God is not defined by distinctions, but by Unity." This is where we begin an exploration of *nama* and *rupa*—name and form—which is so central to the perspective of Enlightened Duality.

The Sanskrit word nama may be understood from more than one vantage point. When it is combined with the word rupa, as in nama-rupa, it refers to the complex of kaleidoscopic appearances in this world we inhabit: the ten thousand things of Creation and their inherent spiritual potential. The supreme advice to repeat the nama of God is found in abundance through the "revealed scriptures" of the Vedic and Upanishadic tradition. The fundamental principle behind the practice of repeating the name of God—as in mantra practice, for example—is based on a profound understanding of the sacred nature of language. This is especially true of Sanskrit, but all languages have this potential, as to "name" something is to "know" it—to recognize its fundamental nature—in the radical sense. Therefore, Sanskrit seed syllables and the words they form are considered divine. One scholar writes of the Sanskrit language:

> *Its very alphabet is a mantra (a sound or phrase of spiritual significance and power) revealing the song that was sounded in space when the world sprang into*

being. The Sanskrit language is constructed in harmo-
nious relation with the very truths of existence, hence
its power of illumination.... In Sanskrit most words can
be reduced to a verb-root (dhatu), *a seed-sound which*
is unchangeable and reveals the origin of the word.
This verb-root is expressive of action (kriya) *which is*
involved in all existences, for the teaching is that every-
thing in its essence is Being or sat *and in its expression*
is Becoming or bhava.[2]

Judeo-Christian scripture also contains this teaching, which is found in the power of the Logos, or "the Word." The word is considered to be the very thing that it names. When we speak the name of God, we are invoking the living presence of that very Reality. There are many efficacious mantras: Om Nama Shivaya; Hari Om; or the mantra repeated by Swami Ram Das, in which he initiated Yogi Ramsuratkumar: Om Sri Ram Jai Ram Jai Jai Ram. The Krishna mantra is known the world over: Hare Krishna, Hare Krishna, Krishna Krishna, Hare Hare, Hare Rama, Hare Rama, Rama Rama, Hare Hare. Some repeat the Jesus prayer as a mantra, "Lord Jesus Christ, have mercy on me, a poor sinner." This principle is also true of Buddhist mantras focusing on a *yidam* such as Green Tara, or the classic Buddhist mantra, Om Mani Padme Hum, or the Diamond Sutra: Gate, Gate, Paragate, Parasamgate Bodhi Svaha.

The purpose of any mantra is to engage the transcendent function of nama as Ultimate Reality. When mantra is repeated until it becomes impressed upon the organic system as a whole so deeply that it is perpetually repeated by the cells of the body, then it is true of us, even when external attention is placed elsewhere; the mantra has become encoded into both gross and subtle form. This is a

---

[2]   Judith Tyborg, *The Language of the Gods*, page 16.

universal law of nama-rupa. It is the way things work. The mantra becomes true of the one who embraces it with the kind of "Faith" described in Lee's poem.

Yogi Ramsuratkumar gave his devotees the mantra: Yogi Ramsuratkumar, Yogi Ramsuratkumar, Yogi Ramsuratkumar, Jaya Guru Raya. He also gave the use of his name as *Satnam*, the eternal name, or *Ramnam*, the name of God. Because repeating the name of God in any mantra or Ramnam practice is considered to be the most auspicious practice in the current age, or Kali Yuga, the repetition of his nama is the one, all-embracing practice Yogi Ramsuratkumar gave to his devotees. "Say this beggar's name, even once, and this beggar will be there with you," he often said.

The invaluable experience of traveling in India with Lee over the years has given Lee's students the direct experience of this truth. On the trip in 1993, when Lee's poetry to his master was first discovered, we spent almost two weeks staying near the Mantralayam, a temple built for Yogi Ramsuratkumar a few miles from Kanya Kumari on the southern tip of India. We traveled around the countryside and villages in a van with the temple "bhajan band," as we called this group of singers and musicians who chanted the nama of Yogi Ramsuratkumar nonstop.

Making stops at temples, schools, businesses or dusty small villages where people were gathered to see and hear the American saint, we would disembark chanting, while Lee distributed *prasad*. Often Lee gave short talks about Yogi Ramsuratkumar to the students or local people. Upon returning to our quarters at night, we were so exhausted that we fell into bed, only to find our sleep permeated by the nama of Yogi Ramsuratkumar. Waking during the night, the nama was resounding within; upon waking in the morning, the first thought was of Yogi Ramsuratkumar's nama. Many of the people in our group had this experience: the name of Yogi Ramsuratkumar was a living spiritual force that flowed through us like a river of fiery sweetness.

This is an example of what the Bauls call *bartaman*: direct experience. We were not repeating a mantra because of a dogmatic creed based on the mind's belief; the mantra was repeated because the devotees of Yogi Ramsuratkumar have faith in it, and they joyously sang this nama "all the twenty-four hours," as they said. Their faith and joy mingled with ours, creating a synergistic, exponential explosion of graceful Divine Influence. The benefits were more than tangible; they were unforgettable, and when I do forget, which we humans are wont to do, the nama of Yogi Ramsuratkumar often arises spontaneously, without being willfully called into conscious awareness at all. Suddenly, the spontaneous arising of the name of Yogi Ramsuratkumar springs to life in mind, body and heart.

When Sanatan Das Baul, a wise elder in the tantric path of the Bauls, was asked what the highest practice of the Bauls was, he said, "Finally, there is only nama." The full quote from Sanatan Das appears in the essay titled "The Bauls of Bengal," but it is referenced again here because it provides an important glimpse into the meaning of nama in the ultimate context. To know the nama of any form is to penetrate the potential of Life, which will ultimately lead to the Supreme Reality. The more nama becomes apparent to the practitioner, the more rupa in all its appearances shines with that nama.

The ancient Indian philosophical system of Samkhya uses the terms *purusha* and *prakriti*, which are parallel to formlessness and form, Creator and Creation, nama and rupa. Yogi Ramsuratkumar was often referred to by his Indian devotees as a *purushottama*—one who dwells in and as the divine purusha, the Divine Person, in a human form. He left many forms imbued with his presence to radiate blessings and Divine Influence in this world. There are a number of *vigrahas*,[3] that are alive with the transmission of his nama, including

---

[3]   Vigrahas are sacred images that are empowered with a divine force that emanates; they are literal containers of the living essence of that which they represent.

the large statue in the temple at the Yogi Ramsuratkumar Ashram in Tiruvannamalai and several smaller statues sculpted by devotees. Other sacred images are called *murtis*; these are photographs, paintings and drawings of Yogi Ramsuratkumar that can be used as a focal point for prayer, meditation or any other contemplative practice or invocation of his nama.

"For God, Name is Form, Form is Name—All is One." One of the most fundamental ways human beings worship is through the forms of images and symbols of the Divine: Lord Krishna with Radha and the gopis; the Lord Jesus feeding the multitudes or seated with Mary Magdalene at his feet, where she holds the alabaster jar of precious spikenard with which to anoint her Lord; the serenity and compassion of the Lord Buddha, gilded and magnificent or plain and stark in simplicity. Likewise, we experience the nature of Reality in the form of Kali, Tara, Sarasvati, or Lord Shiva with Parvati—or in the guru's human form.

Westerners often make the mistake of viewing Hinduism as a polytheistic religion, when in fact it is a vast and deep polyphony of monism, monotheism, polytheism, animism, shamanism, tantricism, and strict nondual philosophy. As we will see in the essay that follows, from Shankara's *advaita* to the devotional bhakti paths of Madhva, Nimbarka, Ramanuja, Chaitanya and Vallabhacharya to the Bauls and Sahajiyas—or any path that combines bhakti with tantra (tantra being "the dangerous fast Path")—Hinduism is big enough to embrace immense diversity within unity.

In Hinduism, the complex divine families of the gods and goddesses—and their extended families of divine beings such as *apsaras, naginis, gandharvas* and *asuras* (to name a few)—are understood as aspects of Reality. These forms represent archetypes or qualities of the Divine represented in twilight language, which finds their origin and apotheosis in the unitive Reality of All That Is. Ultimately, name and form are one.

Because of this fundamental truth, all great traditions become very universal in their highest expression of clarity. When universality is true of a tradition, its practitioners demonstrate generosity, acceptance and compassion toward others. There is a natural feeling of kinship with practitioners of other paths. We run into problems, very big problems, when universal truth becomes obscured by the illusion of separation, giving rise to fear of the other, bigotry, fundamentalism, fanaticism, cultic exclusivity, narrow-mindedness, psychosis and many forms of psychopathology. With the possible exception of Buddhism, all major world religions have a fundamentalist faction that is mired in the illusory labyrinth of rupa at its gross level, and an extremely narrow interpretation of the word, or nama—acted out most tragically in constant religious wars.

When holy scripture is taken literally—for example, to reify the devil as "the other," the stranger, the infidel—then we have a problem with the human shadow, in psychological terms. Therefore it is important to be vigilant in relation to pathological potentials. The vast majority of practitioners on the Path will have the conditioned tendency to take things literally—to become fundamentalist and demand the letter of the law rather than the spirit of the law. This often shows up as conflicts and attempts to dominate others. It is a serious pitfall of the Path and should not be underestimated as a dynamic of the human psyche. The living transmission of the teaching, given by a dynamic teacher, is easily turned into a rigidified code of behavior and ethics that is used to control and manipulate others.

Great scriptures are written in twilight language. It is the language of the deep heart, and every human being has the innate capacity to understand it. The Sufis say that a true teaching story can be understood on seven different levels, and yet the vast majority of Christians and Jews have taken the parables and mythic stories of the Bible as literal fact, which are then used to buffer themselves against anyone who does not adhere to their creed. This is an immense error of wrong view that has resulted in thousands of years of cruelties in the name of God. Sadly, it is the letter of the law, not the spirit of the law, which so often gets extracted from this great book of teachings and sacred stories.

Scripture as sacred art or "dharma art," to use a phrase coined by Chögyam Trungpa Rinpoche, invokes the essence of Reality using the word as form or image. One of the most important qualities of dharma art, Trungpa Rinpoche said, is that it is nonaggressive. This quality of nonaggression is vital to anyone who is attempting to walk a true Path which leads, inevitably, to a universal perspective of nama and rupa.

A consideration of rupa, from a Baul point of view, inevitably leads to an exploration of *svarupa*. Svarupa is the divine quality, the primal pattern, essence or source vibration that informs the subtle and gross worlds of form. Rupa becomes more radiant, more immanent with divine presence, until it becomes svarupa—the innate form, the heavenly form of archetypal origin in the Platonic sense—which emanates from the source. Rupa becoming svarupa is a process of great importance to the Bauls, who revere the human form as the vessel containing the very Universe itself. To realize svarupa is to realize the origins of things, the blueprint of being, the unique nature of each thing—literally, to know one's heavenly form. To realize svarupa is a direct link to realizing nama, in the sense that Sanatan Das spoke of it.

This teaching is found well articulated in the Vaishnava Sahajiya cult of Bengal, which is significantly associated with Baul lineages and practices including the *sadhana* of music, poetry, dance, and relationship practices between woman and man. These traditions are so interconnected and similar that it is difficult to tell them apart even today. Profoundly woven into the prose and lyrical poetry of the Vaishnava Sahajiyas is the teaching of rupa, svarupa and *aropa*, in which it is understood that there are two basic aspects, with many dimensions, of human beings: rupa and svarupa, or the gross physical existence (rupa) and subtle spiritual existence (svarupa). However, to realize svarupa one must come into direct relation to what is called aropa, or the attribution of divinity within the human being.

According to Sahajiya and Baul teachings, woman and man are the gross manifestations of the spiritual principles symbolized as Radha and Krishna. These archetypes are eternally enjoying each other in Vrindavan (their paradisiacal garden); the bliss of that intense love may be enjoyed by man and woman through their mutual attraction and attachment to each other. Man is *rati* (the object of *rasa*) and woman is rasa (the ultimate enjoyer of divine feeling or mood). This teaching becomes extraordinarily complex, with many levels of intersecting symbols and exchanges of roles as man and woman engage the intimate yoga of sexual relationship to realize Radha and Krishna in each other and within themselves.[4] Gour Khepa and Durga Dasi were reflecting this teaching in their earthy metaphors and in their simple declaration, "We worship each other." The bodies of woman and man in intimate embrace become the seal—a *mudra* of invocation—of the literal images of the divine feminine and masculine in union. In the process of this realization, over time, the blueprint of the *sahaja* nature within the individual becomes awakened as a unified whole.

---

[4]   Das Gupta, *Obscure Religious Cults*, page 133.

Das Gupta wrote:

> *This realization of the true nature of man as Krsna and that of woman as Radha is technically known as the principle of aropa or the attribution of divinity to man. Through continual psychological discipline, man and woman must first of all completely forget their lower animal-selves and attribute Krsnahood to man and Radhahood to woman. When the man and woman thus realize themselves as Krsna and Radha in their true nature, the love that exists between them transcends the category of gross sensuality—it becomes love divine, and the realization of such an emotion of love is the realization of the Sahaja.*
>
> *The principle of Aropa is the most important in the process of Sahaja sadhana. We have seen that the Sahajiyas have spoken of two aspects of man, viz., the aspect of physical existence which is the rupa and the aspect of spiritual existence which is the svarupa.... This Svarupa must be attributed to and realized in the Rupa to attain any kind of spiritual gain. But this Aropa of Svarupa to Rupa does not mean the negation of the Rupa; it is rather the act of imbuing every atom of the Rupa with the Svarupa. The gross physical form with all its charm and beauty is as real as our spiritual existence, for it is the charm of physical beauty—the maddening passion, which we call human love—that leads us gradually to a new region where we can find a glimpse of divine love.*
>
> *There is no categorical distinction between human love and divine love—it is human love, transformed by strict physical and psychological discipline, that becomes divine. Divine love is rather an emergence from the car-*

*nal desires of [human beings] as the full blown lotus,
with all its beauty and grandeur above the surface of
the water....*[5]

Rupa becoming svarupa is another way of saying that one's perspective has shifted from duality to Enlightened Duality. Because
of our prior conditioning, it is important to assert that ultimately
both man and woman must discover Radha and bring her to life
within themselves in relation to Lord Krishna. Each individual must
discover and continue to affirm Radha—the feminine presence or
rasa—within himself or herself.

This discovery is made in and through the body, in form, for it is
through rupa that svarupa may be revealed. One perceives the living
truth of the essential form, which emanates or transmits the nature
of Reality. This essentially tantric perspective recognizes the fact that
there are many dimensions of form—from rupa to svarupa, or from
gross to subtle—through which one may traverse a path toward the
Ultimate Reality.

This is a description of tantric practice, which is found in many
different spiritual paths in diverse guises and has a particular flavor in the tantric underpinnings of Baul *sadhana* in the Path of
Enlightened Duality. Aghori practitioner and scholar of jyotish and
Ayurveda Robert Svoboda wrote about tantra:

> *We here in this mundane world inhabit the* Adhibhautika
> Loka, *the "Realm of the Five Elements." Those who
> worship the God-without-Form focus on transitioning
> directly from here to the* Adhyatmika Loka, *the "Realm
> of the Supreme Spirit." Tantric activity centers on the*
> Adhidaivika Loka, *the "Astral Realm," which is created
> from very subtle materials perfused with spirit. The*

---

[5]   Ibid, pages 133–135.

> *astral sits on the border between the attribute-free (nir-*
> *guna) existence of the* Adhyatmika Loka *and the name-*
> *and-form (saguna) reality of the* Adhibhautika Loka.
> *Tantra is all about boundaries, about the places where*
> *two different things meet, and how those different things*
> *interact with one another. Strong energetic potentials*
> *for transformation appear at these margins.*[6]

Tantra is focused more on the transformative process of being and becoming rather than an end result of attaining nirvana and getting off the wheel of successive rebirths due to karmic pulls—the annihilation of any discreet sense of selfhood in an "enlightenment" that delivers one into the relief of suffering promised by nondual realization. This idea of individual release from the terrible burden of existence is not a tantric proposition, although tantra is founded in the unitive fabric of existence, the transient nature of all phenomena and the unborn, unchanging and undying Supreme Reality.

Tantra rejects nothing and embraces all; in the path of tantra the tastes of Life are savored and appreciated. There is a profound relationship to the principle of Life that is rasa. This teaching is often greatly misunderstood, for it is not the separate self who tastes and enjoys—through the principle of aropa, it is the innate divinity that tastes and enjoys. It is Radha and Krishna who taste and enjoy within the practitioner. Because we have the innate capacity for the radical clarity necessary to apprehend Reality as it is, we are given many practices to help us within the complex of nama-rupa—deity worship is one of these. The practitioner, through spiritual disciplines and skillful means, builds a container in which the deity may come to reside and enjoy. This is another way of saying that we are seeking aropa—the attribution of divinity within the human being; we are

---

[6]   Robert Svoboda, *Namarupa*, "Tantric Prospectives," Volume 01, July 2008, page 6.

inviting the Supreme Reality as *ista devata* to arise in and inhabit our bodies, minds, souls.

The form of an ista devata as the doorway to the Beloved is not a reduced version of the Supreme Reality, made palatable for those who fear impermanence or emptiness or misunderstand nondual experience. The ista devata, as worshipped in any form and by any name, *is* the Supreme Reality. To court the Beloved is to court annihilation in love, and despite the prospect of egoic annihilation, we are drawn by the fragrance and sweetness of that *bhava*. We seek to attract the Beloved, because the lightest kiss of the Beloved catalyzes a transformational alchemy within the being. This knowledge lies at the heart of tantric practice.

Dr. Svoboda says, "The best yantra of all is the human body, and nyasa involves taking the human body, which is an ordinary container, and transforming it into a container that is useful for high-level transmutation. Tantra is alchemy—*Rasa Vidya*."[7] He states further:

> *It is not easy to create a simple definition of rasa, but basically rasa represents the world's liquid reality, including all juices, saps and soups; all minerals used in alchemy, especially metallic mercury; the Six Tastes (sweet, sour, salty, bitter, pungent, astringent); the aesthetic "taste"; and emotion. There are many different ways in which to transform the many different varieties of rasa into other rasas; Junior Guru Maharaj,[8] for example, had learned how to convert tobacco's poisonous rasas into that pattern of the Six Tastes that his body most required. Tantra aims to take all rasas and convert them into ekarasa—"one rasa," a single flavor of existence. Once you have achieved this sort of internal*

---

[7]   Ibid, page 6.

[8]   Junior Guru Maharaj is the guru of Robert Svoboda's mentor, Vimalananda.

alchemy, everything you take in and everything you put
out becomes focused on the one thing that is of supreme
importance to you. Only then will you be able to accu-
mulate enough focused shakti to transform the essence
of your being.[9]

The Sanskrit term *nyasa* refers to those rites, rituals or practices that are aimed toward gradually transforming the practitioner's body into the divine body of the ista devata. This is one of the essential aims of tantra; tantra is all about rasa, and rasa happens within the complex of nama-rupa. A true tantric path is defined by unity, in which the myriad tastes and flavors are relished as the one taste: "There is only God."

Name and form come together in art of all kinds and perhaps most potently in poetic language. Poetry brings name and form together. At its best, poetry blends nama and rupa to reach toward transcendence. The reason that the twilight language of poetry and lyrical song is so potent is that the art form draws out svarupa in the power of the nama, for words themselves are a specific rupa of that which they represent. Words are symbols of a manifest aspect of Reality, in exactly the same way that images are symbols for an aspect of Reality. Poetry speaks to us through nonlinear means, bypasses the mind and gets to the heart of the matter, but Lee cautions: "Poetry is the language of the Gods because it speaks directly to the body through the mind. If you think about it too much, you won't get it."

---

9   Robert Svoboda, *Namarupa*, "Tantric Prospectives," Volume 01, July 2008, page 6.

Lee's poetry is a scriptural transmission of his lineage, placed within the form of an intimate conversation between Lee and his master. Yogi Ramsuratkumar said many times, "Lee has done a great work for this dirty beggar with these poems. Lee has written about this beggar for everyone." In 1993 he said to us, "These poems will help this beggar's work." The reading of poems during Yogi Ramsuratkumar's darshan invoked powerful moods among those who were present. Often Yogi Ramsuratkumar fell into powerful bhavas as he listened, in which he became intensely internalized or wept. Sometimes he asked his attendant, Ma Devaki, "How does Lee know so much about this beggar?"

Not only is this poetry full of teachings on the efficacy and practical use of the Name of God, in countless poems Lee speaks directly to Yogi Ramsuratkumar and declares the power of the Name that is ever-resounding within—the refuge and source of Grace. While the poems are transmissions of transcendence, they also offer very real, practical help for the struggles of every day life.

> Oh Dearest Father, Yogi Ramsuratkumar,
>   yesterday Your raving son wrote
> about those one thousand daily betrayals.
>   Yes, this is so, and so what?
> Of what concern need this be?
>   Simply accept, with Faith, with love,
> with surrender and forbearance,
>   and meet all with service and more service,
> and above all, greet every betrayal
>   with Your Name, the Invocation of Your Blessings.
> This turns those small sins
>   into great gifts, gifts from You.
> Yes, to serve with Your Name
>   is to remember and praise You.

Since the betrayals are constant,
  so too is Your Name a constant
Benediction in Your heart-son's life.
  lee lozowick, Your wild Heretic
is ever grateful for Your Presence.
  This little sinner remembers You
out of Love, Faith, Obedience
  and surrender, and remembers You
in the service of others
  where only You comfort and heal.
Oh Beauty Divine, Mercy Incarnate,
  Yogi Ramsuratkumar Maharaj,
lee bows before Your majesty,
  Your Name ever on his lips.[10]

All art forms have the potential to transmit Reality as it is, but this is a delicate potential. Transmission does not depend upon artistic feats of dexterity and originality, although these attributes are praiseworthy and inspiring; transmission depends upon transparency to the Divine. The artist must, at least for the moment in which the art is being created, become transparent to the Source of transmission. Within a lineage, this means being transparent to the root guru, so that the Divine Influence of the guru can come through the art.

In the case of poetry, sometimes the poet tries to say too much, creating concretized images and leaving the words dead and brittle rather than fluid and fiery. The poet may reach too far, and in reaching, miss the delicate potentials of nama-rupa. Often the obscure arrow pointing toward the Unfathomable is more effective than an attempt at direct description. Lee once commented, "Beauty made too public is no longer beautiful," a principle the Japanese poets

---

10   Lee Lozowick, *Gasping for Air in a Vacuum,* 27 October 1998.

understood well and used very successfully in haiku poetry, which is found in a line like "the birches are not telling."

Because of the inexplicable power of nama and rupa to transmit Reality as it is, as Lee said, "You can never get too much poetry." Classical spiritual poetry, particularly found in the East but also in rare Western forms such as the poems of St. John of the Cross, mingles the power of the word with the evocative and invocational image of the ista devata. Whenever we employ the sacred image of an ista devata we enter a full-on engagement in a sacred relationship, which requires a self and an other and finds its fulfillment in the nondual realization of an Enlightened Duality. In other words, the ista devata, in whatever form, will always deliver the devotee or practitioner to the door of unity, and through that door, usher one into Enlightened Duality.

The divine image, whether symbolizing *nirguna* (the Divine without attributes) or *saguna* (the Divine with attributes), whether it is word or picture or sound, will invariably lead to its opposite counterpart and beyond because nirguna and saguna are ultimately one and the same. For the worshippers of Kali, she is both the Mother Goddess and the Transcendent Reality. For the worshipper of Krishna, he is both the personal God and the Supreme Reality beyond form. For those who worship the guru, the guru is both nirguna and saguna; both nondual realization and Enlightened Duality. On the Path we cultivate faith rather than belief—as in the believers of jihad and crusades and inquisitions and holocausts. Pondering the mysteries of nama-rupa, we may accept them as they are: wholly mysterious, unknowable, transcendent, as well as immediate, tangible, beautiful, and feeding the senses by the Grace of God.

Oh Father, Yogi Ramsuratkumar,
    most worthy of Praise, most mad of Sinners,
it is You and You again, always You
    who consume this little beggar's thoughts, feelings, actions,

and thank Father in Heaven for that!
How lost this arrogant Fool would be were it
not for You, Your guiding Light, Your ever-present Mercy,
Your cry of Sorrow and Compassion, Your Call to Work.
Oh yes Lord, Father, Yogi Ramsuratkumar,
even this poverty-stricken lee, Your True Heart-Son,
is grateful indeed, truly saved by Your Urge.
Even such an Heir as I cannot be lazy, self-indulgent,
sloppy, forgetful or too apathetic.
It is always the goad of Your Name, the attraction
of Your Name, the inspiration of Your Name, the honeyed-
sweetness of Your Name and the Absolute Demand
of Your Name, ever Your Name, that helps keep
this wild Heretic true to that very Name.
And True Your lee is Father, True as True can be,
for you are All, One, not-two, not-separate,
everything, anything, past, present, future, unity Itself,
and more than anything You are You, endlessly You.
Pranams in the Holy dust of Your even Holier Feet,
I am Yours without question or doubt,
Yours without confusion or thought, ever Yours
with adoring glances caressing Your Forms.[11]

---

[11]   Ibid, 26 July 2003.

The Caprice of God

Lee Lozowick

When a spiritual teacher realizes Reality, the sacrifice of personal volition—of desire for self—is made. Obviously I still have my preferences. I prefer a room that is comfortable and cool to a room that is hot and uncomfortable, but I am not talking about the superficial form of things. A teacher *is* service itself. Frequently it will not look like I am serving my students, because "I am doing something," but if what I do creates in a student observation of themselves, then it can be said to be service.

Ten years of my life have been spent—and I have just begun—acting like an ass in order to serve my students, with occasional lapses into what looks like a traditional spiritual teacher. People will think, "How does that serve?" Because we *are asses*. If I acted the way I felt, people would have long ago made me into a gold-plated idol, put me on a pedestal, and that's where I would be today, with hundreds of adoring but superficial followers. I don't want followers or superficial people around me. I don't enjoy superficial people; I enjoy people who are just juicy, real, friendly, happy people.

If I only hung out with God-realized people, I'd be alone all the time, and I enjoy company and interchange. But I don't enjoy superficial people, and if I were to act the way I felt, I would have predominantly superficial people around me, and lots of them, because people love sweet holy men. If I acted the way I felt, I would be delicate and sensitive and polite, soft-spoken and gentle, and as reverent and gracious for the gifts of the Universe as a man can be. People would get nothing out of that.

We need to come to terms with our failure. The way I act is by accusation. I am accusing us of a crime—the failure to submit ourselves to God. This is the only real crime. Murder and violence and war are essentially specific aspects of the crime of the failure to submit oneself to God. We need to come to terms with our failure to submit ourselves to God. Never mind Loving God; Loving God is so far beyond Obeying God that, at our stage of the game, to even think about Loving God is absurd. I am exaggerating a little bit, obviously so we will think about it, because it is a worthwhile ideal. The possibility of Loving God before Obeying God is absurd. To Obey God is to submit yourself to the Will of God; to submit yourself to the Will of God is to be not other than that Will, and to be not other than that Will is to be God.[1]

To Love God, you cannot *be* God. I am not splitting philosophical hairs; it is a physical truth. Loving God *is* the epitome of a human relationship to God, but practically, you cannot Love God until you Obey God. To Obey God is to achieve union, and to achieve union is to become God; to Love God is to be returned from union in order to serve God as a slave, as a servant, because the epitome of human action is service. When you Obey God, you cannot serve God because you *are* God. This is not philosophical; this is organic. When

---

[1]   In using the phrase "Obey God," Lee is referring to submitting or surrendering to the Will of God or Divine Will with such totality that one is assumed into the Great Process of Divine Evolution. See *The Only Grace is Loving God.*

you have learned to Obey God—and you can learn to Obey God by practice—God, in God's graciousness, rejects you from His Heart so that you may know the Love of God.

This is God's Gift, if we are lucky, but luck has nothing to do with it. The greatest Gift God can give you is not health, not peace of mind, not the perfect mate or perfect child, not intelligence, not the endless realm of mystical experience; the greatest Gift God can give you is to eject you, to express you like a breast expressing milk, to express you from His Being so that you may turn around and view Him as a servant. That is the only Gift God gives us. There is no Grace but that.

Everything else is the law. Everything else is Nature. The mystical ascent is Nature; it's the law of the nervous systems, subtle and gross. Grace is when you have realized God and you are ejected from the bliss of union into perfect duality, and your realization is not taken away. How could it be? How could you have realized God and have it taken away? Actually you already are God, but the knowledge of that has been taken away in a certain sense. Never mind the whole thing about the birth trauma and duality, the illusion of separation and all that; we are talking about more important matters now.

You cannot Obey God and ever have that taken away from you. When you Obey God, you *own* that; it is yours. When God ejects you from his heart in order for you to view him as a lover to Beloved, that ejection is not exclusive of your realization. You could not suffer the pain of Loving God if you weren't already realized for a moment.

I don't know that pain; I know of it by the virtue of the fact that I have been ejected from the heart of God. The pain of longing, which is sweet but ruinous, is so profoundly unearthing that if you had not realized God, if you were not absolutely submitted in obedience to God, you could not suffer that pain for a moment; you would physically die, you would be destroyed. By no means am I claiming to know that pain—I have never even hinted at that. That is the pattern our lives may take by the Gift of Grace. There is no other Grace but

Loving God, all the rest are mechanics. We are involved in spiritual life ostensibly, but I could introduce you to some pretty good psychics—weird, strange human beings—who could give you the kinds of visionary experiences that you call spiritual. All those lights and sounds are the mechanics of Nature; it's the law.

Sacrifice for the Will of God. Submit yourself to the Will of God in an orderly process, and you will be effected by and heir to everything you have read about in the books on mysticism and spiritual experience. Given a profound enough submission, in obedience to the Will of God, this will happen even to the point of miracles. However, from there you can *consider* Loving God, but you can only consider it because you earn union. You cannot *earn* Loving God as a perfect servant because Loving God is only Gift, Grace—and God is capricious. The best practitioner doesn't necessarily get ejected from the heart of God; the best practitioner gets to Obey God first—gets to realize himself or herself.

Loving God is a matter of Caprice, which is why I don't talk about it much. After all, why talk about something that is entirely capricious? You and I can be a little capricious and we can talk about it, but God's Caprice is beyond any conceivable intellectualization. So I don't talk about God's Caprice. Why bother? I could write volumes of poetry—and I have written some. It's nice. It's sweet. But even that doesn't capture it. God's Caprice is God's Caprice.

Los Angeles, California
September 1985

For the Love of the Lord

M. Young

*A*ll the big problems of a philosophical or ontological nature have been hashed out by our forebears on planet Earth. There are Hindu, Buddhist and Muslim, or Sufi, as well as Western—meaning Judeo or Judeo-Christian and Greco-Roman—ideological positions on all the classic spiritual arguments: nondualism versus dualism, the problem of God or no God, a negative Absolute (an empty void) or a positive Absolute (Brahman), monism versus monotheism, theism versus polytheism, pantheism, animism and shamanism. Or the age-old argument as to which yoga is most effective: bhakti (devotion), *jnana* (knowledge), or karma (work).

The vast body of spiritual literature, tradition and practice found in contemporary Hinduism is a formidable and fruitful source of study. Springing from the Vedas and Upanishads, Hindu traditions—including tribal and indigenous wisdom—have delved into ontological, philosophical, ethical, cultural, and aesthetic considerations concerning human consciousness. The great *rishis* and spiritual realizers of India resolved the big problems of Life for themselves, leaving a heritage of dharma teachings and sometimes vast spiritual movements that flourished and swept across India. These eternal teachings have profoundly influenced seekers, both East and West, over centuries of time.

In the proceeding years, pundits and scholars of many persuasions have been inspired to write tomes of commentaries on the *sanatana dharma*, its expounders and realizers. The study of traditional scripture plays a vital part in all practice—even for the radical, iconoclastic Bauls, who rebel against the soul-deadening rules and strictures of priests, teachers and preachers. There is something of tremendous value to be discovered in studying the pure dharma, especially as it has been lived by the truly great-hearted who have lived among us. Study of the Path and its diverse traditions helps to integrate experience between body, mind and heart; it can bring the mind into resonance with what the body knows. Study is another way of lighting the flame within; we catch fire by transmission from the light that is contained within the word as sanatana dharma.

No matter how deeply we delve, sooner or later it becomes clear that the big problems of Life are revealed to be not problems at all, because everything leads to the same place. *Ekam Sat viprah bahudha vadanti.* "Truth is one, sages describe it variously." So says the *Rig Veda* (1.164.46), and a truer maxim was never spoken, written or in any other way espoused. The more mature one becomes in practice, the more at ease one becomes within the mystery of the whole panoramic display of the Path; what seemed to be a conflict before—for the mind, that is—simply is not a conflict anymore. When one rests in the no-problem state of consciousness, there isn't much to say, because the paradoxical or dualistic nature of things has merely dissolved into Just This.

Every great tradition has some understanding of this at its esoteric core: the ways to God or the Ultimate Reality are infinite. There are many *margas* or paths to the summit, and yet the mountain is the same. Given the modern interest in quantum physics, it is hard to argue against the truth of the unitive nature of all things, or that the polarities of dark and light exist at the foundation of the physical universe as we know it. At the most fundamental ground, everything is One; all of life exists within a field of interconnectedness.

From the *sahaja* perspective, this fact is naturally obvious when we look at the sun in the sky and see a circle of living light, a symbol of eternal oneness. Life is a circle with no beginning and no end, whose center is everywhere and whose circumference is nowhere. Advaita Vedanta, as classic teaching of nonduality, reflects this truth, and yet it simply is not the entire picture. As Swami Ramdas pointed out, there is the sun (*nirguna*) and there are the sun's rays (*saguna*).

The marvelous writings of Swami Papa Ramdas provide a clear view into the firsthand experience of a great nondual realizer of the bhakti persuasion. The knowledge that the Ultimate Reality is a positive Absolute shines through Ramdas' pristine nondual vision, which easily includes the certainty that—through the power of Grace—the Absolute dances in the world of forms as mutual joy or *ananda* between an eternal Beloved and lover at play. Ramdas speaks with deep heartfelt ease in terms that are simultaneously nondualistic and ecstatically dualistic. The Bauls have this same conviction: there is no paradox, no conflict and no problem in the co-existence of unity and diversity in a world that is alive and imbued with spirit.

Before moving on to Samkhya, the roots of Advaita Vedanta, and the bhakti renaissance of medieval India, it should be noted that we are taking a cursory look at immense, complex streams of teachings and religious movements and their historical components, each of which could easily be (and has been) the subject of many tomes. Indepth study of each of these subjects is a highly worthwhile pursuit for anyone engaging the spiritual Path. That having been said, let us turn toward the opportunity at hand: to explore in brief the historical, philosophical and revelatory background of Lee Lozowick's teaching of Enlightened Duality.

Before we explore Adi Shankara, the great Indian nondualist, and then move on to the Vaishnava bhakti *sampradayas*, it may be both helpful and interesting to sketch out a big picture, beginning with the Vedas and Upanishads—the first oral teachings springing from the wisdom beds of antiquity to be written down in Sanskrit as revealed truth. The four Vedas are the foundation of Hindu scripture and are considered to be primordial truth revealed by the rishis, or ancient seers. The *Rig Veda* dates back to 4,000bce; other Vedas were written down in the following centuries, and about two thousand years later, around 1900bce, the spiritual epic the *Ramayana* appeared. Five hundred years later (1500bce) the major Upanishads were written down. Approximately 1400bce is considered the Age of Krishna, the time of Krishna's incarnation in the human world, his love play with the *gopis* in Vraja and his *lila* and teachings in the great Bharata War. The early version of the *Mahabharata* also appeared around this time.

It has been pointed out many times by pundits of Hindu persuasion that the Vedas and Upanishads contain both nondualistic and dualistic perspectives on the Universe. Bhakti or devotion played a tacit role in all the great scriptures and may even be traced back to the *Rig Veda*, which says, "All my hymns in unison praise Indra: as wives embrace their husbands so do my thoughts embrace Indra, the divine bestower of gifts. For the sake of a favor, they cling to the liberal God Indra, as wives do their lords, or as a woman does her lover."[1] The clear metaphor here reveals the dualistic nature of human relationship to the divinity: in praising Indra by clinging to him as a woman does her lover, one may receive divine gifts. This is an early teaching, in seed form, on the human soul as feminine in relationship to God—a relationship that is engaged through service, devotion, attachment, loyalty, passion, worship and praise,[2] the qualities of love between a wife and her husband.

---

[1]   A.K. Majumdar, *Bhakti Renaissance*, page 1.

[2]   Ibid, page 3.

The *Ramayana* and *Mahabharata* address many aspects of life, with the devotional love relationship between husband and wife as the metaphor most poignantly found in Sita's relationship with Lord Rama, but also contained in the rich interplay of teaching-in-life between Krishna and the just Pandavas and the not-so-just Kauravas. Although the bhakti practice of greater antiquity is a bone of contention among pundits, it only makes sense that ordinary village people were reading or hearing the recitation of these scriptural verses in a rich oral tradition, and they were naturally coming to their own conclusions based upon the knowing of their hearts. These Vedic teachings combined with archaic tribal, tantric, and shamanistic streams (another extraordinarily vast and awe-inspiring subject altogether, belonging to a different project) were actively alive as an oral tradition among the village populace; this commingling and cross-pollinating would have naturally produced a strong foundation of worship in diverse earthy and ecstatic forms that are naturally of a dualistic and devotional bent.

The Upanishads also reflect this diversity of teaching. The *Svetasvetara Upanishad* concludes:

> To one who has the highest devotion for God
> And for his guru even as for God
> To him these matters which have been declared
> and those undeclared too
> become manifest if he be a great soul. (6.23)[3]

After thousands of years of Vedic sacrifices and prayers, and a thousand years after the Upanishads, Buddha came along. Spreading like wildfire, the teachings of Lord Buddha had a profound effect on the Vedic religions of antiquity in India. The sublime appeal of

---

[3]   Ibid, page 2.

Buddhist teachings turned popular attention away from Vedic sacrifice and focused on nondual teachings, insisting on nontheism in favor of impersonal although universal karmic forces. We can easily imagine that the Vedic adherents of the era—based in streams of ancestral tradition, knowledge and wisdom passed down from father to son and mother to daughter literally over millenniums—did not appreciate the reforming intrusion of Buddhism into their already three- or four-thousand-year-old tradition.

The *Bhagavad Gita*, which is considered by many to be the most sublime part of the *Mahabharata*, was not composed until much later, between 500 and 200bce—after Gautama Buddha, whose lifespan is considered to be 624–544bce. The impact of Buddhism must have had some influence in the writing of the *Bhagavad Gita*, which seeded an eventual resurgence of traditions springing from the Vedas and Upanishads and the early strains of bhakti practice.

Historically speaking, this brings us to Samkhya, which came into play between 250–325bce, two or three hundred years after the arrival of Buddha on the scene. Originally expounded by Kapila, who authored the *Samkhya Sutra*, Samkhya is one of the six *darsanas* of Hindu philosophy, attributed to the school of Isvarakrishna. In the Hindu system there are six darsanas (ways of seeing or points of view) through which one may perceive and understand reality: 1) Samkhya, which takes the view of ontology, or the science of being; 2) Nyaya, or logic and epistemology; 3) Vaisheshika, or physics and atomic theory; 4) Yoga, or spiritual practice and meditation; 5) Purva Mimamsa, or hermeneutics and ritual worship; and 6) Vedanta or metaphysics. The study of these are immense undertakings; even in the field of yoga alone, one could spend a lifetime, for there is not only academic study but also practice to be mastered.

Samkhya is a dualistic system taught by Isvarakrishna, which states that Reality is not singular but plural, beginning with the two great polarities of *purusha* (consciousness or the transcendental Self, of which there may be endless numbers) and *prakriti* (Nature). Isvarakrishna declared that prakriti is a multidimensional creation ruled by three primary forces: the *gunas* described above. In the *Samkhya Karika*, the three gunas are described as "joy, joylessness and dejection" having the purpose of "illuminating, activating and restricting. "They overpower each other, are interdependent, productive and cooperative in their activities."[4] This ancient text further states:

> *Sattva is regarded as buoyant and illuminating. Rajas is stimulating and mobile. Tamas is inert and concealing. The activity [of the gunas] is purposive like a lamp [made up of various parts that together produce the single phenomenon of light.]*[5]

This teaching provides a glimpse of the large and small cycles of cosmic and terrestrial life and the ups and downs of one's daily experience as well, because everything is informed by the three gunas. Samkhya teaching contains much more detail, which is best left to the study and research of the reader. However, it is interesting that Gurdjieff also spoke of three forces that rule the Universe: the denying, the affirming and the reconciling. These qualities could be said to correspond to the three gunas of Samkhya, which characterize existence: *tamas* (darkness or torpor), *rajas* (excitement), and *sattva* (light). These are often translated as passivity (tamas), activity (rajas) and consciousness or harmony (sattva). By the power of our

---

4   Georg Feuerstein, *The Yoga Tradition*, page 102.

5   Ibid.

own capacity to know and experience these forces underlying life, we come to wisdom, of which awakened faith is one of the grand apotheoses.

Sri Adi Shankara (788-820ce) was a religious reformer and the great expounder of nondual philosophy. His is the great grandfather, many times over, of the popular *advaita* teachings that exist today. Shankara's philosophical teachings of Advaita Vedanta founded a vast movement that strongly influenced the culture, religion and common thought of Hindus of his era all over India, which had been deeply affected by the wide and rapid spread of Buddhism. Shankara led his followers away from Buddhist trends, returning very effectively to ancient Vedic tradition, putting his attention on the classic scriptures of the ten principle *Upanishads*, the *Bhagavad Gita* and the *Brahma Sutra*, and developing his teachings based upon these essential texts.

In essence, Shankara posits that everything is illusion; only Brahman—the nondual ground of being—is real; everything else is maya, a projection of ignorance. According to Shankara, all arising appearances are illusion, and the goal of human life is to pierce this illusion and realize oneness with Brahman through intellectual discrimination or jnana.

Shankara defined *moksha* as the soul's liberation from the bonds of maya or illusion and therefore from the cycles of rebirth ruled by karmic forces, which is accomplished through the relinquishing of all distinctions, differences, attachments to form, personhood, relationships—in fact, every aspect of duality—to merge into the formless, timeless, unitive reality of Brahman. However, if you delve far enough into the life of Adi Shankara, it is of interest to find that he also initiated the worship of the Shri *yantra*, which refers to the goddess Lakshmi and is still today the primary yantra utilized in tantric Buddhist and tantric Hindu Shaktism meditation. He also wrote many verses of devotional poetry to the Divine Mother.

The classical poetic scripture, *Saudaryalahari* (Waves of Beauty), written by Adi Shankara, tell us in its first verse in Part I, *Ananda Lahari* (Waves of Bliss), that Shiva cannot create anything at all without Shakti. The first forty-one verses of Part I provide a detailed account of the worship of the Divine Mother, the concept of kundalini, meditation upon the Shri Chakra, and the devotional worship of Shakti as Divine Mother and Creatrix who is the source of illumination and liberation as well.

> *The dust under your feet, O Goddess great, is like the city of the rising sun that removes all darkness and misfortune from the mind of the poor ignorant one. It is like honey that flows from the flowers of vital action to the slow-witted one; it is like a heap of wish-giving gems, given to the poorest man ....* (Verse 3)

> *O Goddess mine, you live in seclusion with your consort in the lotus with a thousand petals (Sahasrara), reached after breaking through the infinitesimal ways: of the power of earth in Muladhara; of the power of water in Manipura; of the power of fire in Swadhishtana, of the fire of air in the heart (Anahata), and of the power of ether between the eyes (Ajna).* (Verse 9)

> *Using the nectar that flows in between your feet to drench all the nerves of the body and descending from the moon with nectar-like rays, reaching in to where you dwell, coiling your body like a serpent, you sleep in the Kula Kundalini ....* (Verse 10)

Brahma creates the world, Vishnu looks after it, Shiva destroys it, Iswara makes them disappear and also disappears himself, and Sadshiva blesses them all, by your order given to him, by a momentary move of your eyes. (Verse 24)[6]

Shankara continues in Part II, Waves of Beauty, to describe in great detail the many glorious attributes of the goddess, describing her both sensually and with loving devotion as the ultimate source of the gunas, the Source of Life which is beyond birth and death, the liberator of souls. It is interesting that Adi Shankara is said to have considered Samkhya to be the primary opponent to his nondual philosophy, yet in this poem he extols the virtue of the Goddess who is the source of the gunas—the Divine Mother Herself:

Oh Darling of Shiva, those three eyes of yours colored in three shades to enhance thy beauty, in which you wear the three qualities of sattvas, rajas and tamas, as if to create the holy trinity, Brahma, Vishnu and Shiva; after the final deluge they become one with you. (Verse 53)

The learned sages tell, oh Daughter of the King of the Mountain, that this world of ours is created and destroyed when you open and shut your soulful eyes. I believe, my Mother, that you never shut your eyes, so that this world is created by you and never, ever faces deluge. (Verse 55)

Shankara calls his Maha Devi by many names: Tripura Sundari; Saraswati; Uma; Darling of Shiva; Lakshmi

---

6   http://en.wikipedia.org/wiki/Saundaryalahari

and more. He recounts her loving pastimes with the Supreme Lord and her powers to create.

O Parashakti, who is one with Parabrahma, those who have learned the Vedas call you as Brahma's wife, Sarasvati, or call you as Vishnu's wife, Lakshmi, or call you as Shiva's wife, Parvati. You are called forth as Maha Maya, who gives life to the world and have attained all that is to attain. (Verse 97)[7]

This beautiful poem in praise of the Great Goddess with all of her attributes and power to awaken, bless and endow speaks of a human author who knew the secrets of incarnation. Nonetheless, scholarly commentators seem to generally agree that for Adi Shankara, bhakti was considered a step along the way toward moksha—rather like employing maya only in order to realize Brahman and therefore liberation from ignorance and illusion. It is hard to believe, once having read his *Saundarya Lahari*, that this was indeed Shankara's ultimate view; at the very least, we can see for ourselves that Adi Shankara was no stranger to the joys of the bhakti disposition toward Life—or the co-existence of nirguna and saguna aspects of Reality.

In this regard, it is also significant that Shankara is closely linked with the mythologized Dattatreya, the immortal guru and great ascetic yogin worshipped by both Vaishnavas and Shaivites. The worship of Dattatreya (who we will hear more about in the essay titled "Beggary") has endured over the centuries; he is an icon of both radical nondual realization and radical Enlightened Duality. Shankara also wrote hymns in praise of Dattatreya, and in one story of Shankara's death, he disappeared into a cave at Badarinatha led by Dattatreya, who was holding his hand.[8]

---

[7]   Ibid.

[8]   Antonio Rigopoulos, *Dattatreya: The Immortal Guru, Yogin and Avatara*, page 95.

History tells us that Shankara's teachings and his movement took root and flourished as pure advaita, still alive today in India in the active tradition of the four Shankaracharyas, who are rather like the highly revered popes of the four Shankara *mathas,* or monastic seats. Today Advaita Vedanta may be the most prominent popular exposition of Hindu thought; it has gained very strong footholds in the West through its many proponents, loosely including a lot of neo-advaita gurus teaching a brand of nondual philosophy in America and Europe that might make Adi Shankara weep tears of frustration and sorrow over how his teachings have been misunderstood.

Shankara's rigorous and ascetic metaphysical view was challenged in the intervening centuries by visionaries who perceived a possibility of awakened awareness that went beyond the realization of nonduality. The sweeping resurgence of the heart on fire for the love of the Lord ignited a storm of creativity known as the bhakti renaissance of medieval India.

It is impossible to consider a theistic path, or a Path of Enlightened Duality, without this bhakti quality of love, or ananda (bliss). Bhakti means, generally speaking, devotion, worship and love. The devotional tendency has its own pathological potentials: blind following, idolatry, adulation of a cult figure, denial of the psyche's shadow, and so on. When bhakti is the focus, practice is centered on the heart (*hridaya*), the feeling center, or the central notions of *bhava* (divine mood) and *rasa* (taste or essence). The shadow side of the feeling center is to become lost in the emotions of the child. Devotion must be honed by vigilance and the commitment to self-observe and disciplined practice; devotion must be tempered by clarity and deepened through the maturation process in which we become full adults who—as practitioners on the path—cultivate the desire to serve others.

Although the use of the *nama* of Yogi Ramsuratkumar is, as Lee says, "the seed practice of this school," to give in to the desire to just float along is a pitfall of the devotional path. In recent years Lee has emphasized that love alone is not enough to see the spiritual process through to the end. In this regard he is referring to our conventional notion of love, which is tarnished by the smokescreen of maya.

Divine love is a radiance that outshines all else. In its pure form, bhakti has the power to tame, transform, surrender and even annihilate the separative ego. The exalted reaches of the Path are linked with faith and compassion—both of which are conditions of divine love. Both faith and compassion require an integration of those qualities of mind, body and heart that will see us through the difficulties, in the face of which "ordinary" love flees in horror. One yoga scholar writes:

> *In the context of ordinary life, the term* bhava *signifies "sentiment" or "emotion," which includes aesthetic appreciation. According to the Sanskrit dramatists, there are nine predominant emotions: love, joy, sorrow, anger, courage, fear, disgust, surprise and renunciation.*
>
> *In a spiritual context, the word bhava denotes feeling-charged ecstasy or the ultimate mind-melting love-devotion experienced in the presence of, or in union with, the Divine....whose symptoms include spontaneous laughter, weeping, singing, dancing and raving. At times,* maha-bhava *resembles madness, and not a few Vaishnava ecstatics have called themselves madcaps ....*
>
> *A closely related concept in the Vaishnava tradition is that or* rasa, *a term which means literally "taste" or "essence" and here refers to the basic mood of a person*

*or situation. Thus Vishnu devotees experiencing ecstasy
are said to enjoy the mood of love (*bhakti-rasa*).*[9]

From the scholarly perspective, this is information that may be of use. Speaking from his experience of living God-realization, Swami Ramdas writes:

> *Bhakti is an intense longing and love for God which
> enables the aspirant to keep up a constant remembrance
> of Him, thus purifying his emotions and elevating his
> thought to the consciousness of the Reality. Bhakti is the
> adoration of God, who dwells in his own heart and fills
> the universe, and surrender of all his actions to Him.
> Here a fit of renunciation seizes him—a mental recoil
> from the unrealities of life that had so long enthralled
> him. Through the exercise of an awakened intellect he
> now begins to discriminate the real from the unreal—
> the eternal from the non-eternal.*[10]

In *The Only Grace is Loving God*, Lee Lozowick writes about bhakti in his *gita* (song) on the possibility of Loving God:

> *The ancient Vedic scriptures say that God grants Mukti
> or freedom to beings quite easily, but He grants Bhakti
> or Love very selectively and rarely. Mukti or freedom
> frees one from the binds of Earthly or human concerns,
> while Bhakti or Love binds one to the Earthly or human
> expression of the Beloved's Whimsical possibility. And
> God is bound to the Lover and free of the Mukti. Loving
> God is the only Grace there is, and the possibility of*

---

[9]   Georg Feuerstein, *The Yoga Tradition*, pages 385–386.
[10]   Swami Ramdas, *The Divine Life*, page 114.

*Loving God is a Grace to God from Mankind as well
as a Grace from God. Loving God is truly a human,
earthly Grace. We do exist here, despite any number of
philosophies that attempt to convince us that this is all
a dream or an illusion. It is only our relationship to
this that makes it illusory, not the fact of its existence.
Loving God perfects it as it is. And we are already free
of it all in any case! Death finally captures us all in the
perfection of the "Divine Path of Growing Old."*[11]

Lee once had a large sign made and hung on the wall behind his
blues band, Shri, when they performed during a sangha celebration
in a local public venue. The sign said: "The only proof he needed
for the existence of God was music"—a quote from a character in a
book written by Kurt Vonnegut. This is an essentially bhakti sentiment. Music, the innocence of children, the mysteries of birth and
death, the exultation of the night sky and all the inherent beauty in
the world—as well as the fact that human beings, no matter how
low we sink, continue to create art and to demonstrate kindness and
compassion in random moments—is sufficient to invoke praise of
God in the *bhakta*. These experiences alone inform us that there is a
Divine Intelligence guiding Creation, and that Divine Intelligence is
ultimately graceful, merciful, joyous and loving.

At the same time, understandably, many people find it extremely difficult to view the destructive quality of God as graceful and
merciful; life's big battles with impermanence and suffering have
driven many to atheism. Some people feel burned by their concept
of "God" and turn away with bitterness. For others, the faint scent
of the Beloved's perfume continues to lure the heart, and we cannot forget that we have been touched, even when we are perched at

---

[11]   Lee Lozowick, *The Only Grace is Loving God*, pages 44–45.

the abyss of emptiness or in a serious collision with grief—which is where faith comes in.

Faith requires the certitude that grace and mercy take many expressions, and human beings, with our limited perspective, cannot always recognize mercy and grace in the arising of phenomena in life as we experience it. Sooner or later, we must bow in submission and faith in circumstances that remain inexplicable and seemingly inequitable and insupportable. We know that faith can be found in the darkest of crucibles, for there are many people who have survived unimaginable traumas of cruelty and debasement at the hand of their fellow humans—for example the concentration camps of WW II—and in their worst hours discovered the secret of God's mercy and grace because they had faith in the ultimate benevolence of Life.

To quote Lee further, from *The Only Grace is Loving God*:

> *Nondualism is not untrue of Loving God; that is, Loving God is certainly dualistic in its expression and its experience but is not dualistic in Essence—how could it be? Yet at the same time, Loving God is not detached from or does not obscure our humanness either. Loving God, which blinds the Lover to all but the Beloved, nonetheless does not obscure the reality of human life on Earth, as do so many of the yogic states of absorption in the "Self" and so on. Loving God is still full of the apparent contradictions or apparent illusory dualities of life; it is meaty, sweaty, full of glory and praise, full of suffering and blame. Life on Earth is not inherently beautiful or absolutely free of negativity and pain, even Enlightened life on Earth. Blissfulness is a function of being assumed by the Will of God, not a matter of things all going the way we want them to go.... The truth of the matter is that "all things are transitory, including nondual enlightenment." ....*

*Life here is suffering. Transcendence is the true state
of Essence. Slavery to the Will of God is the true state of
existence, or the optimum form of activity possible....*[12]

There are objective experiences on the spiritual path in which
one must face an inner lacuna, which may appear as many different things—impenetrable darkness, grief, doubt, fear, insecurity,
remorse, dread and seemingly infinite horrors, a prolonged clash
with what appears to be unmitigated evil. St. John of the Cross found
faith in the dark night of the soul, when God had disappeared and
left him alone to deal with his demons in the empty yawning crevasse
of the inner world. Dante called this hell. Every person on the Path
has to come to her or his own terms with this part of the terrain on
the way up the mountain—the avalanches, the deep unholy chasms,
uncharted barren stretches of the path, the blinding snowstorms, the
primeval elements unleashed. Ultimately, we find that we must confront and wrestle with that elusive aspect of bhakti called faith.

Papa Ramdas had a practice of greeting everything that came his
way as the Divine, which he referred to as Ram. During his time as a
beggar sadhu, when there was no food for days, this was "Ram in the
form of no food." Every relationship, good or bad, was Ram in the
form of whatever or whomever was appearing before Ramdas. This
is an expression of radical faith; it is "slavery to the Will of God" and
a reflection of the essential state of being.

Yogi Ramsuratkumar, the spiritual son of Swami Ramdas, lived
in a state of what he called "sweet slavery" to "Father in heaven." He
did not leave any written teachings; he often said, "Swami Ramdas
has written all that needs to be said." Yogi Ramsuratkumar asked his
devotees to praise God, and although he did not write books or give
dharma talks in a formal sense, he frequently burst into praise of
God in spontaneous speech. Ma Devaki, who was the attendant of

---

[12]   Ibid, page 43–44.

Yogi Ramsuratkumar for the last seven years of his life, recounted the following story of an exchange that occurred in the early 1990s, when several people were sitting with the master under a tree at the home of a devotee.

Yogi Ramsuratkumar looked at the doctor who was attending to him and said, in ecstatic tones of childlike innocence, "God alone exists. There is nothing else and no one else. He is all-pervading. He alone exists, nothing else, neither in the past nor in the present nor in the future. He is everywhere—here, there...*everywhere!* He is indivisible, indescribable, beyond ordinary intelligence. He is total, beyond words, complete....No one is separate."

While he spoke, the eyes of the beggar saint looked around at each person. Then he said, "It is for people, for ordinary mortals who do not understand this, that name and form are necessary. All are in Father. Father is in all of us. This beggar does not understand advaitic philosophy, but he remembers the lotus feet of his master, Swami Ramdas. Ramdas gave this beggar Ramnam. For this beggar, the lotus feet of his master and Ramnam will do."[13]

These words of inspiration come from a human being whose life was an embodiment of faith; the profound awakening and divine madness that seized his being and transformed his life came through the auspices of Grace—through devotion to the guru and chanting the name of God. Yogi Ramsuratkumar's frequent nondual declarations of the unity of all life were at home in the sahaja ideal: a lucid, natural, unpremeditated relationship to the world around him, which he ever viewed from the eyes of God-realization.

---

13   Ma Devaki, *Saranagatham*, Yogi Ramsuratkumar Trust, Tiruvannamalai, Tamil Nadu, January, 2009.

The passionate, far-flung renaissance of the bhakti tradition that took place in medieval India over several hundred years changed the face of spiritual understanding and practice for millions of people—just as the powerful reformist teachings of Shankara had changed culture and consciousness in his time. Each of the five primary "revelators" considered in this essay founded one of the five major sampradayas of contemporary Vaishnava Hinduism—that is, those sects which worship Vishnu as the Supreme Being. The great bhakti reformers who planted the seeds of Vaishnava worship today are: Ramanuja, Nimbarka, Madhva, Vallachabharya and Chaitanya. While on the subject of bhakti traditions, we will also briefly touch upon the poets Jayadeva and Candidas as patron saints of the Bauls, who fall into the tantric side of the bhakti stream but cannot be considered a sampradaya per se because they are far too iconoclastic.

Ramanuja (1017–1137ce) agreed with Shankara that Brahman, as ground of being, is the Ultimate Reality, but he did not agree that nothing else is real. Ramanuja taught that individual selves and matter itself (described in the terms of Samkhya) are real but rely on Brahman—the Supreme Reality—for their reality. According to Ramanuja, the relationship of selves and matter to Brahman is like the relationship of the human soul to the human body—described as a part to a whole, as supported to supporter. Most importantly, Ramanuja's vision of Brahman was not without qualities (nirguna) but with qualities (saguna); he viewed Brahman as Narayana/Vishnu and understood God as the cause of dependent realities."[14]

Ramanuja expounded further: Although God is beyond description, one can know God by inference and analogous attribution based on God's manifestation in this world as an *avatara* (incarnation) of Lord Vishnu, the preserver and sustainer. In his all-pervading mercy and love of Creation, Vishnu descends into matter in the form of

---

[14]   *The Oxford Dictionary of World Religions*, page 797.

his various avatars. Krishna and Rama are the two most beloved of those and are deified as Supreme Beings in their own right and widely worshipped as *ista devatas*. But generally speaking, it is as Hari and Narayana that Vishnu is more universally known by Vaishnavas as the all-inclusive cosmic Beloved or Divine Person.

For Ramanuja, it was for this reason that God is the source of grace, as God seeks the salvation of those who turn to Him through revelation. Ramanuja gave two means to moksha:

1) Bhakti or devotion to God, which includes:
   a) viveka, discernment, especially related to purity of food
   b) vimoka, non-attachment
   c) abhyasa, constant meditation
   d) kriya, performance of religious acts (ritual worship)
   e) kalyana, auspicious virtues such as truthfulness
   f) equanimity; transcending sorrow
   g) anuddharsa, or joy

2) Prapatti, or self-surrender to God

Ramanuja is essentially describing what Lee calls Spiritual Slavery, which is not a state of total absorption and annihilation in the Supreme Reality; rather it is a state in which the individual self abides in a state of surrender, service and complete dependence upon Narayana.[15]

Nimbarka was a great mover and shaker of the early Vaishnava movement of the eleventh and twelfth centuries. His teaching was similar

---

[15]   Ibid.

to Ramanuja's but differed in that Nimbarka and his followers worshipped Radha, the consort of Lord Krishna. This is most unusual, as Radha symbolizes the Divine Feminine; her image is extrapolated from the earlier archetype of the goddess Lakshmi, the consort of Vishnu. The worship of Radha invokes the Divine Feminine within the body of the worshiper, which automatically insures a divine relationship with her counterpart, Lord Krishna—an early intimation of later Baul practice. Nimbarka's sect caught fire in the imagination of the people, and the success of the bhakti movement in northern India is largely attributed to him.[16] In the worship of Radha and Krishna, this sect sought not union or absorption but relationship: the lover and Beloved in an interplay of everlasting mutual joy. Most likely his views had a strong influence on the later work of Jayadeva, as we will soon explore.[17]

Sri Madhva (1238–1317ce) was the Vaishnava saint who took the most radical position of duality in his teaching. His way is known as a form of Dvaita Vedanta, or dualistic metaphysical philosophy. His particular view of relationship with a personal God as the Supreme Reality is starkly opposite to the Advaita Vedanta perspective, in which the worship of any deity, including a Supreme Deity, is seen as just another illusion born of ignorance, which ultimately must be penetrated if liberation is the goal.

The spiritual epic of Madhvacharya's life began when, as a very young man, Madhva (a Sanskrit word meaning "honey" or simply "sweet") was deeply disturbed by the absolute proclamations of his precursor, Shankara. As opposed to "nothing is real," Madhva's

16   A.K. Majumdar, *Bhakti Renaissance*, page 21.
17   *The Oxford Dictionary of World Religions*, page 701.

essential teaching was "difference is real." His ontological argument was based on the same scriptural teachings as Shankara's, but Madhva's conclusion was different.

Although Madhva used the hermeneutics of intellect to "prove" his argument, the core of his teaching centered around the love of the Divine Person, based on the belief that the individual *atma* or *jiva*—soul or self—knows the truth of the Divine Being by virtue of a native intuitive higher-sense faculty of the jiva. According to Madhva, individual beings have two kinds of sensory faculties: the five gross bodily senses of sight, smell, taste, touch and hearing, and the subtle cognitive sense of intuition. It is this spiritual instinct through which Creation recognizes its Creator—exactly like a newborn animal of any kind knows its mother and naturally takes to feeding from her breast.

Sri Madhva took this even further. He unequivocally stated that there is a loving, personal "Supreme Being who is the source of all beauty, truth, unity and diversity. Further, the atma .... is eternally an individual, both in the material realm and in the transcendental. The names and forms we see temporarily manifested in the realm of matter are reflections of the eternal names and forms ...."[18] He taught that the forms of the worshiped and the worshiper are real, eternal and fundamentally interconnected in a reciprocal relationship that has no beginning and no end.

However, the individual jiva is caught in matter and must work to transcend the karmas that have been engendered in order to transcend to a higher plane of existence, where freedom abounds. In this regard he described a transcendental realm that the Buddhists might call "the Pure Land" and the Christians call "heaven"—an afterlife or otherworld for those who are liberated from the illusion of being

---

[18] Jeffrey Armstrong, "Difference is Real," *Hinduism Today*, June, July, August, Summer 2008, page 39–53.

caught in matter, in which individual jivas are free to experience the cosmic reality of their existence within the divine relationship with Hari, the Divine Person.

Madhva wrote, "The liberated souls, having found their eyes and ears, loving one another, become hierarchically different in various qualities such as intelligence. Some among them play in the huge ocean of milk. Some play near and in the gardens. They bathe and behold themselves in deep, fine lakes fit to bathe in. They behold the Supreme Lord himself."[19]

Madhva taught that the love of the Lord—the devotional relationship itself—is the way to liberation from endless karmic cycles in matter. His basic argument with advaita as expounded by Adi Shankara is that the goal of life is not to realize Brahman, the Absolute and virtually disappear, but to realize relationship with the Supreme Being—in his view, Narayana or Hari.

Following a chronological path of the Vaishnava bhakti tradition, which could perhaps be loosely termed the yoga of devotion, we come next to the Vaishnava poet, Jayadeva, who is of particular importance to the Bauls. All of the great bhakti streams that came after Jayadeva owe much of their religious mythology to the particular stories of Krishna and Radha that have their origins in the *Gita Govinda*, written by Jayadeva in the twelfth century.

This ecstatic poem of erotic mysticism tells the story of the relationship between Radha and Krishna, which is a metaphor for the relationship between the human soul and the personal Beloved.

---

[19]   Ibid, page 51.

The *Gita Govinda* is a celebrated achievement that stands out in the genre of sacred erotic literature in the world. Springing out of a vast transformational process that was occurring at this time, Jayadeva succeeded in bringing the reality of the mystical realm back to the marketplace of human need. The cultural and religious milieu of the times created a fertile ground for this breakthrough of transcendent creativity. Buddhism was not the only contender for religious supremacy in India—Vedic traditions had been equally, although more politically, vanquished by adherents of Islam. The ancient framework of Hindu culture in north India had been decimated by repeated Muslim invasions from the eleventh to thirteenth centuries. There was much plundering and razing of hallowed temples and seats of learning; ancient texts and sculptures were destroyed, and Hindu culture was rocked to its foundations.

Many Hindu monarchs, who had served the culture as patrons of the arts, disappeared into the south at this time, while poets, craftsmen, painters and musicians moved to the safety of mountains and forests of rural areas. Artists who had been trained in classical traditions discovered themselves almost in exile, in a new world among tribal and common people who "lived close to nature and expressed their innermost feelings in a language of refreshing simplicity."[20] This sweeping cultural upheaval had a far-reaching effect on the arts. Poetry was transformed from strict classical forms to a free-flowing vernacular style that was more connected to the earth and took on a new depth of unfettered, uncensored feeling.

Jayadeva came out of this creative outpouring. Like the Bauls of later times, he was born in the Birbhum district of Bengal. In his early life he wandered the roads of northern India, visiting the towns of Mathura and Brindavan, where he was deeply influenced by the enchanting scenery and tales of Krishna. A fervent Vaishnava, he

---

[20]   Amit Ambalal, *Krishna as Shrinathji*, page 12.

went to Jagannath, where he camped under a tree near the Jagannath shrine. There, his life was changed forever when he met a brahmin, who lived at the temple and, after many childless years, had been graced by the Lord Jagannath (Krishna) with the birth of a beautiful girl child. The brahmin had a dream in which Jagannath instructed him to give the child to Jayadeva. Despite Jayadeva's reluctance, the old man left the child with him and disappeared. That child grew up to be Jayadeva's famous dancing consort, Padmavati, whom he married and lived with happily for the rest of his life.

Inspired by Padmavati, Jayadeva became the visionary poet who wordsmithed language into a new, fresh form in which Radha played a central role as the archetypal gopi—lover of Krishna—and Divine Feminine. Although Nimbarka also focused on Radha, Jayadeva forged ahead in boldly presenting a frank, fresh, erotic inclusion of Radha. This earthy metaphor of erotic love for the Divine was one of the primary spiritual inventions of Jayadeva's *Gita Govinda*, which objectified the role of the body in the events of the individual soul. Radha was a human person who became divinized, and everyone could relate with her.

Jayadeva and Padmavati found their way to the court of Lakshmanasena, the Vaidya king of Bengal, where they were renowed as poet and dancer. In India, poetry is almost always put to music, and when Jayadeva sang his poems, Padmavati danced. We can only imagine the soul-stirring inspiration these great artists gave to their audiences. The *Gita Govinda* was considered a lyrical drama and performed as a play; this eight-hundred-year old masterpiece is considered the earliest example of the type of primitive dramatic play that still survives in Bengal.[21]

Jayadeva's poetry spread like wildfire and became so popular that "Poetry began to be written in the local languages based on the

---

[21]   Ibid, pages 337–338.

Gita Govinda, using the same symbolism and extolling love in all its varying moods."[22] The poetic metaphors and imagery of the *Gita Govinda* were reproduced in many different art forms: paintings, songs, rural ballads—all of which reflected this important evolution. Jayadeva's tiny, carved terracotta temple to Radha and Krishna at Joydeb-Kenduli in Bengal is the site of the contemporary annual Baul mela. To this day, the *Gita Govinda* is performed daily before the deity at the Jagannath temple in Puri.

In the fourteenth century, northern India produced the great poet Candidas, who was considered the father of Bengali poetry. Candidas' love songs, which followed the style of Jayadeva, featured Radha and Krishna and are sung in Bengal to date. With Candidas, the Bauls begin to appear on the scene in Bengal. A brahmin by birth, Candidas was heretical and revolutionary; he is often considered a Baul because of the thematic similarities in his poetry and the fact that he rejected caste and rank; his complete rebellion against religious law and social custom was highlighted by his life-long relationship with Rami, a low-born washer maid.

Not only did he turn away from caste privilege and the concretized creeds and rules of religiosity, Candidas' poetic voice was powerful enough to speak about the discovery of the Divine in and through the human body. His frank engagement with yogas of sex and breath placed these strictly "left-hand" tantric practices directly in the stream of the Vaishnava devotional path. The passion of the love union between Candidas and Rami was the inspiration that fueled his masterful writings of bhakti poetry.[23]

---

[22]   Georg Feuerstein, *The Yoga Tradition*, page 388.

[23]   Amit Ambalal, *Krishna as Srinathiji*, page 12.

With Jayadeva and Candidas, the worship of Krishna became an increasingly intimate experience of a personal Beloved—a living God with whom the human person could have an immediate, direct relationship that could include a very mysterious element of erotic sensuality.

One hundred years later, in the fifteenth century another great bhakti visionary appeared: Vallabhacharya, who wrote his famous commentaries on Book X of the *Bhagavata Purnana*, the love games of Sri Krishna and the gopis. As a young man Vallabhacharya was inspired to worship Krishna when he went to Vraja, the historical village of Krishna's childhood and his play with the gopis. The path Vallabhacharya propounded was called the Pushti Marga, or path of grace, in which realization depended not upon Vedic rites and rituals, but upon absolute surrender to Krishna, which then constrained Krishna to grant his grace to the worshipper. This way of radically invoking God's grace required a focus of total attention (*sarvatma-bhava*) upon Krishna alone.

In the latter part of the sixteenth century, the dynamic son of Vallabhacharya, Shri Gosainji, added the element of "regal splendor" to the Pushti Marga, in which he formulated the *seva* (work) in which *raga*, *bhoga* and *shringara* (music, food, ornate adornment and rich attire) were offered to the deity. Furthermore, he emphasized *madhurya* bhakti, wherein Lord Krishna is known as the Beloved of the heart, and all of his devotees, whether man or woman, became gopis. In this path, worship of the deity included not only traditional *puja* but also painting, poetry, music, cookery, flowers and floral arrangements, sculpture, costumes and jewelry—dedicating every possible aspect of life to Krishna.[24] The use of the image as *svarupa*,

---

[24]   Ibid.

or embodiment of God, became empowered in this tradition. Sacred images as invocational objects of meditation and prayer were developed and celebrated through the proliferation of many forms of art as pictorial visualization of the deity.

In the middle of this creative flowering of art, philosophy and awakened consciousness, the great contemporary of Vallabhacharya, Mahaprabhu Sri Krsna Chaitanya (1485–1533ce), was born in a northern region of Bengal. An ecstatic mystic who was disposed toward fits of devotional mood that were so intense they were alarming to those around him, his *mahabhavas*—or objective states of ecstatic love of God—were of such profound objectivity that he became revered as an incarnation of both Radha and Krishna.[25] Founder of the Gaudiya Sampradaya, Chaitanya's teaching (which we will hear more about in the last essay of this book) was dubbed Distinctive Realism.[26]

From around the fifteenth century to the present time, Bauls have sprung up from the grassroots of Bengali religious culture and thrived as wandering beggars and mystic bard-poets. They were minstrels who brought joy and delight, along with a simple but exalted dharma and philosophy, to the common village people in return for a bowl of rice and dahl. Their renderings of religious myths and teachings were couched in the language of the village lanes and city streets, spoken and sung in ways that everyone could understand.

---

[25]   June McDaniel, *The Madness of the Saints*, pages 35–36.

[26]   *Hinduism Today*, page 43.

The Baul belief that every human being has an inborn divine potential fueled their insistence on turning away from rank and caste and accepting all into their communities. For the Baul, the human being is sacred and revered; thus, over the centuries, they have brought inspiration to the ordinary person who has struggled to maintain existence in the face of the fierce vicissitudes of rural life in Bengal. Because of this, the Bauls have always been the heroes of the common people.

From the beginning, the Bauls considered Jayadeva and Chaitanya to be their primary patron saints; at the same time, they were steeped in the tantric teachings and practices of the Sahajiya cults of Bengal. The Bauls were heretical, iconoclastic and revolutionary in their blending of tantric Sahajiya Buddhism and Sahajiya Vaishnava Hinduism with music, dance and transformational mysteries of sexual yoga and breath practice. A further cross-pollination occurred between the Bauls and their Sufi counterparts, the Auls, which greatly influenced the Baul emphasis on longing for the illusive "Man of the Heart," rooted in the nondual realization of the Supreme Reality as a personal Beloved. This synthesis gave rise to *kaya sadhana*, or the path to God-realization through the human body.

Placing a very high premium on devotion and radical reliance on the guru or spiritual preceptor, the Baul ideal is to live from the authentic and original impulse that is called sahaja (innate) in the Sanskrit language. The sahaja principle might be summed up in Lee's words: "We have to relax into the natural state in which the Divine, which is evolutionary, is free to live through us." This impulse takes the true Baul on the *ulta* or reverse path; it is a path that leads in the opposite direction of the rest of the world, or directly against the mainstream current:

> [*The Bauls*] *avoid all religion in which the natural piety of the soul is overshadowed by the useless paraphernalia of ritualism and ceremony on the one hand*

and pedantry and hypocrisy on the other. It is said in a beautiful song — "Reverse are the modes and manners of the man who is a real appreciator of the true behavior. Such a man is affected neither by the weal nor by the woe of the world, and constantly realizes the delight of love; it appears that his eyes are floating on the water of delight; sometimes he laughs alone in his own mood, sometimes he cries alone. Awkwardly wild are all his manners and customs—and the other extremely wonderful fact is that the glory of the full-moon [Krishna] closes round him for all time; and further . . . there is no setting of the moon of his heart . . ."[27]

This describes Lee's relationship with Yogi Ramsuratkumar, who is the sun that never sets in the heart of the disciple. Lee's poetry to his master, Yogi Ramsuratkumar, written over twenty-five years, is published in two large volumes titled *Death of a Dishonest Man: Poems and Prayers to Yogi Ramsuratkumar* (1998) and *Gasping for Air in a Vacuum: Poems and Prayers to Yogi Ramsuratkumar* (2003) and in a smaller compilation in French and English, *108 Poèmes et Prières à Yogi Ramsuratkumar* (2004). These "poems of a broken heart," as they were called in their first editions, are composed in the classic Indian devotional form of *ninda stuti*, or ironic praise. They speak with a voice of radical devotion and worship of God in the human form of the guru combined with a fierce call to the alchemy of inner work on self—a fusion that is unique in the contemporary Western world.

Lee's teachings, music, lyrics and poetry to Yogi Ramsuratkumar flow in the same stream of dharma art as the Baul bards of Bengal; they transmit a teaching for future generations who may long for the

---

[27]   Das Gupta, *Obscure Religious Cults*, pages 162–163.

Beloved and seek the transformational mysteries. The proliferation of art encouraged among his students by Lee will be further explored in other essays.

The introduction of divine images through the tremendous influx of sacred art that Lee has brought into the West vitally reflects the stream of the Pushti Marga of Vallabhacharya in particular and the tantric dimensions of the bhakti tradition. For over twenty-five years Lee has encouraged his students to study Vallabhacharya's commentaries on the love games of Krishna, found in Book Ten of the *Bhagavata Purana*, with which Lee has found a strong resonance, particularly in the precept of total love, attention and reliance upon the Divine.

> *For the one who follows the path, bhakti, devotion, is the well-spring of true religion; but the true devotee is shaukeen too, a connoisseur in every field, one whose heart and soul are fully centred on his Lord. All the arts inspired by Pushti Marga . . . . reflect this attitude of celebration.*[28]

It is a natural human tendency to express beauty in paintings, sculptures and words; art itself is the expression of a sacred culture. As already noted, Vallabhacharya's teachings were manifested in every field of the arts, making the personal God all the more alive and accessible. The importance of divine images as *svarupa* cannot be overestimated, as they confer great blessings and transmission of Reality as it is upon the devotee; these are found embodied in many forms of the arts.

It is this revelry in the beauty and wonder of creation, from macro to micro, which marks the pleasure-as-prayer of the *shaukeen*, the

---

[28]   Amit Ambalal, *Krishna as Shrinathji*, pages 11–12.

connoisseur of life, whose context is to enjoy as a way of celebrating the Divine. It is the *jivan-mukta*—one who lives fully in the state of liberation—who may engage *sambhoga*, or complete enjoyment through the senses, to develop the *sambhogakaya* (divine body of enjoyment). Without this context, revelry quickly becomes the self-aggrandizing activity of the libertine, the rebel without a cause who generates suffering and karmic entanglements as he or she careens through the world, seeking nothing more than the gratification of personal desires. In other words, wherever the *bhakta* experiences bhoga (enjoyment), it springs from love of the Lord.

In conclusion, many inspired teachings and visionaries have influenced bhakti worship over the centuries. Those most relevant to the teachings of American Baul Lee Lozowick are the Sahajiya Vaishnavas, with their underpinnings in Bengali tantrism and deep connection with the Sahajiya Buddhists, out of which evolved the Bauls of Bengal, and the Pusti Marga of Vallabhacharya. However, it should be stated that as much as the bhakti traditions play an important role in understanding the mood and taste of Enlightened Duality, tantric traditions associated with the worship of Shiva, Shakti, Kali and Dattatreya, to name a few, have also been influential in the synthesis that is the Baul way of *sadhana*. Lee has often shared teachings and examples from many tantric traditions, which provide a plethora of experience upon which we may glean insight into practice. As Sanatan Das said in December 2007, "Shiva was the first Baul." For the Bauls, there is no conflict in loving the Lord in multiple images and forms: Krishna, Radha, Shiva and Kali.

In his book, *The Only Grace is Loving God*, Lee wrote twenty-five years ago: "We do exist here, despite any number of philosophies that attempt to convince us that this is all a dream or an illusion. It is only our relationship to this that makes it illusory, not the fact of its existence." The teaching of Enlightened Duality is very simple and yet big enough to hold all the marvelous complexity and diversity of Life in its amazing Realness, from unity to multiplicity. Although there are differences in Madhva's dualistic view, for example, and the teachings of Lee Lozowick, they certainly would agree that "Difference is real." What stands out in the teachings of the great bhakti preceptors is that each one had a direct experience of the Divine that was undeniably Real, and this touches us, even hundreds of years later.

Oh You of infinite forms, of untold mysteries,
    of myriad miracles, oh You, Divine and Holy,
Transcendent and Immanent, oh You, everything and nothing,
    You are still ever in Your folding and unfolding
always He, Father, Lord and King, Yogi Ramsuratkumar.
    Yes, this is Your Name, sweet and tender, Merciful
and Devout, and this is Your Manifestation, tried
    and true, Your son's Adored, Yogi Ramsuratkumar.
This is breath, thought, activity, this is mood,
    emotion and body, this is heart and Heart,
sight and Sight, sound and Sound, Yogi Ramsuratkumar.
    Oh You of wild abandon, of fine purity,
of joyous laughter and of clear eyes, Yogi Ramsuratkumar,
    You have always been, are and will always be,
incarnate and not, recognizable and not,
    hidden or overt, He, the One, Yogi Ramsuratkumar.
You appeared to us for a time, left us Your lilas,
    Your Blessings, the memories of You carved deeply
into our flesh, blood, bones and organs,
    and then You appeared to go, leaving in Your wake
a blazing trail of Faith, devotion, Surrender, Love,
    worship and above all Praise and Obedience.

Father, Yogi Ramsuratkumar, dispel all ignorance,
     banish fear and aggression, let all seductions,
distractions and fascinations be only towards You,
     and Bless our prayers that they be all to and for You.
This is Your bad Poet once again ranting and chanting:
     You, You, only You Yogi Ramsuratkumar.[29]

---

[29]   Lee Lozowick, *Gasping for Air in a Vacuum*, 19 May 2003 VI.

This is a Lifetime Process

Lee Lozowick

Sooner or later you will realize that, if you are on the Path, you are not doing the same thing that ordinary people do. With all confidence, I couldn't say that most of you are being *successful* on the Path. Nonetheless, we are doing it as best as we can, and I think that at the end of our lives, we'll probably find out that in spite of ourselves something very important happened.

One of the ideas of the Path is to help it along a little bit, part of which means developing sensitivity to the dynamics of any given space. Even many people who have twenty or thirty years of experience on the Path and are teaching others do not have this kind of sensitivity. Why? Too much philosophy. The longer I am in this work, one of the things I see is the tremendous limitation of "Blah, blah, blah, blah," as Gour Khepa said to us last year in Kolkata. He was referring to most of what we all have to say, including all the other Bauls: "Blah, blah, blah." What he was saying, as he went from one *asana* to another right there in front of us, was: "This is the teaching. The teaching is in practice. It's not in blah, blah, blah."

Of all those I met in India last December, Gour Khepa was my favorite. He traveled all over the West—in America and Europe—in the seventies. He would have probably been the number one favorite Indian Baul, except he realized that all the fame and fortune he was generating was meaningless—because it was all "blah, blah, blah." So, he came back to India one year, gave away all his possessions and all his money, and started living like a Baul, traveling and singing and begging, instead of coming to the West and becoming rich and famous.

Here's a story about Chögyam Trungpa Rinpoche that I particularly like to use: Toward the end of his life, Trungpa Rinpoche was always complaining about his students' lack of practice and understanding. During one of his bouts of complaint, a student said, "Are you disappointed in us, Rinpoche?" He answered, "I will always be disappointed in you until you are enlightened." Meaning that you cannot stop to rest until you are at the end of the Path. A big part of that is seeing through the blah, blah, blah.

As many of you have found out, we work and we work and we work. In spite of all the hard work that doesn't seem to be producing anything, after a certain number of years, something seems to be happening anyway, because transmission is at the core of our work together. In spite of flopping around like fishes on the beach, wondering where all the water has gone, something happens anyway. In spite of ourselves, the Blessing Force of That to which we have committed our practice somehow works. That's how the Sacred Bazaar works; we are irradiated in spite of ourselves. There is no blah, blah, blah with sacred artifacts; they talk to us through the essential radiance of their being. I would be one hundred percent behind it if for no other reason than that, although it is a gift from Yogi Ramsuratkumar, and that is my primary interest in it.

So, we cannot afford to stop and rest before we reach the end. On the other hand, metaphorically speaking, we have to eat and sleep to survive, and earn a living, and so there are times in practice in which we appear to be doing other things, because digestion takes a certain amount of time. Again, I am speaking metaphorically. When practice has produced a large enough meal, sometimes we need to back off slightly from the immediate intensity of that practice to give our being a chance to integrate and digest. This is very natural and right in the scheme of things.

One of the things we want to continue to focus on is to stay with what is going on now. By now most of you have probably read or considered the "coming bad times," as they say. The new big thing is the black hole generator buried somewhere in the earth between Geneva and France. As you may know, a German scientist went to court to stop the experiment. He hypothesized that if a black hole is actually created, we won't be able to contain it, and it will essentially devour the Earth. That wouldn't be so bad, because it wouldn't happen slowly; it would be instantaneous. If you've ever suffered from a long-term illness, wouldn't it be nice to go instantaneously? No muss, no fuss, no pain, no bother. Not so bad.

Then all the beautiful things on Earth—the flowers and animals and even some people—would just show up somewhere else after a couple of billion years. Maybe this time we would do it better! Maybe after eating the apple and seducing Adam, Eve and Adam would raise their children so that Cain wouldn't be envious of Abel. I blame everything on bad parenting! Well, there was no history in the Garden of Eden—there was no karma at that time. What else could it have been? Today if the parents did a perfect job and the child doesn't work out, we can say, "Oh, it's karma." There are many different factors we can blame. So, maybe if we had started out differently back at the beginning, we would have ended up differently—who knows?

We are always worried about what's going to happen. Instead of worrying about *what* is going to happen, the more important concern might be: are we capable of meeting whatever happens with ingenuity, creativity, maturity and forbearance—and maybe even a little bit of acceptance? If (and it is an "if" despite what all the doomsday prophets say) the proverbial shit really hits the fan—an image that is supposed to depict the seriousness of the situation: you know, the complete crash of the world economy, the elimination of electricity and all sources of power, which would probably mean the poisoning of every water source on the face of the earth—will we be prepared to go on living with maturity and competence and dignity? We need to be prepared. You don't get prepared by worrying about the future; you get prepared by handling your practice and your development as a human being now.

We play bridge night after night, and I keep pointing out people's errors of play. They say, "Oh yes, I know. Okay, yes, I see that," and nothing changes. You aren't going to learn how to meet life with ingenuity, forbearance, and creativity if you aren't able to learn the simplest, simplest, simplest basics of how to adjust yourself to meet the demand. I'm afraid that's not good enough for me. In this community the game of bridge is a practice designed for self-observation. Last night while we were playing I said, "I don't know why they call this a card game. They should call it a mind game, because we aren't paying attention to the cards, all we're paying attention to is our minds!" That is the reason that we play poorly—because we're playing our minds, we're not playing the cards.

It may seem that a lot of the details I'm always picking about are really meaningless; they're just so small, so insignificant. Have you ever had dysentery? Dysentery is a kind of objective diarrhea. In India we called it "Krishna's revenge." Is the thing that gives you dysentery big enough to see? No. It's so small, you don't even know it exists, but *one* of those tiny microbes can completely wreck your system for weeks. It's the same with the tiny little things I'm always poking at. They don't seem like much, but unless they are attended to, they can really sneak up on you and do some damage. If we don't take care of the details, at a certain point we may find ourselves compromising—or maybe even completely destroying—a very important project. So pay attention to the details now. Notice them, handle them.

To continue with the example of bridge, if we would simply pay attention to the cards instead of our minds, then many of us would play bridge extremely well, because we are very sensitive and intuitive. Instead, we're too busy paying attention to our minds, which is all blah, blah, blah.

We were able to interview Gour Khepa, and a lot of what he said was in symbolic language. He referred to his wife as "nitric acid." Nitric acid is what is used to test the purity of gold. He was giving her a profound compliment and telling her he loved her enough to allow her feedback to feed his practice. Of course, she's no sloppy practitioner, and she is also a mother and wife. Gour Khepa, who is a great Baul, is still learning and handling details with the help of his wife.

Let me give you a word of advice about relationship, if any of you can make use of it. I'm not an example of this, but perhaps you could be. In relationship, blah, blah, blah usually does nothing more than create a fortress of defenses and aggression. When you think you're going to get your partner to change by haranguing them, you are barking up the wrong tree—a saying that comes from the relationship between dogs and cats, believe it or not, which means that if a dog is after a cat and the cat runs up *this* tree and the dog is jumping on *that* tree, then the dog is barking up the wrong tree if the dog wants to catch the cat. The best form of communication between partners is the subtlest of looks that passes over someone's face. Any more than that is probably too much—depending upon your relationship. Take it from someone with great experience at failing at that practice: that is all that's necessary. You know how it is: You do something and you look over your shoulder, and someone has one eyebrow raised. Oops! If you have the stupidity to say, "What?"—instead of relying on self-observation and introspection—then you deserve what you get, because it's obvious that something is going on.

If I want to know what is going on without my defenses and my recoil being triggered, then I need to stay with my own experience, dig around, and figure out what's going on. As soon as I try to enter into a conversation I can be very sure that I'm going to be hooked, and in the fraction of a second that I am hooked, it's the end of the conversation, because I'm so busy defending and covering my tracks, verbally or internally, that I'm not able to hear what is being said.

So, details are not irrelevant, even though they can appear to be really insignificant, even meaningless. As most of us have found out from our years on the Path, many things that seem meaningless in the moment turn out years later, in retrospect, to have been very valuable details. For example, when I was a boy and a young man—at different times, but now I'm sort of both at the same time—I observed my environment with the same clarity all of you did when you were younger. Because I didn't have any life experience then, a lot of it didn't mean anything to me. Certain looks on my parents' faces, or certain things they said, went in and out of my awareness, and I had no reference point for them. Twenty years later, after relationship and children and having a profession and earning my own living and paying a mortgage and insurance and getting stuck when my car broke down in the middle of nowhere, a lot of the things I noticed when I was younger suddenly make sense. Not only did they make sense, they had value; they had meaning.

Spiritual work is like that; practice is like that. Often things arise and we notice them, and we don't think they have any value to us because we don't have a reference point for them yet. Ten or twenty years later, those things can be the very things that catalyze a very profound revelation. So pay attention to the details, even if in the moment they don't seem to mean that much to your mind—especially if you are my student and I am pointing those details out to you.

Let's use bridge as an example again. The rules of bridge are not written in stone. They are a framework that, once you have learned them well, is adjustable in the moment you are playing, when those rules are considered within a fairly large body of experience in play. Without that framework, you have nothing to base your decisions on in terms of how you play; at the same time, the rules are meant to be adjusted circumstantially. Without the rules, the circumstance has no framework, no foundation. Many of the principles of bridge apply to business, our professional lives, therapy, self-observation, and everything else. You may not realize this while you're playing bridge now, but if you play seriously, then ten or twenty years from now you'll realize it.

It's like practicing martial arts without a solid foundation in the basics. If you are going to strike somebody very hard in the head or on the hip, and your hand is not perfectly aligned with your arm bone, you could break your wrist if you strike hard enough. That's one out of a large number of very basic framework rules in martial arts. If you kick somebody, and you kick them with your leg, and they are bigger than you, you'll probably bounce off and they will jump on you and kill you. If, on the other hand, you know how to turn your hip so the force of your entire body is behind the kick, you can send someone twice your size through the wall.

My father was a fine artist, not a commercial illustrator— although during the Great Depression of the 1930s he did some commercial illustration to put food on the table. A lot of my appreciation of the value of art in our lives comes from my father. As a child and young man, my father taught me about art without trying to teach me; I learned things from him that I had not the *slightest* interest in or understanding of. My father often sold his paintings to museums, and I would get very upset, because a painting that would bring fifteen or twenty thousand dollars in the commercial market would go to the museum for five thousand dollars. I never talked to my father about these things, but I would say to my mother, "Why don't you sell the pictures to a collector who will pay more money?" My mother would say, "Because your father wants his life work to be located where the most number of people will appreciate it." At the time, that didn't make sense to me *at all.*

So, I've forgiven my mother and father for what I thought as a young man was stupidity, because all I cared about was money—at least on the surface of things. The same is true of practice. People come to the Path and they think all they care about is enlightenment, which is a very selfish concern. It's a concern many of us have shared, myself included. A lot of the things that I say and do now don't make sense, because they seem to have nothing to do with enlightenment. Let me give an example: A wonderful man, a very sweet man with a very overactive mentality, came to me recently and said, "I had an experience that changed my life, and I need to talk to you about it. I'll need at least a half hour to tell you about it." I said to myself, "Hmmph! Do I want to listen to this for a half hour? No." But I liked the guy; he was a nice guy. So I said, "Let me see if I have some time later in the week. We'll see what happens." I knew what he was going to tell me. I've heard it, without exaggeration, thirty times: your standard *satori.* They are all the same—with slightly different personalities, yes, but all the same.

So I decided to write him a letter. "I know what you're going to tell me," I said. "I've heard it from many people. I know the answers you are looking for, but the answers are not a matter of a conversation. I don't need to hear what you experienced, because I know what you experienced. I know how you can use it, integrate it, digest it, but those answers are not a matter of sitting down and talking together, even if we talk for a week." I gave him the letter, and he wrote me back saying that he really enjoyed it.

Perhaps we can help him integrate this event in his life. He won't integrate it in a week or a month or a year; he doesn't have the life experience or the foundation of integral practice on a real Path. He will make sense of it sooner or later, because it was so cataclysmic that he's driven to make sense of it, but making sense of something is very different than digesting and integrating it. If he only makes sense of it, he will never get to the bottom of it. He will throw his life away chasing comets and stars. I know it, as sure as we're sitting here. But if he can integrate it, then something very valuable can be the result. The same is true of all of us. Unfortunately, this is something I did not know when I first started teaching, which is not a pleasant realization: This is a lifetime process.

Ferme de Jutreau, France
September 2008

Impermanence

M. Young

It is extraordinarily beautiful in the green countryside of Rocky Mountain Montana. The views are so panoramic and magnificent, it's like being in a postcard. Wildlife abounds, so that every day the drama of nature unfolds before our very eyes: a mother fox and her band of kits romp in a nearby field; new foals arrive just down the road and stand on unsteady legs, proud and erect with their perfect sculpted bodies. There are bears in the mountains nearby, but I've never seen one on this property in the valley. In past years, I've seen eagles at Trimurti. Now I'm waiting for one to show up.

The spring-fed pond just outside my window is the home of at least two pairs of Canadian geese, many redwing blackbirds and one intrepid muskrat. One pair of geese have a gosling following them everywhere; the other pair are awaiting the new life that gestates within the eggs the female goose guards so fiercely. Mallards also visit. Last week an osprey stopped by—regal and elegant, indeed! Within this prolific natural environment, the *mela* (gathering) of practitioners takes place. Lee is giving talks during the day.

It's a rich, often blissful and auspicious place and time in which to be working—in between the cracks, so to speak, of all the other activities that are ongoing—on this book about Lee's teaching of Enlightened Duality.

Over many years of travel, I have found that there is nothing like a few days in paradise—such as this one—to bring identification with illusion back into focus after particularly sweet, blissful or clear moments. Perhaps this is because we have an expectation of ourselves to be relaxed and ecstatic when we are surrounded by beauty. I have found that beautiful and harmonious environments can have the same mirror-like effect as environments of conflict, stress, pollution, ugliness and decay. This too is very useful: the truth of what is in the moment is all the more impacting when one is surrounded with beauty, but the inner state is not beautiful.

The day was rolling along quite well until mid-afternoon, when a number of familiar skeletons of the psyche came merrily skipping and jumping out of their closets to haunt me with their gruesome dance. Leaving my tiny workspace by the window, I went in search of some companionship. On my way to the group space, in the long narrow hallways I looked out the windows at the breathtaking view of the mountains. It had been raining and snowing for days; today the sky was a deep, brilliant turquoise and the sun was sparkling on the pond. A perfect day to take a walk on the beautiful ashram property.

Arriving in the group room I discovered that people were deeply ensconced in either prior commitments or busy tasks that had to be completed, so I headed off for a solitary walk on the trail that circled the ashram. Immediately I found myself in a familiar psychological state: bone-crushing loneliness had replaced balance and sense of perspective. Writers are a lonely bunch, dear reader. We sit at our typewriters or computers or at some ancient worm-eaten wooden table with papyrus and quill in hand, delving into inner worlds to retrieve that which will become the written word. Loneliness is a rather constant companion or, maybe I should say, worthy opponent. The fact is that loneliness is a very difficult friend to have.

Tears welled up and stung my eyes as I looked down at the deep green grass underfoot, where rich black earth swelled up in mounds and fertile furrows. A doe leapt out of the aspen grove and bounded across the high grass of the field on the other side of a streamlet that borders the ashram. The aspen trees themselves seemed to mock my sentimental mood—they were bursting with new life, their spring buds still tight and pale green, soon to burgeon forth in perfect innocence, perfect peace. Impassive and impersonal, they rustled in the soft breeze.

Upsurging tears accompanied the rush of self-pity. I paused to reflect and re-assess. Okay, here it is, I thought: the moment of practice. What could I get out of this moment? I could either trot out every sorrow and anger and bit of angst I've wrestled with in the recurring patterns that seek childhood's end, or I could engage a creative act: I could practice. Self-observe without judgment. Enquire. I could enter more deeply into the moment as it was presenting itself to me. Yes, loneliness was arising. Yes, judgment of that loneliness was also arising. Yes, yes, yes. Loneliness also had the potential to reveal the truth of the moment.

Reflecting further, I walked on, soon passing by the retreat cabin nestled deeper in the aspens, which was in the process of being built by the specific design of *vastu* principles. Lingering for a few moments, I noticed where the doors and windows were located in the framed walls and thought of how future solitary, silent retreatants would have a marvelous view of the mountains and the ashram building, the green field and pond and grounds where people—adults and children—would be going about their day.

The trail led on until I came to a small bridge made of saplings, where the path, if taken, would lead to an orchard beyond the aspen break. The grass was very green there under a row of small elm trees that were just about to burst into bud. I was drawn by the spirit of the new orchard, trees not more than a few years old, and a certain feeling of *place* that I sensed under those elms. I saw a wooden bench and headed over the bridge.

At the bench I realized with surprise that there was a small grave there. Then I saw the stone, about twenty-five pounds of raw, natural granite, simply engraved with the child's name. I remembered the story of two members of this sangha, whose one-year-old child had suddenly died a few years ago of a strange and deadly virus. Self-referencing emotional obsession dissolved instantly, a wraith of a shadow in the clear light of what is real, which washed over in a wave that left me with shifted perception.

Still raw, tears near the edge, another wave of feeling came, this time closer to the fine knife point of sorrow. What had the parents gone through in letting this child go? How had the relentless truth of impermanence touched their lives? How were they different? Were they transformed by the touch of death, the bittersweetness of having loved a dear child and watched that child suffer and then die?

Sitting beneath the elms in the sun, the words of Japanese haiku poet and Buddhist priest, Kobayashi Issa (1763–1828), sprang to mind. Issa once wrote the following lines, which are said to have prefaced with the line: "On losing a beloved child"—

> The world is
> but a dewdrop,
> and yet,
> and yet

Issa had a profound and intimate knowledge of loss and impermanence: the poet-priest lost three children to death at a very young age. His mother died when he was three, and he was raised by his grandmother in a rural, peasant family. His father remarried, and Issa was sent away to work, eventually becoming a Buddhist priest. Issa seems to be saying to us that although this world is as transient as the morning dew, like the morning dew it is also glorious and tender. His words, "And yet, and yet..." hint that there is more to this dewdrop world than its fleeting appearance and disappearance may imply. Although all things pass, because we have been given the gift of life—we experience, we love and cry and feel—this is real.[1]

'I am not a stranger to death. I have been through the deaths of my parents, the deaths of several dear friends. I have cared for the needs of the dying, spent many intimate hours with loved ones during their final days, keeping the vigil and witnessing. Each time we stand at the threshold with someone who is passing over, we come face to face with the burning mystery of Life which we call death: death, the ultimate doorway into accepting the inexorable fact of impermanence. However, as Lee has said many times, there is something about the death of a child that carries a potency—and a goad to spiritual life—that no other loss or change can touch within us.

The fleeting nature of all that we hold dear will bring into our experience the inevitable sting of irreparable loss. This is the price we pay for the taste of honey, the glimpse of beauty, the precious moments of love—real love, the selfless love of a parent for a child. How rarely do we taste that unconditional love with other adults, and when we do, we are transformed by it—perhaps only just a little, but nonetheless, we are transformed.

As these reflections came and went, I wondered: What was the possibility of practice in this moment? What was Enlightened Duality in this moment? The mountains were somber. They did not answer my question, and neither did the grass or the azure sky. Everything was beautiful, magnificent, and perfectly ordinary. I listened to the sounds of mourning doves cooing nearby, while other birds twittered

---

[1]   Many years ago Lee read this poem and commented on it extensively in one of his bi-weekly after dinner talks to the sangha. It is one of the most beautiful and beloved poems in its genre, having been translated into many difference versions by scholars and Buddhist commentators.

and sang sweetly. The mountains were immovable, purple giants of earth, snow-capped; they were symbols of attainment, ancient of days, speaking also of eternity—but somehow these massive monuments of nature would crumble to dust, blow away on the wind, disappear in time, because all things pass. Impermanence is the goad that pushes us through the door of longing into the unknown. Impermanence forces us to the precipice where we encounter the urgent need to live with courage and joy in the present moment; to live so fully that the unitive nature of things dissolves all distinctions of fear, separation, survival, desire.

If I was looking for the kind of revelation that leaves one starry-eyed, streaming with lambent feeling, heart opened and flowing in the currents of Life's Great River, this was not it. All emotions had dissolved like clouds in a sky; in fact there was no feeling that I could identify. Sometimes real feeling is like that: unidentifiable precisely because of our habitual identification with emotion. After the roiling emotions of moments before were gone—demonstrating, once again, their impermanent and empty nature—all that was left, or so it seemed, was an ordinary orchard, green with the late spring of Montana, rich deep grass and the young fruit trees about to burst into leaf and bloom. The grave too was ordinary. It was very small, like the remains of the child's body it contained, and sunken in the middle where the sod had fallen in. The thick prairie grass had not overtaken it yet, and so it was bare in the middle. I pictured the small skeleton in its place, but it was the stone with the child's name that captured and kept my attention.

What is it all about, this constant creation, preservation and destruction? Life in its coming and going, myriad appearances and disappearances, arisings and subsidings? Even after many years on the Path I could still find myself standing right there, at the doorway, at the threshold of awareness, wondering at the mystery of being and asking why! The fact is that, in *sadhana*, we continue to go back to the basics; again and again we return to the basic practice and take refuge in the dharma. As I stood in that green world with the sun shining down, there was something of beginner's mind, as Suzuki Roshi said, in this fundamental question. There was something very childlike in the questioning, a flavor of innocence and trust.

Waiting for a sense of completion, I sat on the little bench and looked around. Suddenly it dawned on me: every grain of dark soil and blade of grass, every breath and sensation of lungs moving, each furled budded green leaf, the vast stretch of endless sky, the deep silence, the trees, purple mountains, bench, flowers, gravestone—all of it—was Just This. Nature was answering my question with a loud, resounding voice that was at the same time so subtle that if this grave had not appeared, I might have missed it. The only answer to my question, my feeling into that place, was Just This, and it was not going to strike me down like a thunderbolt. It was speaking to me with the gentle, insistent, pressure of clarity.

Sensing it was time to go, I said a brief prayer for the spirit of the child. Where are you now, beloved? In the palm of God's hand. Then, just as I stood up to walk away, the most subtle *rasa* arose. Peace. Peace was this child's gift to me. Peace was the mood of the real world in that moment. Subtle, like a butterfly's wings moving in the sun.

We run after lovers, we make children, we covet
    fame, power and wealth, we collect and consume,
and to what end and at what cost?
    We are born and burn brightly for a time and then
we disappear to this instant, and what remains
    of all of our desires, hopes, dreams, wishes?
And what do we leave behind of value?
    Our houses, cars, properties, works of art?

Let this arrogant Fool and wild Heretic, His
    Fool and Heretic, tell you this:
Only one thing has substance, has true merit,
    that is the service that we offered Him,
that is the Praise we offered Him, that is the Love,
    Devotion, Faith, Surrender that we gave to Him.
When our families, children, professions and acts
    bear His Name and are not separate from Him,
then those very things, objectified, live and thrive
    and sing His Prayers, but without Him
all is for naught, all dies a lovely and useless death.
    Father! Yogi Ramsuratkumar! King, Lord, Guru,
Master — Your True Heart-Son, known temporarily as
    lee lozowick, emboldened by Your Grace,
sees You everywhere and in everything, and always
    and especially as You, Yogi Ramsuratkumar,
and paradoxically, though not separate from You at all,
    bows before You, the dust of the dust of Your Feet.[2]

Sitting at the table by the windows the next morning, I was reading in the Buddhist magazine *Buddhadharma* about the sufferings of people in Burma. Monks and nuns rising up in the "Saffron
Revolution" against the military junta. The oppression, the beatings,
the imprisonment of so very many monks and lay people and of
Burma's opposition leader, Aung San Suu Kyi; the torture, the all-
pervasive atmosphere of fear and dread. By the time I got to the part

---

[2]   Lee Lozowick, *Gasping for Air in a Vacuum*, 19 May 2003 VII.

about the children, tears were coming. I looked out the window, past the fresh spring-water pond just beyond the deck to the snow-covered peaks and burning blue sky, and breathed the Heart Breath. It is difficult to practice accepting what is real when contemplating the truly unimaginable sufferings of people in the world. Nondualist teaching withers on the vine in the face of such a conflagration. At such times, even the treasured pearl of Just This is illusive—and yet, I suspect, more powerful than ever. Compassion, the reconciliation of the broken heart, lies seedlike within the mystery of the declaration of Assertion: Just This.

The Heart Breath, however, is supremely accessible at such a time. In the innate passive action of the Heart Breath, however subtle the breath is, there is a potent felt connection in that moment with all the Buddhists in the world who are doing *tonglin* for the Burmese people—even for the terrorists, the psychopaths, the dictators and those who serve them. Breathing in darkness, suffering, negativity and breathing out light, harmony, positivity. The Heart Breath, which is similar to *tonglin* in Buddhist practice, is a boat across the storm-tossed, turbulent ocean of the world. It is refuge. It is sanctuary.

I looked up at the view of the mountains and pond. A movement near the edge of the water caught my eye. The goslings had hatched! The goose, who had been sitting on her eggs since I arrived at the Montana ashram nine days ago, was nuzzling the newborns. She had been sitting on those eggs with a fierce one-pointed focus, through all the rain and snow of the late spring. Her sitting meditation was about keeping her eggs warm. Now their furry golden heads peeked above the edge of the grassy nest. A few feet away the male partner stood guard in unmoving concentration.

Apparently this nurturing of life was going on everywhere around us. Yesterday, coming back from my walk and contemplations that began with a pervasive sense of loneliness, I had sat down at my desk to write. After awhile I paused and looked up through the window. There in the eaves of the roof was a bird, sitting calmly in her nest, waiting for her eggs to hatch. She alone was ultimately responsible for the new life to come. She was unconscious of her own meditation, but meditation it was—she was brooding upon the coming of life.

Beautiful beyond our understanding, raw, terrible and ruthless in her destructive aspect, Nature is endlessly creating anew. The three *gunas* never stop—creation, preservation, destruction, *rajas, sattvas, tamas*—in unceasing impersonal compulsory cycles of becoming. It is tacitly obvious that the Supreme Reality, that which is unitive, which is beyond all opposites, is compelled to create. There is birth, life and death, and then there is rebirth. That which dies is plowed into the process of becoming. Is there solace in this fact? I wasn't sure today, but as soon as I saw the goslings, joy erupted in me like a fountain and the tears were gone, revealing themselves to be empty, transient. The joy dissipates also, as easily as it arises. Joy arises and subsides, then life is on to the next arising.

The next morning the new goslings were nowhere to be seen. I kept going back to the windows with the binoculars; I even walked outside to the pond and scanned the surrounding spread of lush green grass looking for them. There were three pairs of geese grazing gently in the proximity of the pond but no goslings. Not the older gosling—the only one left of the original brood of three belonging to one of the pairs—or the golden fluff balls hatched only yesterday to my "favorite" pair of geese.

Well, that is the way of Nature. Creation, preservation (in this case, for only a short time) and destruction. Goslings were here; now goslings are gone. Eaten by a hawk, an osprey or eagle, perhaps. Okay, I thought, preparing to write something about the Buddha's teaching on the impermanence of all things. How appropriate that the goslings are gone. I wouldn't want a tone of sentimentality to creep into my considerations of nonduality and duality, would I?

In the perception of Enlightened Duality, there certainly is no room for nostalgia—or is there? Bob Dylan said, "Nostalgia is death." That is truer than true on the Path. And yet, nostalgia too will arise and subside, presenting the opportunity to accept it as it is.

Making my way slowly toward the desk to sit and write, I took one last look at the pond. Immediately I noticed a pair of geese at the water's edge. I got out the binoculars and looked: sure enough, the mother goose was gently pushing a fuzzy gosling toward the water with her beak. The father goose was floating on the water a few inches away, raptly watching the female and babes. One more forceful nudge and the reluctant gosling plopped into the water. A second gosling jumped in behind the first, then a third slipped into the water. The female took to the water in a most natural manner—with total ease and innate grace—and the whole family became a tableau of elegance as they moved effortlessly out across the glimmering smooth surface of the water. So much for reflections on impermanence, because this morning we were clearly in Lord Vishnu's realm: maintaining and sustaining life in its manifold glory of small and great wonders.

Know Thyself

Lee Lozowick

Someone recently asked me if I wanted to help ordinary people. I said, "Ordinary people cannot be helped!" Why? Because ordinary people are so completely stuck in their own world that the only way to get out of their own world is through a revolution: somebody close to them dies, or they are in a car accident and lose a limb. Maybe then they are willing to look at the world differently.

I find ordinary people annoying and irritating; the only thing that is important to them is their own comfort and getting agreement from other people. With no disrespect meant to hatha yoga, people do a little yoga and a little bit of massage, and they do a little of this and that, but it is all to stroke their egos. It's all for their own comfort.

People are unwilling to consider the fact that they are completely mechanical and false. Every breath they take, every gesture they make, every piece of clothing they put on, is completely mechanical and false. If you look around, you see that people are intelligent, attractive and successful. Why would someone who is intelligent, attractive and successful want to consider the possibility that every gesture, every breath, every thought, every feeling is completely inauthentic? Nobody wants to do that—even most people who are following a spiritual path.

I wish I could forget what I know and just sit on the beach, enjoy the sun and the pretty women, drink good wine and good coffee and eat delicious food, read good books and listen to good music, but I can't, because I have a very low tolerance for mechanicality and falseness. I have the misfortune to have a talent for discerning the real from the false; I use the word "misfortune" because there is so little Real in the world. Maybe the Dalai Lama—someone with compassion—would say that everything is beautiful.

My master said that everything has some combination of light and dark, and we must focus on the light and nevermind the dark, so that we see the beauty in everyone and everything. I'm hoping I can do that one day, because I'm a miserable character to hang out with—I'm always provoking people's lazy, apathetic status quo. You may say, "But you do it with compassion." Well…that may be questionable. Time will tell, I suppose.

The Buddha said, "Pain is inevitable, but suffering is optional." That depends on how you define suffering, obviously. Pain is inevitable because we age, the body breaks down, we break a bone once in a while, our lover leaves, a child dies before their parent. Pain is a part of life, but suffering is an interpretation that *we* give to experience that we find painful.

The penitents, for example, after two or three days of dancing and music, get into a devotional trance and stick knives through their cheeks; for that person self-mutilation is an ecstatic act of devotion. They don't feel pain, and the wound heals immediately when they pull the knife out. If you said to the average Christian, "You know, you can show your devotion to Jesus by sticking this knife through your cheeks," they'd look at you as if you were crazy. If they tried to do it, they would suffer unbearably. So, the same act creates ecstasy in one case and suffering—even outrage—in another.

It is possible to change our interpretation of a situation and change what we thought was suffering. In a larger context, if we stop solidifying or crystallizing any situation, then there is no suffering because we transcend suffering altogether. Yes, there is always pain— and, we can change our interpretation of suffering.

I have a very orthodox bias: any real transformation starts with a true master in a genuine lineage. My master, Yogi Ramsuratkumar, has been dead for eight years, but to me, he is not dead. The body is gone, of course, but his presence, guidance, care, and affection are all still very much present. I have been teaching for thirty-five years guided by him. Without my master's guidance I could have made many of the mistakes I have seen my friends make; without him, I could not have done what I have done. As small an amount of wisdom as I have realized, I could not have realized without him. I realize it is a bias that is not for everybody, but for me everything starts with a real master in a genuine lineage, and a genuine lineage is as important as a real master. If a spiritual teacher is not teaching within a lineage and refuses to take feedback from their peer group, which is very common, who is to say if they are genuine or not? Of course *they* say they are genuine, because they want students, but self-praise means nothing. They want to be famous, and they want power and authority. Hitler thought he was the greatest savior of the Aryan people in the history of mankind. Who else did? Anyone ever hear of Lenin?

Pattabhi Jois, among a rare handful, is one of the greatest yogis alive in the world today. By his confession, his mastery of yoga is small compared to his master's, and his master's mastery of yoga was small compared to *his* master's. However, when someone is in a lineage, they are influenced by the entire lineage, so they have a certain possibility that is almost unheard of outside of a lineage. Anandamayi Ma was a rare exception of this; she is an example of someone who had no living master or lineage, although she was in a living tradition, not a lineage.

There is no short, simple answer to the questions of transformation, because the answers cannot happen in a flash; when people realize things in a flash it does not last. We all have realizations along the way, but to realize the fruits of the Path takes twenty or thirty years of rigorous practice with a teacher in a lineage. Even an accomplished yoga practitioner discovers that you really start learning after twenty or thirty years of practice. All the *neo-advaitists* who go to Lucknow for a weekend come home saying they're enlightened—it's a disgrace. It's an insult that they would even use the word "spiritual."

When you receive information in a weekend workshop, it's like somebody giving you the proverbial carrot dangling at the end of the stick. It's a gift, but the carrot is of no good to your body if you don't eat it and digest it. Likewise, we all have realizations, but those realizations need to be literally ingested and digested; we need to absorb them and then practice on the basis of them. If you get a headache, and you stare at an aspirin, the headache doesn't go away. You have to eat the aspirin. Spiritual teaching is like that—except it doesn't take fifteen minutes, it takes fifteen years.

There is a gradual of unfolding of wisdom and maturity and insight into the nature of Reality, which I would call the mystical process, and then there is a big explosion, in which somebody finds themselves literally in a different place and unable to go back to the old place. These two different experiences are usually called "gradual enlightenment" and "sudden enlightenment." Even with the sudden explosion, it is not a mature realization, because the experience is like a baby being born; even though we are intelligent, creative, and competent adults at the time, we still have to learn the new territory.

If someone from Madrid goes to England and sees that people drive on the opposite side of the road, it's going to take them a very short amount of time to figure out that the world of driving in England is different than the world of driving in Spain. Having this blast of insight called "sudden enlightenment" is the same thing: we find ourselves unable to see the world the way we used to even one minute before, but then how we see the world now is so radically different that we actually have to learn how to live there. We don't *know* how to live there; we have to *learn* how to live there.

So, the answers I have to people's questions are not answers that can encapsulate knowledge, like one plus one equals two. Everything I have to teach takes time and experimentation—time to learn the geography. I took a wilderness course years ago with my son, where you jump off mountains, climb rocks, and bond in the process. We were doing this thing called "rappelling," in which you jump off a mountain held by a rope. If you do it the wrong way the first time, you never do it wrong again—not because you die, but because it hurts. The spiritual Path is like that: Sometimes you have to make some really big mistakes, because that's the only way you learn. Nobody makes mistakes in the beginning, because we're too careful. We want to do everything right. We want everybody to like us. We want to please the teacher, be good students and get good grades, just like when we were in first grade. Because of all those psychological imperatives, sometimes it takes a while to make a really big mistake.

If you're with a false teacher—say, someone who has sex with everyone in the community, women, men, and children—and you fall in love with him or her, you are committed. You can just as easily fall in love with a false teacher as with a real teacher, so in your commitment, you bury a lot of your good sense. Then one day the teacher says to you, "I want to initiate your thirteen-year-old daughter." Instead of saying, "You prick, I'm going to turn you into the police," you say, "Oh, my master wants to initiate my daughter! Oh, isn't that lovely—what do you think, honey?" And honey says, "Oh we're so blessed to have our daughter initiated by our master!" You willingly send your daughter into a situation that will probably traumatize her for the rest of her life. Five years later you wake up: "Oh my God, what have I done?"

The situation is not irreparable; it can be healed, but first you have to wake up and say, "Oh my God, what have I done?" Most people who find themselves in that situation turn against the Path. They blame the Path for their inability to learn a lesson. Those who are smart say, "I picked the wrong teacher, I was naïve, I made some mistakes. How can I make sure that this will never happen to me again?" That's the person who, the second time around, is going to find the right teacher, because they're never going to do that over again. They've been much too shattered by their own willingness to be taken advantage of.

One of the great prayers in yoga is "Lead me from darkness to light." We go to the teacher to be led to the light, and then we find out our teacher was a charlatan—but just because we discover the darkness in someone doesn't mean there isn't also light. For instance, every charlatan teacher is not necessarily a bad person, and they're not necessarily psychotic. Some of them were very decent, well-meaning individuals who wanted to help people when they started out teaching. They really believed that their knowledge could serve people. They were very sincere and decent, because they had made it through the minefield of ego once, and by some coincidence they didn't get blown up.

Anybody who becomes a spiritual teacher has got to have some degree of competence: they're good with language; they're charming; they're eloquent. There are those who are not corrupted—if we are lucky enough to find such a one—but they are very few and very far between. When a teacher is corrupt, it's not that they are stupid people who don't know any better; they are people who get caught by their own egos because they haven't investigated themselves deeply enough to have discovered all the hidden bombs that have been there, sometimes for millennia—literally, if you believe in karma.

Many people ask me if a corrupt person can be a guide. A corrupt person can be a guide up to a point, and beyond that point they cannot be. I have some very good students who came from very bad teachers, and they were well-trained by their first teacher, so that when they came to me, instead of stumbling around and banging their head on the wall, they were able to pick up where their other teacher could not go and move very quickly. This principle is true not just in the spiritual field: you can have a good guide who is an artist, a craftsperson, or a chef. You could be trained by someone in yoga, dance or the martial arts.

Many say that God doesn't exist; they say mystical experience and realization are an invention of the mind searching for happiness. They say that we create all of those experiences ourselves, through the power of the mind. I disagree—even though the Buddhists don't believe there is a God, and the Tibetan Buddhists have one of the most sophisticated spiritual systems in the world. It is true that most people's idea of spirituality is completely self-created. Of course, that *is* what most people do, but that doesn't make it Ultimate Reality; all spirituality is not a fantasy just because many people create a whole fantasy world. There is that which is Real and that which is unreal.

The illumination experience does not guarantee harmony in your life. It has the potential to, yes, but whether it does or not depends on the individual, not on the experience. In one sense there is no separation, so the person and the experience are unitive. In another sense the experience is completely distinct and separate from the person, and for the experience and the person to become unified, the person has to do a certain kind of work, which is what Gurdjieff's teachings were about. "The Work" is still very alive today; it is about taking a real experience and a false person and allowing the false person to become real enough to be unified with the real experience.

You have to know yourself. People are false in the sense that their activity is not aligned with the highest possible activity. Who they are in the moment could be different. Maybe a person is a kleptomaniac: someone who steals by compulsion. They can't help themselves, so in the moment that they are stealing, they are not false because they really can't help themselves. However, in a different sense, they are false because their activity is not integral; it's not impeccable activity that is in alignment with the highest principles of life on Earth. Maybe in some other place life is about how much you can steal, but not on Earth. On Earth it is about how much you can give, not how much you can take. Unfortunately, most husbands and wives have not discovered that principle!

People want to know how to help the average person in their everyday life. The answer is always the same: it takes a long amount of time spent studying with a good guide. People are used to the dumbed-down, New Age, psycho-babble version of spirituality. A lot of people think I can help the average person, but that is because they don't understand me. They think that I have a lot to offer the average person. I have nothing to offer the average person. Nothing, nothing, nothing. The average person *could not* possibly understand me if their life depended on it.

A five-year-old child, no matter how intelligent they are, does not have the same sensitivity as an adult because they haven't lived what an adult has lived. They haven't gone through puberty, they haven't had failed love affairs, they haven't had food poisoning, they haven't had friends die. They haven't had the entire spectrum of human experience that crafts wisdom in us. It is the same thing with the average person: the average person wants some money, a decent job that they enjoy, a relationship that is satisfying, and children they can respect, and that is about it. It's a natural human drive to be happy, but the average person does not have the skill or wherewithal to do what is necessary to be happy. It's not that they aren't decent people who love their children and their parents; it's not that they don't have the innate capacity—everybody has the innate capacity—but they don't have the training or the depth and breadth of experience.

In the field of art, how many are equal to the great artists? No one. Who is equal to the spiritual genius of Buddha, Jesus Christ, Shirdi Sai Baba, Anandamayi Ma? How many people in the seven billion people on the face of the Earth are like that? Very, very few. So, the average person is average because everybody has the innate capacity to be a great realizer, but realistically speaking they will not *do* what is required to realize. They won't pay the dues to that club—they just won't.

People want a list of "ten things that will make me happy." Simply giving people a list of things to do or a formula is not enough, but it gives people the idea that it is enough. If there is a list of ten things you have to do to be happy, why would anybody ever look for a teacher or a guide? You'd have to be an idiot to look for a guide if you had a list of ten things that guaranteed you would be happy, because when you find a master, your life is not your own anymore—for five years or ten years or a hundred lifetimes. Sooner or later your life becomes your own, completely, one hundred percent, dynamically, totally your own, but in the beginning, your life isn't your own. If you really understand what it is to have a spiritual master, you understand that it is not about someone giving you a formula, saying, "Here…do this, this, and this, and you'll get your results." Impossible!

That's why I can't help the average person. People would love it if I answered questions the way I used to answer questions. People would read my books and interviews and love them, *and* they would be misled, because I would be giving them the idea that they could do what my master did simply by repeating a few psychological homilies or folk wisdom: "Yes, to be happy we have to be 'one with all there is!' Oh, yes, I like that! What a great idea, yes, to be 'one with all there is.'" Then they go out and spend the rest of their life parroting some phrase.

You have to know yourself, and that takes a long time and a lot of effort. What parent hasn't gotten angry with their child? When you are not angry, you want to treat your child with the greatest respect and honor and tenderness you can. You love them, you worship the ground they walk on—they are your children. However, when you are angry, you are not that loving, tender, parent anymore—you revert to a pre-human condition. You yell at them, you hit them, you turn your back on them, you emotionally abuse them. You punish them unnecessarily, out of all proportion for some little thing, because *you* are angry. That is the average person.

Try this scenario on for size: A man reads an article in a spiritual magazine that gives him inspiration at a time when his life is falling apart. Somehow he is able to keep things together and go on and become a much healthier and happier human being. He believes that he has had something transform inside as a result of this article, and because he believes that, he is not desperate for transformation. If someone believes that they have found the answer to life's problems, they won't seriously seek out transformation. They look for another magazine article, rationalizing, "Oh, that article I read two years ago, that really helped me. I am a much happier person. I'm going to read every issue of this magazine until another article touches me."

What if, instead of reading the article and feeling like he had gotten it back together, everything in his life fell apart, he hit the bottom of the barrel so to speak, and his heart was broken? In Alcoholics Anonymous they say that an addict has to hit bottom before he or she can make a real change. Until we go down to the bottom, we don't really transform. When we hit the bottom there is nowhere to go in ordinary, everyday terms; the only option is to seek out something real that could have a lasting transformational effect in our lives.

This is a true principle I have seen at work a thousand times. I used to teach a seminar in metaphysics that was very effective, called the Silva Method. It's a fabulous course in metaphysics; in its own domain, it is very effective. I was the state director in New Jersey, and once or twice a month I would teach a course, in which people were completely lifted up out of the place where they were stuck. They would come to me some time later and say, "This course changed my life. I swear to it." There was a change, but it occurred within their ordinary context, and they stopped there. Many people had real experiences that were so different than their daily experience that, instead of moving them forward with curiosity and a willingness to investigate, it shut them down—not right away, but over time.

As the state director of the Silva Method, I was totally committed to the system. I saw no other future until I met Werner Erhard and *est*, and in one weekend, my association with the Silva Method was finished. I absolutely could not go back. Thinking of myself as a man of integrity, I went to Mr. Silva and said, "I have to resign, but I'll stay for six months and continue to teach, so that you can train someone to replace me." I left because it became clear that the Silva Method was superb in the domain of metaphysics, but it had an absolute peak within that domain, and it couldn't touch what was *beyond* that peak. The Silva Method never dreamed that something existed above its own peak, so any potential for realization stopped there. When I realized this, I left to find out what was beyond that peak. Then, when I met my master, it changed my life in a completely different context. So, this is the crucial point: The context from which we ask questions about helping ordinary people is different than the context of real transformation, from which I am speaking.

We cannot climb out of the hole we are in unless we have the help of a master. Ordinary help, like reading a book or a magazine on psychology, won't get us out of the hole we are in. In my tradition, which is the Baul tradition, every Baul has more than one guru, because one of the essential elements is that transmission of the teaching is made through poetry, music and dance. Every Baul has an art guru, who teaches them music, sometimes dance, and language, and then they have a spiritual guru who teaches them the yoga of the tradition. Usually the music guru doesn't teach the yoga, and the yoga guru doesn't teach the music. You are not a genuine Baul if you don't practice the yoga, which is a form of kundalini yoga.

Even people who are way above average cannot pull themselves out of the hole they are in without help. Maybe the help is a traditional guru, maybe the help is an artistic internship of some kind; maybe the help is a dying parent. It's amazing how many abusive, rage-filled, alcoholic, rotten parents turn out to be saints on their deathbed. I recommend to my students to be with their parents when they die, if the opportunity is there. Many of those students—who literally have hated their parents all their lives—go to stay with their parents a month before they die, and they come out of it saying, "I never realized my mother really loved me. I never realized my father wasn't just an abusive bastard." Suddenly these people become real, loving, tender, wise individuals, and sometimes that kind of help transforms us in a major way—but not ultimately.

Ultimately we need the guru, and there are transformations all along the way, because of what Gurdjieff called "shock." What he meant by receiving "a shock" is not a violent shock, necessarily, but something that really gets into our hearts and won't let go. We have to come to understand ourselves far more deeply than we are ordinarily willing to. In the Work presented by Gurdjieff, there is a practice called "self-observation." We cannot observe ourselves in the way Gurdjieff instructed if we are judging ourselves. There has to be no judgment. If there is even the slightest degree of judgment, it is not self-observation. To have no judgment means you have to see yourself lying, abusing people, being grossly self-centered, and you say, "Oh, that's me, in this moment, now," without also saying, "Oh my God, what a horrible person I am; I never knew how selfish I was. Oh, I better take this to confession on Friday." *No judgment.*

The average person will not—*cannot*—see themselves objectively. If we don't see ourselves objectively, how far on the Path are we going to get? Not very far. People can have mystical assents from now until the day they die, and if the context out of which those mystical assents arise is ego, when that mystical assent is over…Bang! Everything that goes up must come down, and we are right back in the same old ego. What has that mystical assent meant, objectively? Absolutely zero. Many of us know people who were on a spiritual path with a teacher, and they had extraordinary insights into the nature of reality; then they got badly burnt by the teacher and went back to a life that showed no indication whatsoever of the profundity and the greatness of the visions they had.

The average person will not move from where they are, and the reason is because where we are is perfect. We are completely mechanical beings, and as machines, we are perfect machines. Everybody in this room, myself included, has a psychology that is perfect. We could not be better at who we are—shy, gregarious, full of self-hatred and shame, full of self-adulation and pride—because whoever we are psychologically is *perfect*. Having mastered our neuroses, why would we want to be different? If we take a master, a guru, we go back to the beginning. Suddenly we are nobody, trying to function in a whole new world in a whole new way. Before that we were like a diamond, but there are lots of diamonds in the world. Diamonds aren't all that rare, and there are lots of fake diamonds in the world.

It's the same in the world of antiques and artifacts. I sell genuine, rare, worshipped, sacred artifacts. In China there are craftspeople who can make copies of genuine antiques that are so good that only rare experts in the world can tell the difference. It's the same with precious stones: through the use of laser technology you can take faulty stones and make them look absolutely perfect, but instinctually—if you know your jewels and gemstones—you know there is a difference. To someone with refinement, the difference between a perfect emerald and a damaged emerald artificially made to look perfect through technological manipulation is the difference between the sun and the moon.Diamonds are easy to come by, but on the other hand, a perfect ruby is rare—very rare. A perfect emerald is even rarer than a prefect ruby.

It's exactly like that in the spiritual domain. The average person couldn't appreciate that spiritual difference if their lives depended on it. The average person is lost, lost, lost. I appreciate the sincerity of those who want to help the average person; the world needs decent people who want to help other people. It's a very sweet motive. The fact that they cannot be helped is completely distinct from the beauty of the reality that there are people who want to help them. That's very beautiful! You can't help them, but wanting to help so sincerely is very sweet, very beautiful.

So, we are already a perfect jewel—it's false, but it's perfect. Already being perfect, why would we want to find a guru and start crawling in the mud like a worm again? We wouldn't want to, which is why so few people actually set foot on the Path, much less make progress on the Path. Anybody who makes progress on the Path has had to realize that they are not a perfect human being. They realize that they are a worm—a worm, living in slime!—and having realized that, then they have the potential to realize they can be a perfect, true emerald. Not a false emerald made of glass, or a synthetic emerald, or a flawed emerald, but a real, true emerald.

Barcelona, Spain
June 2008

Seek Beauty and Avoid Suffering

M. Young

*I*n June 2006, Lee used the phrase "Seek beauty and avoid suffering" for the first time, as it became the refrain of many teachings he gave that summer. "Seek beauty and avoid suffering" suggests that we have a choice as to whether we suffer in ways that are without redemptive value. The truth of this must be reflected upon within a larger context, which includes suffering that is objective and of alchemical value, as well as an understanding of the cycles of *sadhana*: there are times when bitterness, disappointment and despair accumulate to tarnish the mirror of the mind. At those times we are effectively ruled by the *kleshas*, those afflictions and obscurations we experience as shame, vanity, pride, greed, anger and resentment, or the yellow-green goblin of jealousy. And yet, the cycles of sadhana are unavoidable, even natural, as they are ruled by the three *gunas* and the processes of creation, preservation, and destruction.

Many years ago Lee described and further clarified this principle by stating three specific phases that are experienced in the Great Process of Divine Evolution: Infatuation—indifference—doubt, which matures into insight—frustration—remorse, becoming free moment—disposition of enlightenment—compassion at the level of the heart. Although the first phase or cycle is considered a "beginning phase," it quickly becomes clear in sadhana that we cycle through these objective processes throughout our lives; the difference is that we find ourselves on different levels of a spiral each time we encounter infatuation—indifference—doubt, then insight—frustration—remorse, and finally a free moment—the disposition of enlightenment—and compassion.[1]

Simply "staying in place" on the Path is ninety percent of the work, as Mr. E.J. Gold says—*and*, we must learn to work with our minds. Finally, in the confrontation with our own misery, in order to "Seek beauty and avoid suffering," it comes down to what Lee has said all along: "All this suffering is needless, useless, and absolutely unnecessary. You have to discipline your mind."

Lee's teaching phrase "Seek beauty and avoid suffering" is succinct and salutary advice on how to lean into the perspective of Enlightened Duality. Like compassion, generosity, loving kindness or other skillful means, the perspective of Enlightened Duality can be cultivated, but the biggest obstacle must be confronted: the dualistic, separating, dividing mind. The taming and training of the mind is the very first front from which the war must be waged. "C'est la guerre," the French say, and any person with realistic time in on the spiritual path can appreciate the truth of this.

As practice deepens in sadhana, layer upon layer of buffers are dissolved, peeled or burned away to reveal the nature of the mind. The mind as we typically know it is brutal—it is a beast in its crude, wild, untamed aspect. Initial efforts at working with the mind are hopeless, useless, pointless it seems—like waving a red flag in front of a bull or using a single spear of wheat to stop a charging elephant. Negativity comes hurling out of the unconscious, that overflowing cauldron of everything good and bad and indifferent: despair, hope-

---

[1]   Lee Lozowick, *Living God Blues*, page 38–41.

lessness, self-hatred and insecurities of all kinds, the agony of believing oneself to be unloved and separate from others. There seem to be endless rounds of these attacks of the conditioned mind, one cycle feeding the next, leaving behind a trail of the bloodied and broken in our interpersonal interactions, believing all the while that "they" are the ones who are hurtful.

For a very long time in sadhana the mind continues to carry on its assault no matter how many insights or forays into its higher dimensions of possibility one may have made. Until the moment of awakening into a true Surrender to the Will of God, the mind continues to resort to its early programming, to return again and again to its default position of habit, like a computer. If we are ruthlessly honest with ourselves, if we are observing ourselves, we know this to be true. The mark of a true practitioner is found in the remorse and sorrow that is expressed by those who have walked the path for many years and can clearly, even dispassionately, admit that the mind, enthralled with egoic identification, is a trickster, an adversary of amazing resiliency and infinite resources. We will always need to return to practice as a beginner, and this process in and of itself is tremendously important, because it builds humility and compassion.

Perseverance furthers, the *I Ching* says, and it is true. It's another way of saying that hanging in there is ninety percent of the struggle. Keep making gestures. "Just try, keep trying," Arnaud Desjardins urged us in 2003 at Ferme de Jutreau. Wisdom and compassion are all around us; by the guru's blessing, we are immersed in grace and inundated with help.

So the work of sadhana becomes mind yoga: disciplining the mind. Sometimes all we need is to ask, "Who am I kidding?" Sometimes we need a stronger, cruder medicine to quell the beast: "Shut the fuck up!" Or, "Stop it!" For some of us this works well; for others it can make things worse.

What does it really mean to "avoid suffering"? This is a phrase that is subject to interpretation; it would be a travesty of misunderstanding the dharma to interpret it as meaning that we are supposed to reject the emotions that arise and shut down the feeling function. Rejection and shutting down are part of the shadow side of this wonderful teaching. There is a dimension of suffering that is objective, and this objective suffering is a feeling, which may be grief, love, sorrow, compassion or anger.

The point is to know ourselves to the extent that we can make the distinction between emotion and feeling. Every person has some experience of the difference between neurotic emotional angst and suffering that is real. We must begin to consciously make the distinction in any given moment of emotion or feeling, which is the indicator of whether it is the child or the adult who is currently in operation. "This is real feeling," or "This is not feeling—this is emotion." The egoic mind is highly creative and flexible, and it will try to convince us that we are feeling grief, sorrow or anger, when really we are caught in the theatre of emotions such as betrayal, vanity, or rage. Once we have identified that what is going on is emotion, as Swami Prajnanpad said, "Give the emotion its full play." In other words, do not repress, reject or deny the emotion, but experience its force and message in order to see it clearly; when the emotion is given full play, it will either pass completely or transform into the true underlying feeling.

When we allow the inner life, when we relax into acceptance, we have some space inside in which the process of that which is arising can reveal itself. Maybe an experience begins with an emotion; we observe it, see it clearly, and then the kernel, the seed of truth within that experience leads us to true feeling, which is a release. If there is something real at the core of what is arising, it will be revealed; if not, the whole charged knot of identification will simply dissipate, like clouds on a windy day.

When Lee says to "avoid suffering," he means that we want to avoid needless, neurotic suffering: self-obsession, blaming others, obsessive-compulsive thought patterns, indulgence in self-hatred or judgments. His advice is encapsulated in the practice of Enquiry as well as in the basic internal process of arduous self-examination and self-reflection. Again, we begin with making the distinction between emotions and feelings. What am I really feeling? What is really going on for me here? For this to be ultimately productive, we have to practice forbearance and restraint. We do not blurt out the first reactive thought that springs to mind; we restrain ourselves from taking action that can cause harm to another. Lee states: "Stay with what is arising, be aware, be conscious, pay attention, but don't do anything."

There is another important dimension of mind yoga, which is the first part of the formula, "Seek beauty and avoid suffering," involving the active cultivation of an inner environment of beauty and harmony, or the geometry of higher principles. With mind yoga, we are beautifying the mind—for example, with the practice of kindness, generosity and compassion. That may seem trite to our cynical ears. "Yes, yes, sure, compassion. You couldn't be compassionate if your life depended on it," our undisciplined minds grumble. The mind is capable of levying cruelties and punishments of many kinds. Before we know it, we can be crudely demeaning to ourselves and others, which creates a very bleak and miserable inner environment. "I'm in a bad mood" is exactly the time when we most need to turn toward loving kindness and compassion.

Compassion for ourselves and others begins to grow when we start to realize that we are nothing—meaning that our identifications are essentially empty. All the hours, days, years of licking our wounds, all those meaningless hurt feelings, all that self-importance and self-pity, when in reality we are less than dust. There is great freedom and luminosity in being less than dust, and only if we are less than dust can we begin to realize that we are made of the stars—the pure stars, radiant and Organically Innocent.

The precious time of incarnation in a human body is wasted indulging in those things that create an inner state of poison and negativity. It seems to take a very long time to become convinced that it is "me" not "you" who needs to be different. Only I can tend the inner garden. First, I have to drain the swamp and clear the land—the weeds and rotten trees, the skanky dead things lying about. Then I have to till the soil, find the seeds (they are given by Divine mandate, already present within us), sow the seeds, provide water and sun in the perfect proportions.

This all takes time and faith in the process; faith in the laws that govern gardening, and faith in the master gardener—that is, the guru. For a long time maybe it seems that we are only migrant workers apprenticing to the master gardener. In the best of all possible worlds, we find the master gardener and stop our migrations, realizing that the search is finally, irrevocably over and this is it. It is the end of the search, but it is not the end of the road, for the road goes on forever, except that at some point we can become free of overweening ambition and the primal knot of survival. Ultimately we discover that the master gardener, the garden, the sun, the rain, the seeds, the soil and everything else is our very self. There is nothing else to achieve, get, know, do, attain. There is only Just This, and out of Just This comes tumbling a cascade of beauty—that which we have always sought.

Once again, we return to practicing restraint. We must restrain ourselves from saying and doing things that may be harmful to others or to ourselves and from acting rashly; in this sense, sometimes it is appropriate to hesitate before we act. If we are practicing conscious restraint (which is different than repression), we will build sensitivity; we will not always be the obvious one, the loudest one, the self-appointed one in the front, leading the pack, the first to jump to the master's aid, knocking others over in our "enthusiasm." We will not be playing the star, because we will be rendered more invisible by the inward focus of attention on tending our own garden. In the process, we learn when to act quickly in service, with dignity and nobility of purpose.

We must be constrained by our own conscience. Pema Chodron says, "Take whatever arises as your path." This is the tantric perspective. There is no separation between every single possible experience and arising of life and the spiritual path. There is no end to beginning with a clean slate and practicing from there. Every single occurrence during a busy day is where practice lies. Jane Heap, a student of Gurdjieff, once wrote, "I am my burden. This is what I am meant to carry." Over dinner with Lee one night in Paris years ago, Alejandro Jodorosky said, "I cannot know truth, but I can know beauty." These sage teachings speak to the essence of the tantric path and are enough to keep us busy for lifetimes.

We must choose the yoga of the mind: to "Seek beauty and avoid suffering." What a delight and joy to discover beauty where once there were only swamp, weeds, rocks, poisonous snakes and crocodiles! When we make the choice to beautify our own minds, in the process we are literally building a soul, for the soul exists in beauty as an expression of God. The soul, in essence, is the principle of eternal beauty, giving rise to the tacit moods, the natural movement, the organic gesture of praise and worship.

Swami Papa Ramdas.

Yogi Ramsuratkumar.

Lee Lozowick.

Yogi Ramsuratkumar and Lee Lozowick, 1993.

On the Caravan to the Divine—Liars

Lee Lozowick

*L*iars, beggars, and poets on the Caravan to the Divine. There's a handy metaphor! It's the name the sponsors gave to this seminar, so let's begin with liars. As long as we are defined by our mechanical behavior, we are liars. It is our mechanical behavior, rather than our egos, that makes us liars, because ego is an element of our existence that can be useful or not useful, depending on how it is used. Our mechanical behavior demonstrates an absolute unwillingness to be real in the essential domains of money, food, and sex. Furthermore, as long as we are dominated by our mechanical behaviour—defined as our unwillingness to function objectively—everything having to do with the truth will be seen by us as a lie.

At the same time, anyone who represents the truth in any tradition—Christian, Buddhist, or Hindu—is a liar to the one who is dominated by their mechanical behavior. This is not necessarily conscious. If you look at the hundreds of thousands of Westerners who have become devotees of Tibetan Buddhist lamas, tulkus and rinpoches, it is obvious that a lot of those people don't realize that, in their mechanical world, their teachers are liars. For the mind dominated by mechanical behaviour, anything that speaks of truth is perceived as a lie.

Let's take the most middle-class, benign, toothless truism: "All is one." Who would argue with that? "Yes, all is One." It's comforting, it's secure, it's true, everybody knows it's true. "There is no separation." You all know that is true, but do you live your life according to that truism? If you are minimally honest with yourself, you would have to say a crashing, "No! I don't even *begin* to live my life according to that truism. I'm identified with my emotions. I'm desperate to be happy. I'm in survival and insecure about money. I'm in love with power." You are under the illusion that you actually *know* something, while every one of those behaviors related to survival, insecurity, power, money, and happiness is completely contradictory to the truism, "All is one, there is no separation." And, we consider anyone who expects us to live according to the truism, "There is no separation," to be a liar.

So, for that reason, on the Caravan to God, those who are serious about the journey through the desert are seen as liars—not by the conscious mind, because we love our teachers; we respect and honor them and have faith in them to varying degrees. We want to serve in genuine ways, and we're deeply touched by the profound compassion of someone like the Dalai Lama. But we don't *live* the teaching, because the part of us that is completely dominated by mechanicality believes all those truisms to be lies.

The question, of course, is: What to do? We find ourselves in quite a dilemma. Everybody is worried about the future. One of the questions a recent interviewer asked Arnaud Desjardins was, "What is the greatest spiritual crisis of the coming times?" Arnaud said, "The greatest crisis that we have to face now is not terrorism, not the economy, not spirituality—it is ecological." If there is no life on the face of the planet, then questions about spiritual crisis are kind of academic, don't you think? We are effectively destroying the ability of our culture to maintain a life of sanity on the face of this planet. So what to do? Obviously, we have some choices to make.

Everybody has a different definition of ego. To me, ego is just a tool: you use it productively and creatively, or you use it destructively. Obviously the good side of ego is when it is used creatively and productively. For instance, when a decision has to be made, you think through what the consequences of the decision are going to be. Often we make a decision that seems good in the moment, but perhaps we are impulsive and don't understand how many people will be affected by that decision. When we are able to think through a decision relative to the consequences, we are using ego in a good way.

If you have a choice between selling guns to Islamic fundamentalists or educating children, which is the wisest decision? Even in business, for instance: if we are producing a product, what raw materials go into the production of that product? Let's say we have a restaurant, and we have a choice between buying food that is naturally produced and buying food that is unnaturally produced. Food that is naturally produced costs more money. Of course we're not in business for the fun of it; we are in business to make money, hopefully for a good purpose. After all, how many shoes can one woman have? I guess if you are Imelda Marcos, you can have a thousand pairs of shoes! She was the wife of the president of the Philippines, and she had one pair of shoes for every hour of the day. So, to make a choice about which ingredients we're going to use in our restaurant or in our manufacturing business can be a good use of ego—if we consider, based on the big picture, whether the use of an ingredient or product is creating damage or is benign.

I'm on a tear about technology. Every school in America has computers in the classroom for every student. How does the school system afford all those computers? They don't. The computers are donated by the computer companies, so when the student turns on the computer, what do they see? Advertising. The computer companies find it very easy to donate even thousands of computers, because the advertising that they write into the computer programs—for Coca Cola and beer and alcohol companies—make far more money than the donation of the computers. If you are the head of a school system, do you agree to fill every classroom with computers? You know that if you decide not to, you will be fired when the renewal of your contract comes up, because the American public is colossally uneducated and ignorant. The parents will form a committee and make sure that anybody who does not allow their children to have free computers in school will not have their job. So what do you do? It's a very real question.

People ask how to open the mind. To open the mind is to be more aware without restriction, which means that you will be more sensitive to the depth of beauty and wonder and majesty in the world, as well as to the suffering, pain, agony and lack of justice in the world. For example, in America, if a nineteen-year-old man rapes a young woman, he can get from five to ten years in jail with time off for good behavior. On the other hand, if he downloads data from a computer illegally, it's a minimum twenty year sentence in jail. There is no justice to that whatsoever—it is inhumane. It's also the law. Guess who influences the law? Corporations, not humanitarians. So the more your mind opens, the more aware you are of the colossal injustices in the world.

The political realities of life are not obscure; most of us are well-educated and aware of the various social and political injustices, and we have a very natural filter system in our consciousness that tends to keep us from being overwhelmed by feelings of despair. When I use the term "open-minded," I am not referring to the philosophy "live and let live," or being culturally open-minded. I mean that your whole system is open to input or stimuli; the more your system is open to input, the more sensitive you are, and the more sensitive you are the more you feel. You have to be a very spacious and open-hearted individual—someone with a lot of faith in the ultimate process of the Universe—to not be completely broken-hearted by what you are seeing.

The spiritual teacher is considered to be a liar because the spiritual teacher wants us to move beyond our mechanical responses to life. The Dalai Lama says that if you want to learn to serve people, then you start serving people. One obvious example of that is found in the relationships between personalities in any spiritual school, where a lot of the work is based. There are those people we like, with whom we are happy to be washing dishes or doing gardening or whatever; on the other hand, we do not want to work at all with the people we don't like. It may be true that if you were not in a spiritual school, your life path would probably never have crossed the life paths of the other people in the school. That's all personality, and personality has nothing to do with it.

If you want to learn how to serve people, you don't go to therapy and deal with your inner child; you learn how to serve people by serving people. After a while you start to realize that you can serve anybody, including the people you don't want to serve, with the same degree of commitment, because service is not about personality. If service was about personality, the only people we'd ever serve would be the very small number of people whose personalities don't irritate us.

In spiritual life, you find yourself thrown into this stew, and some of the spices, according to your viewpoint, don't belong there. If you were a French cook, or a Peruvian cook, or a Mexican cook, and you were very orthodox about your profession, and a Moroccan chef came in and was going to put cinnamon in your stew full of thyme and sage or chili powder and cumin, you'd be shocked. We are thrown into this stew with a bunch of people; some of them we resonate to, some of them we don't resonate to, and some of them we absolutely *recoil* from. Yes, every spiritual school has some very difficult people, some psychotic people. That's life! Those very people realize that there is the possibility for genuine healing in a spiritual school, and so they come. Under the right circumstances, the teacher cannot turn them away.

So, here you are in a colossal mix of personalities and psychologies, and somehow you have to figure out that everyone is here to do the same thing. You are on the same team, and you have to learn that, with a deep and abiding commitment to practice, you can actually serve one another and not start wars with one another. There are always going to be a few people who will not get along with you, no matter what you do, for whatever reason. People are angry, isolated, confused, and they smell! Every spiritual community has got somebody who really smells bad, all the time. Their breath smells, their body smells, their clothes smell, but that person is probably really great at washing dishes. So guess who you get to be next to in the kitchen every time you come to the ashram? The person who smells.

Sometimes it is their personality. The only way certain people can get into relationship is to be critical of everybody they are trying to get into relationship with. Everyone knows how difficult it is to live with someone who is an expert about everything, so that nothing you do is good enough. They tell you how to dress, they tell you how to cook, because the only way some people know how to be in relationship is to be superior. You will find those people in a spiritual school, of course, because it's not an uncommon type. Then you find the kind of person who always wants everything to be nice: they will lie, steal and cheat, they will practically kill, just so everything is nice on the surface. Deep down inside them, who gives a shit? But on the surface—it's got to be nice!

You get all of these people together, and everybody has to realize that we are all doing the same thing; we all have the same aim and purpose. Whenever there are two people or more, individuals work most efficiently and most effectively when they work together as a team. When there is disagreement and antagonism and attempts to power-trip other people in the team, then the efficiency and the ultimate effect of the work will suffer to some degree.

There is tremendous warfare of personalities in my school. It doesn't stop our momentum, it doesn't stop the phenomenal results that we get, but there's no way of knowing what results we could get if the team was completely, fluently harmonious. Our ashram in America is essentially supported by one team's work, and one of the people on that team is the publicist, who sells by phone. She could triple the income for the ashram, but nobody will help her, because everybody is too busy. All of those people who are too busy to help her would be stunned, shocked, even horrified if we lost the ashram because we couldn't afford to pay the bills, but they will not re-prioritize their lives so that they can help. That is the way it is with any group of human beings who are thrown together.

When dominated by mechanicality, our essential priority is personal—it's about us, not about embracing the team. This is particularly true if certain members of the team are personally incongruous with our resonance towards people in some way: the person has dark skin, the person is a Jew or a Catholic, or gay, or whatever our prejudices are. Or the person never listens to us: "I'm the chief of the team, I'm the head of the team, but they never listen—they do things their own way." Have you ever cooked with somebody in the kitchen? You say, "I want the carrots diced …" and they look at you and say, "Okay." When you come back an hour later the carrots are sliced, but your vision of the meal demands—needs—diced carrots, not sliced carrots. Interpersonal *war* is started over things that ridiculous, because we aren't giving people credit for being here for the same reasons we're here.

The person that you have the most negative reaction to among your friends or in the sangha body of your spiritual school is actually there for the same reason you are. If we do not honor that in some way, then we are going to stay at war with different parts of the group body. It stands to reason that if you commit deeply and profoundly to the Path, you are going to want to receive the most optimal and efficient benefit from that Path. That means you will have to deal with people—even your spiritual teacher.

To optimize your personal benefit from the Path, you want to be able to deal with everybody in your life, including everybody you meet, not just people who are in your spiritual school. You have to understand that, on every level, every person born in a human body is here for the same reason—all six billion of us. Every person who finds a spiritual school is there for the same reasons. We could say this in different language or articulate it differently, but whether it's a Christian monastery or a Buddhist retreat or a yoga class, we're here for the same reason. In the big picture, to optimize the benefit of our personal practice, we need to be in harmony with the commonality of purpose. How do we do that?

Somehow we have to figure out that it's not about personality, because personality is probably never going to change: maybe the person who is late to appointments is still going to be late to appointments forty years from now. Maybe the person who is afraid to have sex without a light in the room is always going to be that way. Even though you've always wanted sex in the dark because it is so mysterious, can you stay married to that person for the rest of your life and love them?

If we are expecting people who rub us the wrong way to change their personalities, we may be expecting the wrong thing. Somebody who's a control freak will probably always be a control freak, but they can learn to channel it differently. One of the reasons I'm able to continue to work at the level of intensity that I work at, even though there are times of tension, is because I don't have unrealistic expectations. It's taken me a long time not to be personally broken by unrealistic expectations of individuals and of the Work. There are some people who have a reliable practice, relatively speaking; the rest of us need to get serious, or not have unrealistic expectations. I don't expect all of my students to have a reliable practice—if I did I wouldn't be a teacher. I'd be all alone; I'd have no students.

If you have unrealistic expectations in your personal practice, you will be caught in a conflict that is unresolvable, because by definition your expectations are unrealistic and therefore unrealizable. So, either have a reliable practice or don't have unrealistic expectations. You must have realistic expectations, be willing to work as you go, progress as you go and get what you pay for, without losing your sense of purpose and passion for the work that *drives* you. You say to yourself, "I don't meditate every morning; I'd like to but I don't. There is no reason to beat myself up and suffer over it. I'm on the Path, I love my teacher. I'm devoted to this work. I am who I am, and I'll do what I can." Period.

Personality is not like clay; it's not that malleable. Personality is rather set in stone. You can round out the sharp edges, you can polish off the dull spots and brush off the dirt and things like that, but who we are is who we are. If we're going to work in a harmonious team of any kind, we have to get through our personalities. We have to honor one another's commonality, not react to one another's differences. It's a very difficult thing to do, clearly, but that's the first step.

A lot of people find the Path and get obsessed: "Enlightenment, enlightenment, I've got to wake up." That's like being an engineer who builds large buildings but only thinks about the top floor. If you don't understand and *practically* apply all the steps that create a solid foundation, you aren't going to have a top floor. What if you just went to a field and built a big building on the field. What if the water table was three meters under the field? Just a few months ago the biggest statue of Buddha in the world—which they were building in some Southeast Asian country—fell over. It was two thirds built, fifty meters high, and it collapsed because the foundation wasn't properly established. It's an exact parallel to our illusions about enlightenment.

U.G. Krishnamurti died a few years ago. I never saw him in person, but I really liked him. Without question, he was a brilliant genius in what he did, but I thought he was a rotten spiritual teacher. He knew how to tear down with amazing skill, but that's all he did. As many of you know, when someone is torn down and left to their own devices—without the help of a good therapist or a good spiritual teacher, or friends and family—there is no benefit whatsoever to having been torn down.

In the *neo-advaita* movement, which is very popular these days, there is an assumption that if someone realizes ultimate truth, they will automatically have the capacity, the intelligence, and the skill to know what to do with that realization. Not only is that unrealistic, it's absolutely wrong. It's like putting a four-year-old child behind a wheel of a powerful vehicle and assuming that because they're human, and because their parents drive, they will know what to do and be safe.

On the Caravan of God, before we can fully appreciate the journey through the desert that ends up at the oasis with the water, the palm trees, the perfect dates, and the beautiful tents with nice rugs, first we have to do the preliminary work that gives us the actual capacity and training to manage what we find in the oasis. In the movies they come to the oasis, and when the star goes to drink the guide says, "No! The well is poisoned!" The star is saved, but if the guide did not know how to tell the difference between poisoned water and pure water … oh well!

The neo-advaita advocates say, "What difference does it make? It's all illusion anyway. Okay, so someone realizes objective nihilism and kills themselves—commits suicide—because they can't handle it. So what? It's all an illusion, they never existed anyway, there's no such thing as death!" That attitude is irresponsible to the extreme, because you and I still suffer, even though suffering is an illusion. You and I are still touched by the innocence of children, even though no one is ever born, no one ever dies, and there is no such thing as a child. You and I live in a world in which the illusions of that world are real to us—rightly so, because this is our world. One of our responsibilities is to take care of our world with concern for each and every one of its elements. Any other viewpoint is itself the height of illusion.

How do we get enlightened? You listen to those who are telling the truth, even though the world may be saying that they are liars, because the world is threatened by the truth. Then, as the Christians say, charity begins at home. You start at the lowest level of practice, and when that level is absolutely reliable, you move to the next level of practice. The Dalai Lama gets up at three o'clock every morning and practices until seven o'clock every morning—*every* morning—whether he is in America, Germany or India, or traveling in a car or on an airplane. Wherever he is, the Dalai Lama gets up and practices for four hours religiously. That is *reliable* practice, and without reliable practice, you will not build the structure on which enlightenment must stand. Although there is no such thing as enlightenment; there is what I call Enlightened Duality. As far as I'm concerned enlightenment does not exist, but Enlightened Duality does. Enlightened Duality is Reality, and without a practice that is reliable, we will never realize it.

Freiburg, Germany
August 2007

Beggary

M. Young

The indigent way of the beggar has been part of traditional life in the sacred culture of India for thousands of years. Over millennia Mother India has protected and even revered beggars, particularly the mendicants and sadhus, as an integral and important part of sacred culture. In both Hindu and Buddhist traditions, the householder or merchant or pilgrim who feeds—offers *bhiksu*—to a mendicant, monk or sadhu receives great blessings. The Bauls incorporated this tradition into their way of life as *madhukari*, the practice of begging for alms after singing and dancing. Both the beggar's receiving and the almsgiver's giving are considered sacred acts involving profound blessings for all concerned.

"Beggary" is a term Lee has used to indicate a general disposition toward Life that is profoundly linked with Spiritual Slavery—the core revelation of his teaching. Lee himself is a beggar in a lineage of beggars: Papa Ramdas, the guru of Yogi Ramsuratkumar, was a mendicant beggar for many years of his *sadhana*. After years of traveling and begging as a sadhu, Ramdas' enlightenment experience occurred in a cave on Mount Arunachala. In 1952, Ramdas initiated his young devotee, Ramsurat Kunwer, into the mantra, "Om Sri Ram Jai Ram

Jai Jai Ram," instructing him to repeat the mantra "all the twenty-four hours, night and day." This Ramsurat did for one week, at which time he was taken over by divine madness.

"Ramdas killed this beggar in 1952. This beggar is no more," Yogi Ramsuratkumar often said of this experience in future years. After this spiritual death, a divine fire consumed his life. By strict Hindu conventions of the time, Ramsurat became wild and unmanageable. His devotional *bhavas* were so passionate that Ramdas' devotees at Anandashram were put off, even offended, by this strange person they called "the mad Bihari."[1] Erupting in spontaneous moods of passionate devotion to Ramdas and his female counterpart—Mataji Krishnabai—singing and dancing, disappearing to wander the hills then reappearing disheveled and love-maddened, Yogi Ramsuratkumar disturbed the peaceful status quo of Anandashram. Finally Ramdas sent him away, saying, "Go and beg." When Ramdas then asked him, "Where will you go?" Ramsurat answered, "Arunachala."

For the next seven years Yogi Ramsuratkumar wandered around India begging, until he finally arrived in Tiruvannamalai at the foot of Mt. Arunachala. He arrived as a beggar and he remained a beggar. He lived on the streets, sleeping on the ground in the Arunachalesvara Shiva temple, or outside the stalls in the brass market, or under the punnai tree by the bus station. Yogi Ramsuratkumar referred most often to himself as "this beggar" and "this dirty beggar," because he wore rags and bathed once a year. When asked by a devotee why he did not bathe, he replied that he was too busy with "Father's Work." His old dhoti and kurta shirts were stained and streaked with dust; he ate whatever food he received as alms. He had no money, no place to live. He wandered around Mt. Arunachala and lived in the caves, spending time in the cave where his guru, Ramdas, had his spiritual awakening.

---

[1]   Swami Satchidananda, *The Gospel of Swami Papa Ramdas*, pages 371–381.

Yogi Ramsuratkumar was not speaking euphemistically when he called himself a dirty beggar. He was a modern-day *avadhuta*, in the ancient tradition of Dattatreya—the revered, wild saint of both Vishnu and Shiva lovers. We cannot consider the contemporary sacred beggar, Yogi Ramsuratkumar, without briefly touching on the life of Dattatreya. Deified as an *avatara* and a god, Dattatreya is still considered to have been a flesh and blood man who wandered as a mendicant beggar and yet left behind a significant legacy of teachings.

Dattatreya is the archetypal divine beggar, tantric sage, fierce yogi and wandering ascetic who nonetheless is credited with writing a number of significant scriptural texts. It is difficult to distinguish his historical life from the myth that surrounds him, as his myth was so great that he was made into a full-blown deity.[2] Dattatreya, as both sage and deity, is worshipped as the crazy-wise one who has gone beyond the beyond:

> *A second interpretation of the name Dattatreya, quite current among us followers, is "the one who gave up or surrendered (datta) the three (treya)." In this case, the number three is said to refer to the three gunas which Dattatreya relinquished. The fact that Dattatreya is without or beyond the gunas (nirguna) would then be exemplified by his naked appearance as digambara or "clad in space."*[3]

It is said that Dattatreya authored the *Jivan-Mukta-Gita* ("Song of Living Liberation"), the *Tripura Rahasya* ("Tripura's Secret Teaching," referring to the great goddess, Tripura Sundari) and the

---

[2]   Antonio Rigopoulos, *Dattatreya: The Immortal Guru, Yogin, and Avatara*, pages 28–29.

[3]   Ibid, page 28.

Avadhuta-Gita. The *gitas* are typically a dialogue—between a sage and a disciple or a god and a goddess—in which the nature of Reality is revealed.[4] Dattatreya was a great realizer and expounder of nondual realization while at the same time he embodied the central Baul ideal of *sahajiya*, or spontaneous awakened awareness; he was, perhaps, the ultimate example of this state of consciousness.

Dattatreya is often artistically rendered with four arms, indicating his deity status; he is always depicted carrying a begging bowl with his dogs nearby. Yogi Ramsuratkumar was a dirty beggar who was known to many as a beggar saint. For many years his dog, "Sai Baba," was a constant companion; when one dog died, he was replaced by another "Sai Baba." Clothed in disheveled, street-stained "rags," his only possessions were a coconut begging bowl and a palmyra fan given to him by Gnanananda Giri, the saint of Tapovanum, an ashram near Tiruvannamalai, who befriended the beggar. The only thing Yogi Ramsuratkumar ever seemed to actually want was Charimar cigarettes, for these were mysteriously essential to his subtle work. Spontaneity and childlike delight were two of his most remarkable characteristics, for he was a true sahajiya, living by the currents of the moment.

A beggar is someone who depends upon the goodness, graciousness, and generosity of Life for his or her day-to-day sustenance, place to sleep, clothes to wear; someone who lives a life of spontaneity, largely free of plans and motives—and yet this very spontaneity forces a profound acceptance of uncertainty and groundlessness. What kind of fine edge does this create for people who can truly live this way?

It seems that we have it all wrong in the West, in the way that we look down on beggars and the homeless: we castigate them, cast them out, look away, refuse to meet their eyes when we pass by.

---

4   Ibid, page 195–197.

"Thank God it's not me," we may think in secret. Fear wells up when we see their abject state, the lawlessness, the apparent fearlessness or hopelessness of it, or the depravity. What if the Universe is just full of whimsy, and decides not to feed you for days? Or someone beats you and chases you away, full of fear and loathing as soon as they see one who is living against the tide of "normal, civilized life." What if they beat you just because they can?

Yogi Ramsuratkumar was beaten quite often as a beggar living on the streets of Tiruvannamalai. He was a northerner who was born in a tiny village on the Ganges near Varanasi in Uttar Pradesh; as an adult he lived in Bihar, also in the north, and spoke Hindi. Years later, arriving in Tiruvannamalai, which is in Tamil Nadu, south India, he was persecuted because of the political climate of the times, in which the relationship between northern and southern India was extremely strained, even on the verge of violent revolution. Yogi Ramsuratkumar was persecuted because he was from the north and spoke Hindi rather than Tamil. He never retaliated against his tormentors. He never responded with angry outbursts. He bore their aggression with forbearance, peaceful acceptance, and compassion.

The first time I saw real beggars was on my first trip to India in 1993. I'd seen some beggars on the streets of the U.S. and in Mexico, but India has a true beggar's culture that is quite literally everywhere you go. On a long bus ride from Chennai to Kanya Kumari on the southern tip of India, the bus driver stopped in the middle of nowhere at three a.m. for a coffee break. Everyone on the bus piled out to find a privy spot somewhere among the trees, since the toilets were already overflowing.

There were several tea and snack stalls in the large open area where the bus was parked. Fires burned everywhere, and the smell of dung, wood smoke, and diesel—and an indefinable, pervasive dark musky scent—added to the primal, mysterious feel of the night. Even though it was the middle of the night, there was activity going on. People milled about everywhere; cows slept here and there in big white or tan humps. Farmers came by with their produce piled on bullock carts. Huge tamarind trees grew on the perimeters, and we stood quietly, somber and sobered, with hot, sweet coffees in hand, watching the life of the night.

Suddenly a man stood before me, wrapped in white cloth, holding out his hands and crying, "Ma, Ma…Ma…" He was begging for food, raising his hand to his lips and pleading. He looked like he had just risen from the tomb. His hands, badly decayed from leprosy, were missing several fingers. His face also was eaten away, and his cries disturbed me to the depths, penetrating beyond whatever buffers I had left in this first confrontation with the world of beggars in India. "Ma, Ma…" he pleaded.

I felt cornered. I didn't know what to do. I knew if I gave him any rupees, all the other beggars in the parking lot would have descended upon me. Then I looked into his eyes. Connection. A human being, just like me, looked back. He was completely present and in relationship with me. Our two very different roles in life were juxtaposed in one suspended moment in that mutual seeing of each other. The sparrow wings of compassion fluttered in my heart, and I reached for a few rupees. Suddenly everyone was in motion; the bus was leaving. I was pulled away by my companions. "Hurry, come on! Let's go…" I have never forgotten that person. Since then I've made it a point to act quickly when the impulse to give coins to a beggar comes up.

Beggars are everywhere; their lives are an inseparable part of ours. Beggars are as real and dynamic as we are. Not all beggars inspire one to participate in the relationship of giving and receiving. Angry and aggressive beggars with attitude are so different in mood than those who approach in the mood of Beggary—with acceptance and surrender and, sometimes, even with gratitude or beatitude. There have been times when I have felt profoundly blessed by a beggar to whom I have given alms.

I have seen that Lee gives to beggars whose spirit is shining through their circumstance, like the beggar with leprosy who I met on the way to Kanya Kumari. Later in the summer of 2008 Lee gave money to beggars on the streets of Paris twice. Each time there was a specific intention in his giving. One of the beggars approached the driver's window of our van. He was clearly strung out, his shaggy black hair hung in tatters around his face, his rumpled and filthy jacket and pants betrayed his sleeping on the streets of the city. Lee handed some euros out the window to him, and, driving away, said, "He really needs that. It will go to his next drink, but he *really* needs it."

The Sufis speak of the need to approach the Beloved as a beggar in tatters and ruins. This sounds very romantic indeed until we are directly touched by such a life of beggary. Our small notion of romance is destroyed by the reality of a divine Romance that burns our ideas and concepts to a crisp in its conflagration. Rumi writes that we must come to the Beloved in helplessness and ruin because the urgency of our need and its necessary receptivity—our willingness to accept divine help in any form—carries the most profound depth of feeling. It is a prayer, a magnetic call that is so powerful it attracts the attention of God.

Why do we need to make a place for beggars in our society? Partly because beggars remind us to ponder the most important and deepest places of Life. If we look beyond our fear and repulsion, we can see that beggars have a message to bring to us. They remind us of the impermanent underpinnings of Life. They whisper to us of our true state, which is entirely dependent upon the Supreme Reality for our very being. We are beggars before the Lord. When a beggar approaches, we have the opportunity to be in relationship with a human being, and in the process of that brief interchange, we learn something about how to be beggars before the Lord. Beggars teach gratitude and humility.

It was a rainy, cold, early June morning in Brussels at a brocante fair, where we students were following our teacher in his great passion for objective art. Once again Lee—who deals in sacred art and antiquities and is a Renaissance man himself: poet, lyricist, singer, lover of the formed and formless divinity and general trickster—was scouring the shops and street fairs for an object of heartbreaking beauty. It had rained so much in the past few days that even a reluctant desert dweller like me (who rejoices every time it rains, because after over twenty years of living in a desert, I know the real meaning of bone dry) was ready for the sun to come out and shine its loving rays upon us.

Crossing the wet street to jump back into our van, I caught a glimpse of a swarthy, begrimed street character. He was dressed completely in black with a shiny, bright yellow bomber jacket on top. He had a large dog, a pit bull to be exact, firmly pulled up by a strong plastic leash, with a hat pulled down low over his disheveled black hair. He was heavily adorned with beads and jewels and gewgaws of all kinds that hung from the many chains around his neck.

My friends told me that they had just encountered him at one of the brocante stalls under the dripping trees across the street. He was gregarious and had engaged them in a conversation about Native Americans in Arizona and druid artifacts, some of which he was carrying in his pockets—small tools and strangely shaped objects. It's unusual for people to ask anything about the tribal people when they find out we are from Arizona, but that was, in fact, the first thing he did. "Where are you from?" Arizona. "Oh, what are the names of the tribes that live there?"

My friend had been interested in a stone tool she had found on a vendor's table. It was their mutual interest in this artifact—which he said was a druid tool—that had drawn the man into conversation with her and led him to pull the other sacred druid objects from his pockets. In fact, the vendor later told her that this denizen of the streets came often and bought small objects, which he would pay for over a period of months. I started wondering: Who was this guy? Not your average street bum.

If you are on the Path, at some point you begin to know the meaning of the truism, "Things are not always what they appear to be." Here was a man who was living on the streets (and yet he mentioned that he had a wife) who had what seemed to be a richly variegated life. I notice that street people are often the most interesting of the many folks encountered when one travels a lot. As with any slice of life, human beings will reveal facets of Enlightened Duality if we look deeply enough into them. When it comes to beggars, bums and street people, as one friend said a few days ago about a drunk, whom she had seen on the streets of Paris near a huge street market in Clignancourt, "It depends on how you *see* them." She reported a heartrending scene, in which a vendor was fiercely berating a broken-down drunk who was so debilitated from booze that he couldn't stand. She yelled at him like a browbeating fishwife. Finally another street bum came over and gave him a hand, literally pulling him up off the pavement and helping him to another spot down the street. In the process, the drunk's pants fell off and hung down around his shaking ankles, tangling up underneath the long coat he wore to fend off the spring cold. He could barely stand. It took some moments for him to gain enough stability to stagger, with help, over to the other spot.

The streets of every big city are filled with lives like these. What heartbreak brings a person to this raw and hopeless edge? Is this lifestyle their protest against the brutality and falsity of today's cold, heartless technoculture world? Is it that they just cannot bring themselves to participate in the nightmare of "modern times," to conform, to fit into the narrow confines of societal demands, to be a cog in the machine, a willing prisoner of post-industrial horrors? Is destitution, addiction and depravity preferable to a life of self-betrayal in mind, body and soul as a nameless sleepwalker in some borough or suburb of our times?

Artists like Charles Bukowski and Henry Miller (who lived like a penniless bum on the streets of Paris) refused to live by prescribed standards, in a life of stultifying repression that is nothing less than death to the soul. Instead they chose to live in the underbelly of life in a way that would hone their beings to a fierce edge, or to generate a kind of inner fire on the dry tinder of their existence in order that their art might be ignited, fed, enflamed.

Originating in northern India, the ancestral "gypsies" made their way overland to Europe, where they have thrived despite constant oppression and prejudice from white-skinned Occidentals. It is a well-known fact that hundreds of thousands of gypsies were exterminated in the death camps of World War II. Today, the gypsies, or people of Romany, are some of the countless anonymous human beings who live marginalized lives of wandering indigence, poverty, destitution and homelessness—and yet, something has arisen from within the gypsy culture that captures the soul, something rare that carries a certain palpable quality of longing. This appears most clearly in their music: the soulful gypsy violin or guitar, their poetry and songs, their amazing dance—the Flamenco. Perhaps, when we accept and embrace impermanence, the fact of our own helplessness and impending bodily death becomes the seed bed for an uprising of beauty in the form of art.

Many gypsies of the Roma people are beggars. They are everywhere in Europe, concentrated mostly in France and the countries of eastern Europe. I have seen them on the streets of Paris, Berlin, Marseilles, Montpellier—even in London. Scruffy, bedraggled, sometimes dirty, sometimes not, it appears that the gypsies are not intimidated by modernity, even though they are profoundly at the effect of modern life—like all people who still have a connection to the tribe, the clan, and a rootedness in the Earth. The women stand on street corners or walk frankly down the street wearing dark scarves and long skirts, holding out their hands for money, sometimes imploring, begging, sometimes humble and beaten down, at other times demanding and arrogant.

Most especially I have seen gypsies in Saintes Maries de la Mer, in the Carmague in the south of France. In this tiny village on the Mediterranean Sea, I once saw a gypsy man and a twelve-year-old gypsy boy under the sycamore trees in the Place de la Gitan in the village near the ancient Roman church. The man was teaching the boy to play a guitar; nearby sat a group of gypsy women, dark-skinned, mysterious, in their own world. The man played the guitar while the boy danced, then the boy, taking his elder's instruction, sat down and attempted to play what the man had played. As we left the plaza, I passed by one of the gypsy women; our eyes locked for an instant of connection. Hers were as luminous, green and inscrutable as the sea, except for the gleam of wordless recognition that passed between us.

The gypsies are drawn to Saintes Maries de la Mer by a cloistered, obscure deity, Saint Sarah al Kali, little known outside of French lore on Mary Magdalene. She resides in the crypt of the old stone church. Lee and his students have made numerous pilgrimages over the years to see this divine mother who many say was actually the child of Jesus and Mary Magdalene—the vessel or Holy Grail of the House of David. Saint Sarah is a rare living expression of a feminine archetype, the Ecstatic Mother. It is well worth going out of your way to make pilgrimage there, in order to pay respects and receive her blessing. Once a year in May, one hundred thousand people converge in the village to see the gypsy kings take the deity from the church to the sea for a ceremonial consecration of the icon in the salty waters, exactly like the rituals that have been enacted for thousands of years in India and continue today. It is the gypsies who are responsible for keeping the divinity alive in this innocuous little statue hidden away in a thousand-year-old stone crypt in the Carmague.

Like all human beings, the gypsies are a blend of darkness and light. Gypsies are often outlaws in some way, and yet it cannot be said, necessarily, that gypsies follow Bob Dylan's redemptive words—"To be an outlaw, you have to be honest."But then, honesty is one of those concepts that is quite malleable and subjective, depending on the context of how it is being used. Gypsies have a definite code of honor, but it is quite difficult to comprehend or glimpse its integrity from the *gadjo* point of view. A friend who lives in the southwestern part of France, south of the Dordogne, once told me she knew someone who had her entire house cleaned out of furniture and belongings in one night: while she was away, the gypsies came and took everything. I know others who have had their vehicles broken into at the beach near Montpellier and have had many valuables stolen—again, by marauding gypsies who were roaming nearby. Others who know the gypsies say that they are completely misunderstood.

On the other hand, gypsies create some of the most richly sublime music in the world. Their culture carries a hidden stream of longing for the Beloved, made visible not only in their music, poetry and dance, but in the prayers and praises they offer to Saint Sarah. Their relationship with their *ista devata* is intimate yet reverent: they approach fearlessly, open hearted, to touch her feet and kiss her cheek—or maybe even her lips.

The gypsies are notorious in the south of France for their freewheeling and sometimes questionable ways. At the same time, gypsies are allowed to travel, roam and live freely in France, where most local communities have some land reserved for gypsy encampments—something that probably would never happen in the U.S. Why does the local French government do this? Maybe it's because the gypsies contribute an important element to the depth and breadth of human culture, and the French, who have been around for a long time, know this. In the United States we have completely lost the ancient wisdom that acknowledges the value of the inexplicable, embodied in the stranger, the traveler, the wanderer, the beggar, the mendicant. In the nature of an itinerant person—one who has no home, who lives a truly groundless life—we encounter a mystery, a whiff of impermanence and its kinship with death and longing.

When the event occurred that catalyzed the inception of Lee's teaching work in the guru tradition, the first teaching he gave was termed "Spiritual Slavery." Spiritual Slavery is a term Lee has used consistently over the years to articulate the core of his teaching. "Slavery" is not a word many people care to relate with in any terms. It is an extremely potent and appropriate word, because it takes a word with guts—like "slave"—to intimate the glory that is implied in the paradoxical nature of this teaching. This same paradox is at play in our typical response to beggars and the idea of slaves. From a conventional point of view, nobody wants to be a beggar or a slave, and yet the spiritual Path is telling us that such a disposition yields a coveted dimension of experience in relationship with the Divine. When we are considering such a paradox, it is most helpful to turn to poetic metaphor. Consider these lyrics from a song written by Lee:

> Got a question for you honey
> Please forgive my great emotion
> Is it dangerous to love you
> With such blind devotion?
>
> Ask me to do anything
> Your wish is my command

I will fly up to the sun for you
Bring it to your hand
I will conquer armies
You know what I mean
Allow me to adore you
Be your slave, not your queen

Fingers intertwined, paroxysm of love
That is my idea of praying
Lost in your lover so deeply
You don't even know what you are saying
Don't know much about the subject of holy
But I think I have come pretty near
When I'm looking deep into your eyes
There I am transfixed with fear

Blind devotion, what else is left?
Nothing that is worth very much
Blind devotion, consume me in your path
Let me feel the heaven and sorrow of your touch[5]

A mystery is hidden within these lines: "Allow me to adore you / Be your slave, not your queen." What it means to be a beggar before the throne of God, or a slave to one's Beloved, is a theme that shows up frequently in Lee's lyrics and in his poems to Yogi Ramsuratkumar. It is here, in the poetic form, that we can hear the teaching: the taste of self-sacrifice in surrender is sweet. Such objective sweetness is one of the treasured fruits of the Path, but a sacrifice of the separate self is required. We are truly helpless without God, for He/She is the source of our existence. Only one who courts the disposition of gratitude,

---

5   "Blind Devotion," lyrics by Lee Lozowick, composed by Ed Flaherty, recorded by Shri on CD, *Good Thing*.

of helplessness, of a certain *rasa* of hopelessness, and of surrender, will taste the wine.

> I took one look at him
> My course of action was clear
> I'm your obedient servant,
> Will you let me stay near?
> I will do all your bidding
> I'm your heart-bound slave
> Throw me crumbs from your table
> For I'm foolish and brave[6]

To embrace the disposition of Beggary does not mean that we should wear rags and beg for our food. I look to Lee's example, and I see a man in flames, sitting on a funeral pyre which is slowly burning away any final shreds of dross that may obscure his transparency to his guru. Through his surrender to Yogi Ramsuratkumar, in the relationship of Grace, I see my own teacher becoming more and more a wave of crystalline water with sun shining through it—a vast empty space filled with light. There is an abundance of emptiness, if emptiness can be described at all, and yet there is a kaleidoscopic interplay of opposites that come together in a dance that produces not dark or light but a rainbow burst of radiance.

Beggary is found in my teacher's abiding submission to whatever Yogi Ramsuratkumar, as agent of Divine Grace, will have for him. This shows up in many ordinary ways: On tour, Lee brings simplicity to the stage. He goes onstage barefoot, walks up to the microphone and just starts singing, even in the biggest, most professional venues. Lee does not buy clothes for himself; he wears what he is given as gifts, or what may show up in the "giveaway box" on the ashram. Lee

---

6   "Course of Action," lyrics by Lee Lozowick, composed by Ed Flaherty, recorded on CD by Shri on *Shrison in Hell.*

does not want to know the schedule of events in advance; he is not interested in information (coveted and highly sought by his devotees) about what will happen in the future—the who, how, when and why of everything.

When he is served food, even if several items on his limited diet have been overlooked or forgotten, Lee does not want anyone to make another trip back to the kitchen to retrieve something that is missing from the table. He insists, often much to the chagrin of those who have forgotten to provide a particular item, "I only want what is in front of me." He instructs his students not to ask for special privileges or to be made exceptions: this can show up as simply as not asking for substitutions on a restaurant menu. What a concept for Starbuck's-satiated Americans, who are used to demanding and receiving our own very special version of whatever it is our hearts desire.

Our relationship to food is a domain in which we often see our guru making communications about the principle of beggary. For example, in June 2008 Lee was driving, caravan-style, with a group of students from Barcelona to Madrid. Along the way he decided to stop and have a picnic lunch, which elicited some grumbling amongst a few of his students, because there was no picnic fare planned for the group due to the fact that, when asked before we left Barcelona about buying food for the road for everyone, Lee had said, "Do not pack a picnic. We'll be spontaneous." Now the guru wanted to stop for a picnic, but the only food we had brought was for him. When this was pointed out, he said genially, "No problem! I'll share my food with everyone."

There were thirteen people in his traveling party at this point. We stopped under some sheltering pine trees and pulled out every bit of food we could find in our boxes and coolers. Friends who had arrived from Colorado to travel with Lee for a few weeks brought out their stashes of organic nuts and dried fruits, and everything was piled on the tablecloth until a humble feast appeared out of nowhere, as if by magic.

Once again, Lee had pointed out to us that there is always enough food to meet everyone's needs; we only need to relax and trust the process, trust the guru, and trust the flow of blessings in his company. We don't need to go out and buy more food—we can be satisfied with what we have, which always meets our needs, if not our wants.

These ordinary images of Beggary in action have implications that run in very deep channels, for Beggary informs all the decisions that must be made by the guru. This sometimes causes Lee's devotees to chaff at the bit in irritation at his lack of *wanting* and the seemingly endless waiting, waiting, waiting—for my teacher is a man who can wait, and wait, and wait. He is not looking through the eyes of ordinary concerns, which are tight from the clinch of ego's need to survive at any cost; he is looking through the eyes of Spiritual Slavery.

Lee appears to rest in a state of desirelessness—of not wanting—until desire becomes the natural arising. Quietude and simplicity come naturally to him; he has said that he longs for a life of greater simplicity, but his devotees are still too attached to the superfluities and distractions of a complexity-maddened world, and he does not live separate from us. Every day he denies his own preferences to stay in the nitty-gritty of our lives—to stay in *relationship* with others. Lee is a man who has absolutely no private life. He responds to whatever calls him forth. He is someone who has looked the seductive vamp of power and fame in the eye and said no. If there is a need, he will sacrifice himself to meet it, most obviously in his travel schedule, which would reduce most people to a state of exhaustion and recoil within a few weeks' time.

Sometimes Lee is joyous, even wildly ecstatic, which can be seen in his eyes, not because he is making grandiose gestures that attract all available attention. This is a teaching in and of itself—ecstasy that is mature and elegant, contained yet boundless at the same time. This spiritual maturity was apparent in Yogi Ramsuratkumar: life as a beggar had refined him, honed his life into the finest expression of joy, praise, delight, compassion. He had come a very long way from the capricious, wildly ecstatic devotee at Anandashram, who was struck with divine madness after repeating for only one week the mantra with which his guru had initiated him.

Ramdas sent Yogi Ramsuratkumar away, saying, "Go and beg." Perhaps because Ramdas knew, from personal experience, that begging was the means through which all elements necessary to the process of spiritual transformation would be made readily available to Yogi Ramsuratkumar. Like all great devotees who are obedient to their masters, Yogi Ramsuratkumar took that instruction and lived it fully, to the end of his life. Yogi Ramsuratkumar remains the shining, living beacon of the Path: a beggar king who walked among us in this earthly sojourn and showed the way of Beggary as the great mystery, the paradox of the Path, which it truly is.

> O Dattatreya, O Hari, O Krishna
> O the giver of wild joy, O sky-clothed
> O the silent, O child-like innocent,
> O the one who eats within [7]

---

[7]   After his death in 2001, this verse was found among a collection of drawings, scraps, bits of poems and other writings by Yogi Ramsuratkumar; these had been given to an American devotee, Caylor Wadlington, in the early seventies. This particular verse was written in both English and in Sanskrit, in Yogi Ramsuratkumar's handwriting. Obviously of importance to Yogi Ramsuratkumar, it is assumed that Yogi Ramsuratkumar wrote this verse. It carries the unique flavor of the known poems written by the beggar saint, and although many have sought its origins, to this date the verse has not been found in any extant scripture of India.

On the Caravan of God–
Beggars

Lee Lozowick

On the Caravan of God the next part is "beggars." Yogi Ramsuratkumar called himself a beggar, and for a short period of time, maybe ten years, he wandered around India surviving through the generosity of people. He was literally a beggar when he settled in Tiruvanamalai, and he called himself a "mad beggar" or a "dirty beggar."

It's traditional and understood in India that when you visit a teacher, you bring a gift of food or fruit or flowers or something like that. It's also understood that the guru has projects and the devotees contribute to them. The guru's projects often have a way of becoming larger than life, so to speak. A guru like Ammachi or Satya Sai Baba has projects such as clinics, orphanages and schools, which obviously require a fantastic amount of resources to maintain. If you're a doctor or a teacher, then of course you might feel some pressure to contribute your own personal resources: your time as a doctor working in the clinic, or your time as a teacher working in the school or the orphanage.

Yogi Ramsuratkumar built one of the largest contemporary temples in southern India. The original estimate for the temple was a quarter of a million dollars; after two or three million spent with no end in sight, the project is still in progress. There were times when there was a major aspect of work that needed to be done, like the building of the temple dome, and Yogi Ramsuratkumar would say to one of his devotees, "This beggar needs this much money to finish this project." Some people might have felt, "Well that's not begging, that's asking," because people these days are very easily offended; we live under a lot of stress in very tense times. International corporations are taking over the world, and they don't care about people, they care about profit. People who get in the way of profit just get ground up.

Yogi Ramsuratkumar was a beggar. He still is a beggar through the lineage. Beggary, as an aspect of the Caravan to God, is about being transparent to the Influence of the Divine in the world. Beggary is a quality of being grateful for what you receive without demanding more than you deserve or more than is reasonable for the circumstance. It's hard to do when you feel like a victim, of course, because then you feel that you need to stand up and make your demand.

In the beggar's aspect of the Caravan to God, things are not always the way they appear in the minds of those who are dominated by mechanicality. The mind dominated by mechanicality is completely fascinated by the appearance of things. When Yogi Ramsuratkumar called himself a beggar—and he was able to catalyze a several million dollar project—we might think to ourselves, "This isn't right, he's a hypocrite," or "He's somehow trying to manipulate us," but it is only the mind, dominated by mechanicality, that can think that way.

On the Path, the process of transmission between not only teacher and student but lineage and student is a very multi-faceted, complex, sophisticated process. There are no simple answers, because the process of the representation of Reality by a human being is not cut and dried, black and white, straightforward or obvious. It is tremendously multi-layered, so how something looks isn't necessarily what it is, because we are dealing with human beings.

If we were dealing with art, we could say that different people have different taste. However, if we look on a large canvas, we could say Bach was an extraordinarily fine creative genius, and although Abba may be very popular and enjoyable, they aren't in the same league as Bach. I think we'd have agreement—maybe not by everybody, of course! We could look at the sculptures of Michelangelo or Rodin, or the paintings of El Greco or Rubens, and say, "This is fine work," but human beings are not so straightforward. A piece of art is locked in time; it's got dimension, but it doesn't change. It is what it is, period. Human beings aren't like that. What seems obvious at first glance may not be very obvious. For example, most of you have probably had the experience of meeting someone for the first time and thinking that they are very superficial or very deep, then after you get to know them, you come to the opposite conclusion.

In a recent interview someone asked the Dalai Lama who his greatest teacher was, and he said Mao Tse Tung, because the Dalai Lama was forced to develop compassion under circumstances that were unique. He said that if it hadn't been for those circumstances, he might not have been such a compassionate man. That is very impressive. When Nelson Mandela was released from prison, he was asked if he had hatred and anger toward the jailors who had beaten him in a dehumanizing situation. He said, "If I allow myself to be angry with them, then they win," meaning that violence and abuse of authority would win over compassion and intelligence. If we are transparent to the Divine—so that we are able to manifest qualities such as kindness, gentleness, compassion, humility, and understanding in spite of circumstances that are psychologically provocative—we could say that we are *outshined* by the Divine. It is our job on the Path to be outshined by God, so that God becomes so bright that we become invisible.

It requires humility to be a beggar. After thirty-five years of teaching, I've decided that humility is one of the rarest human qualities. A lot of people who are personally insecure and full of self-hatred might always put themselves second, but that is not humility—that is psychological debasement. Humility is the capacity to be genuinely full of awe in the face of the majesty of Reality, instead of thinking that we are intelligent and powerful enough to actually run the world—for example, by playing around with genetics and controlling nuclear fission, which obviously gets out of control.

In fact there is probably not a one-hundred-percent safe nuclear power plant in the world. Some of them are safer than others, but none of them are safe, as evidenced by all the dead frogs and fishes in the waters that surround every nuclear power plant. If they're not dead, they have arms and legs where they are not supposed to be, or eyes on the back of their heads. Human beings will demonstrate those mutations eventually, but ours will show up last because we are the most complex species. In another one or two hundred years, we'll be the ones with an eye on the back of our heads and an ear on our chins, or fingers coming out of our breasts. You would have to be an ostrich with its head in the sand not to realize that the proliferation of technology these days is genetically mutating the entire human species.

For twenty years I have been talking about how I have a *passionate hatred* of technology. So, how do my students help me? We have a few cell phones now at our ashrams, and someone on my ashram recently suggested that we get more cell phones. That would triple my problems, but this person thought it would be helpful. Sure...

I'd love it if everybody got cancer three times as fast. Would you be happy if everybody closest to you was killing themselves even faster than they already are? Would that relieve you of discomfort and problems? No. Probably seventy-five percent of the cell phone use in my intimate company is absolutely and categorically unnecessary. But we are not grown up yet; we are still kids, and cell phones are our new toys. Instead of playing with dolls and building blocks, we are playing with cell phones and computers—they are nothing more than toys that are entertaining, distracting, and killing us.

I have a passionate hatred of this kind of multiplication of technology. Unfortunately I'm not strong enough or disciplined enough to lay down the law and live without these things—although that would be a good way to diminish my student body from a hundred-and-fifty to about nine. Outlaw the use of computers! Then people say, "How am I going to go shopping?" Nowadays, of course, Walmart is starting to rule the world, although I heard that Walmart got kicked out of Germany. Congratulations! But they will try to get into Germany again, because Walmart will not be stopped. With companies like Walmart and all the other corporations beginning to control the world, of course everything is becoming technologized, and we spiritual practitioners have just moved into the stream as if it were natural.

Before he died, Yogi Ramsuratkumar said he did not want the use of computers on his ashram. The day he died there were three websites up and running—I'm not exaggerating. What does this have to do with being a beggar? To be in the Caravan of God is to be a beggar, because in the face of Reality, who are we actually? A few months ago there was a flood in Missouri—the Mississippi River overflowed and flooded an entire town. That was just from one rainstorm, and we think that *we* are going to control Reality? In the face of Reality, in the immensity of Reality, in the overwhelming brilliance and brightness of Reality, in the face of the awesome potential of Reality, how can we be the mechanical, psychological creatures that we are? How? How can the concept of Beggary be so foreign to us? The antidote is Beggary. Beggary is that which allows us to stand in the face of Reality as we are—one infinitesimally minute particle in a world of infinite particles.

Freiburg, Germany
August 2007

In Praise of Art

M. Young

One could spend a lifetime exploring the world of art as a domain in which the cornucopia of the Divine manifests and spills its priceless treasures upon our senses. All forms of art, classical and contemporary, can be a medium that carries the power to transmit transformational energies and actual blessings; as such, it becomes a valuable aspect of life on the Path. Literature alone offers a vast, deep and complex world that plumbs the depths and soars to the heights of the human possibility. Then there is the world of chisel and brush, color and form, found in sculpture and painting. Literature, poetry, painting and sculpture all work with the power of image: literature by evoking images through the power of the word, and sculpture and painting through the physical representation of the image as a symbolic language.

Music and dance, an art form that uses the symbolic language of gesture and *mudra*, belong in a different essay. It's worth noting that music (meaning instrumental only) is also "the Word," for the word is, in essence, vibration and sound, the origin of which is traced back to the primeval *pranava om*. Dance can also be called "the Word," because dance depends upon rhythm, which brings us back to vibration and sound. This is why all the arts were attributed to the goddess Sarasvati, originally known by her ancient name Vak, the goddess of speech, music, learning and poetry:

> *I am the gold-giving queen of the earth,*
> *I am the knower, the first of those you appease,*
> *The one that the Gods have set in the heart of all things.*
> *I feed you, make light to see by, give something to hear,*
> *For without Me, a man will go down. Here is true faith*
> *For those who can listen; here is what Gods and man*
> *Both look for. He whom I love will be power, be Brahman,*
> *Will see and consider immensely the truth.*

This hymn appears in the Rig Veda, written in praise of Vak, the ancient muse of the *rishis*, the great seers of the Vedas. The *rishis* instinctively knew, with the certainty of direct knowledge, that all sounds are divine in their origins; they are the vibrational equivalent of the very thing that they name—back to *nama* and *rupa*.

Putting aside the importance of music and dance as sacred art, let us turn to the primary consideration here: the transformative power of symbolic language as found in the medium of painting and sculpture. Most of the great spiritual paths have employed art as a means of transmission, but a great deal of truly spiritual art has been produced outside of church, mosque, temple or formal tradition. Shamanic art, such as the aboriginal art of Australia, is one prime example. Classical European art in particular carries tremendous spiritual power—the power to transmit truth or Reality as it is—and in this regard, Europe is truly the land of great treasures of every kind. The museums in Europe are only the most obvious avenue of discovery. It is in the churches and the streets—in stone sculpture, fountains, cornices, facades and all kinds of architecture—where one encounters the centuries of arcane image and symbol that have fired the imaginations of human beings.

Over fifteen years ago I went to the Louvre for the first time with Lee and a group of sangha members. Walking through its hallowed chambers and corridors that late spring day, we came upon the Egyptian exhibit and slowed our pace to take in the stunning display of artifacts. I had stopped to look at a bronze icon of the sun god, Ra, when my attention was grabbed. An inexplicable force caused my vision to fall upon a five-foot-high bronze statue of Horus—it was a stylized, thin, sleek human figure with the curved head of a falcon, reaching one hand up toward the sun. This Horus was alive; he had reached out and touched me as I walked by.

Peering at the four-thousand-year-old statue, I was stunned by the aliveness and the sheer spiritual power of the Horus piece and the fact that an artist of antiquity had made this image. I pointed the statue out to Lee. He said nothing but looked at it closely then nodded, as if to say, "*Bien sur.*" He does not always exclaim or comment on a piece of art on his frequent forays into this domain, although occasionally he will; usually he just absorbs or "eats" the art—a yogic feat that he accomplishes very quickly and invisibly. Talking about it can interfere with the process of ingesting and metabolizing; it disperses or dissipates the energy.

Our group moved on, drawn by the Louvre's vast and overwhelming panoply of treasures. Everyone had told me, "Go see the Mona Lisa." One can easily get lost in the Louvre, although locating Da Vinci is easy; it's one of the main attractions for the immense number of tourists there. Arriving at the Da Vinci collection, I found about thirty people in front of her, jostling up against each other for a peek. I stayed to look at the masterpiece and was surprised by a tiny twinge of revulsion as I looked upon her famous face. The perpetual crowd around her strains and searches for the great meaning, the extraordinary specialness of this painting according to the experts, the art critics and art historians. What do they find? Nothing. That was my opinion, of course. Years later, reading Camille Paglia's commentaries on the Mona Lisa in her marvelous book, *Sexual Personae*, I felt somewhat justified in that response.

I quickly moved on to the other paintings by Da Vinci and found rich forms, dense, rather dark yet with a certain play of light and glow. From one to another I mused along quietly, savoring a lovely solitude with the neglected Da Vinci masterpieces that were not the Mona Lisa, while the crowd hovered around her. Then I came upon John the Baptist. Suddenly my attention—not the attention of the human machine, but a profound attention that seemed to well up from the cells of the body—came to life as if a light had been switched on.

A richly handsome, even beautiful, earthy man of magnetic sensual power and depth of soul, with a hidden radiance that oozed from the pores of his bronzed, ruddy skin, looked out with dark luminous eyes that were pools of wisdom. Passionate, bold and direct, challenging yet seductive in a strange way, his decidedly masculine form was perfection—a sculpted poem of a human body that exuded spiritual authority, glowed with light, and yet carried a sexual charge. He seemed to be breathing, held within the light and dark that swirled and curled in upon itself in a play of such dimension that I was, again, rooted to the spot. Who was this incredible being? He seemed to be asking me a question, or all questions melded down into one question.

On another occasion, at the Musée Guimet in Paris I stood for a long time before a rare tableau of Parvati, sculpted in red sandstone. She was seated in lotus *asana*, hands raised up and fingers stuck in her ears, with a beatific smile on her face. The description told of a myth in which Shiva, her husband, was gossiping cruelly about Parvati. She refused to listen, because her devotion to Lord Shiva was so great that she would not allow anything—even the Lord's words—to disturb her joyful adoration of Shiva, her beloved.

Over the years, given Lee's great love of art and beauty, his students have had the joy of coming into contact with many forms of sacred art. In my teacher's company, I've had the opportunity to see the work of Picasso, Manet, Monet, Rubens, Botticelli, Da Vinci, Michelangelo, Rodin—an all-time favorite—Dali and many less well-known but equally stunning artists, as well as priceless sculptures, in stone and bronze, and friezes from Egypt, India, Mesopotamia, Persia, China, Japan, Central, North and South America. The place where I've had the broadest and deepest opportunity to participate in the world of art has been in the dimension of Lee's teaching work that was dubbed, many years ago, the "Sacred Bazaar" by Gilles Farcet, a long-time friend and disciple of Arnaud Desjardins. The name aptly described Lee's activities around sacred art and artifacts—both collecting and selling them to his students, friends and anyone truly interested—and it stuck.

The Sacred Bazaar came into our lives through Lee after Yogi Ramsuratkumar died. After his master left his body, Lee turned passionately toward what appeared to be an entrepreneurial bent. He said that his time of teaching linearly, through discourse and seminars and talks, was coming to an end. Unsatisfied with the results of this "linear" form of teaching, Lee declared that it was time for a less rational, and to some, more cryptic way of teaching—teaching strictly through transmission. A doorway into the world of sacred art opened for Lee, and it meshed perfectly with this new direction, becoming one of its primary expressions.

At the beginning the Sacred Bazaar came as a great surprise, and Lee's students and friends had to make the adjustment. This was not an easy transition for some, because our ideas about how a spiritual teacher should be and what a spiritual teacher should do are rigid and narrow. However, since the beginning years of his teaching work, Lee has refused to capitulate to a narrow-minded view of spiritual life. My personal experience of Lee in many circumstances over the years has made it clear that everything he does is for and of the Path; it is this inner knowledge that rings in resonance with Lee's clear and consistent assertion that Yogi Ramsuratkumar is the source of every aspect of life he engages. The blessings of the Sacred Bazaar became obvious to many of Lee's students as we began to contemplate and meditate with the divine images that were coming to populate our lives. And although Lee's obsession with art and beauty has demonstrated a fevered divine madness in recent years, he has also helped contextualize the Sacred Bazaar for us, offering countless instructions in the possibilities that are inherent in the world of sacred art. Over the years he has slowly and painstakingly drawn in complex detail the picture of exactly what the Sacred Bazaar is as a particular facet of his teaching work.

One of the teachings he offered to his students during this time was "Seek beauty and avoid suffering"—a phrase that offers succinct and juicy instruction on the Path of Enlightened Duality. In this case Lees' instruction refers to beauty, meaning one of the three faces of the Divine—truth, beauty and love—and suffering, meaning the endless cycles of neurotic, useless suffering that characterize the illusion of separation, in which we wander in various states of confusion and distraction. This kind of suffering, as distinct from what Gurdjieff termed "conscious suffering," drains away life force and leaves the human organism depleted and often unable to function adequately, much less with awakened creative energies. To suggest that we should avoid neurotic suffering is to say that we can choose to rise above our childhood wounds and conditionings and the entire prison of illusion to function as true adults who are free to live a life of authentic relationship to the Universe. As Swami Prajnanpad said, the individual who is one hundred percent adult is a *sage*.

The profound experience of truth and beauty encountered in sacred art has forged a deepened awareness in me. Interacting with the sacred images, I began to realize that there were many fruitful dimensions of Lee's transmission through the world of art, in terms of the communication of the dharma and a life of practice. There is an alchemical dimension that comes into play when we interact with objective art, and in general, there is much that can be learned experientially about Enlightened Duality through Lee's passion for the sacred image.

In June of 2008 the Sacred Bazaar took Lee to Spain, accompanied by thirteen of his students and five teenagers, where his teaching work was introduced in Barcelona and Madrid for the first time, primarily through the auspices of soirees in which he presented sacred art, but also through public talks, dinners with friends and friends of friends, and interviews with magazines and newspaper reporters. In addition, it turned out to be a fertile meeting with the greater world of art.

Barcelona is a lazy, complacent, hot and humid seaport city on the Mediterranean side of northern Spain where we visited for three days while Lee gave interviews to magazines and newspapers and presented an exhibit of amazing objects of beauty in a one afternoon public salon. In between all this activity, two of us walked the lively streets of the gothic quarter with the five teenagers who were traveling with us, making our way to the famed cathedral of Barcelona.

The cathedral was inspiring, as many are, but after seeing Chartres many years ago, all other cathedrals pale in contrast. Chartres is alive: as soon as you walk into the church, there is an immediate sensation of being lifted up, transported into higher realms by the soaring heights and graceful arcs of sacred geometry. You have literally entered another world, which is encoded in the architectural container in which you are standing.

What was most satisfying about the cathedral in Barcelona was that the teenagers were discovering the rich terrain of Western religious art and its symbolic language. In one of the side shrines of the cathedral we discovered Mary Magdalene in a two-foot-high statue of the saint. It was not a piece of art that actually touched the deeper sensitivities, nonetheless, it was a fair rendering and it is always exciting to find the Magdalene depicted in religious art, for she has typically been an underground saint.

Afterward most of the teens went to a café outside the cathedral, while three of us wanted to explore some of the tiny back lanes of the gothic quarter. We had walked for about five minutes when I spied a small Romanesque church at the Placa de la Sant Just. Asking my companions for a moment to stop and explore, we turned and headed into the dim interior of the small basilica. The stone chamber was simple, almost bare, and empty except for one or two other pilgrims. There were no elaborate shrines along the sides as in most Catholic churches, and walking further into the interior, I was drawn, as if by a magnet, straight to the back of the church, where we spontaneously arrived before a large painted statue of Jesus on the cross with Mary Magdalene crouched at his feet.

Mary the Mother and Mary Magdalene, along with John the Beloved, are reported in the Gospels to be the only disciples of Jesus who were at the crucifixion. The Mary before us now had to be either Mary the Mother or Mary Magdalene; one of the clues as to which one was the anonymity of the woman at the feet of Christ. Usually the shrines in Catholic churches give the name of the saint being worshiped, but this statue had no sign beside it. Only a few old offering candles were placed on the iron rack beside the statue. It seems that the church doesn't always want to admit that it is Mary Magdalene who is being worshipped; she is still a hidden saint, even today, when her legend has been coming out of the dusty crypts of ignominy where Peter and his followers successfully stashed it two thousand years ago.

This Mary was wearing a reddish-purple gown beneath the blue drape of a voluminous cape—a good sign, as Mary Magdalene is almost always depicted wearing red, for obvious symbolic reasons, while Mary the Mother is usually depicted in white and blue. Her dress was cut low to reveal a white breast that gleamed in the low light, also not in the style of Mary the Mother. Then I noticed something even more telling: two of the paving stones on the floor just beneath and in front of the statue were carved with skulls and crossbones with vines growing beneath them.

The skull is one of Mary Magdalene's classic iconographic symbols, along with the alabaster jar in which she carried spikenard oil to anoint Jesus as king. She also usually holds a book, which may refer to the Gnostic gospel of Mary Magdalene. The vine, particularly the grape vine, is a symbol of the royal blood line of the House of David and the power of the communion ritual: "This bread is my body; this wine is my blood. Eat and drink in remembrance of me."

The feet and hands of Jesus and Mary were pale and luminous with an inner light, and so realistic it seemed like Mary, in particular, would move or speak at any moment. She looked out imploringly toward whomever would witness the passion of Christ. Blood dripped, a heavy viscous substance, from the forehead of Jesus where the crown of thorns cruelly pierced his flesh. Mary's feet peeked out from her robes; they were translucent and white but smudged, the paint softly worn, almost pearlized, from years of having been touched by pilgrims and worshippers.

Most of all, I was convinced that she depicted Mary Magdalene because of her facial expression and bodily gesture toward Jesus, who, in his dying moment, was gazing tenderly and lovingly down at her. Sorrow, acceptance, great agony and peace were mingled in the face of Jesus. Mary's face was also infused with sorrow and love, but it was mixed with passion, anger, disbelief and shock. This anguished moment was full-blown in her face; with one hand she reached toward her Lord in a gesture of profound intimacy, while the other hand reached out toward the viewer. Her eyes looked directly into mine, and all this she transmitted without shame or remorse. "How could this happen? How can human beings be this cruel?" she seemed to be saying.

Even though in recent decades a new understanding of Mary Magdalene has been emerging, the symbolism of orthodox Christian mythology still carries a potent spiritual charge. In this statue, the artist had captured Mary in a moment of penultimate passion. I had the sense that the Mary Magdalene found in the lore of her later years depicts a woman, a human being, who has walked much further down the Path and reached the peace and acceptance of a saint. Drawn in by the communication of this sculpture for what seemed like a long time, I was surprised to realize we were there for less than ten minutes.

Leaving Barcelona behind the next day, we headed out into the chalky, eroded hills and scorched plains of central Spain toward Madrid. The morning clouds were dispersed to a gauzy blue-white sky, while the terrain grew dry and fierce. Soon we were passing through beautiful agrarian mountain scenes, green and flowing with a harmonious patchwork of olive groves, peach orchards and vineyards. It brought to mind the ancient way of fermenting wine, making olives, bread and cheese-making. Suddenly Spain was opening up in a whole new way. I could imagine the old life, the ancient customs and organic way of life that had endured for thousands of years in this land.

We arrived in the majestic city of Madrid, city of grandeur, to be greeted by our hosts in the spacious, cool, elegant apartment where

Lee would be staying. The evening meal was ready. Luckily, we had time to eat, rest and recoup our energies for the busy schedule of the next two days, when Lee would give a public talk and present the Sacred Bazaar. Lee encouraged the teenagers to go to El Prado, the world-famous museum that he had visited as a teenager, saying, "You have to see the Rubens and the El Grecos there. El Greco made such an impression on me, I've never forgotten it." So it was planned for a few of the adults to accompany the teenagers to the museum while Lee was busy with the Sacred Bazaar.

The next day we spent two hours at El Prado, hardly enough time to really uncover its treasures (although E.J. Gold says it only takes an hour to absorb and decode the transmission of art in any museum). El Prado was thickly populated with treasures—a full display of Rubens (1577–1640), a number of fantastic paintings by Hieronymus Bosch (1450–1516), and of course, El Greco (1541–1614), not to mention the many other great works of art to be enjoyed there. Of the less well-known artists, religious and mythological themes were the most prevalent; the walls were thick with the crucifixion and scenes from the lives of Jesus, Mary, Joseph, and the saints of Catholicism. Mary Magdalene enjoyed a full exposure, but from the conventional viewpoint, as the repentant prostitute, not the partner of Jesus, and—as many scholars now say—a spiritual teacher in her own right.

Having seen Rubens a few times before in the Louvre, I was eager to get to El Greco and El Bosco, as Hieronymus Bosch is called in Spain, but Rubens was not having any of that. I was caught right away by his painting, "Saturno," or "Saturn." The mythological and allegorical themes of Rubens' paintings were as compelling as ever, and this one, which I had never seen before, quite literally stopped me in my tracks as I moved through the room. Old, ugly as sin, with a hooked nose and flabby, fallen flesh hanging off a skeletal frame, crooked and stooped and gnarled in stature, the horrid old man with long stringy gray hair and lust-reddened, maniacal eyes was biting the breast of an anguished child who was bent back in agony, draped across the withered, stringy arm of Saturn and captured in that inexorable grasp. The background of the painting was black, and in the distance three stars shone dimly—probably due to an astrological configuration that was exerting its influence on Rubens at this time in his life.

Even if Saturn has been lenient with us, anyone who has paid attention to their inner process during a Saturn transit (which happens every twenty-eight years by Western astrological reckoning) knows that this is an accurate depiction. We, of course, are the child, which Rubens chose to represent at about one year of age in this particular painting (he painted several versions): tender, helpless, dependent, innocent. That is Saturn alright—merciless, devouring, brutal and generally tyrannical. Character is built through the relentless lessons that ruthless Saturn, the Lord of Time (he was called Cronos in Greece), has to teach us. What is real and what is not real? If we are standing on castles made of sand, glass or any other destructible material, then we are going to find out about it when Saturn transits the particular constellation of the natal chart that symbolizes our individual relationship with the deities, or planets, of our solar system.

Moving on, I came to the El Grecos. If objective suffering can be captured in a painting, El Greco did it. Gazing at the dark, heavy, oblong figures with bold juxtapositions of light and shadow, these paintings were a visceral experience with no mental counterpart for me. They were not only compelling but riveting, inexplicably radiant while dark in their harsh depiction of the crucifixion and different aspects of the life of Jesus. All I could ascertain was that I was experiencing something objective, a particular mood. I absorbed all I could but did not linger.

Soon I came across "La Magdalena" by José de Ribera (1591–1652), depicting Mary in exile, praying in her solitary mountain cave in the wilderness, dressed in iconographic voluminous red robes.[1]

---

[1] Legend has it that Mary Magdalene spent seven years in a cave in southern France. The cave is a place of pilgrimage, near Aix en Provence, that can be visited today.

After this came a whole series of paintings by the same artist, all of a religious nature, which captured my attention because of their luminosity and deep, heartful communication. "La Trinidad" pictured the Father, the Holy Ghost and the brutally crucified son—but death never looked so beautiful, so sensuous, so mystical as in this painting. There was love in death for de Ribera in his vision of Jesus at the moment of supreme passion, for here was an erotic Jesus with lips parted and tender. The translucent glow of his skin spoke of transcendence, and I wondered, did these artists have any conscious intention to create such a juxtaposition, to depict death and eros in this way? The "Penitent Magdalene" was another painting of Ribera's that captured my imagination. There she was with the alabaster jar, head resting on a skull, fingers intertwined, long golden-reddish hair hanging down in waves. A person of many depths and agonies, Mary's eyes glowed with the light of longing.

I was moved by many of Canos' paintings: an expired Jesus in the arms of an angel, another of St. John of Patmos with his crows, and Saint Bernard drinking from a stream of milk that spewed forth from the Virgin's breast. The teenagers were particularly captured by depictions of Saint Bernard, whose devotion to his *ista devata*, the Virgin Mary, was so great that she fed him mystical milk in a stream that flowed from her breasts. It was Vivar's version of Saint Bernard drinking the Virgin's milk that we were most drawn toward of those paintings on this theme; he depicted Saint Bernard and the Virgin in a way that communicated the *rasa*—a divine sweetness, a felt sense of loving surrender, the absolute trust of the child with the mother.

Then there was Pedro Machuca's fantastic painting of the Virgin holding the baby Jesus, while she spilled milk from her sensuous, ripe, exposed breasts to put out the flames in purgatory to ease the agony of the souls caught there. This was an extremely unusual Mary the Mother, for not only was baby Jesus squeezing the erotic nipple of one plump breast, but Mary herself held the other breast with long graceful fingers and pressed the succulent nipple, from which an ample stream of rich milk flowed down to the tortured souls below. Interestingly enough, this Mary was wearing red.

We were powerfully taken by these images. Something in us knew that they spoke of mystical secrets that are rendered impotent if too much mental muscle is applied; in gazing upon them, the impulse to dissect and analyze fell still. It was better to just stand in awe and absorb the images, the light, the transmission of the art itself. I remembered that E.J. Gold said that the transformational power of art happens in the process the artist goes through—the art itself is just the end product. It is what the artist felt and experienced in making the art that is of real spiritual value. There was a tremendous upsurge of spiritual force in the world, it seems, during this time period that manifested in the flourishing of the arts, alchemy, and culture as a whole. What indeed was going on for these Renaissance painters, anyway? It was interesting to encounter the erotic theme in these religious paintings—a theme the orthodox Christian church would deny but that is found in all great religion: the erotic potential of the soul's relationship with the Divine.

Finally, we went to see El Bosco. It was his surreal triptych, "The Garden of Earthly Delights," representing the third day of Creation that drew me inside its world. In the beginning there is Paradise—a primordial yet sublime nature scene depicted in the left panel. The central panel shows the next development of the ten-thousand-thingness of Creation, and what El Bosco gives us is a scene of utter depravity, a world "that has surrendered itself to lustful abandon," as the description said. The third and last panel was hell, pure and simple: a disturbing scene of metaphysical horror.

El Bosco knew something about the journey of the soul. The paintings left me with the sense that these states coexist at all times: paradise is going on right now, as well as depravation and the agonies of hell. After all, the triptych as a whole is titled "The Third Day of Creation." All this happens on the Third Day. In the vision of El

Bosco, what happens on the Fourth Day? The Fifth? The Sixth and Seventh?

For the artists of antiquity—the visionaries, the radical knowers of Reality as it is—worldly life has always been fraught with danger for the soul. I wanted to gaze longer, to write down some description on each of the panels, but several people were avidly hovering in front of this masterpiece. I had to wait for a turn in front of each panel, and even then, there were more people pressing in to see the painting, and I moved on sooner than I wanted to.

There is art that has profound value, which speaks to the soul, such as the art of Ribera and Vivar, for example, and then there is objective art, like "The Third Day of Creation." There is something that happens when we gaze upon objective art. Although the mind is noticing this and that and commenting upon it, simultaneously there is a deep receptivity that turns on, like a lightbulb. It is an instinct that is awakened for the moment and rouses up from its slumber to absorb what it is apprehending through the senses of the body. It's the same with music or dance or poetry. Something gets awakened by the objectivity of the *svarupa* that is being transmitted in the art form.

Leaving El Prado, we walked the immense grounds of the central park in Madrid in search of a statue of Lucifer we had heard was well worth seeing. After an hour of walking through a maze of earthen lanes lined with chestnut trees, arbors and small lakes, we finally came upon the statue deep in the center of the park. Someone had told me it was a sculpture of "the devil," but what I immediately discovered was a classical rendition of Lucifer.

Titled "Fallen Angel," the statue reared up from its twelve foot pedestal. A perfect human form of great beauty, with two snakes twined around his feet and legs, feathered wings gracefully arched, Lucifer looked up toward heaven with the shock of separation sculpted in agony on his handsome face. He was suspended in mid-fall with arms raised in defense. The story of Lucifer goes thus: Lucifer, the Light Bringer, loved the Lord his God more than any of the other angels. Lucifer was known as the brightest angel of all, who stayed at the Lord's side and served the Lord throughout eternity. Then God created Adam and told Lucifer that he must now serve the Lord's creation. Lucifer looked at man and saw that he was flawed, and he refused to obey, saying, "No, I will not serve mankind; I love You so much, I will serve only You." Needless to say, this disobedience angered the Lord God, who cast Lucifer out of heaven and condemned him to hell.

Another version of the Lucifer myth is told by the Sufis, in which Lucifer is called Iblis and is considered not only the greatest devotee of the Lord but also a great ally on the Path. The Sufis say that all great religious stories have seven levels of allegorical meaning that may be uncovered; hidden in the center of the vast park in central Madrid was the extraordinary and unforgettable portrayal of an esoteric teaching.

While we were exploring El Prado and gazing at the "Fallen Angel," Lee was busy putting together a presentation of sacred art for the evening soiree. When Lee heard about Lucifer, he laughingly said, "I'm trying to buy it!" He has often humorously stated that he wants all the great objects of beauty, all the sacred art and icons of the world, for his very own.

The next night Lee gave a dharma talk in Madrid, surrounded by a display of sanctity and beauty in the form of rare artifacts. That night he said:

Every human being has a radiance. Wisdom has a certain quality of radiance; humility has a certain quality of radiance; rage has a certain quality of radiance; psychopathology has a certain quality of radiance. All living beings have a radiance, and every work of art has a certain radiance. It takes more than a symbol to make a sacred artifact; it takes a specific kind of radiance. For example, even something horrible that depicts great suffering, like Picasso's "La Guernica," can be beautiful because the artist imbues that work with compassion for suffering. So many artists have painted Jesus in many different forms, but the quality of that art depends on whether the artist related to Christ as the Beloved of one's heart or the Christ of organized religion—someone who threatens and judges.

Lee went on to speak about how people are deeply worried about the state of the world and the coming times. He emphasized, once again, the importance of creating spaces of sanctuary and sanctity in which we may live and find refuge. The Sacred Bazaar gives people the opportunity to acquire objects of great spiritual power and sanctity, and to then live in close proximity to these beacons of the Path. He continued:

Yes, there are things to worry about. The Earth is poisoned, the water is poisoned, the air is poisoned. Yes, there are those who are trying to clean the air, the water, the earth, but it will take many years to clean up what has been done. Yes, those efforts are being made, but there are no efforts being made to clean up gross commercial materialism and rampant narcissism, which is the underlying problem. When you are worrying about the coming times, you should ask yourself: If there were

> *no electricity, would I rather have sacred artifacts in my*
> *home or a fancy sound system?*

These words are worth considering further in light of how we actually live the dharma in our troubled times. What are our priorities? How, and for what purpose, do we use resources of all kinds? What are we building, on all levels?

In Lee's company, the world of art is populated by images of the Hindu gods and goddesses, along with the classic iconic Buddhas and Vajrayana deities. Krishna, Ganesha, Lakshmi, Parvati, Shiva, Vishnu, Hanuman, Kali, to name a few—these are the agents of transmission for millions of people on this planet who are loosely referred to as "Hindus." Vajrayogini, Green Tara, Mahakala, Padmasambhava, Maitreya, and many other forms of Buddha are the vessels of wisdom that Buddhists revere. They are called gods and goddesses, but another way to understand them is that they are facets of the Divine that exist within us. They are symbolic representations of the divine archetypes that inform Life, as well as divinities that have been worshipped and empowered over eons of time. These divine beings do have an existence in the subtle realms. When we place our attention on them in appreciation of their beauty and sanctity, either in the simplest way or through a more elaborate formal *puja*, they are brought to life. We are invoking their *transmissive* power to bless our lives. When attention is enkindled with intention, this kind of worship is the entry point into the mood of prayer, which could be called adoration.

Robert Beer, a well-known artist who is probably the world's foremost authority on the symbolism and iconography of Vajrayana Buddhist art, has studied and painted deities in *thangkas* for over thirty years. These deities are used for meditation practice, in which the chosen deity, as ista devata, or *yidam*, is visualized within the body of the practitioner. Slowly, over time, the practitioner becomes imbued with the qualities of the deity: compassion, wisdom, perfect clarity, divine love.

In an interview published in *Namarupa* magazine, Robert Beer answered Robert Svoboda's question, "How would you define art?" Beer responded:

> *Art is outside and heart is inside. Art is the outward expression of the inner heart. To me art should convey beauty and devotion, and skill and time, and all of the things that are fine; art should be spiritually uplifting. The Western trend is often for art to portray neurosis. In the West art is often a product of neurosis; the artist somehow has to be tormented or demented. It's all become too conceptual....just thoughts that flash in the mind. Thoughts and ideas are so easy to come by. But to portray beauty, to produce something that carries real peace, tranquility, beauty, grace—to me that's art, that's really art. For me art is uplifting, art is spiritual.*[2]

A symbol of beauty as a facet of the Divine does not have to take anthropomorphic form. A conch shell, when blown, makes a haunting sound and is used in ritual worship all over India as a symbolic and literal call to dharma or truth. The conch is always seen in Lord Vishnu's hand, because Vishnu is the preserver and maintainer of Life, which is maintained by cosmic law, or eternal truth. Since time immemorial the lotus, and its Western equivalent, the rose, have been symbols of the process of becoming—the unfoldment of being—

---

[2]   Robert Beer, *Namarupa*, "Robert Beer Interview," Volume 03, September 2008, page 5.

through the soul's journey over incarnations. Everybody intuitively or instinctively understands these symbols upon first glance because they speak a universal language.

Puja, or worship ceremony, is central to most traditions as the most effective means to focus attention upon the Divine for the invocation of blessings or divine influence. The Hindus and Buddhists in particular have a very complex and compelling array of ceremonial worship, from ancient Vedic rites in which sacrifices of many sacred substances—including animals like goats, which are sacrificed at temples such as those at Kalighat and Tarapith—to the refined Vajrayana Buddhist rituals involving bell and *dorje*. There are many countless forms of simpler, more personal pujas to ista devatas or gurus involving offerings of flowers, ghee, fruit, holy water and flame, or light. These are all ways to focus one's attention toward the invocation of the deity's blessings through an evocation of human energies that can be called adoration.

It is very helpful to use a ritual form to focus one's attention toward the evocation of adoration. It is also not necessary. Through the power of intention, which is a dimension of being, one can focus subtle attention in such a way that the deity is invoked. This can be a very invisible act. Ramakrishna once commented on the nature of ritual observance, saying:

> [T]he tamasic worshiper of Divine Mother, the devo-
> tee who is still violent and unrefined, is convinced that
> Goddess Kali takes pleasure in animal sacrifice. The
> rajasic worshiper, who is still obsessed with personal
> gratification, cooks delicious, expensive dishes to offer,
> with great ritual elaboration, before a regally adorned
> image of the Mother. The sattvic worshiper, who is
> becoming a true lover, no longer engages in any external
> show. The delight of mystic union is inward and invis-
> ible. This blessed person may offer simply a few drops of

*Ganga water and a few green leaves from the sacred bel
tree. Flowers and oil lamps can be dispensed with. After
perceiving that every blossoming plant is a spontaneous
offering to the Mother, I could no longer pluck flowers
for formal worship.*

*No one may even notice that the sattvic worshiper
is performing worship. Occasionally, a small plate of
puffed rice may be placed informally before the sacred
image of Divinity. On the most auspicious days for
praising the Goddess, this lover may prepare some sweet
rice pudding by boiling milk down to a thick cream, just
as his own being as been condensed into essence over
the fire of Divine Love.*[3]

Over years of watching my teacher interact with beautiful objects of
sanctity, I have gleaned something about adoration. This is one of
the important aspects of worship that I've observed in Lee relative
to sacred artifacts: by the simple placement of attention, with intention, the flame of adoration may be kindled.

Adoration through any means, formal or informal, is perhaps
the most elevated entry point into the perspective of Enlightened
Duality. Adoration is a state of being that is evoked from within by
one who participates fully in Life, for its blueprint is innate in all
human beings. Adoration, in this context, automatically implies a
relationship with a living Divinity, a personal Beloved, who resides
at the core of Life and can be invoked through contemplation—or
contemplative praise—of a divine image through mood, rasa, and
the placing of intention. This principle underlies all art that has

---

[3]   Les Hixon, *Great Swan: Meetings with Ramakrishna*, page 130.

transformational power, because it is our adoration that brings the inherent radiance in a piece of sacred art from background to foreground. Another way of saying this is that the deity is literally "waked up." Watching Lee with sacred artifacts in the forms of the pantheon of Hindu and Buddhist deities, or Christian artifacts, is an instruction in how to invoke the spiritual power that is inherent in these artifacts, many of which have been worshipped for hundreds of years. He simply places one-pointed focus of attention upon them.

Music, dance, literature, poetry, sculpture, painting, lithography—the world of art is truly immense. A woven tapestry can communicate mood even if it is an abstract of color and texture. An authentic Navajo sand painting could communicate Reality as much as a Tibetan thangka. The right kachina has as much to say as a Chola period bronze of Lord Shiva worth a half-million dollars at a Sotheby's auction. When we enter this world, we must do so with an open mind and heart, or it will not reveal its secrets to us. If we come with preconceived notions, concepts learned in an art history or music theory class in our sophomore year at the university, we will not encounter the *drala*—the sheer magic—that lives in the world of beauty and form.

Finally, art as a dimension of worship in praise of Beauty is very much part of a life lived fully, which is another of Lee's maxims of Enlightened Duality: "Just live fully." If we are interested in the possibility that the ten thousand things of the manifest dimension of Reality may be inherently Real, art becomes a juicy and vivid milieu to be explored. Learning to see, feel and savor the taste, the rasa, of any artistic expression is a process of refinement of sensitivity, meaning the quality or condition of being sensitive. To be sensitive means that we are capable of perceiving with our senses: sight, hearing, smell, taste and feel. These are the windows of perception in the human body, which have counterparts at a subtle level—exactly as in rupa and svarupa—as intuition and spiritual instinct. Again we are back to the necessity to be embodied, to engage the world through the native instincts of the flesh and blood form that we currently inhabit, because "the body knows." When we encounter beauty and absorb it through our senses, we receive its gift, and as intangible, ephemeral and fleeting as it may be, the soul is nourished and beautified. When we rely upon the wise instinct of the body, the soul is made beautiful.

John Muir said, "We need beauty like we need bread." Appreciating the world of art and artifacts, then, is a way to "seek beauty and avoid suffering." It can become a way of being in life that places us in very close proximity to adoration and praise of all that is praiseworthy. By living a life of praise, we turn away from the distractions, fascinations and seductions of the world and toward the Eternal.

On the Caravan of God–Poets

Lee Lozowick

Poetry is a symbol for all of the arts on the Caravan of God. There are poets on the Caravan of God, and that is a metaphor for painters, dancers, musicians, sculptors, writers, dramatic or comedic actors, martial artists and any form of art that transmits Reality in its highest potential. Art can be created in a way that it transmits and communicates beyond all of the protective mechanisms of the mind, and it touches something real.

Of the three categories on the Caravan of God—liars, beggars, and poets—poetry is the most subjective. Everybody has their opinion about poetry. When people ask artists what they are trying to communicate with their art, most artists attempt to answer that question but aren't able to articulate it in a very satisfactory way because it is something that can't be explained. The art form itself communicates directly; it bypasses the mind, and that's the way we get a transmission or a communication. If we try to make it rational or linear, it doesn't work. Even in mystical writing, they say the highest teaching cannot be effectively defined.

In a way that is true, because one of the weakest human qualities is communication. Even people whose level of intelligence is significantly higher than average have tremendous difficulty communicating clearly—if the definition of communication is that the other person understood exactly what was meant. That is because people tend to jump to conclusions based on their subjectivity. We hear something and interpret what we hear based on our historical database of the information. We are absolutely convinced that we are right, because we have confidence in the information that we have, but we don't listen to what is actually being said. We jump to conclusions, then act on the conclusions we have drawn, and the conclusions are often wrong.

Gurdjieff traveled for many years all over the Middle East and Asia doing research and studying art, music, painting and sculpture—among many other things. He spent a lot of time in Egypt studying the Sphinx and the pyramids, and of course he wrote a substantial amount of music himself. There are many testimonies of people who broke into tears and wept in the presence of Gurdjieff when he was playing music. These people were very embarrassed and wondered to themselves, "What's going on? Why am I doing this?" In fact, Gurdjieff felt he had discovered that one could create a work of objective art that could make a certain transmission to everyone, regardless of their cultural or intellectual state. Of course his music didn't affect everybody the same way on the surface, but he said that the essential effect was exactly the same. Some people felt the music in a way that created a certain physical manifestation and others didn't, but it still had the same effect.

There are different forms of healing, like the Tibetan singing bowls, or drums in the shamanistic traditions, which are used because their quality of sound creates a certain mood, a certain space. You can't just bang a cooking pot rhythmically and have the same effect, because it doesn't have the same quality of sound. Certain animal skins were used for drums and others were not because of the quality of sound produced—the literal vibration of the animal.

Real art has a certain possibility. Who decides what is real art and what is not real art? Time and history. In other words, does the art have enduring power—does it withstand the test of time? Although, they say that Mozart had a sister who was a better composer than he was, but because she was a woman, none of her compositions survived. They were disregarded because in her historical time and place, the subjective opinion was that a woman could not be a fine musician or a fine artist. Her creative work was completely denied any kind of stable circumstance, which is why as far as we know, none of her compositions survived.

Art—poetry, painting, dance, martial arts, sculpture, music, prose, theatre—can touch something in us that is not impossible but is improbable to be touched through the mind. Some of you can remember walking into church as a child—three, four, five or six years old—and looking at the crucifix or hearing the organ being played, and you were transfixed. You can still remember that moment as if it just happened fifteen minutes ago. How many profound, intimate heart-to-heart conversations have you had with your various lovers over the years, and how many of those things do you remember? In the moment, of course, you think that your life has changed forever, but two days later you're the same old asshole. On the other hand, when certain artistic influences catalyze an effect on you, you are never the same.

E.J. Gold once said that art is the shit that is left behind from a moment of objective creativity. However, shit can be analyzed: in the shit is the evidence of whatever created the shit, be it minestrone or muesli! I am in great favour of art and beauty, which is one of the reasons I am consumed by sacred artifacts and art in general, including contemporary graffiti. Graffiti is not called "graffiti" anymore by people who know what they're talking about; it's called "street art." Not all graffiti is great art, just like all punk rock is not great; some of it's just meaningless noise. Every once in a while a real artist comes through a medium that seems to be disturbing and useless, for the most part—like punk rock. Most of the punk rockers are just frustrated and angry at their parents, and they'll never create art, no matter how long they scream or how loud they play their guitars or how many times they cut themselves with sharp glass. They will never create art, but every once in a while a real artist comes through the media.

I'll give you a subjective opinion; you don't have to agree with me. A really good graffiti artist is saying something about Reality. They can't write or create music or go into business and invent things, and they can't be a therapist, so they paint with spray cans. A really good street artist communicates Reality. How do you perceive that? I can't tell you. However, it *is* there, and you have to figure out how to extract it, like somebody learned how to get gold out of ore. Somebody figured how to get aluminum out of bauxite, which is not a very simple process; somebody discovered how to make the steel that is used in Samurai swords. It can be done.

I particularly like graffiti because it's not obvious. We have a big piece of street art hanging in the dining room in our ashram in France. A woman who used to live there said that it made her nauseous the first time she saw it—she couldn't eat. It had such a profound effect on her mind that it completely disoriented her, and she was enough of a practitioner that she wanted to know why that piece of art affected her the way it did. She started living with the piece of art—going into the dining room and sitting in front of it. Once she started relating to the work of art, of course, she had a very different experience.

I like graffiti because it confuses us. We can look at a beautiful Buddha and say, "Yes, okay, this I get," but then we look at street art and say, "but this—I don't get it." In one sense, therein lies its value, because the only way we can get it is by having it *impact* us. It's like a koan in the Zen tradition: you can't figure it out. You either get it or you don't get it, but you can't figure it out. If you figure it out and take it to the roshi, and the roshi is sharp, he won't accept your answer. He'll know that you figured it out, but you didn't get it.

When you look at the sculpted head of a monk and say to yourself, "Oh, there's such a feeling of serenity," which is a nice thing, you have already categorized and boxed in what it is you imagine you can receive from the artifact. On the other hand, you can discover how to draw the essence of the transmission of Reality out of street art. Yes, of course we all want serenity, peace of mind, peace of heart—and, who knows what exact qualities of transmission of Reality any statue of a monk or a Buddha can transmit to us?

When you buy a statue of Buddha you are getting two things: the Buddha and the artist. In the old days artists didn't work commercially; every artist that created sacred art was first a practitioner, who happened to have a certain skill, so they applied that skill within the context of their practice as a devotee or disciple. There are six billion human beings on the face of the earth—six billion facets of Reality. Ultimately they are all the same, and six billion people are six billion unique facets of Reality in the immediate sense. The monk is the monk and Buddha is Buddha and the Bodhisattva is the Bodhisattva. We don't know who the artist was, except we know that the artist was a practitioner. Other than that, we don't know anything about the artist at all. Most of the artists didn't sign their work; they made a piece for a temple as an anonymous practitioner. So, we may have a sense of what the transmission of Buddha is, but we have no idea of what the transmission of the artist could be, except that it's a facet of Reality that may have a unique effect on us that another facet of Reality may not have.

I am in favor of surrounding ourselves with art because I have burned out on communicating the dharma in a linear way. I used to give three seminars a month every summer in Europe. Most of them were three days long but a couple of them were a week long, and it was talk, talk, talk, every day. One day I got to Europe, and I wasn't looking forward to the seminars, so I knew things had changed. Since then the changes have become more and more rapid and more and more dramatic. Now I give less and less dharma talks. My students have been in the presence of the linear communication of the teaching for long enough to have gotten what can be gotten, so now a different kind of impact is necessary for me, personally, which is where all the art comes in.

I particularly look for things that I feel, based on instinct, have the ability to transmit something. Sometimes it's great to have art just for fun, but mostly its things that make a communication that I can't make with language, and, without being overly arrogant, I have above average language skills. There are things that language just can't touch. So, the form of my teaching has taken on a very different quality. Some people are very disturbed by it. They are very enthusiastic about inviting me to their house for dinner, but they are often a little disappointed when I just eat, sit on the couch and don't talk. I don't have to talk any more. Every once in a while something inspiring arises, so I want to communicate it and I do.

Rumi, the Persian poet, was a professor of religion when he met his master, Shams y Tabriz. Rumi was so obliterated by the transmission of Shams that his whole relationship to education and being a professor of religion at a university was completely shattered. He could not communicate in the old, linear form anymore, and because he was a communicator, the new forms of his communication were poetry and spinning. Rumi was the founder of the whirling dervishes; he got into a lot of trouble because the Muslims of the time felt that singing and dancing were the work of the devil—like many fundmentalist Christians today believe that singing and dancing are the work of the devil. So, Rumi got into trouble with the orthodoxy of his time.

Naropa, one of the greatest Tibetan Buddhist saints in the Kagyu lineage, was dean of professors in the Buddhist university of the age. He walked out of class one day holding his book, and an old lady—ugly, smelly, having a very bad hair day, with most of her teeth rotting out of her mouth—stopped him in the road. He was very turned off by her, thinking she was just an ignorant peasant. She asked him whether he understood what was in the book he was carrying, and he said very arrogantly, "Of course I do." She said, "If you understand what is in that book, why are you doing what you are doing in the university?"

He thought she didn't know what she was talking about, so he brushed her off and went home, but her question really disturbed him. It disturbed him so much that he couldn't relax his mind even with meditation. The next day he went to find the old lady. When he found her, he had come to the realization that she knew something that he needed to discover, and he said, "What shall I do?"

"Throw away your books and go find this teacher," she said. As the story goes, he threw away his books and went in search of his master. He probably struggled tremendously for a long period of time before he had the strength and the will to throw away his books and go in search of his teacher. He probably went to hell and back a few times, emotionally, to come to the conclusion that he had to resign his post in the university. So, he went in search of his master and found him. Naropa became the teacher of Marpa, who was the teacher of Milarepa—who wrote one hundred thousand poems to his master and became the most famous realizer of the Kagyu lineage of Tibetan Vajrayana Buddhism, of which the Karmapa is the head.

There are many examples in the Zen tradition of great scholars realizing that their scholarship had a certain value but beyond a certain point was useless. When they got to that point, they were transformed by some catalytic agent, which could be art. So, at its best, a work of art can literally change our lives. At its worst, it can just confuse us because we don't understand what the big deal is. The worst that happens is that we listen to the Bach masses and say to ourselves, "I don't know what the big deal is; this doesn't do anything to me"—but we are still being touched.

Freiburg, Germany
August 2007

Creativity

M. Young

*I*n late May, 2008, en route from the U.S. to France with Lee, after the most easeful international flight in over a decade, our traveling party stopped in London for an overnight in the sanctuary of friends in the sangha. Maybe we earned an easy transit after so many hair-raising, nerve-wracking adventures in globe-trotting over the years. With our feet finally back on solid ground, we had a rainy afternoon and night in Chiswick, a wholesome, simple dinner, and a night of regenerative sleep.

The next morning, before an English breakfast of berries and cream, eggs, and loaves of warm brown bread, I scratched down the consideration of the morning: Can one create art, such as plying this writer's trade, on the run? Is it possible to court creativity in sporadic bursts and fits, without any flow or continuity whatsoever, beyond whatever continuity of formless practice there is in the internal landscape? Since we left Montana, I hadn't written one word for this book during an interlude of a week in the Arizona desert, where temperatures zoomed freakishly from 92 to 42F overnight (more signs of global warming?) as we sped through the preparations for a summer sojourn in Europe.

You know, dear reader, that most writers say that they must have a rhythm, a ritual, with their writing. Many say that they must appear at their typewriter or computer at the same time every day, like having a date with the Muse—to use the term most often employed by artists, while Lee prefers the word "Mistress." Well! Any kind of regular "date with my computer" not to mention communing with my "Mistress" was going to be out of the question. Instead, I would be scribbling notes on the run, pulling out my computer at odd hours, in between the constant action and darting directions of each day.

In the midst of these musings (pun intended), I watched Lee playing cards with his fifteen-year-old daughter. He won, as usual. Joking around with her dad, she complained in a good-natured fashion, to which he responded, "You're thinking too linearly—you have to think more expansively. If you think linearly, you miss a whole slew of opportunities." His glance in my direction was so subtle and swift I almost missed it.

She asked, "Is that something you can learn?" When he answered yes, she said, "How?"

"You just decide," he said decisively.

It's not that there weren't ample moments of inspiration to write during the last week in Arizona—there were many. There was simply no time or space to sit down and write. Clearly, at this point I had decided not to write a series of strictly scholarly treatises on Enlightened Duality, which would have been the easiest route to take: something safe and data-oriented with lots of run-on footnotes—although I suspected those would come into play at some point. Instead, it became clear in Montana that I would dive into my day-to-day experience in living the Path of Enlightened Duality, in the *sampradaya* of the Western Bauls, and write over the period of the summer's travels with my teacher. As a result of that decision, I now found myself venturing down the proverbial road less traveled, while traveling.

Traveling has a way of thrusting me into a depth of intensity that is frightening at times. There is agony involved, partly because

I dearly love the grounded world of the ashram. Every time I go for extended treks, leaving for any period of time longer than two weeks, it is like tearing a tree out by its roots. Travel is a love/hate relationship for me. Admittedly, the torturous aspects of road life are often part of what yields the bounty of a fantastic crop in the gardens of the inner world—if I am willing to really work at making use of the whole panoramic display, most especially in the observance of my own mechanical tendencies.

The constant impermanence of travel throws one back on the necessity to live in the moment, to let go, to cultivate an "equal vision"—to use the term so often spoken by Papa Ramdas, guru of our grandfather guru, Yogi Ramsuratkumar. It offers the opportunity to practice in invisible ways, the way the Sufis do. I remember hearing an American shaykh tell the story of being in Istanbul with his wife's family. There were fourteen people living together in perfect harmony in a tiny city apartment without even a whiff of discord or complaint. The flow between these people was organic, completely natural, and never was there a sense of not having enough space, the way Americans feel they need "personal space." Sufis have a natural understanding of the value of practicing in circumstances that are less than "spiritual," which may appear completely secular. This kind of practice is implied in stories like the great Sufi realizers who appeared to be rug dealers, shop owners, or the baker down the road.

It is not only personal space that ego craves; it is also Western bodily comforts involving food and sleep and showers and time to do yoga. Then there are attachments to certain comforts of the soul: a minimum amount of solitude, peace and quiet, beauty and order. I love the rhythm of a ritualized day, the deep ground that is provided by ashram life with formal meditation, *puja*, time to chant the name of God, to pray. Of course, these aesthetic and ascetic "necessities" can be thin veils over the drive to control one's environment in the turgid world of opposites. When traveling, the rhythms of external practices are sacrificed for a literal groundlessness, and the practitioner is thrown back upon his or her ability and commitment to practice internally without the comfortable seat of external ritual.

Furthermore, the discomforts of travel create an alchemical crucible in which we are put through the grueling processes of transformation. A lot of the fire and water of this process occurs through relationships. When people are stressed out from the exigencies of travel and relationship at very close quarters, conflict can arise. Cooperation, spaciousness, and the many variations of skillful means—which in the Buddhist lexicon are kindness, generosity and compassion—can become quite strained in the purely dualistic human domain of the mundane and our scrabbling and squabbling for the survival of the fittest: in other words, the genetic imperative to dominate rather than serve.

There is nothing to be done about any of the conflicted chaos of our daily world except to say yes to all of it, because, let's face it, if we don't jump into all this crazy opportunity of Life as it presents itself to us and relish its amazing display—its rhythms and dissonance and harmony and melodies and complexities and textures—we will not know the mad dance of our crazy Lord at the center of all this. Then our dying breaths will come along, and we will know the most profound remorse of having missed the greatest opportunity of all.

Indeed, "all this" is grist for the mill of Divine Alchemy in my teacher's world. This subtle form of alchemical transformation is the result of what Gurdjieff called "the Work" and what has more extensively been referred to as *sadhana*, tantric yogas or *rasayana* in the East. Anyone who has really engaged the life of sadhana knows that this is not easy; there may be no tangible gains and successes in this process. The phenomenal world is discovered to be radiantly empty, passing, ephemeral, and yet we do work toward...something. We work toward the moments when duality becomes real—an Enlightened Duality. We work toward the mystical relationship with the illusive bird of Baul poetry, the uncatchable Man of the Heart, the *manur manush*. We wait for a fleeting glimpse of the Beloved.

Outside in the English garden, it is incredibly lush and green. Rain drips from trees, shrubs, and banks of pale pink roses that hang from their vines in wet repose. As I sit here writing, the card game in the garden continues with Lee winning, while the question about writing on the run remains unanswered as life serves up the ordinary reality of transatlantic travel: After seven hours by van from Arizona to Los Angeles, ten hours by plane across the continental U.S. and the Atlantic Ocean, back on land at Heathrow in London and another hour and a half across the city to here, today we begin the next leg of our current journey. Heavily laden with bags and boxes, our group will make another city trek across London to the train, travel by rail under the English Channel to Lille, then take another train—the TGV—to Poitiers, where we will be picked up by the ashram van to ride for an hour and finally arrive in our ashram sanctuary in rural France by eleven o'clock tonight, just in time for tea, made with fresh mint from the garden, and perhaps a little dark chocolate before bed.

It seems the question of how to find time for one's "Mistress" will just have to go unanswered. If there is no time to cultivate the *bhavas* of creativity, no flights of the imagination, no regular appointment with the muse within the grueling demands of travel, does it mean there will be no "art"?

"Think expansively," the preceptor said earlier, with a slight suggestion of a glance in my direction, just exactly as I wrote the question in my journal when I first sat down to write. I get it now—*that* was the answer to the question! Practical instruction for living in Enlightened Duality, a perception of Reality. It takes awhile to catch the drift sometimes, when the guru is answering unasked questions through the byways of synchronicity, when the practitioner holds the question within and the answer comes from an unexpected direction—like a carom shot on the billiard table.

Three weeks later, we were back in London. A pallet made from a thin camp mat with some sheep skins thrown over it has made a fine bed this week in the tiny living room of what was a lovely, elegant, spacious townhouse belonging to a member of the sangha. Now it has been transformed into the nomadic camp of the Bauls traveling in full regalia.

We are in transit mode par excellence: towed along with us are countless large boxes full of all manner of things, including books and CDs that will be for sale this summer, powdered blue-green algae and other green foods, enzymes and dietary supplements, vitamin C, and many different kinds of homeopathic remedies, tinctures, potions and other products designed to boost an immune system ravaged by industrial toxins, pollution, travel, caffeine, short nights and long days and the many varied stresses of egoic self-reference that take a great toll on our health and body-mind harmony—not to mention traveling conditions that disturb *vata* (the inner winds).

And then, amidst all this bulky weight, there are the baseball gloves, bats, sleeping bags and who knows what else for the teenagers who have now joined us to travel off and on with Lee's party for three or four weeks as they skip around Europe on a summer lark, as well as a few laptop computers (including the one on which this is being written), three yoga mats, extra pillows, a premium juicer, flats of organic vegetables and fruits, bags of quinoa for our spiritual master's healing regime, and various other snacks—not to mention our bags, totes, day bags and purses full of clothes and personal care products of many kinds, one cell phone, countless notebooks and reading materials and...perhaps you have gotten the idea by now. Do we really need all this stuff?

Lee is always chiding his students about traveling lighter—with more simplicity and elegance. So far, we have not been able to assume his practice in this regard. My "room" here in London is crowded with many of these myriad and assorted contents of life—particularly group travel life when it is characterized by complexity rather than simplicity. On the edges of all this are several boxes of artifacts, graffiti art, and extraneous bags containing mysterious items, piles of plastic bubble wrap, my personal travel bags (more stuff) and a population of deities belonging to our hostess: Annapurna, Buddha, Tara, a large ferocious dancing dakini, Ganesh, Mahakala, to name a few.

The guru's traveling entourage on the London leg of the summer's tour de force is up to about twenty sangha members and guests who came tonight for a lovely dinner in the lush, chilly garden. It was a passing moment in Camelot, under a Celtic sky. For a long time we sat together amidst the overhanging rose vines, thick Virginia creepers, rhododendrons, herbs and flowers, while fluffy clouds passed gently in the blue rain-washed sky. While we laughed and talked, the long slow evening set in.

Lee sat very quietly at a table under the roses with his guests, two seekers new to this scene and very interested in the master and his most unusual qualities—his soft, often wordless glimmering, his simplicity and innocence, his burning ferocity. They leaned forward, eager, so new and exploring the very first beginning climates of the guru's world. Their eyes stole glimpses of the master or gazed outright in moments, absorbing the mystery of his equanimity, the serenity that is so natural to one who lives in the eye of the storm.

The next day was our last day in London. We were driving to Oxford for the day to visit Lee's dear friend Robert Beer, renowned *thangka* painter and scholar of Buddhist iconography. Often distracted by all the hubbub going on around me, if I don't take the time to sit and write by hand about whatever is coming up in the moment and how it relates to nonduality and Enlightened Duality, the inspiration is lost. What to do in the whirlwind? Keep trying to find what is true in the moment, as Lee advised when we first arrived at the ashram in France.

In 1988 I asked my teacher the question, "How can I serve you?" He responded, "You can write, so just write." In my efforts to do justice to that instruction, I have discovered that writing requires a great deal of discipline. Over the years that directive evolved to include many very specific instructions from Lee on writing and editing. Then, after about ten years and the completion of several rather large projects, his feedback became "just keep writing," and "write this or that," meaning a particular book or article that he would give as a project. At some point this evolved further into "write whatever you want." This has been the most difficult to navigate, because it is so much easier to just do what one is told to do, rather than to assimilate and make use of many years of sadhana in order to find what is true to one's own dharma and live into that. What my teacher means when he says, "Write whatever you want" is: *Do what I want you to do the way I want you to do it without being told—and do all this as an adult, out of your deep alignment with the teaching, the path and the guru.*

This morning we read an interesting interview with Bob Dylan in *The Times*, in which he talked about the exhibit of his paintings that opened in London on June 13. Here is what Dylan had to say about the experience of writing his highly acclaimed first autobiographical book, *Chronicles*: "Writing any kind of book is a lonely thing. You cut yourself off from friends and family to find that necessarily quiet place in your mind. You have to disassociate and detach yourself from just about everything and everybody. I didn't like that part of it at all." As a writer, it was most helpful to hear this from Dylan. Since writing has been a central activity of my sadhana, to have an iconic hero like Dylan say this very thing was tremendously helpful, if only for a fleeting moment before confusion, illusion and all their best friends came hurrying back to haunt me in my road-stressed, self-induced state of unclarity. He was echoing something I have said many countless times, when I have felt like a lone voice crying into the wind, because I've discovered that very often it's only other writers who understand this experience.

Writing requires solitude. Some writers go mad from it. Many of them become full-blown depressives or suicides. It's pretty wild down there, where you have to go to retrieve the soul. Sometimes I feel like I am walking a tightwire with no safety net, and at any minute I could fall into the abyss. Most of the time I have enough sanity to know very clearly that anything I have accomplished in my "role" of writer and editor has been through the direct blessings of the lineage gurus, Lee and Yogi Ramsuratkumar. Quite often I look at books or articles I've written and wonder: Who wrote that? It certainly wasn't *me*. True, it was a different "I" altogether—it was the disciple "I," not one of the many childish "I's," the ones who have an emotional reaction to the prolonged bouts of solitude required for writing.

The vast majority of writers agree that peace and quiet are necessary to the creative task, although my desk at the Arizona ashram is in a tiny, windowless room adjoining "The Office," a somewhat mythical realm where Lee and anywhere from six to fifteen other people work in one room, generating untold waves of chaos and high-spirited, driven, often loud and noisy action. My small space is a thoroughfare through which people must walk all day long in order to get to another small room where important supplies are kept. I have done a great deal of writing at that desk—I don't really know how, except that there is an automatic diving down that happens when I really enter writing mode, so that I am alone in the midst of the fray. When someone comes to my desk and speaks directly to me when I am in writing mode, I am pulled up out of the subterranean world of origins, for it is only from this place that the process of writing can happen.

Lee's instructions to his students over the years has guided us in the direction of cultivating the ability to create art or invoke sacred mood (the same thing, ultimately) at any time, anywhere, on demand. This is the way that Lee writes lyrics and poetry—whenever and wherever. He often writes poetry on the run, literally, while behind the wheel of the van, for instance. He will say, "Do you have any paper? And a pen?" to whomever is nearby and then take these proffered items and proceed to write. He does not need a special place, a primed pump, a certain time of day, privacy or anything of those wonderful things in order to create. It is amazing, daunting and—for most of us—impossible.

However we get there, a writer or artist of any kind has to be willing to go down into the netherworld of the unconscious, which can yield ecstasies, insights and grave depressions as well. That is one of the reasons why navigating the terrain between the inner world of the writer and the outer world of social relationships is extremely fraught with challenges and pitfalls of all kinds. When I extract myself from that inner world and seek reconnection in the world of busy people, as Dylan so aptly said, I am often out of the loop—disoriented and generally clueless about what is going on to such an extent that it can be quite disturbing. When I am functioning on the wavelength of that internal creativity, it requires real presence of mind and clarity of intention to reconnect with everyone else, all of whom seem to be swiftly and successfully navigating the vast honeycomb of interconnectedness that is daily relationship. All this has to happen within the adult who has made a choice to engage this writing practice. Painters are very much like this also, according to testimony I have heard from sangha mates who create in that medium. I have heard Robert Beer speak about the depression of being consumed in thangka painting—an imaginal world of seemingly infinite detail, alchemical heat and intensity—for months at a time.

Imagine it in this way: You are flying above a vast, dense forest, and from that vantage point you see the whole thing, the ever-inspiring Big Picture. Then, necessity demands that you make your way slowly down through the thick branches, tangled vines and leaves to a glade where you descend to the earthy, musky mulch of the forest floor. There you ardently work at examining the tiniest wild orchid that blooms only in this particular place at this particular time of year, each year. The orchid is fragile and exquisite; light shines through its translucent textured petals, and they shiver in the air.

No one knows you are there, or that this infinitesimal wonder of creation is now in relationship with you and you with it, with hearts beating in a circle of reciprocal joy. Does a rare diminutive orchid have a heart? Yes. You have placed your attention upon its possibility, and it has yielded up its secrets to you. It has been born, and in a day or two, it will die. It is supremely impermanent and achingly beautiful. Who is going to understand that kind of experience but you? Or someone else who has seen and been kissed by the *drala* of that orchid…

Of course, this could be a description of any creative process or any dimension of direct experience in spiritual practice. With spiritual practice or any powerful inner event, it is always about how to bring it back into the world of everyday life. This in and of itself is an art form. Whenever we have been internalized, or focused interiorly, we have to reintegrate into the environment around us and bring the jewels of the journey back with us—the jewels being insight, clarity, and hopefully, compassion.

The dynamic of being out of the loop or marginalized, or the sense of being in a completely different orbit, in a world of maddening detail and demand, is common ground to anyone who has ever worked on a creative project that required a great deal of time and solitude to accomplish. When a creative project has us in its grip, we must accept the fact that we really have no life of our own; we are in service to that expression of creation. The project, at best, comes to have a life of its own and is literally pushing its vehicle—the artist—forward in its momentum to be born, to grow and to develop. Mothers and fathers who are in service to the creative act of raising small children have a very similar experience.

It is an experience that I find both extraordinarily rewarding and joyful *and* psychologically painful when primal survival patterns get activated in the process. This shows up in one of two ways: not enough solitude, which makes me very irritable when I am deluged in the process of writing; and too much solitude, which backfires when I resurface to connect with the world around me.

All this talk of lack of solitude or too much solitude, depression, confusion, and psychological imperatives falls into the category that my teacher calls "complaining," no matter how rational or well spoken it may be. To put this consideration in terms of the transformation of our psychological tendencies (and even Dylan has them!) let us turn for a moment to the teaching of Arnaud Desjardins on the ability to bear solitude as the mark of a true adult—a very high state, indeed.

Arnaud's master, Swami Prajnanpad once said, "Adults are more or less grown up, more or less childish, and the Sage is the perfect state of the adult—one hundred percent adult." In light of this teaching, Arnaud commented on the efficiency of this teaching on the Path:

> *Do not feel criticized or humiliated if I speak this way. At the same time, see that becoming less and less childish means moving towards your own wisdom or your liberation, and that the perfect adult is the sage. But listen to me carefully: it is not a case of saying, "adults*

behave like children"—no! It is much more concrete and precise than that. There is a child laying down the law in the heart of an adult. Take a look at what children are like; they will teach you a lot about yourselves as you are today, but, of course, it is below the dignity of a man to remain a child.

A child is incapable of non-dependency because a child has no material independence. For years everything has to come by means of mommy and daddy. Materially and psychology a little child is totally dependent. The goal [of the adult] is non-dependency, autonomy, to find one's own inner strength and inner balance. The goal is to be capable of solitude. This is one of the first criteria: to what extent are you capable of solitude? Swamiji said to me one day: "Wisdom is the possibility of being more and more abandoned, more and more betrayed, more and more rejected and to feel more and more peace, more and more inner security."

Yet you know very well that the idea of being betrayed, criticized, denied is unbearable to you. This is a mark of childishness. The dependency on someone or the dependency of others and the inability to be alone are all a mark of childishness. If you accept this criterion, you will be able to assess and evaluate the level of your being. Am I capable of staying alone, feeling alone? Or is it unbearable? Alone, materially, physically or alone psychologically: nobody agrees with me; nobody understands me. Do I more or less suffer from it? It will always be more or less: more or less childish, more or less adult.[1]

---

[1] Arnaud Desjardins, transcribed from a talk given at le Bost in the 1980s. To be published in *Tawagoto*, Winter 2009.

Generating essays from the day-to-day flow of life experience, most of which is on the road, is risky business. Of course all this travel puts a unique spin on my attempts to write, because ego still struggles against the groundlessness of this sadhana. When ego is pressed hard against the wall of resistance to the process of transformation, we sometimes become like crazy people living on the edge of something fierce, holding on for dear life in the gale. Of course, it is a storm of our own making, as our guru often points out, and if we just let go and trust the wind, everything will be fine. But, because we are in a *sesshin* of a kind—a form of spiritual intensive—we are coming face-to-face with every possible emotion and true feeling state (negative or positive) in a raw, intimate experience of ourselves.

I can imagine that Buddhists who have gone on long-term retreats can relate to this experience of the unraveling of personality. The Buddhists I know are adamant about the importance of, even the necessity for, ongoing retreat practice. Lee's way is to throw his students into prolonged experiences of chaos and intentional stresses, so that we come up against ourselves with such force, again and again, until we *must* see the nature of the mind, the body, the soul for what it is. Illusions become clear over time, slowly—very slowly. Finally, as the sun rises in the East, we begin to make distinctions in the twilight of our own in-between state—the bardos through which we are constantly traveling.

The value in this? To see ourselves as we really are, not as we imagine ourselves to be. "Know thyself" is the prime injunction of the wise. One of the great pitfalls of the spiritual Path is that we create a spiritualized ego and a spiritualized persona, which can be a very effective gloss or lacquer over the unconscious imperatives that rule our actual lives. To be identified with the persona, from a psychological point of view, is death to the possibility of the self. The persona, however good it may look, reaches beyond its native function to become a defense mechanism against seeing and integrating the shadow into the process of individuation—an arduous, long-term task that must be accomplished if we are to allow the self to emerge and unfold. Since Jungian terms are being used, it is important to note that when Jung used this word "self," he was not talking about the personality. He was speaking of the ultimate archetypal principle—the *atman*. When he spoke of the process of individuation, he stated clearly that we do not individuate toward a separate individuality; we individuate toward union with all that is; in the process we become *sat-chit-ananda*.

In the midst of this creative process I hope to carve out some "basic sanity," or "the sanity we were born with," as Chögyam Trungpa Rinpoche sometimes said, some insight into Enlightened Duality that just might be of service to others who are struggling along the Path of self-awareness and awakened consciousness. As Lee says, if it's not impossible, it's probably not worth doing at all, and so, every opportunity at the ashram this summer will find me in the solitude of my tiny room, hammering away at the keyboard.

Paying Attention

Lee Lozowick

We come to the Path with fantastic ideas of what the Path is supposed to provide or produce—like enlightenment or awakening, the biggest fantasy of all. Such things are possible, but our ideas of enlightenment or awakening are so fantastic that I call it a fantasy. We think that if we were enlightened, our suffering, struggles, conflicts, crises and confusion would all be over. Actually it just begins. However confused you are now, however much suffering you are in now, if you get enlightened it will be *six* times as much, *ten* times as much. So, nevermind enlightenment!

Regardless of what we think the Path is supposed to give us, we do what is in front of us. We put up with our eccentric teacher—and they're all eccentric, even the sanest of them. I'm one of the more eccentric, because I'm not a sadist. In this school we're just willing to put up with our teacher's idiosyncrasies and to wash dishes once in a while, serve the community and come to celebrations where we have to eat meat and white sugar! Many of the so-called spiritual masters in the world are sadists whose students are willing to be mistreated.

We come to the Path, and we are willing to go along with the little insults—being asked to walk all the way out to the ashram outhouse to go to the toilet in the middle of the night, working in the kitchen with some tyrant who can't cook half as well as we do. As we are putting up with the small, and sometimes large, indignities that we all put up with, in the back of our minds there is a fantasy about the Path and enlightenment.

Earlier this summer I met for lunch with a very famous neo-advaitist teacher. There were four of five of my students with me, and one of my students—who is one of my editors, so of course she's very involved in the dharma, and the correct dharma—kept asking this guy questions. He had only one answer to every question: "It's all your mind, there's nothing going on, nothing is happening." She asked, "What about all the starving people in Africa?" He said, "Who is there to starve?" My editor was practically tearing her hair out. "What about suffering?" He'd lean forward, his eyes would sparkle, and he'd say, "Who suffers? *I* suffer but there is no I! Ha ha hah!!"

You can't argue with someone like that. There is nothing to say, because there is only one answer: There is nothing. We don't exist. Who is talking? Who suffers? Who's starving? Who just murdered that person? How could anybody murder anybody when there is nobody to be a murderer and there is nobody to be murdered! I could imagine him speaking to a woman who has been raped and saying, "Who was raped?" Bang! "Who was just punched in the nose?" He would probably lean forward with sparkling eyes and say, "Ha ha haa! Nobody was just punched in the nose!" Although, these guys are always surrounded by students trained in martial arts, who would stop you before you could punch them in the nose, so you never get to see if they can actually walk their talk.

There are some people who don't think that there is an environmental crisis because they think that the environment is an illusion. Arnaud Desjardins said the greatest spiritual crisis of the coming years is the ecological crisis; some people think that that's not spiritual. A lot of people don't think that has anything to do with spiritual work. We might think "spiritual" is some kind of eternal, transcendental peace. What needs to be attended to right in the moment *is* what is spiritual. Since you and I live on the Earth and need water, obviously if there is no clean water and no clean air, how are we going to meditate? What are we going to breathe? How are we going to hydrate ourselves?

One of my students—a relatively young woman—was walking around, ostensibly in perfect health and engaged in the struggle with life; the next day she fell down and nobody knew why. That was about a month ago; now she is in a coma and is not expected to come back to consciousness. She may be dead in a matter of days or weeks, since what created the coma is growing inside her. Unexpectedly, without any warning, the Universe could come crashing down on your head.

We've had a terrible drought for many years in Arizona, where forest fires happen all the time. They move quickly, particularly if there's a good wind; by the time you wake up and look out your window, the fire is already burning your house down. In one particularly bad fire a few years ago, some people who lived out in the woods (because they wanted to be alone) didn't have time to get a warning; they just burned up with their houses.

How do we find the balance between self-denial and self-indulgence? Good question! I'm not sure I know the answer. We have ideas about what spiritual work is, and our ideas tend to be projections, fantasies. We are always worrying about what might happen and what is *supposed* to happen. Our work is to handle the situation right in front of us. What is, is. What does that have to do with meditation and all those attractive states of consciousness we read about? Unfortunately, *everything*. Reality is not disconnected or chopped up into different compartments; everything is continuous.

We are always projecting into the future. We read about great saints and think, "I'd like to be in that state of consciousness," but one of the things we don't understand about most of these great saints is that their altered states of consciousness were completely connected to their practical, ordinary lives. If you read about the Desert Fathers of early Christianity, these people lived in the desert. They had to build their own shelters, they had to get their own food, and they had to keep themselves free from insects and scorpions and asps. Does that mean we have to go into the mountains and meditate in a cave? Absolutely not. It means we have to *pay attention* to whatever is in front of us, in the moment—our children, a professional association, a lover, or an altered state of consciousness that intrudes itself upon us.

Saint Paul was a tax collector; he was riding on his ass, going to abuse some poor people, to strip them of the few little coins they had. He was probably not thinking about anything much—which was the secret to his success—then *blam!* He was knocked off the donkey by the Christ Light. He was completely turned inside out and upside down. There was a direct relationship between Saint Paul of Tarsus being *blasted* out of the donkey's saddle by the Christ Light— something as foreign to him as eating the bowels of African monkeys would be to most of us—and the rest of his life. The experience was not separate from the rest of his life, because everything is a piece of the puzzle. When you are irresponsible and disrespecting to someone, five, ten, fifteen, twenty years down the line that moment of disrespect or irresponsibility is going to be part of your experience, to some degree. It is usually impossible to trace, except that we know it is true. Everything that happens to us is not disconnected from everything that has happened to us. Whatever is in front of us, here and now, in our environment, in connected to everything we have done. You might think to yourself, as I often do, having tortured insects when I was six, seven, eight, ten years old, "Gosh, how is that affecting things now?" To some degree, everything we have done in our lives is a part of now because everything is continuous.

Spiritual life is about *paying attention*; it is not about fancy ideas. Paying attention is not a matter of concentration. There are times in which to focus one's attention in a way that we might call concentration is useful and even necessary. Obviously if one is a surgeon or dentist, then one needs to have the ability to focus attention to an astounding degree. At the same time, if you are a therapist of some kind, to focus your attention is often counter-productive to the task at hand. One of the things that I have noticed when people go to therapy is that the last thing they tend to talk about is the real problem. If you are a therapist and you want to help the people who come to you, you need to have the kind of attention that is *diffused*—a kind of field attention—instead of a pointed attention. If someone walks into your office and you say, "So, what's happening?" and they say, "I'm angry! Angry at my parents, angry at my wife, I'm angry!" and you focus your attention on that anger, you are liable to miss the real problem. You need attention that is diffused so that you can pick up things from the field other than the obvious, immediate glaring, noisy thing that is in front of you. While your client is ranting about their father, you can say to them, "So, what about your brother?" Those of you who are therapists and have tried this know that the person says, "Oh! My brother doesn't have anything to do with anything!" Ah! Got it! But you will not touch that point if your attention is so fixated that you are dealing with the noisy part of the person's conscious mind.

Spiritual life is about being able to pay attention, but we are not talking about paying attention by an effort of will, in which you have to struggle to stay with something. We are talking about the kind of attention that perceives the entire field and attends to whatever element of the field is calling for attention, service, help, healing, harmony, balance. Any time we define spiritual life in an exclusive way that eliminates whole domains of life, then we have done ourselves and our practice a great disservice, because we could be given anything at any moment to deal with. In the Tibetan Buddhist tradition, when one begins a ritual, one will first invoke every single guru back to the beginning of the lineage to bless the sanctity of the ritual. If the lineage is a thousand years old, imagine how many names you have to invoke before you start the ritual? That is the foundation. In every true tradition of prayer, once you have covered the foundation then you give yourself over to the powers that be. Who knows what can come to you to be blessed or attended to? The Pope or the Dalai Lama might say that it is possible for life itself to be lived as a prayer. Under those circumstances, anything could come to you in any moment—completely out of the sphere of your expectation or awareness—and demand your attention.

In many traditions prayer begins by bringing to mind the people closest to you, "Oh God, please bless my mother, my father," and then going on to more universal concerns. If your life is a life of prayer, because there is continuity, the transmission of the Divine may flow to a person who makes contact with you in some way. Maybe someone who briefly touches your life in passing is terminally ill, or someone in their family is terminally ill and they are completely broken by it. So, it is important not to separate and distinguish and compartmentalize. When you come to the Path, it becomes your personal responsibility—and the responsibility of the teacher—to help you effect this, so that your life becomes a continuous life of prayer. In a sense, you become one of the antennae of God, so that whoever and whatever you touch in your life is blessed in some way.

Our ashram in France is three hundred years old. It's a farm connected to an even older castle. One of my daughters has the idea that in the old days, when these places were run by royalty, the servants had hard lives. Maybe they were beaten and tortured, and terrible things happened in these old places. She says, "There are bad vibes in these old places. People died in there! People were hurt in there!" It's not just sentient creatures that we touch, it is things—four-hundred-year-old walls that hold a lot of vibrations. You can be sure that when the Dalai Lama walks into a space, the presence of his compassion is not only touching the people who are there but the building itself, the ground that the building is built on, and the sky above the building.

When we have found the Path, in essence we enter a school—a training program. The training program is to develop this diffuse awareness and ability to pay attention, so that ultimately our life is a continuous life of prayer and whomever or whatever enters our sphere of influence is touched. Does it mean if we enter a hospital everybody is going to leap out of their beds and start dancing after us? Probably not, but we usually want to know when someone has been healed so that we can feel good. "Aah! That was me, I touched that person and they walked! Halleluiah!" If you have a personal need to see how your prayer affects everything you touch, then you will not be leading a life of prayer, because that is just the perversity of ego. However, the beneficence and the influence of any individual living a life of prayer is undeniable. Something positive, harmonizing, and healing will happen.

August 2007

City Madness

M. Young

*Any trouble that appears to be going on is just clouds
over the landscape, just a little breeze kicking up dust.
Trying to come to any conclusion right now is useless.
Time will tell, that wicked Bitch! She always does. In
the same way, clarity will come over time.*

—Lee Lozowick
Summer, 2008

*B*ack in Paris today, I feel a definite kinship with a postcard a friend
bought on the streets in the Latin Quarter titled "L'infer"—"Hell."
It was a photograph of a shop entrance modeled into the face of a
devil—the Devil—its open maw being the doorway inside. A man
stood in the closed entrance, and as I looked at it, I thought, "Just like
me." What is arising today is hellish, and as with all experiences of
hell, it feels like there is no way out.

When visiting Montana several weeks ago, Lee took some of his
students to see a movie by David Mamet, titled *Red Belt*. In it the
main character, a teacher of *jiu jitsu*, tells his students that in the
extreme moment of combat, when they are locked into what seems

like an impossible hold, "There is always a way out." At the end of the movie he demonstrates this by emancipating himself from a death-dealing jiu jitsu hold in which his opponent has him locked in what seems like absolute defeat. In the crucial moment, he somehow flings himself up, over and out of the hold to vanquish his opponent. It looked impossible, and yet, he did it.

It's a true metaphor for life. When it comes to hells that are strictly psychological (and for most privileged Westerners, *all* of them are psychological), and other people play a significant part in that hell, then the complications always seem endless. We must want out badly in order to find the secret escape. And, quite often but not always, other people make things worse for us when we are seeking to extract ourselves from Old Satan (who is, of course, none other than the spawn of our own shadowy innards), but there is nothing we can do about the reactions others have to our difficulties.

Today the mind continued to slog its way along familiar pathways of discursive thought. It seemed that my outlook had become progressively murkier during the long city sojourn—from Paris to Brussels to London back to Paris again. After two weeks on the road, wicked combinations of discomfort, personality frictions, old psychological wounds, the general and specific battle of "yes and no" that is part and parcel of all attempts to transform oneself had all folded in upon themselves along with healthy doses of boredom, then multiplied in synergistic evil harmonies that grew until there was no respite from the inner cacophony. Depression and negativity were raging, causing virtues such as patience, forbearance and discipline to flee in terror from the onslaught of sheer, unmitigated self-reference. As a result, I participated in a furious exchange with someone when a communication gaff arose on top of travel stresses and chronic misunderstanding, conflict and lack of resonance between us. Volatile emotions erupted like Mount Vesuvius, leaving me depleted and miserable.

Back on the ashram the next day, I found myself in sanctuary once again, nursing my wounds from the war of *sadhana*, in which the practitioner lost the last battle. At times like these, there is usually a healing process in progress. Seeing myself in the bright light of yesterday's skirmish as the culmination of a very difficult week was not just painful—it was very difficult to accept. In practice, even lack of acceptance has to be accepted without judgment, which is made that much more challenging by the added burden of judgments and projections levied by fellow practitioners. How easily even the strongest practice can fall into the trap of assessing another's position in life, causing our thoughts to zip like arrows and poisoned darts across common airspace and shared daily environments!

We are mechanical animals seeking the survival of our egoic identifications—especially those identifications that are of a spiritual nature. Spiritual pride is the hardest of all illusions to pierce, Chögyam Trungpa Rinpoche says, because we actually have achieved something through our practice, and we have true vajra pride as a result of all our hard work. However, as we know very well (if we are truthful), ego usurps every inch of ground that we have struggled arduously to gain through practice, and before we know it, when someone else is struggling with negative identifications, we self-righteously observe them from a haughty distance. Already the illusion of separation has crept into our context for relationship, setting the stage for something unpleasant, ignoble and decidedly unenlightened to go down. Secretly we are full of fear that we might be infected with their disease! Therefore, shunning is another strategy that the spiritually superior frequently employ. But most of all, we feel quite uplifted by the opportunity to offer insights into the ubiquitous and unacceptable cramp of the other from our lofty height, since, we justify, "it was not me" in the moment who was animating negative psychological patterns in lurid colors. It bears saying here that I can write about this with intimate knowledge only because I have observed myself doing these very things.

At times like these, we are sometimes so threatened by another's demonstration of illusory identification that all semblance of what the Buddhists call "skillful means" (which is rooted in kindness, generosity and compassion) flies out the window, easily tossed there by the hefty muscles of the drive to dominate, subjugate and send out the torpedoes on anything that might spoil our personal party. Do we stop to think of how this particular person might best be served before we launch into invectives in the name of "giving feedback"? What approach, what words, what empathy might really touch this person's heart, which so obviously needs to be touched and coaxed to open?

The pathways of internal practice are many and varied indeed. To use Lee's metaphor, "On the Caravan to God," when one has fallen off the camel on a very long journey toward home, there is nothing to be done about it but to get back on the beast and continue to plod forward on the Path. It does not matter what anyone else in the caravan is doing. Maybe they have fallen from their camels too, just by having seen one of their fellows fall! Perhaps we have even rolled down the precipice a bit and must labor back up the mountain on foot, over jagged rocks and gravel inclines, to get to the Path where the camel is patiently waiting for us. Maybe our fellow caravan traveler is so furious that we halted their progress that they push us back down the mountain, and we must struggle up a second time, even more exhausted from the effort than before.

The tendency to judge others is something that we must know about ourselves. In the necessity to take responsibility for ourselves, we must go all the way. If we have a tendency to be mean-spirited toward others when we ourselves are feeling threatened in any way, this is a serious deterrent to practice. If we do not face this tendency, it will be a bomb ticking away in the unconscious, and sooner or later, it will explode, creating manifold karmas. At any rate, we do whatever we have to do to continue on. For, having begun the caravan journey many years or many lifetimes ago, we cannot stop now without finding ourselves lost in a wilderness with no guide, no food, no shelter, no camel, no candle, matches or blankets, and a long wintry night coming on.

What does any of this have to do with Enlightened Duality? Once again, in the process of writing these essays, that is the pressing, ever-present and illusive question. When events are seen through the screen of illusion, the ability to perceive Reality and then write about it is compromised due to the basic fact that the writer is split off from the very Reality she is attempting to articulate something about. On the other hand, writing from *within* the moment of turning to practice may be of value, both to the writer and the reader.

When dark moods and unstable, negative states take over our consciousness, we have to remember those moments when clarity and stability reigned. Once again, here we are at the threshold, brought to this point by the raging display of emotion. What is different now, in essence, at the foundation of things, underlying the arising of passing phenomena? Nothing. This is nothing more than another passing state, in which the worst aspects of my own psychological disposition have been triggered by other, equally transient passing phenomena, all of it compounded upon itself and creating a complex web of maya.

Arnaud Desjardins says that only a child has emotion; the adult has *feeling*. This is a vital distinction. When emotion arises, and it always does, sooner or later, then emotion is what we work with to find the thread of what is true. Emotion is the arising moment of practice, and when it is accepted open-eyed, with innocence, Just This becomes the ground from which a true feeling may or may not arise. When clarity dawns, it brings with it the possibility of the wisdom quality, or true feeling, underlying any emotional state. What is the price of admission into the realm of clarity, vigilance, even faith, love and surrender? The relaxation and letting go of identification with the whole thing; in other words, surrender at the most basic level.

The only way out of the no exit stranglehold is to drop the identification with it—step outside of the entire picture and into a new frame. In any given moment, we can be different. We can move into another frame of reference; we can assume the character of the disciple, the devotee, the student, the practitioner at any time. We can return to the pristine sanctuary of the dharma. The grand design of Life is that, because of the fact of impermanence, everything can be different from one momentary experience of what is real to the next momentary arising. What is arising in this moment *is*, and, in the next arising moment, it can change. That means: tomorrow is another day, so to speak. Consciousness never changes, but the *state* of consciousness can change, literally from one moment to the next.

What kind of container am I pouring this precious gift of consciousness into, moment to moment? To change the container, all I have to do is be willing to let go, to drop the identification with the old container—shame, guilt, fear, anger, resentment, insecurity, or love, happiness, self-assurance, pride, superiority, whatever it might be, positive or negative. In the inner solitude of the moment we can turn ever so slightly toward a simplicity of being, a not-knowing, a relaxation that is entirely nonlinear and without motivation, and in that moment, as if by magic, the slate is cleared. Letting go to free-float in Organic Innocence, the great flow, the wellspring, the baptismal Font of Creation washes in and sweeps all into the next swirling pool of myriad arisings in the river of Life.

Death

Lee Lozowick

People's sentimentality concerning death is revolting. People's delight in gossiping about those who are dying is disgusting. Having been the object of both of those characteristics in great quantity, I'm ready to really kick some ass. I went to a café a month ago, and my dentist was there. When he saw me, the blood drained out of his head—he looked like he had seen a ghost, because the doctor who diagnosed me was his friend, and he told him that if I didn't do radiation and chemotherapy, I would be dead soon—very soon! Not only was I not dead, I was in a café, walking upright! Poor guy almost lost his lunch.

Two months ago I couldn't eat; a month ago I couldn't talk. I could make noise, but nobody understood what I was saying. I knew what I was saying, but others couldn't understand me. So, unless I drop dead from some unknown cause, things are moving in the right direction. Just because I'm starting to talk doesn't mean I *want* to talk. So please, those of you who have any concern for my well-being at all, spare me the long, rambling questions to things you already know the answer to, when all you want is my confirmation. I'm liable to spare myself, and you may not like the way I do that.

One of the things this whole drama has produced is more of a willingness to be blunt and direct, and less of a willingness to stroke people's egos because I don't want to hurt their feelings. And although I'm acting more in consonance with what I want to do, I am categorically unwilling to change the way I work. In other words, I will not slow down, and if it kills me, so be it. Before we left America for France, people were saying, "Are you going to Europe this year?" Why wouldn't I go to Europe? I have two band tours to make happen, and I expect to be ready to sing by the time the first tour starts—with lots of help from Yogi Ramsuratkumar, of course, since these guys can always help others, even if they aren't willing to help themselves.

You may be wondering why I decided to live and not die, which *was* a decision. I assume that decision will be effective temporarily, thank God; this whole thing about living till you're a hundred—who needs it? If I have fifteen years left I'll be happy, and if I have thirty years left, I'll curse the day I ever decided to live. Hobbling around, bent over, wracked with pain, covered with scars—who needs it? A number of my students swore they would never do chemotherapy, but as soon as they got cancer, what did they do? Chemotherapy! This is like single people who swear that they are devoted to the Work, and as soon as the "right" partner—"right" meaning just another asshole—comes along, where is the Work? Gone!

You can live badly, or you can live well. Death is an illusion, so what are you defending? What's the big deal? What are you trying to preserve? I decided to live because I felt that Yogi Ramsuratkumar was not ready for me to die. That's it! Not for my children, who I adore beyond words and who I felt heartbroken about, and who were all devastated when they heard the news and are now just starting to relax. I didn't decide to live for my students, as much as I love them and wish them all the greatest success possible on the Path, and not even for the Sacred Bazaar or for the music, which are both very dear to my heart.

This whole experience has been a fantastic catalyst for me. A number of things that should have changed years ago are now in the process of changing. The teaching never changes; the delivery of the teaching changes as the person delivering the teaching changes. Back in the early sixties, when Yogi Ramsuratkumar was a relatively young man in his forties, he was occasionally known to make commentaries on some of the great Indian scriptures, like the *Ramayana*. He assumed that he could deliver the teaching—communicate effectively—by using the scriptures. Over time, he realized that he could communicate more effectively without that delivery, and his delivery changed. The delivery of the teaching is liable to change—in some cases, very dramatically—which often freaks out the students of the teacher. In some cases, they begin to act as if the teacher was already dead, when in fact the teacher is more accessible than ever, but the students have to work in a different way to access the delivery of the teaching.

The first couple of months after I started the healing process, people were very responsible. People were really leaving me alone. Nobody was calling me on the phone, because I couldn't talk. I was in heaven! I still want to be left alone. I want to offer you what I have to offer you, uninvited by you—meaning that I don't want you to be the one to ask for it, except, of course, when you ask for more practice. Please feel free to ask for more practice—although, please don't be disappointed if I don't initiate you into all the esoteric secrets of the Work. If you are persistent in asking for practice, and willing to show me that you can practice seriously—an hour or two a day, in addition to doing all the things that need to be done—then I am encouraged to give some of the information that I would like to download.

That's a computer term: download. I don't even know how to turn a computer on, but you can't live in this world and not hear the terminology. As long as I have someone willing to research for me, I will never learn how to turn a computer on. There are wonderful benefits to the internet, such as being able to find out what's really going on in Myanmar or China, which we would never know if there was no internet. On the other hand, the internet is an evil virus that has and will continue to destroy lives. You can't even get a train reservation in France now without using the computer—you can't get a human being on the telephone to ask a question about timing or schedules. There are college students who can barely write legibly, but they can type like hell on a computer. We are human beings; we are not machines. We are meant to think for ourselves and function for ourselves. A large proportion of educated Western adults are losing both of those intuitive capacities. We are handling our abilities over to computers. Would you willingly give your innocents to a sadistic child molester? You would all answer no, I assume. And yet, you are giving your birthright of human ability and human thought to your computers, *willingly*, without even thinking it's a problem!

The point is: practice with no concern for your own death. There is such a thing as living; there is no such thing as death. I understand, of course, that no one looks forward to a long period of pain and suffering before you actually enter into what is called "death." Take morphine! Morphine is not chemo; morphine can be a good thing under certain circumstances. Take LSD, so you don't even know you're sick! If you prefer natural things, take eboga. Of course, if someone you love dies or you lose a child, it is a tragedy, and there is profound heartbreak and grief. In particular, losing a child can drive you mad at first, but if your practice is strong enough, you will return. All that is true, and, death itself does not exist. Knowing that it does not exist doesn't necessarily mean that you will not grieve the death of a loved one, and rightly so.

So, guard your own practice with diligence. I was not guarding my own practice with diligence—my dietary practice—which was one of the contributing factors to the onset of this illness. I am convinced of that, and my convictions have been fairly accurate over the years, to put it mildly. So, eat with great joy and delight, and eat at your own risk, if you are unwilling to seriously consider the recommended dietary practices of this particular path. Just because you had a grandma who drank a half bottle of whisky every day of her life and lived to be a hundred does not mean you are the same person she was. Once again we come to the harsh reality that we are *different* and will forever be different from people who are unwilling to work on themselves to the point of—in Swami Prajnanpad's language—"accepting what is, as it is, here and now."

At the same time, food is great. I recommend you enjoy it. Just because I'm not eating sugar and meat and drinking coffee these days doesn't mean that you shouldn't sometimes enjoy meat or sugar or coffee. An occasional good meal of meat is worth its weight in gold.

Many of you are practicing in some ways and not in others. You don't need to pretend that you are practicing when you are not; that kind of falseness is not appreciated by your teacher. Neither is it attractive when someone tries to pretend that they are more advanced than they actually are, spiritually speaking. I would rather you be honest. I would rather know you are drinking or whatever. We are all in a spectrum. Some of us are more adult than others, and, on the other hand, we are all stumbling ahead, struggling with life's inequities: the horrors in China and the insult to our intelligence that our governments would support the Olympics being held there; the tragedies of hundreds of thousands of homeless people due to hurricanes and earthquakes; or the unconscionable, evil willingness of the American government, as it stands now, to support the torture of terrorist suspects; and with our personal struggles—dying parents, or our own health concerns.

We live in a world of tremendous complexity, and one of the consequences of the complexity that we have taken on for ourselves are illnesses that cannot be diagnosed, which break down the body and mind, and appear to have no ostensible cure. Complexity fills the mind with unusable and irrelevant information and adds to the undiagnosed deterioration of the body, not to mention epidemic cancer. In the American and European sangha in the past two years, we've had five, six or seven cases of cancer of different kinds in the last couple of years. A dozen people in the sangha have been struck with undiagnosable illnesses. People have tried dietary changes, allopathic treatment, naturopathic treatment, bioenergetics, Ayurveda, psychic healers, prayer, everything. Some things work, relatively, but they are still struggling.

Simplicity is something that would serve many of us to move toward in our lives. I always recommend that people surround themselves with holy objects of radiating beauty—and that is not about complexity. I am moving toward simplicity, and I would encourage you to do the same, if possible. I would also suggest you earn as much money with as little effort as possible, and I am not talking about complexity—I am talking about practicality. One of my students runs a business that mediates between the American government and corporations. This is one of the most complex fields of legalities in America. He is phenomenally busy and successful. The reason is that he is honest and will not compromise his principles even for large bribes offered by American corporations. He is an example of someone who is surrounded by complexity but who is very simple in daily life. He has a practice and a family, and he lives a very simple life.

We are going back to basics. We are building a new ashram that will be as self-sustaining as possible. There is no lack of sunshine in Arizona, so we plan to use solar energy supplemented by wind. We plan to prepare our food with wood, not with gas or electric. We are going to live simply—very simply—because complexity itself is a disease.

Ferme de Jutreau, France
May, 2008

Organic Innocence

M. Young

*E*very human being is born with the abiding inner glory of God intact. This is what Lee calls Organic Innocence, which is the mood of all manifestation and incarnation that arises out of the background, or context, of Life itself. The expression of Organic Innocence is the Primacy of Natural Ecstasy. Creation is naturally ecstatic. Nature is naturally ecstatic. This is a revelation that establishes all of Life firmly in what Chögyam Trungpa Rinpoche called "basic goodness" and Swami Prajnanpad called, "intrinsic dignity and intrinsic nobility." This is a teaching that relieves us of a very great burden instilled from birth by a culture that is steeped in Judeo-Christian mythos and mores—a very recent development in the religious ideas of the world as compared to, say, an eight thousand year old Vedic tradition.

In reframing ancient teachings into contemporary terms, Lee has replaced Christian injunctions of original sin with a teaching that says we, as human begins, are born Organically Innocent—our birthright is an original purity and innocence that arises from the context of Life itself. The Primacy of Natural Ecstasy manifested through embodiment is a sacred experience of the Divine, which defines our entire relationship to Life. The body is sacred; sex, birth, death, food, enjoyment, love and pleasures of all kinds become sacred experiences given by the Grace of God—a God of love, truth and beauty, a God of awesome transformative potentials, rather than a God of punishment and condemnation.

We tap into the underlying innocence and ecstasy of who we actually are in many moments of our lives, from watching the birth of a child to any one of a thousand moments in communion with others or with our natural environment. If you have ever gazed into the eyes of a newborn child, or glimpsed raw glory in the face of one who is dying, you have tasted the flavor and texture of Organic Innocence. You might have this experience watching whales surfacing as they swim in the deep, or sitting in the sanctity of an aspen grove in the Rockies or among the sand and rocks beside the swift flow of the Ganges. Equally, the primal dark power of a tornado, the overflow of red hot lava from a volcano or a bullfight in Mexico City transmit the reality of Organic Innocence. The most debased human being, beneath the layers of illusions and pain, is essentially Organically Innocent.

Reflections on Organic Innocence always lead me to a consideration of the fundamentals: earth, air, fire and water, the basic ground of Life in incarnation, in which we rely completely upon the Earth, our Mother, from whose body our bodies are fashioned. As the ecological disaster on our planet has rapidly spread and accelerated over the past thirty years, and especially since the turn of the twenty-first century, I have become more and more irreconcilably heartbroken about the condition of our planet, her rivers and oceans, soil and air, her peoples and their declining cultures. Our organisms suffer the burdens of this Earth from which we have been born. We are the Earth, the Sun, the stars and the vast cosmos. The fact is that we are this Earth's waters and forests and oceans and plains and mountains. When the great whales are beached upon the sand to die of asphyxiation from the hundreds of pounds of plastic bags lodged in their lungs, that is happening to each one of us, our children and grandchildren…literally. When fish are sprouting third eyes and growing cancers on their bellies and the salmon are too toxic with mercury poisoning to eat, that is happening to us all.

These are tangible realities, just as the deaths by starvation and AIDS of children in Africa and India are real. These are our children who are dying, our grandchildren who are left orphaned in war. These are our children who are suffering the effects of plastics leaching estrogens into the water and soil of this planet and into the food we eat, forcing children into early puberty and unseen but certain future problems. Slowly we are realizing that, as J. Krishnamurti said over twenty-five years ago, "we are responsible for everything" that is happening in the world around us.

Not only are we the Earth herself, but the quality of the Earth's soil, water and air is a metaphor for the quality of our own state of being. Sparkling clear water, rich moist earth, fresh, invigorating air—these are none other than original innocence and purity arising from the creation bed of the elemental forces within the individual body. They are our birthright. They are heaven on earth. They are the manifestations of the spirit in matter. They are the agents of the Universe, which call us to—like Lord Vishnu—preserve, maintain and sustain all that is born, grows and dies within this realm of existence so that we may live to praise and adore Life in its infinite plenitude. They are the sacred seals of Organic Innocence, under which we have this life, this opportunity to transform, to become, to flow in the Great Process of Divine Evolution—in what Lee calls "the evolutionary, creative Universe."

Spiritual life naturally includes an innate, inborn commitment to Nature as a fundamental daily *asana* of our lives. It's a matter of commonsense wisdom; a matter of knowing our own Organic Innocence, aligning ourselves to a resonance with that innate condition, and honoring the interconnectedness of life as a creature within the vast holistic web of Creation. Although transformational work is not necessarily about any of the great concerns of the body politic in our times, we do have an obligation to bring integrity to how we relate with money, sex and food[1]—both literally and symbolically speaking—in the realm in which we seek to evolve as conscious creatures.

While there are many people who care very deeply about the ecology of the Earth, growing and eating organic foods or supporting local food economies, avoiding the use of plastics in daily life (to name a few examples of conscience in action), there are also many who are ambivalent, uninformed or defended against making the gestures necessary to support wide-spread, effective change. This dichotomy is found on the Path as well: people who are drawn to spiritual life reflect the common dis-eases, the strengths and weaknesses of the populace in the culture at large. The juxtaposition of profound regard or common disregard for the Earth and Nature as a cosmic principle (or, more simply, in terms of dealing with money, sex, and food) is found to be true also within the Path.

Wide-spread cultural addictions to personal comfort and selfish concerns have created a general malaise that contributes profoundly to the fact that we are "killing this beautiful Earth," as Krishnamurti said in 1982 in Ojai, California, in a heartfelt call to practitioners to take personal responsibility for *everything* in our world. Growing and buying organically produced food—specifically, food grown without the use of chemical fertilizers, pesticides and herbicides—is not just about personal health and well-being. Far from it. The commitment to organic food—as one example of many life-positive actions we can take—is a gesture of responsibility, an act of conscience born of deep heartbreak.

---

[1]   The phrase "money, sex, and food" was originally coined by Adi Da Samraj in reference to the fundamental domains of life experience.

The spiritual Path inexorably opens the heart and tenderizes the hardened buffers of psychology, giving rise to what Chögyam Trungpa Rinpoche called "the tender and vulnerable heart of the spiritual warrior." As human beings, our native soulful instinct is to be in *relationship* with Life. We can only fail to feel moved at the level of the heart by all this if we are disconnected from our own Organic Innocence.

There are numerous arguments put forth to either avoid the "green" concern altogether or shunt it to the back of our priority list, ignoring the fact that it represents a fundamental call to right action in the domains of money, sex and food for every practitioner. Some feel that ecological concerns are another egoic identification, or that a real warrior of the Work doesn't care what he eats, because from the nondual viewpoint, it doesn't really matter—it's is all impermanent and empty anyway. Or, the justification may be: It's too late for the Earth; the damage is already done, so let's just get it over with.

What attitude do we take toward the demise of planet Earth? Are we are aware of the massive carbon footprint that we are personally leaving behind us? Whose side are we on—the continuity of Life, or the corporations, profit mongers and war-making governments? Because it is a war—"a war against nature," as many visionaries have pointed out. The fact is that we are resistant to change, and we want our comforts and indulgences to stay in place—which, in the case of food in particular, involves contributing through our daily habits to the wholesale death of soil, water, and air by poisoning on a grand scale. One of the resulting tragedies is that today's children are developing a myriad of bizarre new illnesses related to toxins in air, water and food as well as to growth hormones in milk, eggs and meat products and foods laced with chemicals, sugar, dangerous additives and carcinogenic dyes. The children are the ones who will inherit this world for which we are responsible; it is they who will have to carry on in the face of the seemingly irreversible destruction of natural environments and ecosystems—including the human body.

There is a deeper underlying reason not to change our habits in relationship to food as an overarching principle of daily life that must be examined: the separative ego can and does use spiritual rhetoric to justify and rationalize decisions that are motivated by the deep-seated drive to keep our cynicism and psychological buffers in place. When we are defended in this way, we do not feel the very real suffering of the world around us, including the Earth herself. The less we feel, the less we must forge the conscience that will build the chalice of love and compassion for all of Life. The more compassion we are capable of carrying as living artifacts of the Path, the more transformation is demanded of us in our own lives—the more purity and nobility and generosity and selflessness we are asked to embody. We resist the great responsibility, the simplicity, and the reduction of personal will or control that is thrust upon us as a result of our own transformation.

Over the years Lee has given countless teachings and recommendations regarding what he calls "the Conditions"—a pure vegetarian diet, meditation, exercise, and study—which cultivate a mature, sane and balanced foundation from which one may engage practice. In this regard he has also been outspoken at times about the importance of eating organically grown food, avoiding irradiated and genetically modified food, and the dangers of toxins in one's diet. At the same time, the context of the Conditions are not necessarily moral or ethical but are based on the practical benevolence and alchemical efficacy of such a lifestyle in terms of the greater Work. The Conditions establish the body in a receptive and clear state to receive the subtle influence of the Divine. Similarly, he has spoken many times about gardening as a sacred activity that should be primary to any ashram; likewise he emphasizes the importance of conservation of resources, simplicity and Earth-friendly lifestyles.

At the same time, Lee views all this from the ultimate context of the Path. When Lee admonishes us about idealizing the "Green movement," or the next charismatic politician or any other form of engagement with the concerns of this world, it is always about calling us to a higher context. It's not about what we do, but how we do it. We are called to right action in the domain of ecological and social concerns, because when we destroy the natural integrity of the planet upon which we live, we are destroying our own Organic Innocence and our opportunity in this incarnation to align with the Great Process of Divine Evolution; we are living in opposition to the dharma.

The great teaching of Samkhya states that *prakriti* cannot be separated from *purusha*: God is Nature, Nature is God. Swami Papa Ramdas, the guru of Yogi Ramsuratkumar, lived in this state of realization. His life was a paean in praise of the Divine manifested in all things. Ramdas once wrote an essay called, "Nature Smiles—God Smiles," in which he says:

> *Nature smiles—God smiles.*
>
> *My heart is aglow with joy when I witness this wondrous phenomenon, God reveling in His own beauty and luxuriance....*
>
> *O God of plenty and abundance! None can rival Thee in Thy rich, free and reckless liberality. Thou art marvelous in Thy infinite variety—in shapes, colors, movements, ways and natures.*
>
> *I saw and saw and my dazed eyes became dim, and I beheld a halo spread over all space that resolved the multifaceted worlds into one radiance, one presence, and one truth.*[2]

---

[2] Swami Ramdas, *The Divine Life*, page 43–45.

Praise of the Divine is a sure tonic for the maladies of seriousness and sorrow that can become quite pervasive when we are sensitive to the decay of the world around us. Praise is intimately linked with prayer, and many would say that the most responsible thing one can do for this world is to pray. One way to pray is to praise the beauty and wonder of the natural world and its inhabitants.

Yogi Ramsuratkumar reflected the teachings of his master, Swami Ramdas, in many different ways, including his love of the natural world and his prime instruction to praise. Praise is one of the open doorways through which we may find an easy reconnection to our own Organic Innocence. Praise is a state of being; it is one of the primary ways that we, as practitioners, may produce *rasa*, and rasa is truly needed in this world ruled so ruthlessly by the analytical mind separated from the heart.

Innocence and solitude are two of the conditions necessary to the production of true rasa, which feeds and nourishes the world soul, which is not separate from the planetary being of the Earth, the individual, or ultimately the cosmos itself. In the external realm, there may be tremendous sadness and heartbreak about the loss of innocence and solitude in our world today, which is reflected in the destruction of natural environments, the deadening of our night sky by glaring city sprawls, the hell realms of cities everywhere. People are drawn to live in urban environments like moths to a flame, which is an apt metaphor, because, as Lee points out, cities are getting worse. When we turn and face the abject condition of the world today, it is only natural that great sorrow arises. When this happens, the most potent, beneficial response is to pray.

It is easy to pray in nature. Everyone has a reference point for having touched the sacred while walking in the deep woods, on the seashore, down a hidden path beside a flowing river, or meditating under venerable old trees, or in a magnificent rose garden. In these and many other ways we have felt the transmission of the sacred in nature. If we pay attention, the natural world will transmit the truth of nonduality to us. Chögyam Trungpa Rinpoche once said, "Nature is silent, free from kleshas."[3] Jeremy Hayward writes that Trungpa Rinpoche had a particular love of nature in all forms. He would sometimes, when out driving, stop to sit on a rock beside a lake, looking silently out across the water until he was moved to leave. Once during a time when Trungpa Rinpoche was recuperating from an illness, he would ask to be driven to a specific tree located in the foothills of the Rocky Mountains. He would lie down beneath the tree for "considerable periods of time."[4] If we observe the patterns of Nature, the changing seasons, the creating, growing and dying away of all things, Great Nature will reveal every great secret, including the emptiness and luminosity of *shunyata*. In its expression of sheer beauty, which is *sat-chit-ananda*, Nature eventually calls us to adoration and the secrets of Enlightened Duality.

Mid-June finds us in London again, where conflicts are brewing among our party of traveling *sadhikas* as the stresses of groundlessness, homelessness, and lack of privacy, quiet, peace of mind, extract metaphoric blood from our veins and sweat from our brows. It's rather like a coming storm, when electricity almost crackles in the air. The madness and toxic background of the cities we've been visiting—Paris, Brussels, London—take a toll on the organic system as a whole, and there is no time in each busy day to get grounded and back on track with our usual regenerative practices.

---

[3]   Jeremy Hayward, *Warrior-King of Shambhala: Remembering Chögyam Trungpa,* page 245.

[4]   Ibid, page 243.

Cities are a hard place for me. It's not that I don't also enjoy immensely much of what cities like Paris or London have to offer, but quite often as I travel around, I feel like someone from a different century—a time when things were less complicated and we lived closer to the natural world. Traveling brings into focus just how pervasively techno-culture is running amok on this planet. Two weeks spent in Kolkata six months ago was enough to make me swear off cities for the rest of my life, but we travel into cities with Lee quite frequently, as his work calls him there. It strikes me that the only reason one would want to be in any city on the planet these days is if there is a possibility of serving others in some way.

Today in particular I am contemplating the frustrations and joys of working with others—that is, attempts at teamwork in the highly competitive circumstance around the spiritual master. Problems of relationship are the same everywhere, of course, whether in a professional situation at a job, within a family, in a marriage or just dealing with the clerk in the check-out line at the grocery store. Karma and karmic ties can be the bane of existence, without question. Of course, relationships hold the greatest possibility for spiritual breakthroughs of the ultimate kind, for if we can remain poised and calm in the midst of the storm, then we have really achieved something. This kind of equanimity depends, in part, on the ability to see one another with clarity and to acknowledge the fundamental ground of each other's Organic Innocence.

In all sanghas, as in all households and in all human beings, the sacred and the profane exist side by side. In exactly the same way that ashrams are not separate from Life, and in fact are perfect microcosms of the macrocosm, so is the individual practitioner a reflection of the world—a microcosm of the macrocosm. The world, even the Universe as a whole, exists within each one of us.

I heard a spiritual elder—a devotee of Swami Nityananda, guru of Baba Muktananda—speaking about ashrams and spiritual life last year as we sat with friends on an ashram patio in rural Gujarat.

He said, "As soon as you walk through the gate of the ashram, you are greeted with maya, and that is what you have to work with in sadhana." After many years on the path, I am still learning, in an excruciatingly slow and hard way, to accept this basic truth of the human condition: that while we are mired in maya, aswirl in the currents of the illusion of separation, at the same time we are the ever-changing, ever-creating, ever-inspired condition of already present enlightenment. Spiritual life is where we go to embrace this truth whole-heartedly, whole-bodily, before we can make any true, lasting headway at all.

Sadhana does cultivate the inner life of mystic reverie and all those wonderful pearls of the Path, but mystical ascent is the easy part for many of us; human beings are natural mystics due to the fact of our God-given birthright. We have the innate blueprint in place; all we have to do is pay attention, open up a little, and the cosmic sea comes flowing in. It is the integration of those experiences into daily life and allowing those experiences to inform our actions and relationships that are the hard part of maturation on the Path. In all this travel, Lee gives his students the opportunity to be and exude the environment of the ashram—with its subtle fragrance of the Divine—whether we are physically residing there or not. It is a *lila*, a game in which, perhaps, the goal is to reside in sanctuary in the interior sense no matter where we are.

Over time the body of a practitioner becomes a beacon of the Path, a symbol, a fragrant icon. We are surprised to find that this is true even on a bad day, when practices seems to slip through our fingers and we give in to moments that are less than kind, generous or compassionate, not to mention less than dignified and noble. These moments are the place of practice—the point of departure, the dock, pier, and quay from which the voyage on the sea of practice commences.

People are drawn to spiritual life for all kinds of reasons, some true and some false. Some of us come seeking personal power; some come for the love of God, while others come because they are suffering and have nowhere else to turn. Yogi Ramsuratkumar once said that all human beings have both light and darkness, and it is important not to deny the light because we see a dark aspect. A truly generous, mature integration of this truth of human incarnation is extremely difficult to achieve. At the same time, it is vital that every person who genuinely wants to practice on the spiritual Path comes to grapple with this in relationship to self and other: the acceptance of our enlightenment *and* our endarkenment.

It's all too easy to see the endarkenment and dwell thereupon, because that is what the mind does endlessly: obsession. There are two ways that the shadow side shows up: obsessing or rebelling. We obsess by fixating our attention on the negative or positive of any given detail of our lives. We go over and over some event or conversation or entanglement we are in. We talk to ourselves, playing out imaginary conversations. Our obsessing is usually highly charged with energy. If we look at our obsession closely enough, we see that it is always really only about *me*. It is never about anyone else but me.

Rebellion is also about me; we rebel most fundamentally against the absolute sovereignty of God, the fact that there is only God, which brings into sharp relief the truth of Spiritual Slavery, the necessity to Surrender to the Will of God. We rebel against the absolute utter truth of these statements in countless myriad shifting ways. Therefore, it is easy to see the darkness in others because we ourselves are dark, and we project our own darkness on whatever comes into contact with us.

Perhaps it is much more threatening to see the enlightenment in ourselves and in others—to honor the fact of our Organic Innocence or "basic goodness," as Chögyam Trungpa Rinpoche put it. If we did, we would have to be responsible for the gift of incarnation, for our potential and real enlightenment. The addiction to self-indulgence and self-reference would be finally and forever quelled. We would be called into the service of Life in an all-consuming and all-pervasive way, because to live our Organic Innocence is to live in Surrender to the Will of God, in the flow of the Great Process of Divine Evolution.

Leaving our quarters at seven a.m. this morning, we followed Lee around London. The kaleidoscope of maya's best that had been parading across the screen of my mind urged me to volunteer for time in the van, where I would guard the bags and bundles while Lee and his group prowled the antique markets of London. It was a perfect time to contemplate and write the following journal entry:

> *Watching my own passing states, I sit alone in the front seat of the van and reflect on how we human beings will occasionally awaken from periods of sleep. Even when awareness is dormant, submerged or buried beneath veils of illusion that seem as real as ten tons of solid granite pressing in on the soft and delicate tissues of this frail human body, we can have a sudden moment of illumination.*
>
> *Only when love and its handmaiden innocence are alive in me is there any sense of wonder and the basic goodness of existence—the place from which bodhichitta might be cultivated. Then, the heavy aromatic heads of red roses hanging in many-petaled glory on a wood fence, just at the edge of this parking lot where I sit, seem somehow dazzling, filled with drala, rather than rendered flat and foreboding, as they are when I am clouded over with negative emotions.*
>
> *If I can stop long enough to appreciate beauty in any of its appearances, then a window opens to reveal a fresh view: an opalescent dawn, the redolence of tangled*

honeysuckle, linden trees in bloom, abuzz with happy bees. Like the chestnut trees that are blooming just now all over London: their pale lavender spikes point toward heaven against a backdrop of glossy dark leaves, catching my eye as we drive by on streets bustling with busy people. All the meaningless activity of crowds in the city—all the self-important hurry here and there under a lowering sky that broods of coming storms—only points toward our desperation, until suddenly everything is transformed by the sun that peeks out from behind clouds to shine down hot on England's emerald world.

Contemplating nature is a return to innocence, for nature is pure, uncomplicated innocence. If we know how to place our attention in a certain way, Great Prakriti transmits the fundamental auspiciousness and truth of the cosmos. Nature is unconscious divinity. Nature reveries may catalyze a fleeting image from last night's dream, bringing insight or wisdom to bear, or call me away from the sulfuric, smoking brink of a hellish mental dialogue. Any contact with Organic Innocence—a child playing, a great piece of art, the unexpected sound of Andean flutes that delights my senses in the subway—moves consciousness toward the glimmer of intelligent awareness, toward remembrance of a deeper nature than what the mind will tell us is true. Mind: the most fickle and dangerous opponent to living the truth of who and what we are. And what are we? Fragments of divine light scattered across the living web of God, living hidden behind veils thick and murky as the night of our slumbering awareness of what is.

Most of the time in this vale of tears, love and innocence sleep the death of opium addicts, as if poppies in the somnambulant vein—sweet as death with that

musky scent of decay—have lured them away. Instead
of a brief candescent moment when I might glimpse the
Mystery that gazes at me perpetually, I am gone into
whispers of an old sad song with small fragments of bone
in the throat. When this happens "I" am nothing but
a drifting wanderer gone astray on a well-worn path,
suddenly deep in the thickets, torn and bleeding from
brambles, lost beneath glowering trees that breathe the
terrors of mankind and his cities, just as I do, insurgent
and longing for an earlier time when inborn innocence
held sway and the word "machine" meant a plow, a
wheel, a wagon ...

My guru's love for his master, Yogi Ramsuratkumar, is so great that
there is no sunrise or sunset, no rainbow or grandeur of mountain
and ocean, no canyon or forest that distracts him from the inner
view of his Beloved. This I have found to be absolutely true of Lee, as
he describes in his poetry to Yogi Ramsuratkumar. He is often irreverent and jocular, sassy and cynical in his poking fun at our attachment to nature and the beauty of nature, and yet I have also seen Lee
deeply enjoying the spread of a rainbow across the sky. I have seen
him standing beside the Ganges with bare feet in the sand, absorbing
the holy river. I have heard many a soft, quiet comment come from
Lee when he takes in a beautiful sight—the night sky in the high
desert ablaze with stars, seen through cold, fresh air. He is constant
in his statements about the insanity of city life, and he has spoken for
years about his own wish to live a life of greater simplicity.

It is my experience that Lee's concern is that we are not distracted,
fascinated and seduced away from the hard work of the transfor-

mational path by Mother's Cornucopia, because prakriti is asleep without purusha. Without purusha (pure consciousness, pure context), prakriti (nature, which is none other than Organic Innocence) will lull us into sleep, and the flame of consciousness that might be "real only then, when 'I am'," will not be awakened into being.

At some point on the Path, the love and enjoyment that we experience in the myriad displays of complexity is subsumed by a one-pointed focus on the Divine. This does not mean that enjoyment of beauty and nature's gifts cannot still be enjoyed, but everything is enjoyed through the perspective of Enlightened Duality: "There is only God." I remember Yogi Ramsuratkumar listening to the birds singing during darshan on his ashram; I was moved by his tenderness, delight and joy when he commented on their songs. I remember as well his profound love for Mount Arunachala and his enjoyment of certain flowers that were brought to him daily: the red hibiscus and white sampanji. And then there was his inexplicable devotion to his dog, Sai Baba.

As Swami Prajnanpad taught, one must have both *bhoga* (enjoyment) and yoga (union). At the same time, for the great realizer, there is only one taste, and that is the taste of God. Once when we were in Kanya Kumari, where the three oceans converge at the southernmost tip of India, a devotee of Yogi Ramsuratkumar and good friend of Lee's was traveling with us. He said to Lee, "Come up to the rooftop to see the sunset. It is especially beautiful here at the ocean." Lee politely declined, saying, "I don't need any sunsets. All I need is Yogi Ramsuratkumar."

Lee's love and devotion—his great capacity for enjoyment within the world of forms—is concentrated, focused like the beam of a laser, in one direction: Yogi Ramsuratkumar. Love and devotion to the master, in Lee's case, subsumes everything else so that nothing is left out of this love. Consider the following poem written to Yogi Ramsuratkumar on June 14, 1996, in which Lee begins by extolling the beauty of nature:

Here we sit in the lush countryside
    of Central France
viewing the magnificent valley
    from our equally magnificent hilltop.
The green is brilliantly aglow,
    a carpet of rare richness.
The scene is sprinkled
    with equally brilliant sparkles
of red, yellow, purple and white
    from the trees and flowers.
This is beauty;
    Nature has outdone herself.
Now as always, this bad Poet's
    mind drifts to You.
You are Beauty also,
    but You are different, unique.
All other beauty is seen
    in relationship to something else:
good against bad, lively against dull,
    attractive against ugly;
all aspects of a perception
    of duality, of opposition.
But You are different, unique.
    Yes, You are Beautiful as well,
but You are Incomparable,
    You are singular, One.
There can be no opposite to You
    for You subsume all, You are All.
Yes, You are Incomparable,
    You are Beauty Itself.
This little sinner has tried
    to find such Beauty

amongst the wonders
of the world
but he cannot.
The mere thought of such Beauty
turns him from the visible
to the vision of You —
You as That, You as This,
You as You.
Multiplicity is not as attractive
as it once was!
Multiplicity has died
in its meeting with You.
There is still Beauty, of course,
but it is all You, only You.
This is true Joy, Father.
Your son is too Blessed
to do anything but sing Your Praises
and lay himself before You.

This is a poem that rides the fine lines between duality, nonduality and Enlightened Duality, weaving in and out of the vision of these perspectives. At the end of the poem Lee resolves this, speaking again of nondual vision and its great possibility of Enlightened Duality, making them both real: "There is still Beauty, of course, but it is all You, only You." One does not deny the other. Speaking to Yogi Ramsuratkumar—the living symbol of the Supreme Reality—Lee writes an unforgettable line: "Multiplicity has died in its meeting with You." It is a contradiction in terms, actually, because it speaks of unity, "multiplicity has died," and in the same breath of "You," signifying an Other—a divine Other. How is this possible? Grace.

Organic Innocence and its expression, the Primacy of Natural Ecstasy, is a great secret which informs Lee's poetry to his master, which continually amazes in its expression of natural innocence and original mind. His poetry, taken as a whole contains everything we need to know about sadhana. Virtually every poem is written in this same format with simplicity and great intention.

The format of Lee's poems in itself is a teaching: Life is extremely repetitive, and as we get older, this basic fact comes into focus more and more. Within spiritual practice, the ego-driven need for constant stimulation, variation, new and bigger highs, and more and more complexity is confronted as the addiction to illusion that it is. If we are courting wisdom as a way of life, then we will learn to drink from Life's cup in a different way, which is only possible if we too are informed by Organic Innocence. Instead of divorcing our wife or husband of twenty-five years, we discover a way to reinvent the relationship. The reward of this effort is born from great courage and creativity; what it builds in the spiritual domain is priceless.

The key to unlocking this door is given to us in the poem. The poet says, "The mere thought of such Beauty turns him from the visible to the vision of You—You as That, You as This, You as You." In this statement, Lee takes us from the visible world of form, *rupa*, to the invisible world of transcendence. Bringing attention to bear on *rupa* brings *svarupa* from background to foreground. When we see the world and all it has to offer from the view of the unlimited, unified field of transcendent Reality, then even the most ordinary thing, which we have seen and experienced a thousand times before, becomes fresh. It seems entirely made anew, when actually the view has become clear enough to see it in its original radiant pattern. We are able to *see* it with the eyes of the heart, informed by Organic Innocence and the wisdom of original mind.

Practice and the Path

Lee Lozowick

The Natural Flow of Life

*A*t some point on the Path it is like a battle of titans—an equal fight between the great adversaries of ego and self. For most of us, that's where we start with practice, but we don't want to get stuck there. If you get stuck there, you can go back and forth for years and years. You have to get to the point where you can't cheat anymore, which is a great advantage on the Path. If in fact it is true of you that you cannot cheat anymore, then you can progress in your practice. As long as you have a strong ego and a strong commitment to practice pitched in a battle with one another, you won't move on to the next stage, in which it is not a matter of which one wins; it is a matter of both sides of the conflict being established in a higher context, so that neither needs to assert itself independently, in conflict with the other.

In a relative sense, the world is a world of dualities. Many dualities are not in conflict—chocolate and sugar, for example, and mothers

and daughters, hopefully. In many other aspects, dualities are in conflict: fire and ice, tractors and grass. In reality, there is no conflict. It's
not paradoxical, it's not confusing, there is no problem. There is simply the arising of phenomena, each arising having a certain essential
nature. No winning or losing, no conflict, no fight. Ultimately that's
the only genuine resolve in which ego doesn't lose, because ego finds
itself established in its natural state, in which whatever of value it has
is offered and animated, and whatever is confusing and counterproductive and damaging simply doesn't get any traction—it doesn't
manifest. You want to consider this "battle" within the framework
of the higher context, in which there is no battle because there are
no opposites; in which the urge to practice easefully and gracefully
manifests. Then ego rests in a state in which it serves.

The easiest component of our makeup to manage is our body. As
things get more and more subtle, they become more difficult to control. Ultimately the answer is not *controlling* the mind; the answer is
found in surrender to the natural state of what is arising. But in the
short run, when you just need to get something done and the mind
is getting in the way—you are not finding the "to be one with," you
just aren't hitting that groove—the mind will not respond to gentle
or pleading requests. The mind responds to firm commands. If you
can be intensely firm, the mind will listen.

Whenever you are working with the body, mind or emotions,
you always want to remember that in the context of practice, it is not
about having control over mind, body and emotions. It's about estab-
lishing all the components of who we are in their natural arising in
the flow of life itself. When we are established in the natural arising
of the body, mind, and emotions, they will not be counterproductive
to the process of the Universe. In the beginning it requires trust and
a bit of faith in the ultimate unicity of the Universe. The Universe is
not like a big corporation that has some kind of perverse motive, and
we are going to get ground up in that motive. God is not a sadistic
dictator, who took my mother or my daughter or my brother, or who

won't let me be in relationship with a wonderful person—or whatever we curse God for. The Universe doesn't have feelings, emotions and mind.

While you are working with the body and the mind and the emotions, you want to realize that this is an on-the-path measure, which in itself is very useful but is not the ultimate practice. Every time you define something as being a means to an end, it builds your intention and the magnetic force toward the end. In India there is a practice called *neti neti*: "Not this, not this." Every time you say, "Not this, not this," you automatically reflect on, "Then what? If this isn't it, then what is?" It's not simply a negation; in fact it is a prayer to the Real.

Unicity in the Field of Practice

Reality is completely unitive. At the same time, we are always practicing and working within the world of duality: we have professional lives, relationships with people and social lives, and we live in a cultural milieu. We want to work intentionally in the world of duality; we do not want to be captured or hypnotized by the world of the relative. Because it *is* the world of the relative, we don't want to mistake the relative for the Absolute; at the same time, neither do we want to discount the relative as being meaningless, because the vast majority of humanity is identified with the relative.

Maybe we have a beautiful clarity—a pristine, enlightened viewpoint. One of my criteria for how enlightened people are is: How do they relate to people who are not enlightened? You can be sure that if someone is really enlightened, they are not looking down on people and thinking, "These poor unenlightened slobs. What do I have to do with them?" They have the same feelings and the same emotions and the same minds that we do. As Arnaud Desjardins said, even if someone's suffering is illusory, it is not illusory to *them*. They are suffering an illusory suffering as if it were completely real.

We remember ourselves every time we function intentionally in the relative world in a relative way. We can affirm, "This is not the ultimate practice, *and* this is what I'm doing right now, this is what I need to do right now." That act of awareness is, in fact, automatically and naturally drawing us toward the Absolute, because you cannot have one pole of a pair of opposites without the other. They both exist. When "yes" exists, then "no" exists. When light exists, darkness also exists. When the relative exists, the Absolute exists. When we consciously recognize the relative, we are also—perhaps unconsciously, but definitively—recognizing the Absolute in some way.

Of course, we want to realize the Absolute consciously. We think that we want to realize the Absolute because we have the idea that realizing the Absolute is the end of the Path: that's winning, that's enlightenment. If we ignore the relative and only look at the Absolute, believing that we can leave this disaster behind us, then we become oblivious. That may not be such a good idea, because we become focused on "God, God, God," while our family is falling apart, we can't support ourselves, we can't even pay the rent. We create all kinds of suffering around us while we are saying, "God, God, God."

When we are conscious of the relative world, and we accept that it is relative, we are automatically reinforcing our commitment and intention to realize the Absolute consciously. The aim of practice is about consciousness; it's not about winning or reaching a goal. Even then, when we are really conscious about the relative, the distinction starts to fade because it is all unitive. If someone says they are conscious of the Absolute, and it's obvious that they are *unconscious* of the relative, then we have to look at their declaration with some question. When there is consciousness, those distinctions don't get made, except to make conversation. Yes, we need to make distinctions to write a book or make a definition, but in fact those distinctions don't get made. What difference does it make if something is relative or absolute if we're conscious? No difference. That's one of the secrets of the practice.

It sneaks up on you. There you are, all concerned that you're stuck in the relative and not making progress and being a terrible candidate to discipleship, then one day—*if* you're practicing right-ly—you just realize that the distinctions you've been making have been unnecessary and unrealistic in fact. You realize that "what is *is,* as it is, here and now." You realize it's all Just This. To say, "This is relative, this is Absolute," is labeling—that's all.

That's a little heady—a little heady for me! But it is really impor-tant, because people get stuck on not wanting to do "lower" practice. We only want to do "higher" practice, but we don't even know what higher practice is. There is no such thing as lower practice, except maybe no practice! The important point is that there is unity within the field of practice.

We tend to transpose our ordinary psychological relationship to life onto the Path: we are very concerned with our reputations and with being good little boys and girls who won't go to hell. It is help-ful *not* to do that. It's not necessary to keep demeaning ourselves, assuming that we've got a terrible practice because we're not surf-ing on rainbows and communing with diamond Buddhas! Would you know the results of practice if they showed? Often the results of practice are dramatic but subtle, and the external appearance of things doesn't change all that much. If practice produced profound results and those results were interior, would you even know?

It's very common for people to make bad decisions because we don't trust our impulse. The impulse is telling us one thing and the convincing outer world is telling us something else. Even though we have an impulse to realize that we have had profound changes take place, the mind is looking for confirming results. We expect the clouds to open up and rain gold and diamonds on us, or for people to say, "You're so different!" Or we want our relationship to work. Maybe none of those things are the result of practice. Would we even recognize the results of practice if they showed up? My recommen-dation is to stop looking for results. Just practice, and assume that the profound Benediction of the Path and the lineage is taking care of things in its own way and time.

Attitude and Practice

When the flame of your enthusiasm for the Path mellows, don't make an unnecessary effort to bring the flame back. You look at the situation with clarity and honesty and ask yourself, "Where is this lack of enthusiasm coming from? Is it me? Or have I just been in this phase long enough, and I need to move on?" You ask yourself those questions whenever you're feeling this lack of enthusiasm here and now, when it's really with you. Don't make it a problem or try to bring back the past—which you can't do, because even if you hit a new wave of enthusiasm, it's going to be different because the past is the past. Now is not the past.

So when this feeling of lack of enthusiasm comes up, you just look at it—straight, clear. You don't judge it as wrong or wish it would go away, you just look at it, without judgment. Simply say, "This is what's here now." There is an inherent question, which you don't even have to language, which is: "What is this? It's different than it used to be, so what is it now?" If you're able to see it that way, then the answer will come, in one form or another. Maybe the answer will be a new wave of enthusiasm that is different than the last one, because this is now, that was then. Maybe it will be an offer for a different kind of work that seems very attractive to you.

When you are looking for an answer to a question, you want to relax the rigidity of your attitudes and expectations, because the answer comes through circumstance: something happens, or we find ourselves with a certain opportunity or lack of opportunity. Maybe the house burns down, and that is the answer to a very deep and searching question we have had. Many times the answer comes circumstantially, but we still have the question because we are looking for an answer in a particular form and our vision is narrow. Because we have a fixated and rigid idea, we don't recognize the answer.

For example, a lot of single people are looking for a relationship, but they have very rigid criteria for what kind of person they are looking for. Many of us have found through personal experience that we can be very happy with someone who is not our "type." If we had studied that person deeply, we might have said, "No, they're just not my type," and yet once we are involved, somehow we find, "This is really working; this is great!" The way we establish criteria is sometimes very conscious: "I want this kind of person with these kinds of qualities." Obviously if you read the personal ads in magazines, you see that people have very specific requirements, but when we have such rigid definitions, we miss *fantastic* opportunities.

Again, we want to cultivate a mood of relaxing and just seeing what shows up; be prepared to check out what shows up right there on the spot, when it shows up. Chögyam Trungpa Rinpoche called this "on-the-spot-ness." Cultivate an attitude of openness and possibility so that you can see what happens in the next moment, because with professional work, relationship and many things, our greatest life opportunities come when we least expect them and from the least expected place.

So, the practice is to cultivate the mood of, "Let's see what's going to happen next." It doesn't take a lot of physical time to consider most opportunities. If you are buying a building, it takes some time to check out the roof and foundation and make sure they aren't eaten away by termites. You need to check out the plumbing and electricity, and there is some time involved in that. If you are offered the opportunity to get into business with somebody, or take over a business, yes, there is some time involved in investigating possible partners. Is some debt associated with the business? What is the market like? If you are considering a relationship, you want to know how many times the person has been married in the last two years. In fact, are they still married? And how many children do they have? How deep in debt are they?

At the same time you want to cultivate this attitude: What could show up here? It might be renewed enthusiasm, and it might be something completely beyond your imagination, something you never thought of. We want to cultivate the attitude of investigation, so we can leap on an opportunity in a moment; at the same time, we do not want to be impulsive, because if we are naïve relative to the consequences of the opportunity, we can get carried away in some infatuation or impulsiveness and make very big mistakes.

Many opportunities can be essentially seen as they are, including whatever consequences might be associated with the opportunity, just in the moment, on the spot. At the same time, we can get into a lot of trouble if we are impulsive about engaging opportunities, based on an emotional response instead of seeing clearly and knowing what the consequences of engaging the opportunity will be. So we also want to observe ourselves when we are cultivating this attitude of wonder and here-and-now-ness. Are we the kind of person who is impulsive and doesn't check things out? Do we see clearly? We want to have a sense of ourselves, of who we are, when something comes and we're feeling the pull to be carried away.

Of course it's possible to make an error, realize that you've made an error, grow up and go on about your life—but I wouldn't count on the consequences being that simple. It's better to avoid the error in the first place. Once an error is made, it's better to cut our losses and walk away as adults than to get stuck in some swamp—feeling like a victim, that our lives have been ruined, and all that nonsense.

It is easy to say "yes" about wonderful things. "Yes, I have great job. Yes, I have great kids." But practice is about accepting whatever life is, in this moment, here and now. Life is what it is, therefore "yes," because "no" creates conflict and emotionality and struggle. So the intelligent response is "Yes, this is what is," because no amount of wishing it wasn't makes it any different than it is. So you want to cultivate the mood or practice of acceptance *and* a sense of who you are, your tendencies, your psychological labyrinth.

Of course, knowing human nature, anything can become just another rigid attitude. "Let's see what's going to happen next," can become just another dogmatic obsession, so you also want to cultivate a mood of softness and vulnerability, so you aren't waiting for what's going to happen next like a cat ready to jump on a mouse. You're just moving through life with a sense of wonder and possibility and openness, so if an opportunity shows up, you're willing to genuinely consider it. Big, life-changing opportunities don't show up every week. In fact, you may go twenty years before an opportunity shows up, or it may never show up. You cultivate an *attitude* of being-here-now-ness, rather than waiting with a demanding expectation: "Okay! I know something is going to show up, and I'm going to *grab* it."

If nothing happens, well, at least you can enjoy the majesty of a perfect sunset, or a beautiful moon on a clear night, because something that ordinary and unadorned could be the very opportunity we are waiting for—except we think it's going to be the perfect partner, or winning the lottery or the perfect profession. Yes, it could just be the moon on a clear night that we are waiting for. Or it could be a selfish, wicked bitch. After all, look at the poetry that Baudelaire wrote—ahh! And what was the catalyst? A selfish, wicked bitch! But oh, that sublime poetry! Of course, some people don't like to read Baudelaire because it depresses them; they find him dark and negative. I don't. I'm just completely stirred by him. The way I read Baudelaire is as a testament to the Beloved.

Compassion

It is my opinion that the guru/disciple relationship ultimately leads to a greater, deeper understanding of Reality, which allows one who has such an understanding to align with the natural process of universal unfolding, instead of getting in the way of it. The other opinion is that everything—no matter what it is—is perfect as it is. In such perfection, no one could interfere with the natural unfolding of the Universe, because no matter what everyone is doing, it is part of the natural unfolding of the Universe. That is a very reasonable philosophy, and it might be true, but it's not my philosophy. My philosophy is that we can either help or interfere. We can serve the Universe or we can slow things down; we can be annoying little insects in the face of the Universe.

The whole reciprocal process of student/teacher and teacher/ student is about the Blessing Force of the Universe creating greater alignment amidst great dissonance. Of course, that is just philosophy, because what does it mean when you and I get up in the morning? We are trying to deal with the demand to practice, the demand to bring integrity to our professional lives, to respect and honor those with whom we are in relationship, personally as well as professionally. Not to mention that we are paying bills, which for some people is very easy and for some people is a little more problematical. We are not so completely detached that these kinds of demands do not touch us, so the real issue is: How am I going to manage today?

There are two poles to this consideration: the ultimate pole, in which all of the effort that we put into practice has a certain effect down the line, and ultimately there is some transformation going on; and then there is the pole of day-to-day life. How do we handle emotional upsets? Crushing disappointments? Profound losses? In the past year, three people who are very close to me have had daughters in their early twenties die in unexpected, sudden circumstances. How do we deal with something like that? The teaching has a lot of deep ideas that are fun to consider sometimes, but practically speaking, how do we deal with the shocks of life in the here and now? Somebody who loses a child never gets over it; it is with them for their lifetime. The immediate emotional devastation will be contextualized and absorbed in the process of grieving, but although in some ways we recover and go on, we will never get over such a loss.

My whole teaching process has moved very dramatically since the beginning from an almost exclusive engagement with mystical philosophy—which is all true but not practical—to an emphasis on practical application. How do we deal with disappointments and betrayals and good fortune? Good fortune is just as hard to deal with as bad, believe it or not. For example, the research in America has shown that in almost every case when somebody who is not wealthy wins a lottery of millions of dollars, it usually ruins their lives. So, it's not just about how we deal with disappointment; how do we deal with good fortune—or really *big* good fortune? Most people sabotage it through emotional warfare. What goes along with fame and fortune? Some pretty big demands, not just to have integrity and to use your ego well, but to grab onto the devil's tail and hold on for the ride.

In a very practical sense, how do we take care of the ordinary aspects of our lives in the context of this higher vision? How do we deal with the fact that people we love are late all the time, and it drives us crazy? There are little things that go on all day long, from the minute you get up in the morning to the minute you go to sleep at night. Suppose you're a therapist and a control freak, and your schedule is very regulated: somebody calls up five minutes before their appointment and says, "Sorry, I can't make it today." Ah, that must drive you crazy! How do you deal with it? Some people eat doughnuts.

My teaching is becoming more and more tacit and less and less articulated. It is not about eloquent discussions of the most refined cosmic principles of Reality; it's about dealing with real daily problems. You're married and you haven't had sex in two months. How do you deal with it? If you're my age, it's a big pain in the ass, but for young people? When I was young, I would never go without sex. If I was fighting with my partner, I'd say, "Who gives a shit, let's have sex and fight later!"

So, how do we deal with the immediate circumstances of our lives? For instance, if we find ourselves without money. We were in a gas station a couple of weeks ago on tour, and I pulled out my money to make the proper change. I said to myself, "As soon as I get the change, I'll put it back." When I walked out of the store, I realized I had left my money on the counter. Fortunately I don't carry a lot of money around, so it wasn't very much money. I ran back in the store.

I was in France, and I can be understood in French, but not when I'm asking somebody if they saw my money. So it was like, "No, I don't speak English—is that French you're speaking? Don't understand a word of it!" I said, "Was there some money on the counter?" "No."

One of two things had happened: either the person in line after me took the money, or the girl behind the counter took the money. I wasn't annoyed with them; I was annoyed with myself for leaving my money on the counter. The money was gone, so I shrugged my shoulders and said, "Well, somebody had a good day!" I hope the person who got the money really made good use of it.

So, how do we deal with day-to-day occurrences? That is the dilemma we find ourselves in. How do we deal with traffic jams? How do we learn to deal with the ordinary things that provoke us and shock us and alienate us in life? That is where my teaching is aiming these days. Obviously some degree of education is useful, but that's not entirely it. You can't give a class on peace of mind. You can't solve everybody's problems, but you can give some useful hints and some great examples and maybe even some little exercises to do.

The higher ideas can be exhilarating, and they have their time and place—but, unless the higher ideals are integrated into our ordinary mode of life, they don't help us deal with the immediate circumstances of our lives. Higher ideals can help us profoundly, for example, if you understand that to take from somebody is to take from yourself, then you think more deeply before taking. Higher ideas can help if they are integrated into our ordinary mode of relationship to life, but most of us never let those ideas get in that deeply because the implications are uncomfortable.

If you study astronomy, for instance, and you look through a big telescope at the vastness of space, our little solar system and galaxy is only one of an infinite number of galaxies and solar systems. Let's face it—in the big scheme of things, how important is any one individual anyway? We typically don't want to be confronted with the reality of that. Even those among us who will never produce a real work of art, who have failed relationships all of our lives, who will never add *anything* to the quality of life on Earth, still feel that we are really important! We don't want to integrate into the big picture, in which we're just one of an infinite number of sentient creatures struggling along, or to realize that the greatest contribution we can make to the Universe is not a function of our intelligence, our creative skills, or our capacity to produce. We want to serve the Universe by writing the perfect song, or painting the perfect picture, or coming up with the greatest invention for serving human comfort. We don't want to realize that the greatest form of help we can offer the Universe may be something as nebulous as having compassion for others. We just don't want to realize that, because we're too attached to our identification with the personal elements of our existence. But maybe that's it—the most profound way we can practice and serve the Universe is to feel compassion for others.

Mechanical Habits

To get with the Program in a very real, practical way is to allow yourself to be expressed, manifested, moved by the Blessing Force of Life—or the Intelligence of Life, we could say—in a way that serves the Work and is consistent with your skill, talent, intelligence, and health. "What's the Work?" you may ask. In essence, "the Work" is getting with the Program.[1]

The dilemma we find ourselves in is this: We are profoundly committed to the Path, to being decent human beings, and to service, whether the object of our service is a spiritual teacher, a spiritual

---

[1]   When Lee uses the vernacular term, "the Program," it is capitalized here to make the distinction that he is referring to the teaching phrases, "Surrender to the Will of God," and "The Great Process of Divine Evolution," which refers to the Will of God as it manifests in the ongoing sweep of time in a process of becoming—birth to death to rebirth—at all levels of being. To "get with the Program," then, is to Surrender to the Will of God and enter into the flow of the Great Process of Divine Evolution.

community, or the staff and clients in a psychiatric hospital, or the students in the school where we teach, or the plants in our garden. We wish to serve optimally, but nobody stops us from serving except us.

We keep ourselves from getting with the Program. Is it difficult to act in a way that is inconsistent with our psychological script? Yes, very difficult, no question! Can we do it? Yes, absolutely, we can do it. James Hillman said that when you start to function objectively, it will feel wrong to you because it's dissonant to your habit pattern. If you have a habit pattern of self-hatred and you find yourself acting in a way that is full of confidence and personal authority, it will feel to you as if you are doing something very wrong, because what is comfortable is your self-hatred. Hillman said that when you start to be different, you will need to have discipline to stay with it, because it's going to feel wrong. The mind will say, "See, this is wrong. This is not right."

Even though the mind and emotions are telling you it's not right, you have to stay with it until you build a new habit in the domain of objective behavior instead of animating your usual psychological script behavior. That's what we're up against—a big wall that you can't get above or below or around because you can only go through it. Since the mind is very certain that you cannot move through walls, it seems impossible. I have students who are profoundly devoted to this Path, who genuinely want to get with the Program. They are sincere, hard-working and dedicated, and everything they do is a function of their mechanicality. They keep saying, "How can I be different?" and I keep saying, "By being different."

We are up against our gross external habits, which would be obvious to us if they were someone else's habits. Because they are our habits, we don't see them. How do you be different? You start where you can. How difficult is it to watch yourself for a couple of weeks and figure out your patterns? Look at what you always do. For example, when you brush your teeth at night, first you use the brush, then the floss, then the sonic—in that specific order—and that is what you do every night. How difficult would it be to see that for twenty years, every time you brush your teeth, you brush, floss, sonic—*every* time? How difficult would it be to floss first, and then use the brush, then the water?

You may say, "That's not difficult, I could do that." But the thing is, we don't do it, even when we're given an exact picture of our habitual behavior. In the Gurdjieff Work, self-observation is the essential foundation upon which all other practice takes place. You watch yourself for a couple of weeks (or a couple of years!), you observe yourself, and you see your gross external patterns. Watch anybody eating: some people make sure they separate every pea from the potatoes, while others always have the peas and potatoes mixed. Some people always cut their food, put the knife down then pick up the fork, take one piece, put it in their mouths, put down the fork down. We all have absolutely mechanical patterns of eating. How difficult is it to figure out your pattern and do something different?

How do you be different? Be different. How do you know what to be different about? It's as obvious as the fact that you're sitting in a chair semi-conscious, fighting off sleep. It's obvious! You watch yourself. If you are vain, you are always watching yourself in a certain way. Your whole life is about your hair or your clothes or your complexion or your ass. Start paying attention to the things you usually don't pay any attention to. You walk into a room and scan the room; what are you looking for? Different people look for different things. When you walk into a room, most of you are looking for some advantage, even if the advantage is to be invisible because you're so full of self-hatred. Sometimes you are checking out where you can hide. Then you look at the people. How difficult is it to figure that out? If you're minimally self-conscious, it's obvious! If you're a single woman or man, and you don't want to be single, the first thing you do when you walk in the room is to scan the room for who's single. Are they good-looking? Could it work? You might think you're being subtle, but you aren't.

So, watch yourself for a couple of days, figure out your pattern, then make an agreement with yourself: "I'm going to walk in a room, and I'm going to look for something different." You force your mind to look for something different—anything, it doesn't matter what. The point is to interrupt the absolute mechanicality of the pattern. As James Hillman said, it will seem wrong to you; you might feel tremendous insecurity, because it feels wrong. It only seems to feel wrong because it's different, because you aren't following your habit pattern.

Everything starts with self-observation. You don't have to make gigantic gestures. You can do small things: the way you shift your gaze, the way you put your mind into a different thinking pattern, the way you hold your fork differently. Very small things have gigantic repercussions. You don't have to be some kind of hero; you don't have to climb Mount Everest: "Okay, I'm going to confront my fear!" You can just make small gestures. If you're afraid of snakes, how do you confront your fear? You do not say, "Okay, I'm afraid of snakes, so I'm going to milk the poison out of cobras!" You go to a reptile zoo and find someone who's trained and knows snakes and will help you play for a few minutes with a snake that is not poisonous and will not bite.

You don't have to make dramatic gestures. Look at small things in your habitual behavior. How do you recognize your absolutely mechanical behavior? Watch yourself, pay attention. All the little rituals that we have are obvious. How we get into the car; how we sit behind the wheel and check all the buttons. Everybody has a pattern. Even meditation can become a habit. We can meditate just as mechanically as we do anything else. In the Zen tradition, before you sit down to meditate you pick up the pillow, mush it around, put it down and then you sit. That relationship to the pillow wakes you up for a second and tells you, "Don't sit mechanically." If we don't enter into the process of meditation being reminded that meditation could become just another mechanical habit, it will.

You can use anything as a reminding factor, like looking at a picture on the wall. Obviously the argument is: "What if that becomes a habit?" Anything could become a habit. Something you use to remind you not to be habitual can become a habit! When you sit to meditate, you need to be conscious, but only for a second; you don't have to stay conscious when you're meditating. You only have to be conscious that you do not want to be habitual in your meditation during the moment that you are sitting down. If you're conscious in that second, your body takes care of the rest of it.

Yes, new habits can develop. Gurdjieff said that new habits form in two weeks and become just as mechanical as what you were doing before the new habit. We are all mechanical. Part of working with that is accepting it without judgment. To self-observe and make a small change in a habit pattern does not mean that what we work for is changing every small pattern that we have, so that we are just exchanging one set of habits for another group of habits.

You are a holistic being: mind, emotions, feelings, aura, causal mind, astral mind, etheric mind—all of that is a part of you, holistically, but none of it *is* you. You are non-problematical, tacit awareness of Reality, completely transcendent to time and space. Transcending time and space means in every moment, without effort in a natural process. Awareness *is*. We don't have to do anything about awareness. Awareness has been covered up with layer after layer after layer. The typical metaphor is the onion—you peel one layer then there is another and another and another.

When you interrupt the pattern it creates a crack in all the layers, and at the base of that crack is you as perfect, pristine awareness. Whenever there is even an instantaneous crack in the pattern, you have the opportunity of being that which is already perfectly aware. None of the rest of the layers disappear necessarily, but they stop dominating and running you. That's the point.

Suffering

Someone was crying over a feeling of humiliation that she had failed in her practice. If a tidal wave came and swept someone away, and they were powerless in the face of such a natural force, would you say that they were humiliated? No. So why would you feel humiliated in the face of such natural forces as anger, fear, pride or vanity? What can we ordinary people do in the face of something like that? One of the mantras of the ordinary neurotic is, "I couldn't help it." When we are carried away by our passions, instead of saying, "I can't help myself," say, "I *can* help myself, and I'm going to practice, practice, practice until practice is non-problematical. No matter how many times I may miss the mark, I'm going to continue."

If you are a tightrope walker working without a net, if you miss the mark the consequences are extreme. If you are working with ego and you miss the mark, what can happen? Maybe we feel some shame, humiliation or disappointment, but none of that need alter the course of our lives. In extreme cases of psychoses people allow those emotions to create harm, burning themselves with cigarettes or taking it out on others, but that's the exception to the rule. Ordinarily, for ordinary people, when we are working with ego on the Path and we fall short of the mark, the consequences are minor.

Having fear, anger, pride or ambition is not a problem; just don't give it authority over you. Recognize that you are suffering. When suffering arises as a result of various vectors of life that intersect, then we do our best to meet it with maturity and to practice with and through it. It's never pleasant. When it's there, it's there—so we try to make it useful. Many people on the Path ask if there is value in suffering. Suffering either drives us to practice or away from practice. When it drives us to practice or a deeper reliance on the master, then it has some value.

There is no more inherent value to suffering than to beauty. If we make use of suffering, then it has value to the Path; it's the same thing with beauty in all its forms, living and not living. For example, many people become parents for the wrong reasons. Any parent who is open and heart sensitive will be completely transformed by the beauty of the child. If not, they keep abusing their children. Just having a child does not mean that we learn anything at all—we have to make use of the situation. If not, they don't. Similarly, the common belief in some spiritual systems is that suffering is good. Like the Christian penitents: people gave themselves pain because they believed that God wanted them to suffer. I've never been able to support that philosophy—*and*, suffering arises, in the body, in the mind, in the world. When we intersect with suffering, whether we make it useful or not depends on the strength of our practice.

Any trouble that appears to be going on is just clouds over the landscape, just a little breeze kicking up dust. Trying to come to conclusions about the future in the present moment is useless. Time will tell, that wicked Bitch! She always does. So, clarity will come over time. Trust the Universe.

Practice Becomes What We Are

There is a tremendous amount of help available, and you have to use the help for it to be effective. The primary form of help is practice. Whether we feel the practice is effective or not, we have to keep practicing. Sometimes we are practicing and the practice is effective, but we don't know it because we are looking for some result. In our fantasy, we imagine that if we were practicing correctly we would be happy all the time; we would be in ecstasy, with our feet barely touching the ground when we walk. Everything would be crystal clear, and we would never have any inner drama! Maybe we are doing the best we can, and we're actually practicing pretty well, but we are looking for some different result than what is present. Maybe we're not trying to practice at all, because we're insecure that we're not doing it right, so we don't bother trying—which is very common, everywhere. Or, we feel confident that we are practicing as well as we know how, and in spite of that, we are struggling with some things in our lives.

The core practice—*dzogchen, mahamudra,* "accepting what is as it is here and now," Just This, or whatever the essential practice of the tradition may be called—is always the primary and basic form of help that is offered on the Path. Then there are derivative practices, because the simplicity of the core practice is simply beyond most people. The core practice is so simple we can't believe that's it! So, derivative practices are given to help us, to always point back to the basic practice. There are other forms of help: the guru and senior students of the school. If we are not using all of those sources of help, then we have to cut through our dramas as best we can—sort of shooting in the dark, as we say, expecting to hit the target when we can't see anything.

When we were in India in January, 2008, I was still eating anything I wanted to eat. My favorite Indian dessert is called gulab jamen—fried cakes soaked in thick, sweet syrup. We were in Bengal, walking in the temple markets in Tarapith, and we saw gigantic woks filled with gulab jamen. Some of them were big balls of cake and some were long rope-like cakes. I bought some for the teenage kids and myself. The cakes were warm and soft and just soaked with incredible syrup. I was so absorbed in eating them that I remarked to one of my students, "Boy, I hope this isn't the last thing I think of before I die, because if what they say is true, I'm going to come back as a big, fat, juicy gulab jamen!"

In any event, there is no need to worry about death, if you are practicing. If you're not practicing, you *may* want to worry a little bit, just in case it's true that how we show up next is defined by our last thought. Maybe it's true if you believe it's true; maybe it's not true if you don't believe it's true. We create more of the world of duality than we can possibly imagine. But, if you are truly practicing, you don't have to worry about the moment before death, because every moment is a moment of practice, and whatever the last moment is will be perfect for you as it is. If practice is true of you, then you don't have to design or engineer some program so you will be thinking the right thing at the moment of death.

I took a program once to train my voice, in which one process involved getting into a human-sized gyroscope. Once you were in the gyroscope, the voice teacher would spin it, and you would have to maintain certain tonal qualities while it was spinning all over the place. I'm not crazy about spinning things under any circumstances. When my kids were small and we used to go to carnivals, I never went on the rides because I don't like those things—but, I was committed to the program and trusted the teacher, so I said, "I'm going to get in this thing and do what he says."

As he was walking me up to the gyroscope, I was imagining what it must have been like walking up to the guillotine, because I was really in survival. All the way up, I was singing the tone he told me to sing, and I was singing it perfectly. I started to get really confident: Okay, I've got this tone down, no problem. So he strapped me in, and the gyroscope went upside down and I was singing the tone perfectly. Then, the minute he spun the thing—gone! I wasn't gone, but the perfect tone was gone.

I imagine the moment of death is something like that—you're saying the mantra like crazy, you know you're going to die. The mantra is going, you're on automatic, "I've really got it!" and at the moment of death...gone! All you're thinking of is your mother! Your family gets to say, "The last thing he said was, "Mommy!" A friend of mine was with a very famous Sufi when he died, and he said that the Sufi was weeping for his mother, like an abandoned baby, at the moment of death.

If your practice is steady and reliable, then the moment of death is yours. It belongs to you; you possess it, completely, entirely, totally. If you are not practicing, it doesn't matter, because a stimulus as profound as the moment before death is far too big for the mere mind to override it. Again, it's back to practice. All the great, searching questions of life are resolved in the moment of practice: to become one with. Then whatever happens at the moment of death, it doesn't matter. What happens at the moment of death only matters in *time*—in the flow of past, present, future. When we are remorseful about our past and hopeful about our future, then what happens at the moment of death matters.

It doesn't matter why you came to the Path. If we are realistic, most people's initial motive for coming to the Path is selfish. Mine was power. For others it is health or security or to be relieved from suffering. When I first came to the Path, I didn't know there was any suffering to encounter—I was great! My motive was power. Of course there is something subtle, something essential that attracts us to the Path, while in the gross world we are usually attracted to the Path for reasons other than what the Path actually is.

Sooner or later we will want what the Path has to offer to us instead of expecting the Path to give us what we want. What the Path has to offer is to disappear into Just This, into "what is as it is, here and now." By definition, to "become one with" is to lose the sense of perspective that keeps us stuck in illusion and duality. Yes, death and birth are profound changes, shifts, in the world of duality. To "be one with" as a state of being, not doing, is to be the same under any circumstances: life, death, the moment of birth. We are simply present with what is, as we are, essentially connected to the field of all that is. Just This.

This does not mean that we are entirely passive. When you are one with, you are not like a piece of wood floating on the ocean; you are the ocean itself, responsive to various currents. If there is a storm, at least on the surface, the ocean is responsive to the storm, which is different than when the ocean is calm. When there is an earthquake on the floor of the ocean, there is tremendous passion!

We are the same. When we are "one with" life, we are moved relative to our circumstances. The ocean is never other than the ocean, and given its ocean-ness, it responds to stimuli based on what it is, as an ocean. We are human beings: we respond to stimuli given our human being-ness. We are in relationship with people and things and art. We are sometimes active, sometimes passive, sometimes suffering the cruelty of nations and genocide, sometime elated by someone's smile, the beauty in the song of a bird. So, if we really have a sense of the Path, everything comes down to practice, until practice is what we *are*, not what we do.

Hauteville, France
July 2007

Are You True or False?

M. Young

The first day of June 2008 finds us at the Baul ashram, the jewel in Lord Vishnu's crown called Ferme de Jutreau—two three-hundred-year-old country farmhouses and a large stone barn set in the lush green world of Douce France. A few days at the ashram after being on the road for two weeks make a big difference in our quality of life. Living in the verdant countryside, bare feet on the sacred earth of the ashram with green grass underneath, we have the chance to breathe clean air, gaze at the sky and trees and gardens, eat the clean and natural diet of ashram fare.

Most importantly, when we arrive at Ferme de Jutreau, on Sunday nights Lee gives darshan. Being on the road for extended periods of time, my appetite for dharma gets sharpened; tonight we were hungrily poised for the banquet as we gathered in the meditation hall—a large room in the ashram's big stone barn. Large bouquets of flowers from the ashram gardens graced the shrines and dais, while a hundred ghee flames danced in the four-tiered black stone *arati* lamp, cheerfully and steadily sending their golden glow out into the space.

From his seat on the dais, Lee's first words to the gathered pilgrims were, "We are always being given opportunities by Life to see whether we are false or true." He continued:

> *We are always being given opportunities to see if our discrimination is true. It really should weigh on you to be accurate in your perceptions, to be able to represent that perception diplomatically if necessary, bluntly if necessary and with stunning sophistication if necessary. Are you true or false? Is your discrimination reliable?*

Lee's words could not have more apropos if he had looked at me intently, assessed my inner state, and then commented to me personally. Instead, he tossed out into the general space of the gathered sangha this perfect teaching commentary for whoever could make use of it. He presented these teaching statements, so very salient for practice on the Path of Enlightened Duality, then posed the following questions:

> *Are you here for the right reason? It would appear to the outside observer that you all have great faith in me. You've made the decision to be here, and it is the right decision—the right choice—but it's like in relationship: What's love got to do with it? There is a song I wrote on the new CD, called "So Hard," which is about how easy it is to fall in love, but it's so hard to stay in love—with the same person, that is! So, what's love got to do with it? Because the Path is like being in a relationship. Once you get into it, you feel kind of stuck! It's easy to get into, hard to get out!*
>
> *How many of us are here because of poor discrimination? There is no question that we are in love, but this is not romance—this is the Work! This is guru yoga! If*

you don't contextualize love in its proper domain, you
can easily make good choices for the wrong reasons.
Gurdjieff once said that making the right choice for the
wrong reasons is not good enough; in order to mature
in the Work, you have to make the right choice for the
right reason.

It was a useful series of questions that Lee posed to us: Is your discrimination true? Are you true or false? Are you here, on the Path, for the right reasons? It is one thing to fall in love with a dynamic spiritual teacher; it is another thing to commit oneself fully to the Path which the teacher embodies. The Path has many different dimensions—it is both empty and full, simple and complex. With Lee, many of us fall in love with the devotional aspects of his teaching and then come up against the ferocity of the nondual underpinnings of the Path or the razor's edge of its tantric dimensions—the hard work of radical transformation.

Lee often articulates this in the Gurdjieffian language of "the Work." If we are engaged with a real teacher, sooner or later we will come up against aspects of his or her teaching or manifestation of spiritual work that we find extremely difficult to savor. Maybe we have fallen in love with the community of the sangha. Lots of people visit our ashrams and comment on what a great community we have, how loving and kind we are, how beautiful and bright our children are. But this is seen without realizing that the foundation of that community is built upon a life of discipline and stringent self-examination.

"Practice" is a very big word. It refers not only to specific disciplines or yogas but also to an entire lifestyle, a way of being, a mood and context underlying every action, breath, thought. The ongoing flow of our lives is the ground of our practice. The context of true spiritual life is that everything is God-referenced rather than self-referenced. This is not just a huge challenge, a seemingly impossible goal, a daunting journey of a lifetime; it is a commitment to a certain interior annihilation of egoic concerns. If we come to spiritual life seeking another version of "the good life," we are in for some serious shocks as time goes on and we are confronted with the demands of the Path to become *sunyas*—nothings.

Lee's discourse had segued into another arena altogether as he continued:

> *As every good Baul does, we use whatever we find that is useful, wherever it comes from. Sometimes couples go into psychotherapy and realize that they got into the relationship for the wrong reasons, and they begin to question the basis of the relationship. I say: So what? If you are in love, who cares? If you are in love, protect what you have. My viewpoint is: Love matters; psychology does not matter.*
>
> *Relationships need love and sex. We are neurotic animals, and at the same time, we are sublime, potentially enlightened God-creatures—we are sages! We need love for the sage and sex for the animal! If you are in relationship, you can't pretend that there isn't an animal that will rear up and tear the face off anyone who tries to hurt its children. That animal needs sex once in a while, and if the sex is great, the animal wants it all the time. So, a working relationship needs love and sex. It's better if the sex is good, because the better it is, the more trust you have in your partner, and wanting sex becomes a sweetness instead of a bitterness.*
>
> *If you are in love in any way, you are a fool to allow your psychology to destroy that love—and it can destroy it, because love can be the strongest thing in the Universe, but it can also be extremely delicate. So if there is love, you want to protect it. Of course, there*

are times when we can't stay in a relationship, if we are in a relationship with an alcoholic or drug addict. Sometimes it just doesn't work.

Discrimination is important, so you make the right choices for the right reasons. Being here on the Path, you have made the right choice, and if you made it for the wrong reason—no problem! Simply learn and re-make the decision for the right reason. Every morning when you get up you have to re-dedicate yourself to the Path, as an act of devotion—as a vote, as a sign to the Universe. "You can still count on me, God. Still here." That's what morning puja is all about.

A few days later, back on the road, Lee's words came back into focus during an early morning *puja* in the stone surroundings of an eight hundred year old windowless underground room in the belly of Paris, called "the Crypt," where we were spending the night as guests. There are many such places in Paris, where centuries ago deep cellars, storage rooms, vaults, wine caves and crypts were built to accommodate many different needs of city dwellers in those eras. Unimaginable numbers of lives have come and gone in the archaic underground of these city dwellings, many of which have been remodeled and turned into spaces used today for many practical purposes, including the Crypt—a psychotherapy space where people come for group or individual counseling sessions.

Like many places in Europe, there was a tangible presence of ancient life that had imbued the walls with subtle energies over the centuries of birth, life and death. On this morning, it was just me and the ghosts, those denizens of the underground, in the Crypt, while others of our party took a walk on the streets or slept one level above. Feeling a bit provoked by the unseen companions, I chanted the name of Yogi Ramsuratkumar through sun salutations and a string of *asanas*.

The question Lee had posed days ago reasserted itself: Am I true in this moment, or am I false? Can the Divine count on me today? I felt pretty silly, being squeamish over a little ghost or two, when my teacher has trained me to handle this and much more over the years—like the *smashan* (cremation ground) in Tarapith, Bengal, which easily comes to mind. Even more, we have had encounters with entities and beings of many kinds in steamy dark bars and clubs where Lee's bands have played over the years, in America and Europe.

Like the club in Amsterdam, where the blues band Shri was booked to play from midnight to three a.m. many years ago. The scene on the dance floor was out of a sordid movie. We were tightly packed together with the crowd of about two hundred, right in the pulse of things, sharing sweat and breathing each other's carbon dioxide along with the thick smoke from cigarettes, cigars and marijuana. Men moved through the throng of people, trawling for easy sex, while women ran back and forth to the toilets to snort another line of cocaine.

Danger flowed on the currents of the night like a dark, heady wine. One man stood in front of the band and screamed at the musicians and dancers; he threw his body into spastic gyrations in an imitation of dance, his passions roiling up and spilling out in frantic distortions of movement. His anger was hot and explosive; it seemed as if his aggression could turn ugly and spin out of control at any moment. But he was just the most obvious element of the dark entities that prowled the surreal night, tinged as it was with people's desperation and a dark kind of wonder. The opportunity, of course, was to practice right there, on the edge.

Back in the present moment, in the unseen world of the Crypt, I considered: in every situation we are given the choice to practice, or not practice. I considered further: There are many types of smashans. This is just another opportunity to accept whatever situation I find myself in and understand that this too is empty: fear arises and subsides. Fear of the unknown, like all things, is essentially empty. It is another opportunity to recognize that "I" am not separate from whatever I encounter.

Continuing on with the practices, I kept chanting, "Yogi Ramsuratkumar, Yogi Ramsuratkumar, Yogi Ramsuratkumar, jaya guru raya," the mantra given by Yogi Ramsuratkumar to his devotees. All other images dissolved, and I soon found myself transported back to India. Scenes from Tiruvannamalai sprang to life, creating a sensation so vivid and real it was as if I was actually there again, living those moments and days in the physical company of Yogi Ramsuratkumar. In the early morning on the Yogi Ramsuratkumar Ashram, waiting in the sun for him to arrive by car, we stood in long orderly lines, breathing in the lush, moist air and looking up at the green flanks of Mt. Arunachala. Its rough peaks showed through drifts of white cloud as the mist dispersed in the growing heat, while black crows cawed raucously in staccato counterpoint to the melodious sound of our chanting.

As soon as Yogi Ramsuratkumar arrived our attention became sharpened and sweetened as we, the assembled devotees, stood with hands in *anjali mudra* to greet him while he was slowly driven past. Blessing us with upraised hands, his kind dark eyes looked out upon us with truly infinite compassion and spoke of universes upon universes and a flow of knowledge that coursed far beyond the known boundaries of this Earth. The car disappeared behind the temple where we would join Yogi Ramsuratkumar for *darshan*.

Yogi Ramsuratkumar always told his devotees, "Say this beggar's name one time with faith, and this beggar will be there to bless you." Suddenly, the strong loving presence of Yogi Ramsuratkumar dawned like the sun in the windowless, airless underground world of ancient stone.

The presence of the lineage gurus had imbued the space with a subtle radiance that slowly permeated the dank traces of existence emanating from dry crumbling bones, mold, and insects you could not see but knew were there.

Memory is a very mysterious dimension of life. Memory is a function of both the mind and body and the capacity for awareness of each. Somehow memory is a living thing—it is not limited to the constraints of linear time. Sacred memories live like seeds in the body-mind complex and can spring to life when they are watered with the rain of our focused attention, particularly when attention is imbued with intention. It is a form of invocation. Memories of Yogi Ramsuratkumar, for example, spring to life when I meditate upon him, as the *Guru Gita* says, "Like the wasp upon the worm."

There is an old gospel song called "Precious Memories," sung by Aretha Franklin and recorded many years ago. It says: "Precious memories, how they linger, how they ever stir my soul!" The song goes on to tell us that in the stillness of the midnight, these memories return to tell us "sacred secrets of the soul." For most of us, solitude and quiet are essential to retrieving these memories.

Sacred memories are linked to the transmission of the Divine which has been made to an individual. A *jivanmukta* such as Yogi Ramsuratkumar transmits his state of Surrender to the Will of God to anyone who places their attention upon him. The guru transmits through glance, touch, sound and through invisible means that may be telepathic or energetic.

It is a viable form of invocation to remember moments when we were aware of the guru's transmission, or moments of *darsana*, or seeing Reality as it is, often in the form of receiving the guru's darshan. The key is to remember in a very specific way, as an act of intention, an act that can bring us into direct relationship with the vivid realness of the moment at hand. It is like fitting a key in a lock and turning it, so that the catch releases and the door opens. To remember in this way, we literally access sacred memories that contain the seed essence of a moment of divine transmission, when the soul has been touched and illumined. Remembrance, or Remembering God, can then be a doorway to "Life is real only then, when 'I am.'"

In Hindu traditions it is said that the guru passes the *jyoti*, or light of awakened consciousness, to the devotee. It is this moment of transmission at the most sublime and subtle level that is imprinted into our beings when we *see* the guru in the moment of darshan. We are illuminated by that seeing. Darsana is not the kind of seeing we experience when we look merely with our physical eyes; darsana may come through the physical eyes, but it is the intelligence of the subtle heart, the being itself, that receives when darshan occurs. In the presence of great realizers, there are many moments of true seeing and receiving, which might also be called moments of the guru's tranmission and can happen in the most ordinary of circumstances. Some of the most powerful moments of transmission in Lee's company have occurred in cafés, over dinner, riding the Metro in Paris, or when Lee was singing onstage with his bands.

Transmission of the sacred in any form that we experience receiving it is encoded deeply in the wise cells of the body, which have a great capacity for memory, from microcosm to macrocosm. The cells of the human body carry cosmic memory, archetypal memory, ancestral memory, and racial memory. They also carry what we might call alchemical memory. To tap into these is to make a gesture toward a moment in which we may bring the quality of enlightened awareness to our experience. Once we have received the guru's darshan, it is always happening; it is always accessible to us because it exists in the eternal now. Lee uses the phrase, "Remembering God," or simply, "Remembrance," to point toward this principle. Calling to Remembrance a powerful moment of the guru's transmission opens the door to what may be possible in any given moment.

The moment in the Paris underground world passed, like all things do. That's the thing about Ma Time: She is ever elusive. One minute Remembrance is alive in the body, then the moment passes and memory fades back into its hidden secret recesses. Finished with yoga, I rolled up my mat, extinguished the candle on the small puja, and walked up the ancient stone steps, smoothed and molded by countless climbing feet over eight long centuries. The spirits hovered about on the edges of perception, nothing more than incognizant shreds and wisps. They had no real power at all—just enough to make me aware of them. I wondered if the charged, subtle energy of Yogi Ramsuratkumar's name had attracted them, and now they were more curious than ever. Perhaps they were hopeful of some bit of light, or they were seeking liberation from their bondage in maya—a way to return to the source of all.

How does it happen that the spirit which animates an incarnation can be gone for hundreds of years yet something still hangs around in bits of a self that is not a self at all but only a poor remnant of lost possibility? It's a sobering glimpse into what it means to be a "lost soul"—lost in the labyrinthine hallways of time, unable to find one's way out, unaware of the liberating, shining light of vast space in Ma Kali's dark eyes. The scriptures say that it is only with the guru's grace that we can cross the ocean of samsara. Gratitude for the dharma, the guru and the company of *sadhakas* came into my awareness. Maybe the blessing of Yogi Ramsuratkumar's name was the possibility for those remnants—those lost revenants—to move toward cohesion and wholeness.

I made my way back to the upstairs room, where finally the natural light of day flooded in through the two barred windows that looked out upon the Paris street. Thinking of Lee's recent talk, I could testify today to the efficacy of morning puja, which might take many different forms for an individual on the Path. It might mean an hour of meditation, or chanting the gayatri mantra, a prayer to the deity of the sun, at dawn: *Om tat savitur varenyam bhargo devasya dhimahi dhiyo yo nah pracodayat om.* It might mean praying to Jesus or Mary Magdalene, or saying a hundred times, "Hail Mary, full of grace, blessed art thou among women, blessed is the fruit of Thy Womb, Jesus ...." It might mean loving service to one's family each morning, greeting one's children with kisses and hugs, preparing the food for the day, caring for others in any one of a hundred ordinary ways. Any genuine act of attentive kindness toward others can be a prayer, a kind of puja, a ritual of invocation. For today at least, in my corner of the world, I could say, "I am still here. Still here, Yogi Ramsuratkumar. You can count on me."

That night in the Crypt in Paris, after a meal with Lee and a number of his students in a space that resounded with silence and stone, we sat now in the very same room where the ghosts had emerged in the morning. A psychologist was talking about her clients with Lee and a few others. She said that she worked for a therapy center where her clients received free therapy.

I commented, "Well, that's the benefit of socialized medicine in France. But, do you remember what Freud said, about how clients do not benefit from therapy unless they pay for it?"

This inspired the psychologist to passionately assert that her clients were greatly benefiting and she could see it in them. Lee broke into her emphatic statements with the question, "How do you *know* you are helping people? Do you follow them home and watch them there, with their families, their children, their wives and husbands? No, I didn't think so. Psychotherapists are some of the most pretentious people of all—they think they know people, and they don't."

As she began to reassert that she was sure she was helping people, at least at the psychological level, Lee interjected again, saying, "She's all fired up now!" Good humor gleamed in his eyes, and he smiled at her in a way that invited her to parry with him further.

She looked at him and, attempting to relax her posture a little, said, "Okay, I'll calm down."

"I'd like to *see* you calm," Lee rejoined gently. His voice resounded with the timbre of compassion, which vibrated in my heart like a tuning fork. It had the effect of waking me from my slumber of the moment, so that I was paying attention in a whole different way. Suddenly the consideration was taking a much deeper turn as he continued, the context of his words becoming more and more crystalline as he spoke, his voice carrying with the strength of clarity and kindness, "Are you calm? Are you calm in the core of your being? Are you *ever* calm in the core of your being?"

She was listening very closely, and her face reflected clearly that she understood—as we all understood that this question was for each one of us—that she was not calm in the core of her being. He continued, "That's exactly what I'm talking about. Is the core of your being calm?"

She said, "No, I'm not calm, but I didn't know anything about spirituality before I met you only a few years ago."

Lee responded, "Insight into the depth of humanity doesn't have to come only from a spiritual master; it could come from a good criminal or a good farmer, for that matter. A good farmer knows more about people than a psychotherapist because a farmer deals with the essential nature of things. Even a good criminal has to know people, or they will get killed by the first person they do business with."

Someone else asked, "Is it the civilized world that separates us from our essential nature?"

"Yes," Lee answered, then he seemed to be considering further. Pausing, he then said, "A lot of Native Americans were close to their native roots until casinos came along. Sure, they take the money and build schools and hospitals for their people, but what are they teaching in those schools, and what medicine are they giving to people?"

The psychologist continued to argue the point that she was only trying to help people in the psychological domain; she did not feel capable of doing anything for them spiritually. Lee again turned the tables on her and said, "Why not? You don't have a very high aim!" Almost immediately Lee left us with this hefty morsel to chew.

The consideration of being calm in the core of one's being dovetailed perfectly with Lee's teaching at the ashram days earlier: "We are always being given opportunities to see if we are true or false." These two teachings struck me as very immediate, practical help, pointers on the map of practice.

We do not know how pervasive is our lack of true calm, true composure, true repose, until the right stimulus reveals us in its bright light. We can go along for so many years believing we are calm—assisted by our pursuits of psychotherapy, body work, aromatherapy, healing environments, quiet homes, even meditating and doing yoga and *pranayama*. Above all, we are bolstered by our intellectual understanding of dharma—what the Bauls call *anuman*, or understanding that has not come from direct experience (*bartaman*). Because we heard about it or read it in a book, or the priests and scriptures told us so, anuman is considered gossip, hearsay, or secondhand information. It is "gossip" until we have a direct knowledge ourselves. Until we find the real teacher who provokes us to see ourselves clearly, we have illusions about our state of calm. This is what the spiritual master proposes for us: "Let's see just how deep your calm really is." The master does this simply by virtue of his or her presence of being, because the true calm of the master's being is a constant mirror of our own state.

When we really give ourselves over to the velocity, heat and pressure of the tantric path in the company of a true teacher, we find out that we are not really calm at all—in fact, we are not surrendered to the process of transformation to which we have dedicated our entire lives. Not only is the constant mirror of the teacher showing us this, but practice is actually designed, in part, to stir it all up so that we can see it. Jeremy Hayward, a long-time disciple of Chögyam Trungpa Rinpoche, wrote:

> There is, naturally, a lot of resistance to this surrendering process and the practice arouses, so that one can clearly see them, a tremendous amount of coarse kleshas, mental defilements. In a traditional analogy, it is as if, wishing to build a palace, one first has to clear the ground of all the big rocks. These kleshas are offered up as food to that wisdom-mind embodied in the lineage. As Rinpoche once said, "We eat anything."[1]

As Lee says, we do not realize what possesses us at subtle levels until we have gone all the way to the bone with ruthlessly self-honest observation of our actions, motives, postures, gestures—however well-meant and positive they may be in many ways. Even when the teacher gives direct input, if we are stubborn enough, we go on for years ignoring the specific instructions, hints, sound advice, eloquent dharma expositions and sheer transmission of the teacher in favor of our own version of reality. After years of arduous efforts on the Path, we can find ourselves still steeped in ordinary dualistic life that

---

[1]   Jeremy Hayward, *Warrior-King of Shambhala: Remembering Chögyam Trungpa*, page 107.

is riddled, pock-marked, shot through and through with the illusion of separation and profound, but unnecessary, suffering.

In the process of *sadhana* we discover that we do not have a dependable, unshakable "calm abiding," as the Buddhists sometimes say, within us. There is no one "I am" but an incoherent bunch of internal characters, like in a play, each with its own agenda. *Sahaj samadhi* is an attractive dream, a fantasy, while "I" am a turbulent, often violent, aggressive and defended animal—a machine programmed at a fundamental level to respond to stimuli, to the threat of bodily extinction or ego death at the level of sheer incarnation.

The Buddhists speak of the precious nature of this human life; the Hindus also understand the fundamental truth of this enormous opportunity. We must enter fully into the ocean of experience and willingly begin to see ourselves as we really are, from ground to sky and beyond, if we deeply wish for transformational alchemy to take root, bud, flower and bear fruit. When we realize our predicament as timeless beings, caught in time and space with no way out of endless karmic reckonings except through Surrender to the Divine Will, then higher laws slowly become true of us. Slowly, painstakingly, over a very long period of time we stop separating ourselves from others, and begin to put others first. Slowly we wean the mind from its habit of demeaning, degrading and damaging ourselves and others with insults to our fundamental Organic Innocence.

Being calm at the core of one's being depends completely upon whether or not we are being true. Being true, we are brought to life in a new way: strength, courage and purpose flood a vessel that may have been weak, unsteady, lacking integrity, tarnished with afflictions of character. Being true in the moment re-establishes us in the original state of intrinsic dignity and intrinsic nobility—basic goodness. Being true places us firmly in mythical Camelot or Chögyam Trungpa Rinpoche's vision of Shambhala; suddenly we embody the knight's code of honor and chivalry and being true ourselves, we can perceive the innate truth and royalty in others.

Am I true, or am I false? When it comes to the play, the game—the divine *lila*—of awakening consciousness, sadhana teaches us that the answer to this question is always yes or no. There is no in between. I am either on the mark or off the mark. There are no degrees of integrity or honesty: I am either honest, or I am dishonest, and the truth or falsehood of this can be read in the mudra of the body, in every gesture, word and deed.

Lee used to say of his master that Yogi Ramsuratkumar fine-tuned him every time he would visit, "like a mechanic with a car." This is the guru's job, to keep asking us, "Are you true, or are you false? Are you calm in the core of your being? Are you unshakable in your Faith? Are you impeccable, reliable in your integrity to the Path?" It is the sign of the guru's undying loyalty, his love, and his sacrifice that he continues to show us what is real in a myriad of ways, whether by instructive teachings such as these, or by subtle glance or by direct intervention. It is the guru's job to finally convince us that, despite the fact that we are, as Lee said, "neurotic animals," we can come to live as "sublime, potentially enlightened God-creatures…" We can grow into sages. As the Bauls always say, "Jai Guru!" Victory to the guru.

Getting into the Guru's World

Lee Lozowick

One of the phrases in Vajrayana Buddhism that I've used on occasion is "getting into the guru's world." Unfortunately, getting into the guru's world is not done by simply sitting around, light as a feather, waiting for a beautiful spring breeze to pick you up and drift you into the guru's world. You have to have obedience and dignity, because the door to the guru's world is locked shut if you don't have dignity.

There are several elements of dignity: one is a certain politesse, which is a refinement and polish of decorum. "Politesse" is a good word—you'll find it in the Rolling Stones' song, "Sympathy for the Devil," which is a great song, by the way. It is a song that a good Sufi might listen to over and over again, until they understood what it meant. Another quality of dignity is the ability to appreciate the position of others. In order to enter into the guru's world with dignity, we have to understand the position of *others*—so that, when the guru shows deference to someone, we have a sense of perspective.

In the contemporary world, beauty is considered to be power, and if someone is beautiful enough—a man, woman, child, dog or horse—the average person will overlook anything beyond the most superficial surface appearances in order to be "in relationship" with Mr. or Miz Beauty, whatever "in relationship" means. So, an aspect of dignity is to be able to see beneath the surface of someone's physical appearance and psychology. Another aspect of dignity is the ability to say yes or no, not based on transference or psychological weakness but on personal integrity. When entering into the guru's world, one aspect of dignity is to also appreciate the guru's position. If we are running around like a mouse saying yes out of fear of condemnation, how do you think that makes the guru feel? The same as it makes you feel. If you ask someone to do a favor and they say yes out of fear of you, how does it make you feel? It's very unpleasant when someone is doing something they don't want to do, even if it helps you ostensibly.

Curiously, I started teaching before I met Yogi Ramsuratkumar in his body. At the time I started teaching, I didn't even know about him, even though now I attribute the catalyst for teaching to him. As you can imagine, people who teach without having a master are often the more arrogant of the species, believing they have a direct relationship to God without this insignificant intermediary—the master! So, when I met my master, I was not looking for a master. I was already teaching transformational work, not metaphysics. I had visited with many saints and sages in India, some of whom I was very touched by—like Anandamayi Ma and Baba Muktananda—but none of whom really struck me as someone I could work with personally, in terms of time and energy. Being very selfish, when I met my master, I had the sense that I could get something from him—something that would add to my treasury of profound and extraordinary spiritual brilliance! And, now, in retrospect, I mean that with some humor.

So I began to work with him, not by spending a lot of time in India but by putting my thoughts and attention in his direction.

I visited him in 1976 and in 1979, but the third time I visited he sent me away and told me not to come back—literally—so that I could not make the mistake of misunderstanding what he was saying. There was no symbolic dream or cryptic message: it was extremely direct. By that time, it was obvious to me that, in spite of all the extraordinary people I'd met in India, he was my master.

Besides being arrogant, I'm also lucky to be very conservative and well-mannered, if I do say so myself, so instead of forcing myself on him—which most Westerners would have done—I decided that my relationship to him for the rest of my life would remain subtle, and that the influence that precipitated my teaching Work and guided me to him in the first place would continue to function. This was my experience with my master, how I handled my own desire for attention and regard from him, and how I got into his world.

Two years later, he called me back to India. I was so happy, because in my mind—since he'd sent me away—I had said, "I'm never going back to India again, I'll never see him again. And, he is my master." So when I got called back to India by him, I was tremendously grateful, but I still wasn't sure what our relationship was on the outer level. It was a three-week trip, and I planned two days at the end of the trip to go to Tiruvannamalai to visit him. The rest of the time I planned to spend with his devotees, because I was scared he wouldn't see me. I didn't want to go see him in the beginning of the trip, only to have him send me away again and get all bummed out.

We finally got to Tiruvannamalai where he lived, and when I knocked on the door, he came running out, grabbed my hand and said, "Thank you, thank you! Thank you, Lee! You've been so kind to this beggar!" I thought I was the grateful one! So I decided that I would serve him however he indicated that it was useful—and that's what I did. When I went to India, I did not go as a teacher; I went as a disciple. Whatever he indicated, I just followed his direction.

There is a difference between you and I, of course, because you're in a room of Westerners and I was one of the only Westerners in a

room full of Indians, and I did receive a very immediate kind of recognition. A few Westerners came by now and then, but they weren't
even worthy of licking my boots! Of course, I never, ever, demonstrated that arrogant attitude in the presence of my master, but if I
thought it would have served him, I would have. I would have done
anything in my power to please him in areas in which he thought I
could serve.

One of the most important ways to get into the guru's world is to
serve, so students will often ask the guru how they can serve. When
your service is effective, even if you only see the master once a year,
the unlimited being of the master will never disregard your offering.
If you do not serve in any other direct way, the primary way you can
serve is to practice, whatever the practice is. In this school there are
the basic practices, which have been articulated—Assertion, Enquiry,
the Heart Breath—and the basic conditions: meditation, vegetarian
diet, exercise, study. To engage practice is to begin to align yourself
with the guru's world.

The wisdom of the guru, if he or she is a true master, is not limited by
a narrow stream of perception. In the guru's world there is a vast and
deep inner landscape that the majority of people who call themselves
devotees, disciples or students have no idea about and don't want to
have an idea about. But to enter into the guru's world demands that
we have the perception of the vast profundity of the guru's inner
landscape—at least the dimension of it, not necessarily the details.
To enter into the guru's world in this particular school requires both
an appreciation of an inner landscape and an outer landscape which
is—or at times may be—fairly surreal. The outer world landscape
has a lot of elements that appear contradictory or paradoxical. Part
of what is required to be in the guru's world is to have the dignity to

appreciate and understand—and *accept*, if we don't understand—all of the elements of the guru's world.

There are many saints in India who appear to be angry and resentful; people come to see them, and these saints throw rocks or shit at them. Sometimes naive people say, "That person can't be a saint, because they're always angry and throwing things at people." But they are not seeing their inner world. My opinion is that in certain cases the inner demand is so extreme that it warps the personality. Without equating the artist with the saint, I am sure that certain artists feel this at times. When you are in the midst of a creative surge, you can be very unpleasant on the outside, even to your children and your lover, because you don't want to lose that taste, that inspiration. You don't want to eat, except when you want to eat. You don't want to talk to anybody, except when you want to talk. And everybody and everything except the emergence of that inspiration is a big pain in the ass. So you are liable to be a bit cranky and annoyed.

When this little health theatre of mine became obvious to everybody, of course people wanted me to essentially go into retreat for healing, so I could have adequate amounts of rest and peace and quiet. I did actually cancel three trips I had planned, but I assured everybody that I was not planning to slow down. Some people were very upset, but life doesn't mean that much to me! At the consideration of dying, I wasn't heartbroken for any of my students, because my students should know better.

People were upset because they value life. I don't value life, unless—and there is an exception—life is devoted to what we call the Work. So, I'm willing to live. I'm not ecstatic about it. I didn't decide to live because I love life. When I thought I might die, I tried loving life! I watched the sunrise and sunset and really tried to get into it. I looked at dogs and cats and really tried to appreciate their value to the human race. In the end, I just kept taking refuge in the beauty of the sacred art, and my family, believe it or not (I'm not as tough as

I talk). The rest of it just wasn't that big a deal. I was very happy that I lived long enough to see the last Rambo movie, which I enjoyed immensely, although the critics tore it to pieces!

So, I live for what we call "the Work," in Gurdjieffian terms, and I will live for my students' work, but not for life. Why? Life never ends. Death is not the end of life; birth is not the beginning of life. So why live for Life? Life is a given. You can't not live for life anyway, no matter what you do, so instead of living for life and grasping for every last second—as some of you have seen your parents do before they die, even those who have lived very full and rich lives—why not live for what Life *is* in every moment, which is another definition of the Work. The Work is about living for what Life *is*, not for the extraordinarily dazzling illusions that Life has the capacity to shower you with, which aren't bad! When Life showers you with those things, hallelujah, and be very grateful, but that's not the point, because that's not what Life *is*—it is what Life *does*. If you're living for something that might be or could be or was, that's not what Life is. The Work is about what Life *is*: Just This. In Swami Prajnanpad's language, "What is, as it is, here and now." That is the guru's world.

Ferme de Jutreau, France
July 2008

Divine Folly

M. Young

Given a choice between a folly and a sacrament, one should always choose the folly—because we know a sacrament will not bring us closer to God and there's always a chance that a folly will.

— Erasmus

In the summer of 2008 on tour with Lee's band, while devouring Tom Robbins' paean to the power of the word in his divine book, *Fierce Invalids Home From Hot Climates*, I ran across this quote—words of wisdom from Erasmus that carried the reverberations of lucid insight into Enlightened Duality, in which the great possibility is getting "closer to God."

If I may speak for long-dead Erasmus, it seems that he is referring to sacraments as those religious forms that have been dogmatized, concretized into a credo, written in stone, from which the petty tyrants, the Pharisees and Sadducees of the world, successfully rule by the letter of the law rather than the spirit of the law. Erasmus' declaration against stultifying rigidity, in this case, reflects the fundamental, iconoclastic Baul perspective on *sadhana* and relationship with the Divine—the very view that refutes the necessity of inter-mediaries who overshadow rites and rituals tyrannized by the caste system.

The Bauls have a keen insight into the dead end of religious injunc-tions and churchified rituals—they refute the pedagogy of priests, teachers, preachers and lawmakers, for these are the ones who have wielded big sticks over the native intelligence and spontaneous joy of children for thousands of years. Human "society" today is defined by politicians, popes, preachers, most scientists, medical people, and teachers—and let us not leave out the worse of all: corporations, the military and media. This is exactly what drove the Bauls to insist upon music and dance and poetry as a way of life, a way of worship and God realization. It seems that, all in all, Erasmus would approve of the Baul spirit.

That having been stated, lest the baby is thrown out with the bath-water—or the poison mushrooms get cooked along with the edible ones—it is important to make some distinctions. Bauls engage rituals of many kinds, because a sacrament can carry tremendous spiritual power, and like all things, depends on the context—and the authen-ticity—of the person who is enacting it. A ritual may be flowing, fluid, an invocation of divine energies, an evocation of great *rasas*, blessings and grace; a ritual may unleash transformational pow-ers of multiple dimensionality. Ritual isn't limited to ancient Vedic, Catholic or Buddhist ceremony per se. A ritual can be many things, in fact—from making and pouring tea to sun salutations to the enact-ment of a myth or a Shakespeare play. A ritual can be created in the way one tends a garden, irons a shirt or prepares a meal. A ritual can be enacted when we read a favorite book to a child. It all depends on one's context and the placing of attention and intention.

In the play of the Real, in the possibility of Enlightened Duality, mood is everything, and a transformational ritual is that which invokes energies powerful enough to change the state of awareness of those who are participating in it. Such a ritual has true alchemical power. One of the most powerful rituals with transformational potential known in the contemporary world is the performance of rock & roll—the illegitimate love child of gospel, blues scale and rhythm. Therefore, as in the case of rock & roll—or Shakespeare's tragedies and comedies, for that matter—transformational ritual could be taking place in secret, hidden underneath the appearances of a concert or a play.

Human beings have worshipped the Divine Mother since the beginning of time as clefts in rocks, deep holes in trees, fissures, caverns, ravines, cenotes, lacunae, spring-fed pools or other natural formations. As symbols of transformation, these are the places where the peoples of antiquity the world over have worshipped the pervasive power of Devi—the Divine Shakti, both as Earth Mother and Cosmic Mother. The *dhuni* fire is an example of this ancient knowledge that endures today as an earth-based ritual linked to Hindu tradition.

The dhuni is worshipped because it signifies and exists as the living symbol of Shakti or awakened Prakriti. The dhuni fire as a rite is so ancient its origins are lost in the misty veils of Ma Time; in fact, it could be said that the dhuni fire is actually a manifestation of the Grand Dame herself. Worship at a traditional dhuni is a sacrificial rite, in the sense of the word "sacrifice" meaning "to make sacred." The dhuni ritual fire may include making offerings of incense, flowers, ghee, drops of water, herbs, or other suitable substances. The dhuni also receives names or prayers spoken silently or written on paper for specific blessings we wish to invoke. Singing, chanting the names of God, ecstatic spontaneous dancing and prayerful gestures have traditionally been a part of worship at the dhuni fire. As with any authentic gesture toward the Divine, it is our individual intention that makes the difference between a dead, dogmatized form and a living form, a *pitha*, seat or throne from which the goddess may arise.

The dhuni fire is a natural part of life in India. When Yogi Ramsuratkumar was a child growing up on the Ganges, he sat for many countless hours around the dhuni fires of the sadhus and mendicants who populated the sandy shores of the great river. It was there that he learned many things of the life divine; these were some of the primal experiences that shaped his destiny. Meher Baba instructed his devotees to light a dhuni fire on the twelfth day of each month to symbolize the purifying inner fire of Divine Love. This ritual began in 1925, when local villagers approached Baba about a severe drought that plagued their area. He told them to return home and build a dhuni fire; within minutes of lighting the fire, the rain began to fall.

The dhuni fire is one of those rare sacraments that is quite open and free of stultifying religious rules. There is room to breathe and to be in relationship with a dhuni fire, perhaps because it is the primal Mother Goddess who is invoked in a very personal and immediate way for each person who participates. We make our own prayers or internal worship—no priest or *pujari* prays for us or mediates with the gods. The relationship with elemental forces—earth, air, fire, water and deep space—and with the body of the planetary being of the Earth catalyzes a direct experience that is visceral, felt in and by the human body. There is no intermediary; there is only you, the Earth Mother and Cosmic Mother, and the tacit presence the blessings of the guru and lineage.

Before Lee and the band ventured out on tour this summer, a ceremonial dhuni fire was performed at the Guru Purnima Celebration on the ashram in France. The fire pit was dug in the courtyard facing east, toward the rising sun, then lined with white limestone rocks from the garden. After a short *puja* to consecrate our intention and invoke the lineage, we spread blankets on the grass around the dhuni. For four hours we chanted the name of Yogi Ramsuratkumar to call on the blessings of the lineage gurus for our ashrams, families and friends, and for the well-being and cleansing of the Earth and her inhabitants. While the twilight faded into a long purple dusk as we chanted, a tangible force began to grow. Finally the stars came out to glitter in the distant background of the velvet summer night.

The mood seemed to grow exponentially as the melodies lifted and carried us along. While people made offerings to the fire, there was no wild display of dance that can turn a ritual like this into another stage for ego's grandstanding; instead it was sober, contemplative, yet deeply joyful. By midnight, when the fire was burned down to red-hot coals, I walked up to the edge of the dhuni to make a final offering, only to find myself rooted there, feeling connected earth to sky and held in place by the living deity. Nothing existed but the fire and the point of perspective that witnessed the fire, because there was only the sanctified shrine—a living symbol, understood in a way that was alive, newborn, fresh. The dhuni was a burning volcanic portal, from which emanated the wild glory of a formidable mystery. The simple firepit had been transformed and now resembled a yoni after giving birth—raw, as if torn with primeval power rushing through.

Looking up at the sky, the stars were another kind of fire, burst into diamond points in the black night. I had the sense that we humans of the twenty-first century, gathered together on the grassy ground, had invoked an ancient rite of Mother worship in the cosmic and terrestrial sense. When the final coals were extinguished well after midnight, there was nothing left but grace and gratitude. Divine Shakti had come to bless us this night; she was called forth, awakened, by the blessing of Yogi Ramsuratkumar.

There are countless ways to invoke transformational energies; most of them are not encountered under the auspices of formal religious rites. They are moments in which life is concentrated by intention in such a way through the human lens, like light focused through a prism, so that a fire catches hold and a transformational process bursts into flame. This can happen any time the name of God is chanted, especially for long periods of time. It is a mystery that we do not want to pierce or understand, because to understand would impinge upon and limit its primordial potential for pure magic.

The whimsical, spontaneous nature of any venture we might call "folly" plays an extraordinary role in the magic of life—of living a life of *drala*, to use a Tibetan Buddhist term. As Erasmus says, there is always the chance that folly—especially divine folly, or objective folly—will bring us closer to God. The possibility of invoking divine presence, of realizing our innate intimacy with God in any given moment, lies at the core of the teaching of Enlightened Duality, for the pinnacle of that state of being is about being "closer to God." If folly gives us the best shot at getting closer to God, then surely we want it.

The best example I know of folly is manifested in the way my teacher works in general—the "Systeme D" method, as they say in France. Systeme D is the method by which one uses whatever spare materials, loose odds and ends and seemingly useless junk one might have lying around and combines them with the unusual resources dredged up by magic to create something amazing. In folly, there is not a lot of advanced planning and no contingencies, failsafe or safety nets. "Fools rush in where angels fear to tread" is a saying that is intended to scare us away from such foolhardy behavior, but if we have taken Erasmus' words to heart, then folly and foolishness go together like birds of a feather. In Lee's world, the vision shows up, unerring and true, he takes the first opportunity that life throws in his direction, and—*voila!* Something useful, beautiful, amazing, extraordinary and maybe even magical has been created out of nothing. Lee's ashrams in Arizona, France and India—which took form, arrived and thrived against the odds with minimal or nonexistent resources at hand—are manifestations of this principle at work.

Most especially, divine folly is found in the way Lee has sponsored, encouraged and participated in his students' various art projects, particularly the music. Maybe all art is divine folly; one could certainly make a good argument for that. We can say with certainty that rock & roll has always carried with it a powerful element of folly, magic, foolishness, mayhem and paradox; perhaps we can also say that rock & roll as dharma art is divine folly at its best.

Rock & roll has a long history of those who have embodied or come very close to embodying divine folly in their music: Bob Dylan, the Rolling Stones, the Beatles, Jim Morrison and the Doors, Janis Joplin, Jimi Hendrix, David Bowie, Led Zeppelin. Then of course there are the African American gospel greats, blues and jazz heroes who came before, in the middle, and after rock & roll, who were the innovators, the originators of rock & roll as a stream of musical expression, with all its variations including soul, pop, hip hop, punk and so on. These great African-Americans were the real movers and shakers of divine folly in the musical domain: Big Mama Thornton, Robert Johnson, Mahalia Jackson, Muddy Waters, Screamin' Jay Hawkins, (to name only a very few) and much later, greats like Aretha Franklin, Otis Redding and Buddy Guy.

Inspired by the blues, gospel and rock tradition, Lee started the musical projects in the sangha from nothing—a big zero, a divine emptiness, a void. Many of the musicians and singers in these bands had no background or experience in music and performance. Drums, mouth harp, bass guitar, banjo, and keyboards are some of the instruments that have been learned in the process of performing original rock & roll or the blues under the auspices of Baul music. Twenty years ago we had no fixed idea about what was going on, except that our guru wanted to play rock & roll. Over the years, it became clear that we were encoding the teaching in poetry, lyric and song, using performance art and the music that has naturally arisen in the Western cultural milieu as a way to reach ordinary people and maybe, in some small way, help relieve some of their suffering.

The Bauls, who are the rock & rollers of Bengal, encode their teaching in poetry, song and dance. They call their gurus *sunya* (empty) because it is only from emptiness that real creativity can spring. It is an apt appellation for Lee, whose first foray into the rock & roll world began with a mishmash of thrown-together musicians from the sangha body who played at a marriage feast in 1986. It was great fun for everyone, but more significantly, it fanned a creative fire in Lee, who had been writing poetry for some years. The doorway was opened for a gush of lyrics that came from Lee—a creative flow that has not stopped over the years.

A year later Lee inaugurated the Living God Blues Band, which came together and played for the first of many times at the Guru Purnima Celebration in July 1987. That night kicked off a long love affair with rock & roll: the band gelled and evolved over time under the name of *liars, gods & beggars*, or LGB, with Lee writing lyrics for original songs that were performed on three tours in the U.S. and six in Europe. LGB played in honky-tonks, bars, restaurants, street festivals and private parties all over Arizona for ten years. On countless star-studded nights we arrived home with Lee at the ashram at three a.m.; four hours later we were up and on our seats for an hour of formal meditation. Our sadhana was a woven tapestry of steamy rock & roll, dancing our hearts out in the smoky quartz atmospheres where Lee and his band made a divine madness of song, and a disciplined life of practice. In twelve years *liars, gods & beggars* recorded fourteen CDs of original music.

Then came Lee's blues band, Shri, which continues today and has recorded eleven CDs of dominantly original music. For the past twelve years Shri has toured for six weeks in Europe each summer, performing extensively in France, Germany, and Switzerland

and making forays into Spain, Italy, Ireland, the UK, Norway and Austria. Shri paved the way for other projects spearheaded by Lee's students, including the band Attila the Hunza and the Denise Allen Band, along with various other musical projects, in which numerous CDs of original music have been recorded. After a seven-year stretch of performing and recording three CDs of original music and one European tour, Attila the Hunza disbanded. Its members moved on to various other creative projects, including the Denise Allen Band, which currently tours every summer in Europe and has four CDs recorded to date. At Lee's instruction, the European sangha has also initiated musical projects that are in their beginning stages. All this has happened within the busy, committed lives of householder yogis who are raising children, engaging spiritual practice, working and running businesses, and putting time into *seva* (service) at the ashram. These are ultra busy individuals whose lives are committed to Baul sadhana and guru yoga.

In 2006 Lee's first solo CD was recorded at Trimurti Ashram, with Lee's lyrics put to music composed by Paul Durham. Three CDs of original music have been recorded by Lee and Paul, titled: "Crushed by Love," "Broken Angel," and "Tongue of Poison, Soul of Love." This tremendous creative burst gave birth to the Lee Lozowick Band, a patchwork of French musicians who were brought together to play with no rehearsal before their first public gig. Since then the Lee Lozowick Band has toured for three consecutive summers, 2006–2008, with a fourth tour pending in 2009 as of this writing.

Lee comes naturally by his use of music and poetry as a mode of teaching and transmission of dharma and engagement in sadhana. His spiritual father, Yogi Ramsuratkumar, "the Godchild of Tiruvannamalai," was a master of divine folly who loved music, singing and dancing. For many years the divine madness that captured his heart and soul was demonstrated by spontaneous *bhavas* (divine moods) that manifested in song and dance.

In December 2000, two months before Yogi Ramsuratkumar died, Lee went to visit his master for three weeks in Tiruvannamalai, taking a group of students with him. We had the auspicious opportunity to witness and participate in the master's last darshans. This was a very rare occurrence and a great gift indeed, as Yogi Ramsuratkumar had not appeared in public darshan in the ashram temple for a year. One day about midway through the visit, Yogi Ramsuratkumar called me to the big dais where he sat. His brown eyes shone with the light of infinity and seemed to contain every arising and subsiding of divine activity from then till now. Looking into those eyes caused my mind to stop—until he said, "You can sing." The pause was so brief it was barely there at all, then he added, "And dance." Then for emphasis, it seemed, he concluded, "Sing and dance," meaning that two of us should chant his name and dance, which we did. There was a certain mood of folly and foolishness in this, since chanting his name came easily and naturally, but the "dancing" had to be made up on the spot, and it had to arise out of the mood of the chanting.

This instruction led to a whole series of requests for singing and dancing from Yogi Ramsuratkumar that year, both to many of the Westerners traveling with Lee and to his Indian devotees as well. In one way, we were singing and dancing for him. At the time he was confined to a reclining chair on wheels, as he could no longer walk. Only two months away from shedding his physical body, the delight on his face as he watched the devotees sing and dance seemed to carve deep grooves and unknown pristine forms in our hearts. This sense of being *changed* by these simple acts was supra-real; it seemed he was building a temple in the interior world of his devotees—a sanctuary for the *ista devata* after he left the physical body.

The reverberation of that instruction to "sing and dance" went far beyond the moment, carrying with it the sense of divine mandate: Yogi Ramsuratkumar was telling us that he wanted us to rejoice, to celebrate the living Lord in this world, to move our bodies in praise of Creator and Creation. Looked at in one way, singing and dancing is exactly what we *do* with Lee's bands—in an especially one-pointed way every summer on tour.

Since Yogi Ramsuratkumar left his body and moved into the unseen worlds, my teacher has become far more enigmatic, cryptic and generally difficult to live with and understand. He has made it clear in countless discourses and talks and through his action in the world that his days of teaching in a more linear way are over. Therefore, what we have seen is a lot more divine folly, which has continued to proliferate in the creation of art, literature and music. Is is also widely demonstrated in his passion for acquiring and passing on sacred objects of beauty of many different kinds. This love affair with the world of the sacred as it is expressed in art led to the Sacred Bazaar, which Lee repeatedly declares is entirely the gift of Yogi Ramsuratkumar. Many of his students have followed him down untold roads and highways in hot pursuit of objects of ultimate beauty, but this sometimes inexplicable drive with which he pursues his treasures is the tip of the iceberg. His one-pointed focus on the Path as it is revealed in these ways frazzles the ordinarily constrained mind. As Regina Ryan wrote of him in her introduction to Lee's book, *Feast or Famine—Teachings on Mind and Emotions*:

> For all his enormous compassion to me and wide-ranging skillful means, which I have witnessed firsthand in countless circumstances, I don't hesitate to admit that he has been and is a hard teacher. Not only because he is uncompromising in his dealings with ego—in all its guises from arrogance to naivete—but because he is often so maddeningly nonlinear in his teaching style.

The seeker or student who comes to this well to drink
will first have to unravel the knotted ropes that keep the
bucket secured.[1]

Lee Lozowick is an extremely demanding teacher in many ways. He can be very difficult, irascible, grouchy, touchy, picky and critical. In other ways, he is the gentlest, shyest, most refined, compassionate, generous and exquisite individual—along with his master, Yogi Ramsuratkumar—whom I have encountered in my years on this planet. I have learned that if I am unable or unwilling to respond to Lee's most gentle, kind admonishments and guidance, then the work gets harder and harder. The more resistance his students have to the Work, the more abrasion and irritation there is coming from him, and the velocity of the Work becomes more terrifying and at times horrifying to ego. Situations of life in which our sadhana occurs become more difficult and unpalatable, because the friction between my lack of surrender and the discomforts and demands of life's situations grows proportionately larger and larger. I am creating my own hells.

Traveling on band tours in Lee's van is one of many examples of alchemical stresses my guru offers to his students. The van is a microcosm of the ashram; it is a symbol of any milieu in which the practitioner finds her or himself working and living. On the road, we travel in a caravan of cars and vans, sometimes as many as six or seven. We are literally careening through space and time, buffeted about as our guru himself does the driving of his van, and it can get high spirited in moments, to say the very least. More accurately, the van full of people is a metaphor for something much bigger—working within the crucible of community, sangha, tribe or group of any kind—that the teacher offers to his students as a way to refine our

---

[1]   Regina Ryan, editor, *Feast or Famine—Teachings on Mind and Emotions,* page xiii.

lives, our practice and ultimately our being within the Great Process of Divine Evolution.

The metaphorical "van" is our vehicle—the tumbler in which we are stones turning, being ground down and polished by the constant abrasion against one another, to finally turn into a precious object that might even be polished enough to set into gold. We have to be a little bit crazy to choose this madcap caravan of souls. But, we are striving to be divine fools, bound together in the smoldering ruins of the guru's nightly bonfires of music, sound, and rhythm, where we sing songs to Life and send our prayers and adoration to soar into the spheres to draw the attention of our ista devata.

I've come to view "understanding" the guru and his activities as an unprofitable enterprise, because who can "understand" divine folly, much less someone who might be referred to as a sunya—or a *khepa*? To understand is to render a mystery into the mundane, to shear its long and flowing dark locks until all you have left is a heap of tangled hair lying on the floor. One might as well throw ash and mud on the honey cakes and wine prepared for the marriage feast with the Beloved.

Bauls use the word khepa to refer to those who live in a state of divine madness, or they use the word *pagal*, also meaning mad. Lee, who once called himself "Pagala Lee" in a poem to his master Yogi Ramsuratkumar, lives within the field of divine folly with wisdom and intention.[2] Divine folly is something that springs out of an intimate knowledge of Reality as Enlightened Duality. Such a one appears mad to the conventional world precisely because he or she has transcended conventional, middle-world definitions, including the defi-

---

[2] The word "intention," often used in these essays, carries the very specific meaning of an intention that is free and unmotivated, completely devoid of aggression or any self-propelled action. This kind of intention is in the background; if intention is brought into the foreground of the action, then it becomes willpower, which is another thing altogether. Intention is a state of being, not a state of doing.

nition of enlightenment. This is someone who has gone beyond, into a state we cannot know or describe, pointed toward in the famous *prajnaparamita* mantra of the Heart Sutra: *Gate gate paragate para-samgate bodhi svaha*: Gone, gone, gone beyond, gone completely beyond enlightenment, *svaha*. The Tibetan Vajrayana Buddhists call this state "crazy wisdom," meaning, again, "gone beyond."

Jesus Christ once said to the thief who was dying on the cross beside him, "In my Father's house there are many mansions." Applied metaphysically, this statement means that there are many realms in heaven, or we could apply it in a more transcendental, universal or ontological sense. We could say that there are many different experiences of a multi-faceted, multi-layered Reality that can be entered into and experienced, even savored, from the perspective of Enlightened Duality. Perhaps we could further declare that one of the primary entry points into those endless possibilities of dimensions is divine folly.

When we look at the lives of those who are characterized by divine folly, the chief characteristic of this state is a sublime madness, which manifests in many different forms. Divine folly is not just the domain of world saviors like Jesus and Krishna. Krishna had his *ras lila*, in which he duplicated himself a few thousand times to dance in the moonlight and make love with each individual *gopi*. Jesus had his resurrection from the dead, his calling forth of Lazarus from the tomb, and perhaps above all, his relationship with Mary Magdalene. Divine folly is also the domain of countless artists, scientists, visionaries, and holy madmen and madwomen across the centuries—like Hazrat Babajan, who threw the rock that catalyzed Meher Baba's awakening and subsequent divine madness—who have been driven there by the untameable raw force of the Divine.

Meher Baba's divine folly took him to impossible lengths with his male *mandali* to discover and retrieve the mad saints, or *masts*, of India and help them move beyond the plane of *samadhi*—where their consciousness was stuck—and back into the world, where "emptiness is form." This was something Meher Baba understood: when divine madness came upon him, he would pound his head on a stone for hours to bring his consciousness back into the human realm, where he could work for the benefit of all beings as a source of divine influence and blessing power.

Paramahamsa Ramakrishna's divine states left him singing, dancing, swooning and unable to walk or stand. His ecstasies were so overpowering that he had to be attended to almost constantly, because one never knew when he would go into samadhi and lose bodily function. Like Yogi Ramsuratkumar, Ramakrishna's bhavas rendered him into states of childlike innocence that profoundly touched the hearts of his devotees. Ramakrishna said once of his constant adoration of Kali, his ista devata: "The supreme lovers, however, transcend the three categories of tamasic, rajasic, and sattvic worship. They are so childlike that they can only cry Ma, Ma, Ma while dancing, weeping, and laughing."[3]

This could be a description of Yogi Ramsuratkumar, whose divine madness was legendary in his own time and manifested often in his spontaneous singing, dancing and blessing "fits," when he would raise his hands in the air and bless whomever was before him, saying, "Ram, Ram!" Most of all it appeared in his smoking of cigarettes, when he smoked away the karma of his devotees—a gesture that communicated innocence and purity while at the same time transmitted spiritual authority.

Swami Ramdas, the guru of Yogi Ramsuratkumar, was no stranger to divine madness. After he received the transmission of Ramana Maharshi, the wandering sadhu climbed Mount Arunachala, where he stayed in a cave. Sleepless, eating nothing but a small amount of boiled rice, he was fervently repeating the mantra, Sri Ram Jai Ram Jai Jai Ram without cease. After twenty days in the cave, sud-

---

[3]   Les Hixon, *Great Swan: Meetings with Ramakrishna*, page 130.

denly his eyes were filled with a radiant light, and he realized that the Presence of the Divine was everywhere. He ran about the mountain embracing rocks and trees, shouting, "This is my Ram!"[4] Years later, he wrote in *The Divine Life*:

> *When the devotee has realized the full splendor of God and is surcharged with ecstasy, and has merged in Him, he cannot contain himself. He dances, being seized with a rare rapture, his entire body thrilling with bliss. The very name and thought of God sets him ablaze, as it were, with this exalted experience. In this state the line of demarcation that divides the devotee and his God disappears and God reveals Himself as the devotee.*[5]

Although this is divine folly at its most joyous, these great ones often appeared to be suffering. Yogi Ramsuratkumar sometimes cried when he was deeply moved, either by joy or sorrow. He fell into deep bhavas in which he seemed to be carried away by a flood of feeling, sometimes heavy and anguished as if he was bearing the pain of the world, and sometimes full of delight and joy. The flow of these apparent states were continuous demonstrations of his nondual realization of God. Yogi Ramsuratkumar frequently stated, "This beggar is no more—only Father exists. Father alone." This awakening into the greater life of unity brought Yogi Ramsuratkumar's innate oneness with the whole of life into the foreground of his consciousness; for him there was no separation between the suffering of individuals, humankind as a whole, and himself.

In the company of Yogi Ramsuratkumar it became clear that there are many ways to suffer consciously. We might ask ourselves if this is something we really want to court in our own lives. For most of us,

---

4   Swami Ramdas, *The Essential Swami Ramdas*, page xlviii.

5   Ibid, page 46.

the guru role is not likely to be our destiny; the fruits of the Path will be put into service through different roles and means in our lives. Perhaps our destiny will be to act as an "enlightened witness"[6] for children, or one particular child, or for a dying elder, partner or close friend. Maybe we will serve others invisibly for an entire lifetime in myriad ways—simply through silent acceptance or silent witnessing and blessing—and that becomes the expression of realization. The bodhisattva vow is inherent to all true Paths: "Turn the other cheek," and "Do unto others as you would have others do unto you," are prime examples of this. Most practitioners of the spiritual way will manifest this profound commitment—which is one of the most crucial fruits of the Path—in ordinary life as an ordinary, invisible person.

Lee often seeks out meetings with representatives of many different paths, offering opportunities for his students to meet and sometimes come to know different teachers. The teachers I have met on the Path in my guru's company who have impressed me the most, who have inspired me to carry on, who have provided real help and transmission of the fruits of the Path, are those who are unafraid to be truly human. Though they are formidable in their own right, they are transparent, earthy, humorous and vulnerable about their foibles and their own suffering. Their spiritual authority is found, to a great degree, in their willingness to be an adult human being.

At the same time that the true sage is an adult, the gurus, saints and spiritual masters who have gone beyond are difficult to comprehend. Their activities may appear quixotic, crazy, foolish, and yet all beings benefit from the incredible blessings that are produced through their divine folly. Both their joy and their sorrow are ultra, mega, meta, *maha*—great beyond measure. On the path we cultivate the capacity to bear great sorrow and joy. Most people can only sustain relationship to conscious joy or conscious suffering through images and symbols and twilight language: Jesus Christ on the cross,

---

6   "Enlightened witness" is a term coined by psychologist Alice Miller.

suffering for all of humankind; Buddha as the bodhisattva who returns forever, until all sentient beings are released from illusion. Chögyam Trungpa Rinpoche gave us a powerful example of this kind of activity in the Tibetan Vajrayana Buddhist tradition of crazy wisdom, as did Yogi Ramsuratkumar, smoking away the karmas of those who came to him for blessings. These are bodhisattvas, whose sole purpose of existence is to serve Life, to bless and to miraculously take on the suffering of the many. As Chögyam Trungpa Rinpoche said, "My body is the whole world."[7]

After six weeks on tour with the Lee Lozowick Project, in the crucible of divine folly, we arrived back on the ashram. In the sanctuary of that pristine environment, I reflected on how the process of maturation requires acceptance of that which we cannot change. The frail human personality, with its likes and dislikes, its peculiarities, its difficulties and struggles, will always be with us to greater or lesser degrees, as long as we are in these bodies. There will always be abrasion when two very different machines try to get in sync, and the design of their mechanical parts simply do not fit together, because the personality is mechanical, like a clock, and self-observation reveals this to us time and time again.

The process of transformation is excruciatingly slow. Sometimes it seems like nothing is happening, while dismay and remorse grow as we see more and more of the motives that drive our behavior. Regardless of this, transformation is the natural movement of Organic Innocence; it is the inevitable result of the graceful Influence

---

[7]   Jeremy Hayward, *Warrior-King of Shambhala: Remembering Chögyam Trungpa Rinpoche,* page 122.

of the lineage of gurus and the living, symbolic structure of spiritual discipline—the *asana* or sacred gesture of practice. Although it is often largely invisible, once we have discovered the Path, this secret of transformation is happening, hidden deep inside the being.

Slowly we are building a seat or throne for the deity within our own being. We are coming into perfect resonance with the vibration—the sound and light—of the lineage, or of the Divine, depending upon the language and structure of the Path in which we find ourselves. These principles are true, ultimately, whether it is Hinduism, Buddhism or mystical Christianity within which we practice. Realization of the Divine is the incarnation of spirit into matter, whether we call that Buddha, Vajrayogini, Green Tara, Kali, Krishna or Jesus Christ. These are the luminous symbols of an ultimate numinosity: the self-radiant, all-pervasive, omniscient, omnipotent, loving Intelligence we might also experience as the personal God or Beloved.

During the touring sojourn, I was convinced in precious moments that the Creator moves or intends Creation toward a balance and harmony of opposites interacting: the Great Process of Divine Evolution. Dark and light together fluctuate in rapid rhythmic movement, and the asanas of practice—the sacred gestures of practice—restructure and align us to that harmony. Spiritual practice literally arranges or choreographs the vibrations of the human organism to resonate with the original balance and harmony that is Organic Innocence. We need more of those gestures that align us to the essential harmony of opposites.

Darkness is so so pervasive in the Kali Yuga that we need a lot more light and radiance produced by prayer and adoration. I am convinced that prayer, praise and adoration are the ultimate answers to the problems of the world—the inner world, the outer world, the world at large, and even the horrifying world where we are killing our Earth. The global problems of today are problems of a spiritual nature. Humanity must return to the dharma, to the Way. We must realign with Creator and Creation and cosmic law.

Music, song and dance are prime magical ground for alignment with the Great Design, for opening a channel through which light and radiance may rain upon the Earth. Movement and dance—when it is organic rather than purely egoic and mechanical—also opens these doors and windows so that light may stream in. Any truly creative act opens the channel to the divine impulse: the painter, sculptor, poet, writer, weaver, cook, potter, the mother and father with their children. Friendships are ground for creativity to be expressed through kindness, generosity and compassion, fidelity, nobility, and dignity in the relatedness of the moment.

This is always a matter of divine folly, because creativity which is completely nonaggressive and radiance-producing requires a radical shift of perspective. It will always seem to be folly to the egoic one who operates by standard procedures of self-survival. To create, in the objective sense, one must be nothing and no one, and this intending of self-sacrifice will always seem foolish, dangerous, threatening to the ego that wants to survive intact and in control. Folly requires that we let it all go and trust.

These are the creation beds of our lives. Transformation is written in the *act*—the sacred gesture, the divine folly—of creativity that allows light to come shining through. The products or remnants of that act of creation will gleam and glow with divine light, but the actual unleashing of radiance happens in the body, in the moment of creation. This potential for prayer and adoration of the Divine is the essence, the lotus, the jewel at heart of Enlightened Duality.

Just Live Fully

Lee Lozowick

Just live, and live fully. Living fully, by my observation, doesn't mean that sometimes things aren't difficult, or there aren't crises; life is full of ups and downs. As long as you are reacting to what is, then you have internal warfare. As long as you are judging, you have disturbance. If you are practicing Assertion—Just This—or accepting "what is, as it is, here and now," then a creative solution always becomes obvious.

People are afraid to live fully. We're afraid of disappointment, betrayal, abandonment—especially when it comes to relationships. We're afraid that love won't last. Someone asked me if love has a certain value on the spiritual Path, and if it does, what should one do to make it last? I'm a romantic. Love—what a wonderful thing! For me there is nothing *but* the Path, which I could also call Life, so of course love is a very important quality among the various things with which we could occupy ourselves in living fully. It's certainly better than politics—although that doesn't mean we can't be ecologically concerned, and really should be these days.

My approach to dealing with thoughts like "Love won't last," and the mind in general, is: If something arises in my mind and I don't want to give it any energy, I say to my mind, "Shut the fuck up!" And it does! The thought, "It's not going to last," is not uncommon for any of us who find ourselves experiencing particularly good fortune. This is especially true when it comes to love. You don't want to give that thought energy. The thought by itself, discrete, unassociated with energy of any kind—emotional indulgence, drama, projection, expectation, judgment—has no power or authority. Don't feed the thought with your energy; when you feed something you give it health and life, and when you starve it, obviously it dies.

In the practice of Assertion, of accepting "what is as it is here and now," you notice that a thought has arisen, and you can't pretend it's not there. Well, you can pretend it's not there, but it doesn't do any good to pretend it's not there. If it arises, it arises. The thought is there—it has arisen, and you can't make it go away because it is here, now. When you indulge it in some way, you are giving it authority over you—you are giving it life. If you don't give it any energy, it will naturally subside. It will arise, and it will subside.

Accepting what is as it is here and now has implicit questions within it: What is thought? Who is thinking? We don't have to say those things to ourselves every time, but those questions are implied in our Assertion of what is, here and now, in this moment. If you accept a worm for what it is, as it is, you aren't only accepting the visual perception of a worm; you are accepting the entire complex of wormness that makes a worm a worm. In the acceptance of what is as it is, relative to our own tremendously complex and sophisticated system of mind-body-psychology-emotion-essence, it's not that you have to be a scientist of being, in the sense that you have to study Jung and Freud and every psychologist and philosopher, or you need to read every book on psychology. It's that you have to connect to the essential wisdom, true of all of us, which tacitly knows Reality as it is and does not need to rely on information for definition.

For example, the thought, "Love won't last." Who is thinking that thought? The obvious answer is: "Me. I'm thinking that thought." The second response is usually to drag up some philosophy you have read in a book: "No, it's not my thought; thoughts simply arise. I can't hang on to them, I don't possess them." We trot out the teaching as a philosophy, but not as a tacit knowing, and often we are very glib about it. "Yes, yes—I know the teaching." Intellectually, yes, we all know the teaching. I've had times in my community when I hear a new student explaining the teaching to an even newer student, and I'm amazed because their articulation is brilliant. I think: How did they ever learn all that so fast? They didn't learn it; they just remembered it from reading a book.

If we have a curious mind and we have a philosophical leaning, there is no problem with learning. Many wise people have a tremendous amount of learning and information at their fingertips, but having information is not problematical for them; they use it as a tool. They know that the information and learning is not what defines their being and presence.

So, we have to mind our thoughts. A part of us that is not conscious feeds thoughts energy until they do have force. Don't feed that thought, and remember that to accept what is as it is here and now is not a superficial thing. The word "acceptance" is a common word. Accepting what is as it is here and now is not like accepting a dinner invitation: "Yes, I'd love to come." Even in that kind of acceptance there is an implied consequence of very simple social etiquette that you'll be well-mannered and you'll respect the space. When we practice accepting what is as it is here and now, the implication is much more sophisticated. What is thought? Who is perceiving this thought? The answers that we want to these questions are found in the presence of our *tacit* knowledge of Reality, not in what we've read in a book. The point is not to deny information. We are social creatures who enjoy talking to one another, and information is very useful in conversation, for example. Information has a certain usefulness, and, under certain circumstances, information can also compromise what we are trying to see and understand with the heart.

In current cell research, what neurologists are finding is that the exact same cells found in the brain are found throughout the spinal cord and in the heart. When we speak of the heart, we are not just talking about the physical organ; we are talking about the entire physical system through which consciousness expresses itself as love, intelligence and all objective sentiment. We begin to understand with our minds, and then we come to understand with our hearts. You don't have to understand with your mind what it means to understand with the heart; you will come to understand. If the love you feel for your partner is radiant, that alone can be enough to open the door to understanding of the heart.

Whatever the past history may be, there is the possibility of a radical difference for every person in their life. In spite of what seems to be a pattern that is not viable, your life can be different. Maybe you've had a lot of relationships. Every time you fall in love, you should assume it's with the right person. Maybe the right person is the one who comes along last, after all the other ones have left. It's possible! Yes, of course, there may be fear. "Love won't last." Fear is everyone's response, with very rare exceptions. We are comfortable with our rigid and predictable machines, because ego defines whether we feel fear or not.

How profoundly you want your love to last is the degree to which you will allow yourself to be ravished—to be a bit mystical about it. Ravishment is one of the only things worth going for. Very fine sacred art draws us to it because we can feel or sense the ravishment of the artist, the devotee, the disciple, who created it. Baudelaire was ravished. He is someone who lived fully. He couldn't become healthy on the basis of it, although he wrote some inspiring poetry. Even though he as a man was the sacrifice, one could argue that it was a worthy sacrifice, because so many people have been nurtured and fed by what he left as a result of that ravishment.

There used to be an American television show called "The Twilight Zone," which was about parapsychological events and circumstances. In one episode, a man dies and finds himself in the afterlife, which is fantastic—everything he has ever wanted is there: good food, beautiful people, fast cars, everything. There is no qualitative difference between things—everything is perfect, and there are no challenges. After a while he starts getting bored. So he goes to the boss and says, "I want to get out of here." The boss asks, "Where do you want to go?" He responds, "Down there," because he assumes he is in heaven. The boss says, "You *are* down there." The point is that hell is the *same thing* forever—like eternal love.

Another consideration is to know that the person who is your "one," your "significant other," might be your "one" forever—of course in different forms and with different faces and names and so on. Ultimately, that person is the same one for ever. They say "variety is the spice of life." A lot of people think that means different partners, different excitement, different vacations, a different car every year. It might be worth your while—it might save you a *tremendous* amount of suffering—to cultivate the ability to accept the person you are with now, as they are, without reservation and without qualification, because you will probably see them again. And again and again and again and again. Anything you don't solve this lifetime, you will get another chance and another chance and another chance, until you solve it.

It probably will become obvious to you at some point, if it hasn't already, that much of who you are now—not psychologically, but in large brush strokes—cannot be traced to your childhood. Mozart is a classic example: no child can create what he created without bringing it with him from somewhere else. There are two-year-old

Tibetan children, discovered as reincarnated *tulkus*, who are able to identify artifacts that belonged to their past incarnation. These same children are able to do a six-hour Tibetan Buddhist ritual perfectly without moving.

Sooner or later the feeling will arise for you that a lot of your experience is the result of something that happened sometime or someplace before you were born in this lifetime. It might occur to you that what you're doing now—everything you're doing now—is creating a setup for some other time. I'm not talking about heaven and hell; I'm talking about an eternal process to which there is no beginning and no end—and the bad news—from which there is no exit! What to do? You get with the program, or you suffer. Ultimately, that is the choice: surrender to the truth of Reality, or suffer misery, confusion, crisis, conflict, emotional angst and everything else.

To be born in a human body is to have a commonality of purpose with every other human being—which, by the way, is not merely to eat, drink and be happy. Although, if you can eat, drink and be happy while you are realizing the aim of what it means to be human—hey, take it! It is an absurd concept to believe that you can't be fulfilled as a human being on the Path. If you can be comfortable, happy and creatively fulfilled on the Path, it is not a problem.

Let me say that again: Living fully is not a problem on the Path. Some people have such a strong sabotage mechanism that they actually keep doing things to destroy their potential happiness. They have an unconscious belief that to succeed is to fail; to be happy is to be a mediocre human being. For some people, every time they start to get a little ahead of things financially, a catastrophe happens in their life. They have an unconscious association: to succeed is to fail. In conscious, intelligent, linear terms we say, "That's ridiculous!" Yes! It's ridiculous, and yet for many of us, it's not uncommon.

So I would encourage you to consider that the ease of your life may be in proportion to your ability to accept your life as it is. Will it ever change? It might. It can change as easily as it might not change—why not? Anything can happen! However, the more committed you are to having a different life than the one you have now, the less likely it is that anything will ever change. The good news is that it's never too soon or too late to start. You're never too old or too young. If you're twenty-one years old, you don't have to go out and live your life first before you start to practice. If you're sixty and all full of creaks and back pain, it is never too late. It is never too early or too late to start living fully.

The definition of living fully is found in practice. In every school there are practices that are articulated. In our school the practices are Assertion, Enquiry, the Heart Breath, the cultivation of kindness, generosity and compassion in relationship—and a whole score of others. There is a distinction to be made between living fully and *ego's* idea of living fully. Obviously it's natural to want happiness and satisfaction and success, and there is no reason we should not have those things when we are living fully.

At the same time, one of the things I suggest is: don't *reach* for things. Don't reach beyond your space, because when we reach, we tend to alter the Universe's sense of timing, which is perfect. When we are really reaching for something, the tendency is to try to alter the natural, appropriate timing of things. When we reach, we tend to use our personal force of will to make something happen that may not be ready to happen yet. When you are *given* something, then to work hard and really push may be a perfectly appropriate course to take. That is not what I mean by "reaching." Once the door is open, run through the door! But before the door is open, don't try to break it down with your head. It's entirely possible that there is something that wants to express itself.

Everything works in the proper timing and pacing. One of the hardest things to do is to wait for Life to give us the timing of things.

It's very important to be sensitive to the signs. There is an obvious distinction between an intense effort to create or accomplish, and reaching for something before it is right. Sometimes we have to do both in order to have the experience of both, so the distinction between them becomes obvious.

Whatever the Universe has designed for us, the Universe will demand that we express. For most people on the Path, that expression is about the fullness of Life. You may ask, what about those saints in India who appear to be angry and resentful? People come to see them and they throw rocks or shit at them. Sometimes naïve people say, "That person can't be a saint, because they're always angry and throwing things at people." But they are not seeing the saint's inner world. My opinion is that in certain cases the inner demand is so extreme that it warps the personality.

Without equating the artist with the saint, I am sure that many artists feel something like this at times. When somebody is in the midst of a creative surge, they can be very unpleasant on the outside, even to their children and lover, because they don't want to lose that taste, that inspiration. They don't want to eat, except when they want to eat; they don't want to talk to anybody, except when they want to talk. Everybody and everything except the emergence of that inspiration is a big pain in the ass, so they are liable to be a bit cranky and annoyed.

Like the artist, the saint is always—twenty-four hours a day, forever, nonstop, no vacations, no breaks—in an almost compulsive relationship to divine inspiration in the inner world. In my opinion, that possession warps the personality, and the saint becomes a cranky, angry, put-offish person on the outside. For some teachers, their job is to work with people; for other teachers their job is not to work with people but to work in a whole different way, in a universal way.

People are intimidated when someone is living fully. I consider myself an incurable romantic, and people have been trying to cure me of that romanticism for years. I have a big life, and, in the magnitude of that life, my love of beauty and freedom and spontaneity—

my romanticism, which is very precious to me—is constantly under assault by the "supposed-to-be" police. Those are the people who are always policing you because they think you should be a certain way. There are people who would do anything for me, but they won't relax and let me be romantic, even for five minutes, without putting their metaphoric hands around my throat. That doesn't mean life isn't being lived fully; it's just one of those unpleasant things that we all have to put up with in some small form or another.

So, just live fully. It's true that it is better to have loved and lost than never to have loved. Right now, in this moment, we are the result of every experience we have ever had. When profound experiences have faded or even disappeared, it is just the movement of things on the surface. The effects and results of all experience rests in our beings and continue to add to all that we are. That is one of the consequences of embodying faith.

When great mystic experiences, including love, come and then go, we don't regret their leaving, because we know that we have grown as a result of them. Those experiences are still implied by our being now. People say they want to fuse with another person, or they want to fuse with God. The only reason to look for fusing with God is if you want to disappear into Reality. A lot of people say, "I don't feel really alive." If you can live full out, even if in some cases that means an explosion, then live full out. I'm not talking about taking stupid risks; I mean living full out in terms of love, service, beauty. If you have come to the conclusion that the Path is about what it *actually* is about—not what we want it to be about, meaning our personal suffering—then go for it! Just live, and live fully.

Hauteville, France
July 2008

Be That Which Nothing Can Take Root In

M. Young

*L*ee's caravan of two vans and three cars drove up the thickly wooded hillside and parked by the orchards near the mansion. We tumbled out, disheveled and a little road weary, to take in the grandeur of the scene around us. The chateau and its grounds spoke of aristocratic old Europe. Nestled on a mountainside, the terraced gardens, greenhouse, and formal "silent" garden were impeccably manicured with a sober attention to detail that was echoed throughout the chateau itself. Spacious hallways and rooms with high ceilings were sparsely but richly adorned with well-placed, extremely valuable artifacts: a large, golden standing Buddha, a gorgeous painted tapestry depicting Krishna as Jagannath with the *gopis*, a rare Russian icon over the fireplace in the drawing room. This sanctuary—mansion, gardens, retreat cabin, trails—was dedicated to the study and practice of the Path.

The scene presented quite a juxtaposition with the band of Bauls, in the form of the Lee Lozowick Project, who had been invited to perform then stay overnight at this pristine European ashram. After an austere meal with our hosts in the garden under white canopies, the mood among these Belgians was so formal and somber that it was amazing to see them spring to lively action the moment the music started. Crushed up against the band in the small meditation hall that had been turned into a soirée chamber for the evening, over a hundred people danced, jumped and shouted to the sound of Lee's band. As the band and audience flowed into one reciprocal circuit, our lambent energies were gathered together, fired, shaken, and spun—like sugar into cotton candy—into a most refined and ebullient atmosphere. In that *rasa*, we were joining heaven and earth.

The joy and heart-cracking gratitude that I experienced in the heat of the music and merriment threw into sharp relief recent sorrows and struggles of the day. After the music passed and weary singers, musicians, dancers, children and revelers were making their way toward their slumbers, the troubled and insatiable discursive mind returned to plague me again, like the Red Sea rushing back into place after Moses had passed through. When shining moments have revealed that which is beautiful, they are not uncommonly followed by the return of the dark, most often in the form of the mind's relentless dialogue with its identifications, expectations, assumptions, and projections. Just like in the Dylan song Lee likes to sing, it's "trouble, trouble, trouble."

Lee continues to tell us that even though there is trouble, there is nothing to be troubled about, because most of the problems we perceive are a matter of attitude and not seeing clearly, which is the result of the mind's dividing, dividing, dividing. Yogi Ramsuratkumar often said, "There is only Father," while "Relax!" is Lee's most frequent teaching statement to me these days. If we can truly relax, we naturally fall into the disposition of enlightenment that exists prior to the conditioned mind, which knows that "There is only Father."

That night in the luxurious surroundings in which we found ourselves, I reflected for a long time on the purity and freedom of my guru's teaching phrase: "Be that which nothing can take root in." When we are not practicing moment-to-moment, every passing impression that impinges upon our senses takes root, flowers and bears its unhappy, twisted fruit within the bed of our identifications. Such "flowers of evil" (in praise of Baudelaire), can only leave us poisoned in some way: crazed by the pain of the world, bleeding from the shards and cruel edges of our equally broken companions, and worst of all, the heartbreak of personal failures to inhere in the wisdom of the Path.

Equanimity is one aspect of the wisdom that is cultivated on the Path—and, like peace and compassion, it is maddeningly elusive because the usual state of mind is here today, gone tomorrow, depending upon which way the wind blows. Maybe the hard part of maintaining equilibrium in this mad play of glaring opposites is simply the sticky nature of all things created—which is to stick to other created things. Perhaps this is precisely because it is all one—but isn't it true? There is some cosmic glue, obviously, that holds it all together, and it is this viscous natural fact that causes things of all kinds to adhere, grasp, and glom on for a ride, like cockleburs or a clinging vine.

Things are sticky. Like honey jars and little smears of jam. Like scotch tape, glue, gooey candy, mangoes and sweat. Like bodily juices. Life is sticky, and this is most poignant and true in the domain of human relationship. Of course, in the world of duality—where there are things we like and things we don't like—interrelatedness is the absolute law. Life itself does not seem to discriminate but rolls and rollicks along, playing the game as it is informed by its own inexorable forces. In fact stickiness, or relationship, is all about maintaining and sustaining life. In its essential nature, stickiness is love—the glue that holds everything together; the very interconnectedness that we worship and praise as Parvati and her Shiva, Radha and her

Krishna, Sita and her Ram in other contexts and vectors of experience. At its worst, this stickiness is the maddening chaotic unstable mess of entangled manifestation—a kind of insanity, a lack of clarity due to the madness of an overwhelming plethora of things that have obscured our vision.

The gods and goddesses have an infinite capacity for creating and sustaining life—like Apollo, the sun god, riding in his chariot across the sky each day, or Demeter, who presides over the fertility of the plant and animal world. In their capacity for destroying life, the gods have a rather immense penchant for initiating humans into realms of higher consciousness, which they regularly do. Take, for example, the way that Eros and Aphrodite awakened Psyche's consciousness—through erotic love, trickery and betrayal. The gods and goddesses do whatever they damn well please, and if you look into Greek and Roman mythology, you find them doing some pretty questionable things. Rape, jealousy, back-biting, intrigue, betrayal—these are just a few of their regular activities. Both their praiseworthy and nefarious acts seem to be reflecting something to us about the human dilemma.

But let us return to stickiness. In the created world of infinite diversity, all manner of things seem to sidle up as close as possible, wrap themselves in our soft furs, thick or sparse, and burrow in like worms or spores or some other symbiotic creature looking for a place to take hold and gestate, beginning their life cycle. There they feed off our life's blood, ensuring their progeny many fertile generations to come and even the hope of permanence—longevity at least, if not immortality—as they carry on in the natural expression of life propagating and preserving itself.

In other words: Relationships of all kinds are the stickiest, most intertwined, complex, fertile, seed-sprouting gardens of all. The more conscious we strive to become, the more we wish to engage a transformation of self, the more the trolls and ogres and pixies and elves (not to mention Oberon and Titania, who are real trouble when they arrive) that reside in each of us come out to play. We human beings seem hell bent on dragging each other into our briar patches because, as the truism goes, "misery loves company."

Many people who are on a genuine spiritual path do not live lives of seclusion and solitude; most of our spiritual practice actually occurs in the daily marketplace of relationship with friends, family, children, co-workers, clients, sangha mates, husbands and wives, life partners and everything else. The more receptive to our interconnectedness we are, the more we get entangled. Once entangled, we may be smothered to death from lack of air, or bleed to death on the thorns, depending on which metaphor works in the moment. It is in this fertile field where everything beautiful and horrid may grow, cross-pollinate, fertilize and generally intermingle—and it is in this fertile field where practice may yield up its bountiful harvest.

"Be that which nothing can take root in" is a practice that informs us of how to be vulnerable and compassionate, generous and receptive, heartful and feeling without getting entangled and dragged down into each other's muck and mire. In order to practice in this most sublime way, one must be an adult. Arnaud Desjardins spoke on this:

> *Here is another one of Swamiji's statements: "A child lives in emotions, an adult no longer has any emotions." These words are extraordinarily efficient in helping you to progress on your own Path. I realize it is quite hard for you to understand. We went to Swamiji to hear him speak about Vedanta, wisdom, Brahman, Atman; we did not go to hear him speak of childishness. But when speaking of childishness, I find myself in the heart of*

Swamiji's teachings, in remembrance of Swamiji, in communion with Swamiji. Emotion = childishness; dependency = childishness; the inability to be alone = childishness; the inability to postpone until the next day = childishness.

If you go back to these different themes, you will be able to see that "having" is childishness and "being" is the adult state. Because a child is [naturally] dependent, its imperative need is to have. An adult has less and less the need to have and finds increasing joy, fullness and security in being. Of course, it is perfectly normal for a child to be childish. It is no longer a normal state for an adult to be childish....

Here is another one of Swamiji's definitions: "The child is meant to ask and to receive; the adult is meant to hear the request and to give." Once again, assess your existence according to this criterion. "....To what extent do I still need people to listen to me, to show an interest in me and be giving toward me?" Each time you will find "having" and "being" at the heart of these questions.[1]

At the most basic psychological level, we have been hearing for years that we need to establish proper boundaries as an individual in order to function as an individuated self. When we withdraw our projections and expectations from others, and we realize that we have no power to change or affect others ultimately, a certain freedom begins to dawn. We begin to see both ourselves and others with more clarity because we have stripped away the projections of our own psyche upon them.

---

[1]   Arnaud Desjardins, "From the Child to the Sage," to be published, *Tawagoto*, Winter 2009.

Very likely it will be necessary to start over, many times, with basic psychological clarity. With intention and the teacher's guidance, we will move into the practice of "Being that which nothing can take root in," which will lead, sooner or later, to the experiences of Just This or Assertion. In Vajrayana Buddhism of the Kagyu line, Assertion is called *mahamudra*—perfect clarity of awareness, the realization of the nature of Reality. Arnaud Desjardins calls this "accepting what is, as it is, here and now." Any truly pithy practice will lead to this core of practice.

To be an adult is to make the distinction between emotional dependence upon others and the truth of our interconnectedness. To be an adult is to stand firm in what is true for us without taking on the reactions of others, which can cause damage to our inner world. This requires the ability to let things pass us by, to "Be that which nothing can take root in." Sometimes we have to witness another's suffering and offer up a silent prayer. Often, to simply refuse to play the game of one's neurosis interacting with another's neurosis is the hardest thing of all, leading to endless permutations of stickiness. We want to remain open, resilient, receptive and flowing in relationship without getting tangled up, tripped or ripped to shreds and then losing precious life force. Therefore, it behooves us to cultivate an awareness of life in its myriad manifestations within the context of practice: "Be That Which Nothing Can Take Root In."

The primal psychological imperative of the body-based ego has done its job well by creating complex strategies of survival during childhood. As an adult, ego stands in the way of transformation because in order to transform, one must die, and ego seeks to avoid death. The demand of self-preservation is always behind the deep-rooted part of us that shouts "No!" to the raw awakened state, in which the separative identity has died for all effective purposes. And so we say "no" to transformation; "no" to a life of self-sacrifice in service to others; "no" to discipline, "no" to radiant happiness, "no" to luminous emptiness—"no" to surrender to the Will of God. We want to remain children rather than take up the obligations of an adult. What we must do is say "yes" to being an adult.

The impossibility of the task and the ephemeral nature of all passing phenomena (which includes the fruits of the Path such as compassion, equanimity and inner peace) can become an almost unbearable experience as we trudge along, dragging behind us the immense burden of our psychological strategies that are fraught with their own stickiness, lending themselves to every manner of enmeshment, co-dependence, general confusion and chaos. Gurdjieff referred to these as "the body of habits" and the multiple "I's," that are animated in interactions with others. After a certain amount of time in sadhana and spiritual practice, there is a perception, maybe even a literal sensation, of dragging the corpse of our body of habits along with us.

Even after the practitioner has lost interest in them and the self has gone on about greater work, the body of psychological habits still animates its tendencies and addictions, based on those strategies or decisions made at a very early age or even brought into incarnation as karmic tendencies. It can be an unpleasant surprise to find ourselves doing something that is beneath our dignity, which points toward the fact that we have not persevered fully in observing ourselves. So, the corpse becomes our constant companion and goad to practice, until any weak foundations have been discovered and replaced with strong, true foundations upon which a trustworthy practice can come to fruition. That is, a practice in which calm, equanimity, discernment and abiding insight are not wishful thinking but a real ground upon which to stand.

Beyond psychological efficacy, "Be that which nothing can take root in" captures an essential underpinning of tantric practice. One cannot navigate through the complexities of life and remain free to engage higher work in service to the Divine if we are constantly finding ourselves trapped in sticky situations in which we have lost our clarity of mind and purpose. Therefore, to live with the awareness, awakened receptivity and heartfulness demanded by the Path of Enlightened Duality, we must learn to discriminate and make distinctions, for only if we are making proper distinctions can we "Be that which nothing takes root in."

Essential discrimination is the child of clarity. My master will sometimes say, when I am fretting over what someone else is doing and whether or not I should interfere, "It's not your business. Leave it alone." Or, he will say, "You are not seeing clearly. You cannot accept what is until you see clearly." He has consistently taught us that we must learn to make the proper distinctions between what is important and what is not important before we act and perhaps find ourselves entangled in ways that are unproductive.

Making these distinctions is one of the important ways that a practitioner guards his or her energy. Every day we lose tremendous amounts of life force in casual social interactions, emotional entanglements, romanticism, nostalgia, worry, projection, expectation, and assumptions about ourselves and others. When we are tied up in knots in these emotional states, we do not have free attention. When the natural reservoir of life force is leaking or dwindling, we do not have the energy reserves that are necessary in order to work in the spiritual sense. We can see this principle at work in a river that has been dammed to generate electricity: when there is a drought, there is not enough water in the reservoir to create the force necessary to generate electricity as it flows over the dam.

Building and conserving energy is a fundamental element of tantric practice, because without energy, we cannot act in either gross or subtle domains. In tantric work one of the primary aims is to be in active internal relationship with the *ista devata*—the chosen deity or *yidam*. Without energy and free attention, we cannot place our attention on the deity and we do not have the energy necessary to make or distill rasa to attract the attention of the Beloved in the form of the ista devata. How do we make rasa? We make or distill rasa from basic life energy by placing our attention on the ista devata—or that which we adore, which could be a particular piece of art or music, a child or partner or dear friend.

Energy is generated through being. Being and doing are another pair of opposites that interplay in the realm of duality; the organic system of the body generates energy through the state or quality of being, whereas when we are busy in the activity of doing things, we are expending energy. Because being generates energy and regenerates the organic system at all levels, when we are in a highly active mode, it is important to bring balance to our organism with moments of simple beingness. When being and doing are in a reciprocal, complementary dance, then energy is both expended and renewed by the creativity that is generated between the passive (receptive) and active states. Even though it is possible to generate energy through activity, there is no substitute for large doses of meditation, contemplation, reflection and contemplative silence and solitude.

As Swami Prajnanpad said, the adult does not "want" and is able to find complete satisfaction in being. Herein is the secret of the sage. So often we function as if we are abandoned children who are focused on getting our desires fulfilled rather than acting as adults who have cultivated the qualities of patience, generosity and inner quietude. The degree to which we are fixated on our unmet psychological needs is the degree to which we live out our fundamental childhood trauma in the dynamics of our daily lives. If we look deeply, we see that the need to do, accomplish, act and achieve is driven by a need for acknowledgment; all this driven activity of doing, doing, doing—while being is ignored and even feared—is the thin veil that covers our need to be loved and acknowledged. We have not yet truly learned the secret of being, which leads to the discovery of innate wholeness and Organic Innocence.

As long as we live from the context of self-reference rather than the context of God-reference, we are limited in our ability to cultivate the rasa that will attract the attention of the ista devata. Most of the self-obsessing and loss of vital energies necessary to the production of rasa is due to unresolved psychological conflicts reflected in the entanglements, misunderstandings, resentments and subtle combat that so commonly occurs between people. Within the crucible of sadhana, spiritual friendship—which carries so much potential to be a place of refuge and even transformational alchemy—is often fraught with serious difficulty.

When we are seriously engaged in the Path and practicing within a bonded sangha (or a bonded relationship with mates, children, family members, friends, or a group of some kind, for example a band or publishing team, or it could be the church choir), we cannot walk away from troubled relationships. In ordinary life, when we encounter a difficult person, someone who we feel brings out the worst in us, we just get rid of them. We fire them, quit our jobs, move away, get a divorce, end the friendship, don't return their calls, refuse to visit (as in the case of relatives, for example) or in some way just cut them out of our life experience altogether.

It seems there will always be those individuals who bring out violent emotions; whose subtle inflections of gesture, tone and facial expression are enough to send us into the ninth ring of hell. But in sadhana, we cannot run away or ask that person to kindly exit our lives. We have to hang in there and keep chiseling away at the matrix that surrounds the jewel of understanding, the gem of insight, the turquoise necklace of "being that which nothing can take root in"— a very high practice, indeed. We must hang in there until we can be a free adult.

Once I asked my teacher what to do about a chronic negative relationship with someone. I was expressing my disappointment in myself and how my negative responses to another person seemed to point toward an abject failure in my sadhana. It was a true enough assessment of myself, yet also a thin veneer over the blame and resentment I felt toward the other person. After briefly describing my misery, I said, as if I'd never practiced a day in my life: "What do I do with such negative emotions with someone I have to live with for the rest of my life?"

"Nothing," he snapped. "So what? So what if you have negative emotions? The Work doesn't care about your negative emotions! Do nothing," Lee concluded. "Just go on." This ferocious answer came without his even looking at me, but continuing with what he was doing, as if to demonstrate the absurdity of my predicament. Of course he had already given me enough teachings on this subject to last five hundred lifetimes. To be asking at this point was an insult, therefore I considered the fact that he answered at all to be a demonstration of his immense generosity and compassion. The emptiness of my question ricocheted back at me like a sharp sound in a tunnel.

At some point in all tantric practice, it becomes necessary to call forth the rasa of the heart so that the ista devata is pleased—so pleased that He or She will come to reside within the body-mind-soul matrix of the practitioner. The crux of the matter may be: what brings enjoyment to the deity and what banishes the deity? This is the fundamental demarcation line from which all discernment follows and from which "be that which nothing can take root in" follows. Therefore, in the constant interplay of intricacies in the field of sanctuary that is the radiant being of the spiritual master, we are challenged to cultivate the rare sheen of a clear vessel, one in which the elixir of life—the secret of the golden flower, the essential quintessence, the rasa and mood of inner being that is pure praise—may entice the Beloved in such a way that His or Her radiance burns forth from our being.

When we are practicing "being that which nothing can take root in," we become sanctuary. Not only does the teacher need sanctuary—every human being does. For the spiritual master, this quintessence, this rasa of sanctuary, is essential to his work, for the Divine is drawn to the perfume of that rasa. The wellspring of rasa that may relieve the suffering of others is made possible by virtue of its clear vessel of containment; a human being who becomes such a vessel offers the solace of compassion, spaciousness, clarity, and nonjudgment to others when they are sad, angry, caught in greed, pride or hatred. Over time, we become capable of being sanctuary even when others are projecting their sorrows and the furious, banked fires of their suffering out upon the world around them. Isn't this what we ourselves long for when we are lost in our own murky swamp of illusion—compassionate loving-kindness that is borne of clarity? Yes, and how to achieve and maintain enough clarity in the hurly burly grinding away of the ten thousand things? "Be that which nothing can take root in," and from that grand sweep of fecund emptiness, all things are possible.

To "be that which nothing can take root in" is to be a *sunya*, a Great Nothing. This is the good news: if we are practicing when the stickiness of others is coming toward us (which may be only a response to our own stickiness having gone out toward them), we will be creating a generosity of space—a spaciousness that can be filled with light, an internal environment or atmosphere that will naturally clear away our unconscious motives to ensnare, capture and therefore share our personal suffering with others. We could say that "be that which nothing can take root in" is a bodhisattva practice of the most delicate and exalted order.

How to "Be that which nothing can take root in"? In strict nondual-ist teachings, love and attachment are viewed as problems or obsta-cles that must be overcome through cultivation of nonattachment. Human beings naturally desire to be loved, respected, appreciated, understood, seen at the most essential levels; likewise, we have an innate impulse to love and respect others. Because we are all con-nected, we naturally desire harmony and heart-to-heart commu-nion with others. It's a complex blend, because many of these desires are natural and inherently good; they live very close to Organic Innocence within us, and will ask for expression. From the Baul per-spective there is nothing "wrong" with these desires or the fulfill-ment of these desires. The answer to the problem of relationship is found within relationship itself. To kill our desire with suppression or denial in order to become completely detached is not the way of tantric practice, nor is it the way of Enlightened Duality.

In tantric practice we do not turn away from desire, emotion, or entanglement within life's complexity. The way is to say yes to it all, but this requires courage, vulnerability and energy. The way of Enlightened Duality is to be completely attached—to love with total ferocity, total commitment, with the bone-deep knowledge of impermanence guiding our knowing that this moment is all that we have. Instead of seeking to be loved, we turn toward loving the other; instead of craving respect, we give respect. This is the path of free-dom and fulfillment.

We love and are attached within the knowing that all this is fleet-ing, and it is this knowledge itself which is heartbreak. In heartbreak we know the bittersweet rasa that is compassionate love. We have compassion for ourselves and others because we know that we are all broken, flawed, wounded. If in no other way, we are wounded by the very fact of impermanence. We are mortal beings, our time is finite. Our time to love the other, to know and be aware of the Divine Play, will come and go. We will die and watch those we love die. This thick, overspilling, graceful moment of God's flaming love for us, within us, living us, as imperfect and broken as we are, is all we have—and it is more than enough. It is Grace.

The spores and seeds and all kinds of effluvium of love attachments are drawn into the juicy gestalt of the embodied organic being—the matrix of corporeal awareness in which we breathe, sense, cognize and ultimately love with compassionate discernment. In the thicket of life, it may be that we are so bemused, confused, enthralled, and enchanted by the Dance of the Mad Lord that in moments we forget everything else. Forgetfulness makes us sticky, so that anything and everything may take root within the matrix we understand as "me." This too will arise, and we can surrender to it all: the aching pain of our confusion and imprisonment within illusion and the radiant soaring moments of freedom as well.

It's true that forgetfulness makes us sticky, but then so does eating ripe peaches—a true metaphor for divine rasa, the holy juice, because what is stickier than the nectar from a sugary, sunstruck, wind-rain-and-starlight-grown summer peach? There aren't many good peaches left in this world of woe ruled by monstrous Monsanto and other corporate techno-evils! This summer, amazingly enough, we had all the sweet, sun-ripened peaches, nectarines and apricots we could eat as we tumbled down the roads of France in our vans on tour with Lee's band. That is where gratitude comes into play in this crazy quilt of freely associating reflections and metaphors. Compassion blossoms from gratitude in these moments of reflection.

That night on the mountainside in Belgium, when I stepped back into the soirée after playing in the orchard with the children, I was happily surprised to be swept up into the sweet relief of gratitude. Gratitude was the mood of the prayer that ascended from the synergies of molten jubilation as the audience was melted down in the last few songs of the band's glory parade. There, in the midsummer night, we were at the borderline between Belgium and France, at the borderline between human and divine where transformational potentials had lain secretly in waiting for the right call, the perfect note to draw them forth and into life. There, in between polarities in rapid motion, dark consorting with light and light consorting with dark, yin and yang oscillated so fast you could hardly see the distinctions. We were a hummingbird in flight.

Context

Lee Lozowick

*E*verything is about context. When your context is viewing Reality as it is, everything in Reality takes on a different radiation, including you. In spiritual work we use words like "surrender" and "sacrifice," but we are not talking about the renunciation of things such as joy or beauty or happiness or love. We are talking about the renunciation of illusion, the renunciation of lies. It is important to understand this distinction, so we don't define our lives by the need to have nothing. We don't have to be a struggling spiritual student, having nothing.

Reality is a very big environment that includes everything in Creation, and in that everything there is a large spectrum of thingness. Obviously there are vast areas of the world that live in extreme poverty. When my master was building his ashram, he would only hire local people. The average salary was one and a half euros a day—much higher than the workers were used to getting. All of them had families to support. Their day started at seven a.m. and they worked until they got the job done, sometimes until one or two a.m. And they were thrilled to have the work.

Just as there are vast areas of the world that live in extreme poverty, there are areas of the world that live in extreme wealth—Monaco, Lichtenstein. There is great diversity in terms of what people have and the resources that are available to them. Obviously there is tremendous diversity in health, from those who have no arms and legs, who can only eat and look around, to those who have vital health: climb mountains, jump out of planes, perform amazing feats of physical activity in the Olympics.

Within all that diversity of life, Reality embraces everything. Without getting into karma and what karma means in detail, let us say that sometimes we find ourselves without any effort in enviable circumstances—healthy, successful, with great children who are healthy and happy; we have love and friendship. Sometimes we find ourselves in circumstances that are not so healthy: we are struggling, neurotic, psychotic, pathological.

In the New Age, metaphysicians say that anyone can change their circumstance. After thirty-five years of teaching, I'm not convinced that we can change our circumstance; however, Reality is malleable, and there are things we can do to change our context without changing our physical reality. When you change your context, Reality will look different to you from the new context. For example, it's very common that when a relationship breaks up—not necessarily because there isn't love, but because people can't live with each other—still there is heartbreak. For the first time in their lives, people realize that they were not innocent in the tensions of the relationship; it was not all the fault of their partner. This can be very useful, especially for the next relationship.

Reality is vast and deep, and any aspect of Reality can potentially be a part of our own personal reality. Catastrophe, ill health, a life full of fear, stress, unhappiness—any of those are lawful in our own personal reality. No matter what is happening, Reality will without question look different when your consciousness perceives holistically what is, without dividing it into separate elements. You will see things differently. On the other hand, if you look at the appearance of things, and you don't look into the essence of what you are seeing, then you will be very confused by what you see, and you will be disturbed.

When earthquakes or tidal waves or a natural disaster hits the world and thousands of people are killed or homeless, even if you don't know them, you feel some heartbreak, some horror, some sensitivity for the suffering going on. At the same time, you understand that you have a life, and in your own life there are things to take care of, people to respect, agreements to keep, and responsibilities to uphold. As much as your prayers might go to people affected by natural tragedies, you also understand that for human beings to control the weather—as if we could control the world so that there are never spikes of activity like earthquakes or hurricanes—we would create more problems in the long run if we did.

If you don't understand the principle I am describing, look at the way the world is now: We, in our unspeakable arrogance, have attempted to control every natural force in the Universe. We are so stupid that we have failed to realize the obvious [tragedy] of that, and so we are now considering nano-technology and implanting computer chips under the skin and genetic research that would give us the power to decide the genetic make up of the human race! It's parallel to a child who doesn't like the way the game is going and says, "I'm going to take my game and go home!" We are effectively destroying humanity. Life may continue, but it may not be life any of you with any sensitivity would want to participate in. We won't have a long discussion of "Is it too late?"because tribal elders all over the world are saying that it is already too late.

Reality is what it is, and how Reality manifests is directly relevant to context. You, as an individual, can only change your context; you cannot change anyone else's context. Relative to changing the cultural context, it is probably possible but it is very rare and unusual. An example of changing cultural context is the industrial revolution: an agricultural, rural-based culture was turned into an urbanized, industrialized culture in a very short period of time.

We were reading the statistics on how many people are leaving their villages and countrysides all over the world and moving into the cities. The statistics will scare the hell out of you. Within forty years, seventy percent of the population on the Earth will live in cities! If you have been to L.A. or Kolkata or Delhi or Mexico City or Tokyo—big cities—you see that people are mad in those environments. Paris is a lovely, romantic city; I love Paris. Even in Paris, people are insane! They are full of tension, stress, disease, pain, resentment, anger. Every major city is going to be enlarged by fifty to seventy percent in the next forty years!

If you have studied psychology, you know what over-population does to rats, and rats are very simple creatures compared to human beings. The problems that rats have in over-populated situations will probably be multiplied a hundred times for human beings living in the cities of the future. It's not an attractive equation. Those of you who want to live in the country now are intuiting the future, because everything, in all the major cities, will be madness. Those who hold the power will be particularly mad. George Bush was not elected by the people; he was elected by other politicians. Those who have the power are not interested in changing the cultural context.

I have been teaching for thirty-five years, and lately—though not in the beginning, when I thought I knew everything—I am continually open to the possibility that there might be a form of teaching I could bring to people that could be more effective than the form I now bring. The form of my teaching is always changing; to perceive changes over weeks and months is not possible, but over longer periods of time it becomes obvious. The form changes because I am interested in efficiency, not in how eloquent or dynamic I am.

What interests me is you: In your lives, can you align yourselves more immediately and directly to Reality as it is? When the context of your life is "me and mine," your choices are very limited because of the grip your psychology has on you. You are constantly making choices relative to action around money, food and sex, which covers everything. People usually think money is about power, but it's not; sex is about power. When your context is Reality as it is, then your choices or options relative to action in all those domains become almost unlimited. Your ability to mold Reality becomes vast and dynamic.

So, saying yes means accepting the nature of Reality as it is now, and acting. If you are trying to act from a narrow and limited position, how creative or influential are you going to be? If you are able to act from the unlimited, then you can be a Mozart or a Bach. The greatest artists in the world, as extraordinarily technically competent as some might be, are great because their context is unlimited possibility. They are not bound by the constraints of a narrow and limited worldview.

Paris
September 2008

Heartbreak

M. Young

When it is dark, you can see the stars.
—Persian Proverb

The air has gone chartreuse and silver. Thunder cracks and rolls across the sky, obscuring for a moment the susurration of the wind in the trees, the pattering language of leaves in the quicksilver rain that falls. Autumn has arrived, and it's a poignant and lovely mood that greets us, coming home in mid-September to our country ashram in France after three weeks on the road. The first thing I find out is that the toilet doesn't work. It's a great metaphor, because there is a pressing need to digest and eliminate the detritus of many impressions from our most recent travels in Germany.

A long van ride brought Lee and his traveling party back from Hamburg, where we had spent four days at the end of the Shri tour participating in a conference titled, "The Path of Transformation." There were a wide range of paths represented: Buddhist, Christian, Hindu, Sufi and shamanic. Lee was the rep for the Hindus. Each of the presenters was given a euphemistic name: Lee was called "the Alchemist." He had been asked to speak on the alchemy of love and sex.

Our teacher was in arch form. After two days of listening to the other presenters, he strode across the stage and took his seat, threw a nonchalant arm across the back of the black leather couch and said, "Okay, the women can take off their blouses!" Leaning back further and turning casually, as if he was yelling at some invisible waiter, he called out, "Hurry up with the popcorn! The show's about to start!" He then proceeded to say, "I've been looking at this couch for two days and wondering if I would feel like I was watching TV up here. This would make a great reality show: 'The Conference'!" In his inimitable and most insolent style, Lee proceeded to insult, implicate and provoke his audience with off-the-cuff theatrical stream of consciousness, tossing in some scintillating bijous here and there for anyone willing to make the payment, up front, of loss of ego-face to receive the teaching. About a third of the people in the room walked out during the first of two talks Lee gave that afternoon.[1] Some left in a hurry, making irate statements like, "I didn't come here for this!"

It was a most interesting phenomenon to watch—and one that Lee is rather infamous for serving up to audiences over the years. People in general are not prepared for an encounter with a true teacher, one who carries the spiritual power to initiate transformational alchemy at a level that is beneath the radar of the thinking mind. How easy it is to forget that the first thing occurring in an alchemical process is a breaking down of the old structure, the dissolution, which involves a destruction of that which was before—whether it is self-image, world view, religious and moral beliefs, general mindset, or any small detail within those big categories of identification. We like the sound of the word alchemy because it is very romantic and engaging, but when we are faced with the real thing, we flee for our lives—the comfortable, well-established life of ego, that is.

---

[1]   Excerpt from Lee's discourses at the "Path of Transformation" conference held September 6–9, 2008 in Hamburg, Germany appears as the essay titled "The Alchemy of Sex" on page 407.

This is often the way Lee works in public talks. He throws out a lot of bait, like peppering the water with corn to see what fish rise to the surface. If we are easily offended by seeming insults, we will take the bait and get angry. Then, if we want to work on ourselves, we get to see the dynamics of our anger; it's a way to gauge where one's self-importance and identifications are lodged. Some leave, and those who remain experience how Lee's modus operandi changes to give a jewel-like teaching. Even those who take it personally and leave in a huff have the opportunity to see how easily they can be manipulated by words alone.

Those who are willing to stay in place and feel beneath the words of denunciation, who are willing to receive Lee's derisive accusations of our chronic mechanicality, sleep and selfishness, then become the recipients of not only the jewels he will spill out before the end of the talk but also of the rare moods he invariably invokes in such teaching spaces. In Hamburg, by the end of Lee's second session many people were so moved they had tears in their eyes. The remaining group of about a hundred people were given a glimpse of the true teacher, and their gratitude and amazement was palpable. Many approached Lee after the talks to thank him profusely.

When Lee steps into this function of trickster and alchemical maestro for me personally, I often do not welcome his penetrating intrusion into my "blissful" ignorance until later—after I've had a chance to digest and integrate an exchange with the guru's burning fire. Sometimes "after" means five or ten minutes later; sometimes it means an hour or a day or a week later. At this point in the process of sadhana, I am interested in just how fast I can shift from ego's recoil to the practitioner's context.

I often see Lee's brash style as a disquieting and sometimes deeply painful, even heartbreaking, demonstration of sacrifice for his students. Not only does he enact the rogue, fool, hard-ass cynic, antagonist and general bad guy for ego, he also has to endure people's projections and negative thought-forms that are then directed

toward him. But, he does what it takes to get the job done—that
is, the job of confronting our illusions so that there may be some
chance, however slim, that we will be moved one step closer to that
which we really are.

In the early spring of 2008, shortly after we returned from the trip
to Bengal, Lee initiated a strict natural healing regime. Because he
was unable to speak with ease and he was carefully conserving his
energy and speech, he chose to handwrite his weekly addresses to the
sangha. When he began to speak again publicly, Lee gave his first talk
of the summer in France, which appears in this book under the title
"Death." It was a penetrating response to the well-meaning concern
expressed by students and friends for his health and an assertion of
the context of Reality as it is.

Since then the sangha has been thrust into a much greater daily
confrontation with impermanence and uncertainty. Lee asks us to
live easefully within the great unknowns of our lives; he has repeatedly called us to have faith, to trust completely, to live into the teaching of Spiritual Slavery. We really have no idea what the future holds
for any of us. This is as true in our particular sphere as *sadhakas* as
it is true in the global sense: the world teeters on the brink of great
changes. Every moment is a new moment, and to bring nostalgia
and sentimentality to whatever is arising, including our guru's health
and the impermanence of his body, is to deny and suffocate—even
murder—the delicate environment of our inner work.

Chögyam Trungpa Rinpoche was famous for making such com-
munications, in which he contextualized practice for his students, as
Jeremy Hayward reports in *Warrior-King of Shambhala: Remembering
Chögyam Trungpa*. The story that follows is placed within the
Buddhist teaching of the *kayas* (bodies) relating to the awakened
aspects of being. These can manifest as either enlightened aspects or

neurotic aspects, corresponding to mind, speech and body: respectively, the *dharmakaya*, the *sambhogakaya*, and the *nirmanakaya*.[2]

> *Once, when Rinpoche was ill, one of his close students was concerned about his health and asked him to take more care of it. Rinpoche said, "Why is everyone so concerned about my health?" The student replied, "Because we care about you, we care about your body." Rinpoche responded, "My body is the whole world." That is the point of view of a being who has fully accomplished the realization of the nirmanakaya. This brings with it tremendous compassion because there is no hang-up, there is no "me"; so compassion, love for our world and for others, radiates naturally. Compassion has expressed itself, at the nirmanakaya level, in all of the physical manifestations of dharma, texts, statues, and great dharma teachers.[3]*

These days there is a profoundly renewed feeling of urgency around Lee, sometimes ecstatic and sometimes disturbing, which is clearly communicated in his speech, gestures and teachings. Unequivocally, Lee is letting us know that there is work to be done,

---

[2] Jeremy Hayward, *Warrior-King of Shambhala: Remembering Chögyam Trungpa*, page 122. Hayward explains further that dharmakaya relates to awakened mind; sambhogakaya relates to awakened speech and emotions; nirmanakaya relates to the body and is often referred to as the "emanation body" of one who has realized the Buddha: the physical form of the teacher, guru or tulku. "At this level there is pure energy, which is undistorted by 'me'/'I.' The energy normally experienced as the unawakened or negative emotions—passion/lust, anger, ignorance, jealousy, pride—are felt from the perspective of awaken mind as energies at play in the sambhogakaya, and as wisdoms of the five Buddha families...."

[3] Ibid. (It is noteworthy that Hayward makes the point of including texts, or scriptures, and statues as emanations of *nirmanakaya*, or manifestations of Buddha wisdom—a principle examined in depth in the essays of this book.)

on many different levels; he has been abruptly and ruthlessly making those communications that penetrate to the bone of our illusions. Lee's heartbreak at the "Path of Transformation" conference was apparent in his irascible manner of confrontation that communicated a profound frustration at the misunderstanding and misrepresentation of the teaching. If we are seeing clearly, the teacher's heartbreak is poignantly evident in these moments.

Many years ago at his ashram in southern France, Arnaud Desjardins once gave the teaching: "Do not be afraid to love the human guru." It takes a lot of courage and maturity to love the human guru, because to do so demands that we step out of our idolatry and fear, that we relinquish the steel-trap grip we have on life, and that we let go of our projections on the guru: savior, cosmic hero, divine lover, just father, holy mother and on and on, including all the negative projections that are foisted upon him. To love the guru as a human being requires the largeness of our inner being to hold, accept, even nurture in a way, the pressure of extreme paradox, which the guru appears to be in his or her manifestation as tangent point with the Divine. The *satguru* is the living embodiment of *purusha* and *prakriti*, which places at the guru's fingertips the potential to mirror to the disciple whatever is necessary to transmit the Supreme Reality and to catalyze a process of radical transformation of the being. Within the guru's attempts to guide and enlighten, he or she may exhibit a great deal of sound and fury for the benefit of the disciple's transformation. The guru's activity appears to be paradoxical from the perspective of ego, and yet when we see from a larger, more spacious view, that which seemed paradoxical is revealed as Just This.

The guru is a miracle of Grace, a living, breathing enigma: the guru is the giver of light and dispenser of blessings beyond our understanding; the guru is also a human being made of flesh and blood, born of woman and man. The miracle is that this human being embodies the qualities of awakened being and has the innate capacity to transmit those qualities to others. We can only truly see the guru and his sacrifice—the guru's absolute, irrevocable commitment to our growth and awakening in every moment— with clarity if we are willing to love the guru as a human being.

Love will break your heart. The more we are aligned with the guru in the mood of love and devotion, which tenderizes our hearts and makes us receptive to the guru's transmission, the more we are infected with his context. The guru's context—"my body is the whole world"—causes us to look upon the entire world through the eyes of heartbreak and compassion. Many years ago Neil Young wrote a song in which there is the line, "Only love can break your heart." It is an objective truth that we discover on the Path, but most of us will not understand the profound spiritual value of having our hearts broken for many years. Our romantic nostalgia about love limits our understanding so severely that we—as products of Western culture—are crippled when it comes to giving and receiving the true power of love. Love can and will break our hearts. It is the force of annihilation. It is the power that moves the planets around the sun, the glue that holds everything together. Love is a force that demands our utter respect and awe. We should be longing for love, yearning for love, aching for true love—not because we want the consolation of a new love affair to distract us from the real work of the spiritual Path, but because we want to be radically transformed by love.

To be Surrendered to the Will of God is to be moved by love. Not insipid, milk toast love, not the love of crocheted hearts and flowers and Hallmark cards, but love with no options. Kick ass, whole body, up against the wall, ferocious, galactic, stars burning into eternity love. Love without beginning or end. Love that leaves no stone unturned. Love of ruthless abandon. Love that reveals all. Love that makes the ultimate demands upon us. Love that gives rise to dignity and nobility. Love that endures all. Love as the power that causes the sun to burn in the sky as an act of praise. This is not where most of us live, because the only way to live in radical love is to have a wound that only God can heal.

The more love we feel, the more sorrow we feel. Before the conference in Hamburg, Lee was on the road with his blues band, Shri, for ten days. While traveling with them in northern Germany, I got the news from home that an old friend was brutally murdered one night in her home in Prescott. Her ex-husband, also a former acquaintance, turned out to be the prime suspect. (Two months later he was arrested for first degree murder.) There was a time when these two people were the perfect couple: attractive, genial, well-educated, interested in spirituality. They had kids together. They taught at the local college. Everyone loved her. He was a handsome, brilliant man. I knew their divorce had been a bitter one, but the shock of this news brought to mind the realness of my deep-rooted, visceral response to Lee's renditions of Jimi Hendrix's "Hey Joe" ("where you goin' with that gun in your hand?") with his band this summer. I heard this news, and my heart broke a little more.

Lots of things make me cry these days. News of a death. Children playing on the street. Prostitutes walking by, both ravaged and stylin', dressed to kill. Nuclear power plants billowing huge streams of smoke into the air. The sounds of birds at dawn. Children especially make me cry. They are so incredibly beautiful. The fact that their innocence will be crushed, even brutally destroyed, is almost too much to bear. How do we walk around, day after day, seeking our successes, justifying and defending against our failures, when children are being tortured, prostituted, murdered, sold into slavery? I don't think I will ever get over the suffering of children in the world, nor do I want to. I am willing to shoulder the burden of their suffering, to feel some of it, because maybe, just maybe, I can mitigate it in some small way through a conscious participation in it. This too is a form of prayer.

Weeks later, back in Arizona, Lee played a video of J. Krishnamurti's 1982 talks in Ojai, California. Krishnamurti spoke of the responsibility we have for everything that is happening in the world. His words communicated with a wrenching heartbreak as he spoke of how we are killing the planet and each other. He told the audience that we are murderers; we are violent, obsessive, brutal and primitive creatures. All this he said with perfect compassion while sorrow poured from his eyes, emanated in light waves from his fragile, elderly form.

The Path demands so much of us. It seems to take everything, each attachment, one by one—or in batches, for some. The Path says, "Oh, and I'll have this…and this…and this. Oh yes—and *this too*, because you don't really need this anymore, do you?" The Path loves us with ruthless abandon, and this is how we know it. When the Path wants to say, "I love you, you are precious to me," our illusions get dispelled, crushed, dissolved, destroyed—one way or another.

The Path takes our attachments and grinds them to dust in its maw in order to make room for love. Love and Grace would like to come and live inside us, but they will not as long as we are obstructed and afflicted with false identifications, attachments, addictions to the fool's gold of worldly life. We have to seek real beauty, not fake beauty, to make ourselves attractive to love. Lee says, "Seek beauty and avoid suffering." This is not a superficial statement to be taken narcissistically, as a path of denial and self-gratification; the context in which Lee gave this teaching is just the opposite. If we seek beauty and avoid suffering, we will find the treasures of annihilation promised by the Path. Our hearts will be irrevocably broken by beauty and impermanence. We will turn away from the needless self-obsessing that we usually call "suffering" and toward objective suffering. The precious nature of this ephemeral, passing life will break our hearts with its promise and its failure—its failure because, as the Qabalists know and as Bob Dylan said, "Everything is broken." We are cracked vessels full of light.

At Ferme de Jutreau in September 2008, a married couple—students of Lee—were telling him about a recent visit to see the woman's father at the family's country house in the lake region of northern Poland. They were smiling as they spoke of catching fish in the lake, then walking the woods to gather wild mushrooms for their dinner. In this pristine rustic setting, the meals they prepared over wood fires were "four-star"—delicious enough to satisfy the tastes of any gourmand. They discovered that they were deeply nourished by this way of life—with no electricity, resting in the hands of nature. They were touched as well by the gifts of handmade cakes, fresh eggs, milk and cream that came from their generous neighbors' chickens and cows. They baked cakes to give as gifts in return and carried them to the neighbor's house. It is a traditional, old fashioned way of life all over the world—even in America, in rural areas to this day—to share one's bounty with friends and neighbors.

After returning to Paris from Poland that same day, the man went back to work as a flight attendant for Air France. Hopping on a seven-hour flight to Luanda, the capitol of Angola, he was powerfully confronted with the disparity between the idyllic interlude in rustic northern Poland and the depravity and avarice of the modern world: the greed for "black gold" and all of the entanglements of the oil industry in Africa. On his flight were five women, five Africans, and 315 white men, all destined for the petroleum platforms near Luanda, where they would spend two months working for Total, Shell or some other corporate mega-monster. Tickets for this flight started at three thousand euros and went up to ten thousand euros for the eight first class seats on board. The oil companies paid for it all.

These workers would not see the truth of conditions in Angola—the poverty and crime of the streets, death from AIDS and starvation, tribal genocide, oppression of the people. They would see nothing but their Western-style sleeping and eating quarters where they lived off-duty, sequestered away from all unpleasant realities. He said that it is the same in all the oil-producing countries of Africa: Nigeria, Equatorial Guinea. The juxtaposition of these two experiences was shattering in a way; he went from Eden to Armageddon in twenty-four hours' time.

These images stayed with me. Later I checked some facts with them, knowing I wanted to write something about this. They started talking about many other aspects of the world at large, including the EU experimental lab that is far underground between France and Switzerland, where scientists want to create small "big bangs" and "black holes." These scientists want to find out whether Einstein's theory of relativity is correct, or if quantum physics is correct; once the high priests of science know which one is correct, whether time is circular or linear, then advances in technology would increase so fast it will seem like we are moving at the speed of light.

When I commented, "What a nightmare! How depressing," Lee, who was sitting nearby listening to this exchange while going through a box of artifacts, looked up and said, "If you don't want to get depressed, then don't ask about such things."

Someone else who was sitting in the room asked him, "You don't want to know about those things?" Lee answered, "Me? No. I don't care. I'm just living, and if the world ends, I'll be very happy. Bring it on." He picked up a Tibetan prayer wheel just then and started whirling it around and around. "Om mani padme hum…This is a nice one! It works well."

This is how Lee often makes the most powerful statements to us: through oblique and symbolic means. If we look only at the surface, we could take his statements out of the context of his overall teaching and believe—if we wanted to—that he is cynical or that he doesn't care. My experience in the moment was that Lee was communicating two things: the context of transcendence, and that prayer is the real answer to the problems of the world. He has said many times over the summer that he is going "full steam ahead" with his work, what Yogi Ramsuratkumar called "Lee's mission in the West." His almost constant teachings to us this summer about taking responsibility for what is going on in the world does not mean that he is saying we should strike out into social activism, but that we need to dig more deeply into our practice—to turn toward prayer. Lee, the bad Poet, prayed once to Yogi Ramsuratkumar thusly:

> Oh Yogi Ramsuratkumar,
> > Master of Hearts, Quieter of Minds —
> You have made such a multitude of cracks
> > in Your son's hard heart.
> For that lee is ever-grateful,
> > Your Mercy is great.
> Still there is a nagging question
> > which is this:
> it seems that as much of Your Love
> > as can get into these cracks
> is exactly the amount, Transformed,
> > that can get out to benefit others
> in their pain and suffering and
> > in their endless need.
> This is not enough,
> > I tell You this now.
> Break this stony heart wide open
> > so Your Love will pour in unobstructed,
> not leak in in the small amounts
> > that Your son's arrogance allows.
> Break this heart so completely
> > that no heart remains,
> no inside and no outside,
> > but only You and no-one and nothing else.

Then Your Love won't merely leak out
  but will rush like a torrent
drowning everything in its path
  with You, only You.
This lee asks of You, Kind Father.
  Listen to his prayer.[4]

How do we deal with heartbreak about the decay and decline of sacred culture in our contemporary world? I was reading the December 2008 issue of *EnlightenNext*, the magazine published by Andrew Cohen and his students, in which I noticed a short review of a new video game called "Spore" under one of the magazine's feature sections titled "Technosphere." "Spore" is a game that recently hit the market and has excited the general public because it is all about giving the player the egoic thrill of their lives—they get to play God in the game of evolution:

> *Simulating the vast multibillion-year trajectory of life's development—"from cellular pipsqueak to land-walking animal to tribal half-wit to civilized sentient and finally to space-faring ultra-being," as UK reviewer Alec Meer put it best—Spore offers an experience like no other, one that actually achieves that rarest of gaming goals: a seamless synthesis of education and fun....*
>
> *Not only does the game allow kids to play God, but it lets them give the evolutionary process a clear direction*

---

4   Lee Lozowick, *Death of a Dishonest Man*, October 21, 1995.

> *while doing so, consciously evolving their intelligently*
> *designed creatures through increasing orders of com-*
> *plexity and expansions of consciousness.*[5]

This gives one pause to question: Fun? Education? The review goes on to state that a *New York Times* article written just before the new game hit the market raised objections from evolutionary biologists who were questioning the so-called "educational" aspects and the over-all value of such a game. University of Chicago professor Neil Shubin stated, "Playing the game you can't help but feel amazed how, from a few simple rules and instructions, you can get a complex functioning world with bodies, behaviors and whole ecosystems." Omnipotence for dummies? That pretty much says it all about modern culture.

Dr. Shubin particularly cautioned against the idea, inculcated by the game into the mind of the player, that the evolutionary process proceeds in a linear ascent from oceanic cellular organisms to "galaxy-spanning civilizations of self-aware beings."[6] Biologists are now aware that evolution is "more like a tree than a line," as the article in the *New York Times* stated. *EnlightenNext* tells us that biologists describe evolution as "meandering in all directions over eons of time, with some branches bending backward and others never bearing any fruit."[7] Dr. Shubin concludes, "There's no progressive arrow that dominates nature."[8] Maybe that is because Creation is the work of God, a Great Mystery, an unfathomable Unknown? Instead of competing with God, we should be bowing before God's creation in awe and praise, but like Lucifer, we say "no!"

My eyes settled in on the troubling term "tribal half-wit," and I wondered how the Navajo, Hopi and Zuni people of Arizona would

---

5   "Spore—Playing God with Evolution," *EnlightenNext*, December 2008, page 24.
6   Ibid.
7   Ibid.
8   Ibid.

feel about the use of such a term. Hopefully, when Alec Meer made the statements quoted above, he was just trying to provoke the reader—to capture our attention in order to make a point about how deeply flawed and deadly this game, ostensibly designed to merely entertain, actually is. The entire context of this game is built upon the premise that human intelligence knows better than Divine Intelligence what evolution is all about. We are being trained and prepared for a society that is entirely run by the high priests of science, controlled by the greed for power of those very few who run the corporate megaliths. It is tragic that children will be further indoctrinated to believe that evolution means greater technological complexity instead of greater potentials of being.

It's great that the biologists have made critical statements about the game, but it won't make one bit of difference to the vast majority of parents and teens who will buy this game. Many parents will buy the game for their small children, aged seven or eight. The trend now is to start children with computers at age two. Our bodies and minds, our innate capacities for learning, thinking, doing, feeling, intuiting, languaging, relating, communicating, cognizing for ourselves and with each other are all being reduced to dependency upon a man-made machine.

Modern science is telling us that the goal is to build space ships that can navigate deep space to conquer new territories there; the governments of nations are competing for power in space for fifty years or less. As much as I enjoyed the movies and the myths they portrayed, "Star Wars" has quite adequately prepared us for a techno-future ruled by machines, spaceships and computers. If we are willing to consider that the solution to serious global problems is spiritual, not technological, then we can also consider that the way to connect with the cosmos—to realize our interconnectedness, our oneness with all Life—is not through technology. Nor is it the way to take our place in the greater universe.

It should go without saying that there are benign forms of technology, which began however many eons ago with the use of fire, making of stone tools, creating the wheel, which then evolved into the arts of agriculture, astronomy, astrology, languages, writing, music, mathematics, architecture and all the rest. Now there are such things as washing machines, refrigerators, stoves and even the computer upon which books get written. The pressing question is: Can we, as a global society of human beings, decide when and where and how to apply technology? The good or bad of advanced technologies depend upon their judicious, wise application and a profound consideration of their long-term effects upon the entire world and its inhabitants—animal, vegetable and mineral. Decisions of that magnitude depend upon the spiritual context of the human beings who are making those decisions.

Modern science and techno-culture does not function from the context of the dharma. As a whole, our culture has turned away from God and toward a completely secular, materialistic, reduced view of the grandeur and magic of the Universe. We think the only way we can evolve is to conquer space itself...through machines. Once again, the inner life is abandoned to atrophy and ultimately wither away in favor of dependence upon that which is false and will only lead, sooner or later, to a dead end for our potential to awaken into greater awareness of pristine consciousness and real wisdom.

From the perspective of sahajiya, the way to take our place in the cosmos is to go within and develop the technologies of the soul—the innate, God-given abilities that have lain dormant for so many eons of time, with truly rare exceptions. We might consider that the Mayans were not the only ancient culture that had the ability, now lost, for intergalactic travel in the subtle body. These ideas are accused of being far out, idealistic, woo-woo, and New Age, but they are not; they are found throughout the great teachings of Hinduism and Tibetan Buddhism, in shamanism worldwide, as actual facts of human life. The tantric traditions are full of accounts of dakinis, yogis and yoginis who could fly long distances in their physical bodies. We reduce these accounts to myths, meaning untruths. What if we are wrong?

"Spore" is one particularly virulent example of the poison our children and teenagers are being spoon-fed by marketers, most public school systems, the media at large, and the hideous corporate agendas that seem to run everything from behind the scenes. The "education" our children receive from "Spore" is designed to appeal to an ego that wants to play God, while effectively indoctrinating children—and adults—in the scientific worldview that the evolution of human consciousness is inexorably tied to and dependent upon machines, advanced hardcore technologies and so-called "scientific progress."

We need to think for ourselves. We need to turn off our TVs, ipods and computers and listen to the cosmos that is speaking to us from within. When we consider the wisdom of tribal people and tantric teachings, lived by flesh and blood individuals, how can we possibly believe that "space-faring ultra-beings" are more spiritually evolved? What authority decided that complex machine technologies have anything whatsoever to do with intelligence of a truly higher order? Why isn't it obvious that the real evolution of consciousness is an inner event? We urgently need to be asking ourselves these questions.[9]

My guru often says that he is a dinosaur. He says he is a throwback to another time. He says that he is alone in his desire to live a simple life. He refuses to use computers or the internet. He often says, "I don't even know how to turn a computer on." He plans to build a new ashram in Arizona that will be designed by ancient *vastu* principles and will function entirely off the grid, powered by solar energy and wind, with compost toilets and no internet hookups. A

---

[9]   The idea of evolution as a process of the soul is well-explored in the writings of Sri Aurobindo—one of the three gurus Yogi Ramsuratkumar considered to be his spiritual fathers. A prolific writer, Aurobindo left an immense legacy that may be studied in this regard.

stellar practitioner himself, Lee's impeccability in every domain is awesome and inspiring—and more than a little daunting.

Western technological culture is, if nothing else, materialistic to the end. We are hell bent upon forcing a materialistic, man-made evolutionary process upon Nature, one that gives us instant gratification in concrete terms: the next new gadget, another machine toy to distract us from the pressing need to go within and find out who we really are. To face the bitter truth and heartbreak of what we have lost and what we have become; the bitter truth and heartbreak of what we are doing to our children and grandchildren with our lies and violence and emotional abuse, our addiction to cell phones and Blackberries and laptops and GPS tracking systems and airplanes and bombs and spaceships. The unconscious cultural attitude is to forget about the sun and sky and air and water and earth, about real experiences of birth and death: we'll just start cloning ourselves, sooner or later—get rid of the messy blood and guts stuff and live a completely antiseptic, sterile life. Science fiction is upon us, and it is heartbreaking.

There is a common mythic theme, found in many cultures and religious traditions, of a fall from Grace. Imagining ourselves to be separate from God, refusing to serve the Divine Will, we asserted our individual will; the higher intelligence of our original state of Grace is now lost in the obscurity of eons. We have to *return* to the original state of Grace, not discover it anew for the first time in interstellar space travel and bionic bodies encoded with computer chips. There are a hardcore few, a minority for sure, of people who believe that the aboriginal people of Australia, the Hopi and Navajo, and other tribal or indigenous people of Central and South America, Africa, India, Tibet and China, carry the remnants of original wisdom that survives from those lost cultures. The biologist said that evolution meanders like a stream in the high meadows of the Rocky Mountains, wandering everywhere over eons of time. Some of the branches of evolutionary trends bend backward, while others never bear any fruit at all. What if the old myths are true and original wisdom was lost because human beings turned away from the soul, from the subtle world, from the Will of God?

Human beings are a race of creatures who are still falling from Grace. In fact, the velocity of our fall is accelerating at an alarming rate, and we are taking all life on this planet down with us. If we aren't brokenhearted about this, we should be. At the Path of Transformation Conference we heard Malidoma Somé speak. An African shaman, Malidoma was forcefully taken from his tribe at age four to be educated by French Jesuits. At nineteen he miraculously escaped and found his way back to his village. He had to be completely re-educated by the tribe to connect with the esoteric life of his people. In order to re-enter their world, he had to go through the dangerous process of male initiation—usually engaged by boys at puberty—at the age of twenty. He survived and was initiated into the spiritual mysteries of his people, but the elders of the tribe sent him away. They sent him back to the West to plead their case; to attempt to educate the Western world about the worldview of tribal, earth-based people. They hoped that somehow, Malidoma might make a difference.

One of the things Malidoma emphasized was the form of knowledge his people have held over generations, which is a form of technology—a subtle technology. Listening to him play the drum and speak, I was struck by the reality of just how much we have lost. To a great degree, we have lost our soul connection to the rest of the cosmos. We have abdicated our birthright in favor of a lie. Lost in the ocean of samsara, the collective race of human beings are living out the illusion of separation. Human ignorance, greed, affliction, aggression…these are the forces that dominate this planet, and we are all responsible. As Lee said, somewhat humorously, a little tongue-in-cheek, as cool as dolphins are, they can't do anything about it. Only human beings can do something about it.

This is a perilous time.
　The roads are uneven and broken
and the waters are troubled and rough.
　The skies rock with storms,
thunder and lightning abound.
　War is everywhere, profit
is the god of modern man.
　In these days, these troubled times,
Your Name, Yogi Ramsuratkumar,
　is a life raft, a beacon of Light
that guides us safely and purely
　through the labyrinth of darkness.
You point us to integrity,
　kindness, compassion, to love
for our fellow creatures,
　for animals, plants and to
true worship of Father in Heaven.
　Your Name, for Your Name is You,
is our salvation, our Faith, our goal —
　You, Joy of our Hearts,
delight of our eyes, comfort to our souls.
　You, Your Name, ever with us,
soothes our worries and
　heals us, bringing us to harmony and peace.
This is lee lozowick, Your true heart-son,
　not just Praising You today,
but thanking You with deep gratitude
　and with pranams at Your Holy Feet.[10]

The perception of Enlightened Duality demands that we take complete responsibility for our lives, for the world we live in, for

---

[10]   Lee Lozowick, *Gasping for Air in a Vacuum*, 10 October 1999.

our relationships with others, for the problems and the solutions. To take responsibility is both personal and impersonal; it impels us to act in a genuine way, with integrity, with honor, with dignity, with kindness, sensitivity, awareness of the other. The "other" is a very big category: it includes the whole planet and every being and nonbeing upon it—animal, vegetable, mineral.

Jacques Cousteau, guardian angel and international advocate for the oceans of this world, once said, "We protect what we love." We are rarely willing to take responsibility until we find love in our hearts. Being responsible means that we are willing to love and therefore protect, preserve, maintain, defend, and sustain Life. This is Lord Vishnu's realm, and we are called to enter into it through the doors of love and heartbreak.

Love and heartbreak go hand in hand, because only love can break your heart. Heartbreak is, finally, the great gift of the Path. Lee once said that his master, Yogi Ramsuratkumar, gave him a wound that only God could heal: this is one of Lee's most poignant and penetrating teachings. Everyone, sooner or later, must have a wound that only God can heal. In our mad dash through this life, in all the confusion and distractions, or when adversity strikes, when we weep for the hardships of others, we bring this wisdom to bear upon all things, and somehow, miraculously, we are turned toward God's love. This is what heartbreak is ultimately about.

> Dearest One, Father,
>   Yogi Ramsuratkumar Maharaj,
> as the devotion grows deeper
>   the heartbreak grows stronger as well.
> Suffering causes one kind of heartbreak
>   and joy, ecstasy cause another kind.
> In any case, heartbreak
>   is Your most Merciful Gift.
> How broken can a heart become?

So broken that there is no heart
unless it beats by Your Blessings
    and with the repetition of Your Name.
May You touch Your son,
    this little beggar lee,
with such a Grace,
    and may lee bring this glory
to all those who hunger so greatly
    for You, even if they don't yet know
Your True Name, Your heartbreaking Name.
    This is this bad Poet's wish, Father.
Do not deny him for he lies prostrate
    at Your Feet, his only sustenance
the dust of Your Rags, his only breath
    that which You breathe as him.[11]

---

[11]   Ibid, 2 August 1999.

The Alchemy of Sex

Lee Lozowick

For some of us, sex is our favorite subject matter. It shouldn't be, because it's only sex. It's a nice thing. It's a great thing. Sometimes it feels good, but it's only sex. If you have a spiritual practice, what is the single-most difficult obstacle to practicing the way you want? Your partner! One solution to the alchemy of relationship is: don't get into one.

When I was quite a bit younger, I thought I was an expert on the subject of the alchemy of love and sex, and I would have appreciated it very much if other people considered me an expert on the subject. I thought I knew a lot about sex and men and women. That was forty years ago. Thirty years ago I still thought I knew a lot, twenty years ago I was beginning to get the picture, but I still acted like I knew a lot because I wanted to be some kind of a spiritual expert on love and sex. Now I don't know what in the hell is going on.

One of the most dangerous elements of relationship is expectation. When we start to expect things of our partners that are not directly relevant to who they are, we are bound to be disappointed. Sooner or later, our disappointment is probably going to be the end of the relationship. Here is an interesting true story: A couple was together for fourteen years, but they were not married because the woman had a history of not trusting men—she didn't want to make a mistake. So neither of them had been married before. Finally, after fourteen years of a loving, intimate relationship, the woman felt safe enough to marry the man of her life. They got married, and two weeks later the guy had an attack of rage and physically beat the woman to the point that she had to go to the hospital. It's strange how marriage, which is really nothing but a legal piece of paper, can change people.

In Tibetan Vajrayana Buddhism there is an image that sometimes becomes a part of a practitioner's *sadhana*, which is a male deity and a female deity in sexual union. Whenever I get a statue of that image, I always sell it very quickly, because people love them. The really fine statues have definition to the sexual organs, however, the symbol of that statue has nothing to do with men and women; it has to do with the universal union of opposites. It's actually more about physics than it is about sex. So, when we try to have a conversation about the alchemy of love and sex, we already have a problem, because we are talking about two different things: sex and transformation. Alchemy is a word related to transformation, and the symbol of the male and female deity in sexual union is about transformation. I am sorry to say that most of us will not understand, in our lifetime, the transformational possibility of love or sex.

So, sex and breath. There are two parts of the body that breathe: the mouth and nose, and the sexual organs. That's a metaphysical reality. Given that reality, why wouldn't everybody who is interested in sex as a doorway to understanding Reality be passionately interested in oral sex? I leave the implication of that to your imaginations. Breath/sex; sex/breath. Breathe in, breathe out, breathe in, breathe out—that is what we do, right? The spiritual utility of oral sex depends on naturalness. A lot of men think that women smell bad; I think that particular scent is one of the most subtle and beautiful perfumes in the world, especially when combined with a menstrual period—now we're getting to something! American women tend to be extraordinarily full of shame, probably because childhood sexual abuse is epidemic. A lot of women, before they are going to have sex, wash themselves down there with soap because it's antiseptic. I'll tell you, when I'm diving for the bushes, I don't want to get there and have it smell like a fucking hospital! That can ruin a good night.

So, we are talking about the alchemy of love and sex, but we've got a problem to *begin* with. The body is a wonderful thing, especially when it's healthy and full of life and vitality. It can be a little problematical when it starts to disintegrate—you know, dust to dust, ashes to ashes—but it is still the body. It is still a fantastic instrument with an extraordinary capacity for the appreciation of beauty. I used to really like to look at the women I found very attractive. Every woman has got something that is beautiful—the curve of the back, the shape of the hips. And the smile...every smile is beautiful. Now I'm much more interested in the transition knowledge, the transition experience, which helps us make the distinction that the body is *only* the body.[1]

On the one hand, every human being is discreet—meaning independent—while at the same time, every human being is continuous with all of creation. My master, Yogi Ramsuratkumar, said that he was "everything," although he never used the word "I" when he referred to himself. He said, "this beggar." I never had a problem with the statement that he was everything. My master was not an egotist; he was actually nobody—there was no ego left. Well, that's not entirely true, because there was ego left, but that ego was at the service of his attempt to help other people pursue Reality to the end. He was a Hindu; he loved Buddhists, he loved Christians; he loved Jews.

---

[1]   Lee is referring to the death transition.

He loved everybody, and he never wanted people to leave their Path to become a Hindu. He loved Jesus so much that every Christmas when we visited him, he asked us to sing Christmas carols. He would sit there, weeping while he listened.

When the body is free to follow its natural inclination, sex can be a doorway to a kind of realization. I'm not talking about an enlightenment realization. I don't even use the word "enlightenment" anymore because it's absurd. It's ridiculous. There is a wonderful story told by the wife of Chögyam Trungpa Rinpoche, published in an article in the *Shambhala Sun*. It's the story of how Diana Mukpo and Chögyam Trungpa Rinpoche met, fell in love and married. She was talking about their first married night, when they were in a hotel room and the phone rang. Trungpa picked up the phone, and he was talking very excitedly to a friend, telling the friend about this wonderful person he had married. He turned to his wife and said, "Honey, what is your name?" Chögyam Trungpa Rinpoche loved his wife; they were married until the day he died. He had complete and total regard for her, but he was living in the Reality in which all things are continuous. The Tibetan Buddhist term for my use of the word "continuous" is "dependent arising." Diana Mukpo also said that what was intoxicating about sex with Trungpa Rinpoche was the vastness of his mind. He took you where *he* was.

I'm not a yogi like Chögyam Trungpa Rinpoche was. I'm a dyed-in-the-wool romantic, but after forty years of teaching Americans and Europeans, my romanticism has been driven deeply underground. Years ago I gave a talk titled, "We Always Try To Kill What We Love." We don't do it on purpose. We're not bad people; we are not aggressive, vile beings. We are intrinsically noble and intrinsically dignified, and we are profoundly disengaged from the essence of our being. Having worked with people for thirty-eight years, to be exact, my approach has been to get down in the mud with people. I have to say that I don't like it. It is not my preference. It's not even natural for me. I was given a mission by my master, long before I had any idea of what in the hell that meant. Like Sisyphus, I was chained to the rock and had to roll it back up the mountain over and over again before I knew I couldn't leave the mountain whenever I felt like it. I don't like dealing with people's swamps—and our neuroses are a swamp, beautifully disguised of course, but with tremendous pitfalls and traps.

People often ask me when they see my community, "How can you let these people transfer on you like this?" I say, "Go ask Carl Jung!" That's not what I say, but it is what I feel like saying; I feel like being insulting, because it is obvious that we transfer. When I started teaching, I said to myself, "Transference, projections, expectations will be gone in a year." After ten years I said, "I think it'll take fifteen years." After forty years, I'm thinking, "Maybe never." I think that we're going to have to get used to flawed spiritual masters—except for Arnaud Desjardins, by the way—and flawed spiritual students and just live with the way things are.

Swami Prajnanpad, who is the guru of Arnaud Desjardins, said. "Every human being is intrinsically dignified and intrinsically noble." I love that phrase. Chögyam Trungpa Rinpoche, one of the Tibetans of the last century whom I most admire, used the phrase "basic goodness" to address the same quality. Even though we have basic goodness, at the level of mind and ego, most of us are profoundly ignorant. We may have a two hundred IQ—we may be a genius in a variety of areas—but that does not make us any less ignorant. That in us which can know and live Reality does not need to be educated in a linear, rational, articulate way. That which is essential within us responds instantly to that which is essential in others, including those others who happen to be spiritual teachers.

So this is the problem: We are divorced from that in us which relates to Reality in truth. You may have read some of the Taoist books on sex, which are very popular—Mantak Chia, for example. If you have read some misleading book, which implied that sex could be a path in and of itself, then you have missed the point. Sex is fine.

Even bad sex is only mediocre, and great sex is fantastic! So what? Reality does not revolve around sex. In a tantric path (and I use the word tantric very rarely because it's been so completely commercialized) sex is one possible element of practice. Osho Rajneesh, for example, was an extraordinary spiritual genius. On the other hand, he could not communicate any better than anybody else, and most of his students didn't have any idea what in the hell he was talking about. All this *sannyasin* shit that passes as tantra is not tantra. Great sex is just that—great sex. If you must have sex, then have great sex. Why bother with the mess and the emotional entanglement if it's not going to be great?

There are Buddhist and Hindu paths—and, believe it or not, other religious paths—in which the use of ritual sex can be an important part of the transformational process. What passes for tantric ritual in most of India these days is a bunch of horny guys using tantric practice as a justification for getting drunk, eating meat and having sex with somebody besides their wife. This is the kind of catalyst that has driven my romanticism deep under ground. I still love India. The first time I got off the plane in India, I took a deep breath and said to myself, "I could live here." The second time I went, I thought, "I'd like to stay here for six months." The third time I went, I thought, "Two months is good." I still love India with a passion, but one of the things I've realized is that people are the same everywhere. That was a disappointment.

Many years ago I gave a talk at a gathering to celebrate my master, Yogi Ramsuratkumar. The essence of the talk was: "My master broke my heart in a way that only God can heal." (If the word "God" offends you, you can use the words "Truth," or "Reality," or "Life," or whatever you want—it makes no difference.) As most of you have noticed, our world is struggling these days. A practice that is isolated from the awareness of the world that we live in is not a practice. I am not crazy about the "green movement," and I don't march for clean air and the cleaning up of the ecological systems—and it is obvious that the world is in crisis. Animals are not going to be able to do anything about it. You and I, human animals, need to be aware of these kinds of things. I don't want to be. I want to bury my head in the sand. I want to be a raging romantic. I want to be naïve again and look at all things through rose-colored lenses, but I can't.

C.S. Lewis, who is a wonderful author, wrote a little book called *Surprised by Joy* about one of his realizations. It's nice to live that way—surprised by joy and beauty—and the opposite, because genuine transformation happens across the board, in every domain. You can't just pick the nice things and avoid the things that are not so nice. If joy is that much more brilliant, so is pain that much more brilliant. If we can believe the Dalai Lama (who seems to be one of those spiritual teachers who walks his talk), the more one is transformed, the more one has a *field sensitivity* rather than a point sensitivity. A few years ago there was a big hurricane that devastated New Orleans. There was the unconscionable response by the American government; there was tremendous suffering as a result of homelessness and lives blown away in the storm. Forty years ago I would have said, "I don't know anybody in New Orleans. That has nothing to do with me." I can't do that anymore.

This principle of interconnectedness is also true in relationship. When a relationship is full of expectation, the other person is defined by your expectations on them, to some degree. Even if they are not insecure—and it doesn't really trouble them that you are projecting expectations on them—if they love you and want to remain in communion with you, some part of them will want to fulfill your expectations. The same is true in sex. Sex is a very delicate field of interaction. If you are sensitive and you are not just being a tough guy or a pushy woman, in the act of sex—especially in prolonged sex, which could be anywhere from fifteen minutes to several hours, depending upon who you are—you will be entering into communication with many different subtle vectors of energy. Every one of those vectors is extremely fragile and subtle. The least bit of authoritative activity will banish the presiding deities of those vectors of energy.

Here is an example: Findhorn in Scotland first became very famous for their big vegetables, and everybody who had a garden wanted to know how to grow vegetables that big. How did they grow a cabbage that big? The vegetables at Findhorn were fantastic because of the delicate balance between the presiding deity of the land and the presiding deity of the vegetable. It wasn't just the fertilizer, the water and the prayers. It is the same in the act of sex.

In my tradition, we would say that during the act of sex the room is full of deities. Those deities are not voyeurs—they want to play the game or get the hell out of there. If you don't allow them to play the game, they will get the hell out of there. If you are a woman, and you don't want your husband coupling with a *dakini* now and then, you are going to have a problem—if you want sex to be what it essentially can be. But don't worry girls, the dakinis are on your side, and I sure as hell ain't talkin' about dakinis clothed in human flesh. They are not trying to take your husband away, they're trying to allow the realization of Reality as it is—but you have to help. The way you help is to get out of the way in terms of your expectations and projections.

A friend of mine, whose words are jewels of experience and realization, said that you are perfect as you are, defined by your neurosis. In other words, you are living out your neurosis perfectly; you couldn't be better at who you are than you are. Your self-hatred is perfect; your pride, vanity, and greed are perfect. Your aggression— perfect. Why would ego want to change something that is perfect? It wouldn't and it doesn't. On the other hand, we want to change. We find ourselves shouting at our child or hitting them, and we are horrified. We're completely divided: a part of us has lost control, and another part is saying, "Oh my God, what have I just done? I've just hit my child! Oh my God, I can't believe it."

Who we are is perfect. Ego does not and will not change that. If we are starting to notice things about ourselves that are disturbing—our aggression in various ways—the teaching says that unless you accept "what is, as it is," your aggression will not become workable. You accept "what is" not relative to some kind of perfect ideal but exactly as it is. Unless you do accept what is, it does not become workable. Workability is not a function of ego; when you accept what is, as it is, you become relaxed. You aren't holding on, gripping for survival; you are just present. When you animate who you are naturally, then intrinsic nobility and intrinsic dignity, or basic goodness, will raise its magnificent head—and there you will be, acting in a way that is resonant with your highest being.

So, if transformation in the act of sex is interesting to you, the ideal position to be in is to allow the confluence of vectors of energy, which I would call the participating deities, to have their way. Sometimes there are so many deities there it's hard to breathe, and the better the sex, the happier the deity. You don't want to be pissing off those dakinis, because they can get a little fussy. I have this favorite saying, which is: If you don't do what you need to do, the Universe will do it for you sooner or later, and believe me, you do not want the Universe minding your business if you can mind it yourself. The reason should be obvious, but if it's not, I'll tell you my opinion: The Universe is a completely impersonal force. It doesn't have a mind, it doesn't have a heart, and it doesn't have a form; it just rolls on, arising, sustaining and subsiding. Nothing personal. An earthquake happens and thirty thousand people die—it's nothing personal, to the Universe.

Relative to sex, somehow you and I have to figure out how to live in the paradox of the personal and the impersonal, in which things are not separate; in fact, they are in no way distinguishable from one another. You cannot wrap your mind around that; the only thing you can wrap around that is your body, when the body is no longer dominated by the mind, thoughts, and emotions. This is not the easiest thing in the world to do. Keep trying. If you're dealing with sex and it is not what you want it to be, keep having sex and deal with it there. Yes, therapy can be very helpful in its time and place, and lots of external guidance can be very helpful in its time and place. I am not suggesting that education isn't extraordinarily useful—and, if the problem is with sex, then the solution is with sex.

So, we are talking about a ridiculous subject, which is being sensitive to the presiding deities in a given space. Really, you should do a quarter of a million prostrations and about a million and a half mantras and a lot of ritual puja before you even *hear* about this subject matter. We are attempting to talk about sex. Why? People love it, people want it, it is a big thing. Even when we have a very serious, dedicated spiritual practice, which for most of us does not exclude sex, we tend to be far more affected by ripples in the sexual field then we should be or need to be. It's important that this issue be clarified.

The song I played in the beginning of this talk, "Come to Me," [2] says it all: your relationship should be the source of comfort, refuge and sanctuary. Of course the implication is that you come to one another undefended and free of aggression in any form. Chögyam Trungpa Rinpoche, who was one of the unexcelled dharma geniuses of our time in my opinion, wrote a book called *Dharma Art*, in which he says that real art—dharma art—cannot be aggressive in any way. In exactly the same way, if relationship is to be the doorway to genuine and lasting abidance in that which is true and real, it cannot have any quality of aggression—because relationship and sex can be a doorway to the Real.

---

[2]   "To Me," lyrics by Lee Lozowick, composed by Denise Allen-Incao and Everett Jaime and recorded by Denise Allen on *Not Just Another Diva*.

I didn't make sex a doorway to the Real; neither did Mantak Chia or Osho or Gurdjieff, for that matter. Sex is objectively what it is. Obviously, different things have different potentialities, different seeds. If you plant an apple seed, you don't get a peach tree. In sex being what it is—not what we project onto it and make it up to be and wish it were and all that nonsense—it opens a window to Reality. In the ultimate sense of things we could say that about any aspect of Creation.

Everything is about context. Everything, everything, everything is about context. To try to play with the presiding deities from the position of ego is ridiculous. "Oh yes, that sounds cool! I'd like to meet some of those dakinis! Look at them in the thangkas—their faces are a little strange, one looks like a horse and another looks like a lion, but their bodies—hah!" Ego might think, "Oh yes, I'd like to play with these goddesses and gods." From that context, all you will get is a little buzz. Many of you have had what could technically be called an enlightenment experience, in a traditional, mystic sense. That is not to say you are enlightened; it is to say only that you have had a glimpse of Reality, free of all projections, expectations, and illusions.

When I was in metaphysics, back in the Dark Ages—when I was in my early thirties, before gas stations were open twenty-four hours a day, and before credit cards—there was a man who was very well known locally. He was driving late at night and the gas tank was on empty. There were no gas stations open anywhere, so he prayed and kept driving. He drove two hundred kilometers on an absolutely empty tank, and for the rest of his life, every single time he gave a talk, he relayed that experience. Nothing like that ever happened to him again, and he was living his life constellated around that night. Think of what he missed! If you have had an enlightenment experience, that was then, this is now. Everybody asks, "How can I live there? It was so radiant, so bright, so ecstatic, so wondrous!" Yes, now it's not—that's life.

Everything is about context. When we live in the context defined by Reality as it is, things are not what they are when we live in the context defined by ego. Because we don't live in the context of Reality as it is, we can't really say *what* things are in that context. We can't wrap our minds around how someone can be in prison, brutally abused, and write a lyrical poem like Jimmy Santiago Baca wrote, because when we suffer, we suffer in the ordinary context of me, my, mine. We suffer in the context of wanting to control everything: " I want to manage my own experience I want to rule the world—or at least *my* world."

Many people think that lust is the problem. There is no problem with lust. Lust is a great thing, and there are two kinds of lust: 1) greedy and possessive lust; and 2) lust that is pure, radiant feeling. Greedy lust and radiant lust can feel the same. The distinction is this: in the context in which lust is a brilliant feeling, whatever arises in consciousness does not have to be engaged and followed through. Lust can be lust, stay lust and not be fulfilled or acted out. Lust is intense and powerful, and if we don't act on it, instead of being frustrating, it can be sublime.

I was visiting Yogi Ramsuratkumar in India once when a Theravada Buddhist monk was also visiting him. The monk was in his thirties; he had been a celibate for twenty years. He was happy, laughing, smiling, radiant—he was not an angry renunciate, as many are. He said that when he was seventeen he went to Burma to study *vispassana* meditation with a group of friends. They went out to the jungle to meditate, and one by one, they decided that they couldn't take it. Everyone left but him; he was the only one who stayed, who made it through that knot of feeling, which tells us that we have to act out the lust in some way. When he got to that point, celibacy was not a problem

For those of us who are not celibate but are in a relationship, if you want your partner to give you what you give to your partner, you will almost never be satisfied. Any two people are almost never going to be equal. Love is a radiance, and radiance has nothing to do with receiving. If you really love someone, that love shows up as a radiance. How they dress or speak or whether or not they give you affection should have nothing to do with how you love them.

Love is an infinitely faceted jewel, and all the facets aren't pleasant or sweet or good. We have to be able to be with what is without judging the relationship based on one feeling—even if the feeling is intense or uncomfortable. You have to be able to pay attention to your partner. The Tibetan Buddhists say that in the afterdeath state, in the *bardos*, if you aren't able to maintain your attention on the clear light of truth, you are instantly drawn into rebirth. Imagine if something attracts you here, in this life—a piece of art, a painting. Those things that attract you here will be a million times brighter and more vivid in the bardos. If you apply that principle to love and sex, the ability to pay attention to your partner becomes crucial. For example, if you are at a party where everyone is talking and socializing, your partner has to be more important to you than all those exciting people.

You have to pay attention in the middle of sex, so that the act of union with your partner is more important to you than your mind. My experience of women is they are maddeningly sensitive. If you are a man, you might be thinking that it's going pretty well, then all of a sudden your partner says, "Hey, where are you?" It is a very useful skill to be able to pay attention and stay with the attention you are paying. There is a kind of "going away" through fantasy, boredom, worry, and then there is going away in the best sense, into Reality, so that there is no "you." If that is the way you go away, then wonderful! If you go away in those other ways, then it is back to working with the mind. It's always about bringing your self back to what is right now.

All of this relates to sex. To really touch the edges of alchemy in sexual relationship, you have to be out of your way, without definitions. You have to be able to go anywhere without compromise or boundary. The alchemy of love and sex is not about great sex. Yes, if you have sex for three or four or five hours nonstop, and you are able to keep your attention there, you are going to be altered. For most people that alone is a miracle in itself, because after an hour or two most men are asking, "How long is this going to go on?" Even after a few hours of sex, you are altered in a positive way. You're flying in some universe, completely out of your normal range of reference. Yes, that's great sex, but that is not Reality. That is not Enlightenment. If great sex is enough for you, and you are on the Path just for great sex, then disregard what I am saying. Please. Don't ruin it. But if you want more than just great sex, then the first thing you have to do is redefine the whole sexual experience.

Hamburg, Germany
September 2008

Shunyata

M. Young

*E*arly in the summer, as we drove on a narrow, winding road through the Ardeche Mountains of southern France, the sun played brilliantly on the river that tumbled over a stony gorge at the bottom of the canyon. The coruscating radiance, which lit so vividly the green trees, terraced vineyards and sloping mountainside orchards, captured my attention and quickly took me into a mood of remembrance.

Serendipitously, a friend and I were listening to a song written and recently recorded by Lee titled, "Take Me Away."[1] The focused attention of our listening combined synergistically with the music, lyrics and the opulent display of *drala* to move my awareness into the underlying unity of the moment, revealing also the *shunyata* of the rampant beauty all around. Ecstasy welled up, and along with it came the insight that the roots of our individual beings are commingled in shunyata, the place of origins, where all image, sound, and light spring forth toward becoming.

---

[1]   "Take Me Away," Lozowick and Durham, *Tongue of Poison, Soul of Love*, 2008.

Letting go into the experience, relaxation flooded into me like a warm balm. In these troubled times when tension, worry, dread and fear hover like vultures waiting for an old horse to die, relaxation is a divine state of being indeed. It is one of Lee's most potent reminders, in fact: "Relax." Relaxation is very close kin with that even more sublime state we call "peace." When relaxation arises, the nobility of friendship comes easy and service is the natural response to life. Relaxation opens the doors of perception to the abundance that reigns supreme, as the inner sun is shining, shining, shining upon the shores of being.

In the relaxation of that moment, the feeling of interrelatedness with all of Life became so delicately honed and juxtaposed with a perception of underlying emptiness that it burst forth into joyful elation. It was then that insight arrived on the scene and said to me, "My guru has married me to the entire world in the circle of eternity." Some hours later, as I started writing, insight returned for a follow-up visit and insisted, proceeding like ripples on a lake, until it became clear that this declaration of the nature of tantric *sadhana* was rich ground for a consideration of Enlightened Duality.

Tantric practice is a way of life that is all-inclusive, non-rejecting and embraces everything the Path has to offer, from nondual to dual, because tantra is about continuity. Tantric sadhana on the Baul path marries the practitioner to the entire world within the circle of eternity, while conventional marriage passes sooner or later into the foggy mists of Ma Time—"that Bitch!" as Lee said lovingly and reverently, although with tongue most definitely in cheek, for he is adept at making statements that encapsulate ironic praise while making a teaching.

From the tantric perspective, there is no reason to reject marriage, but clarity demands a revolutionary relationship to it. Like all things that are of this world, marriage dissolves into impermanence: sooner or later, our loved one will be as desiccated, worm-eaten and blackened as a corpse left out in the desert sun for forty days. Even if love for a partner is deep and mature, sooner or later the certainty of "forever" will be bluntly and inexorably called into question by the loss of death. Or, perhaps our marriage is broken asunder by betrayal in one form or another. These days, most conventional marriages simply wind down like mechanical toys, their creative juices seeping and weeping away into ennui and mediocrity. We outgrow one another. We get bored. We move on. We change. We die.

The conventional world places enormous importance on marriage to one person—what Da Free John called "the cult of pairs." Marriage is a religious and secular institution that carries great nostalgic power for us all, as we idealize this contract and project absurd romanticisms upon it—in fact, societal norms would have us convinced at an early age that we will not succeed in life nor probably even survive if we are not married (heterosexually speaking, of course). When we seriously engage the spiritual Path, we investigate the teaching and begin to forge a different view of the societal expectations that rule the lives of the masses of people—such as marriage. Certainly marriage has a sacred, objective possibility, but it is unlikely that we will discover that possibility if we have not examined the societal indoctrination and rigid definitions of marriage as an institution.

The truth that tantric practice marries one to all of Life communicates the basic contrariness of the Baul way, which is called *ulta* because it goes in the direction of flow that is opposite to that of cultural expectations and demands. Bauls definitely do commingle in pairs—sometimes they marry, sometimes they just cohabit for a long or short time—all for the sake of their sadhana. Lee advocates committed, monogamous relationships between mates, and at the same time, if we are interested in transformation, we want to court a radical vision of what may be possible in relationship, including that relationships do not need to take the expected forms.

In January 2008, when the sun struggled to glimmer through the blanket of smog in Kolkata, Gour Khepa and Durga Dasi made it abundantly clear to us that relationship is vitally important to Baul sadhana. As they said, Bauls who are practicing within a coupled relationship worship each other as god and goddess—usually symbolically depicted as Krishna and Radha but also sometimes as Shiva and Shakti. This means that each partner invokes the divinity within the other, and through the close proximity and intermingling of *prakriti* and *purusha* in the act of bodily love, each partner discovers the relationship of Radha and Krishna within themselves as an individual.[2]

This is the secret (that is not really so secret) behind the depiction of Radha-Krishna as one deity, or of any deity and consort image, whether from Vajrayana Buddhism or tantric Hinduism. These images serve to remind us of the union between spirit and matter, between masculine and feminine, *nirguna* and *saguna*, purusha and prakriti. In the Western traditions this has been called "the mystical marriage" that is discovered within the individual. Each person contains within themselves both masculine and feminine essences, which have the capacity to produce a divine child—the golden child of awakened consciousness alluded to in Gour Khepa's quick metaphor: "We are like the father and mother of Jesus."

It's understood among mythophiles that when a god and goddess of most any pantheon commingle, depending upon the status (or qualities) of the deities involved, they beget a divine child that operates at some level of realization: the symbolic Jesus, the symbolic Horus, the symbolic Ganesha. If we consider Jesus (the Christ consciousness) as the model for our own possibility of awakened consciousness, we can understand that within the practitioner the masculine force (Logos) marries the feminine force (Eros), and the

---

[2]   It is important to note that what we are considering is human sexual relationship engaged primarily for the purpose of sadhana. The committed love relationship between human beings on the spiritual Path can yield profound self-knowledge, and although typically this will be done in pairs of woman/man, it could be man/man or woman/woman. The sadhana could also be accomplished by an individual who is not functioning in a bonded pair.

product of that interplay is the divine child that opens his or her eyes and realizes she is awake to Life.[3]

One of the primary ways Bauls discover this secret is by engaging in sexual yoga. Tantric practice is a vast field of endeavor that includes many different disciplines, of which sexual yoga is one small, even minor, part. However, it is being explored herein both as an exacting practice and as a metaphor for the principles of tantric practice in general, which apply across the board in any techniques, rituals, or yogas that one might engage on the Path.

One of the big misunderstandings about sexual yoga is that people place primary importance on a technique in a willful engagement with *doing*, when it is *being*, alive in the body, which is the actual catalyst of alchemical process in sexual yoga. The mood of being, or the state of consciousness, is vital to sexual alchemy, and nothing is really possible if you are not willing or able to surrender to shunyata, or emptiness, which catapults one into the transcendence of the personal self. When Lee speaks of Baul practice being about inviting the deities to participate in the act of sexual yoga, he makes it clear that we must allow that to happen:

> *In my tradition, we would say that in the act of sex the room is full of deities, and they aren't voyeurs—they want to play the game or get the hell out of there. If you don't allow them to play the game, they will get the hell out of there.*

---

[3]   Lee frequently speaks of the awakening of consciousness in his own case as "the event that catalyzed my teaching work." He says that whenever a radical awakening of this nature occurs for anyone—loosely termed "enlightenment" by many, this newly awakened consciousness is like a baby (a divine child) that must go through a process of growth, development and maturation before it can really be of help to anyone else. Because of this, there are many who begin to teach prematurely, which causes a great deal of problems, abuses and suffering for both teacher and student.

How do we "allow" the deities to participate? In essence, the practitioner must become a *sunya,* to use a Baul term—an emptiness. How do we ordinary practitioners do that? By emptying ourselves of identifications, expectations, ideas, concepts, even needs and wants. Desire and passion—*kama*—is allowed to arise and move freely in the body without the interference of the mind, which is a hindrance to the process. The mind can be extremely treacherous when we are concretely identified and attached to our identifications; when we feel that we possess and *own* our partners, for example—when our sexual partner is "my husband" and "my wife" rather than a great mystery of being with whom we are in loving interplay.

It is not enough to say to ourselves, "Oh, I will let go of my possessive control of my wife or husband during sex," while we are still controlling, manipulating and domineering her or him all day long. When we try to cheat our own sadhana in that way, the deities feel, know, and sense the dross we carry. But primarily, the two human participants will find it extremely costly, difficult and highly improbable to clear the mind and body of tension and resentment so that innocence, trust, tenderness and vulnerability can give rise to mood, or rasa.

The deities (or the *ista devata*) are drawn to radiance and purity. Every day we build intention and gather energy for the sacred moments in which sexual union will occur; if we are not building a reservoir of radiance over days, weeks, and months of practice, the invocation will most surely not happen. In fact, how we are being— in mood as well as in gesture, word and deed—during the everyday grind, is exactly how we will be in sex. If we are not building a resonance with our partner of trust, respect, dignity, affection and mutual daily enjoyment, we will come to the alchemical chamber with nothing much to offer the deities. Instead, the mind will be remembering and voicing its litany of complaints, worries and obsessions, nursing resentments, fear and anger, and seeking nothing further than the gratification of egoic desire.

If we feel empty in the psychological sense after sex, it is a clue that we need to re-evaluate and examine our relationship to daily life, sex and sexuality. Free, unconstrained, passionate sex is an encounter with primordial, natural forces and the transformational potentials of shunyata, and when we are emptied of the roiling contents of ego and mind to receive the alchemical blessing of the deities, we leave the exchange—the great dance of interplay between opposites—regenerated, full to the brim and overflowing with light, energy, creativity and Blessing Force. We have touched the auspiciousness of our deepest nature, and we have received the fleeting kiss of the Beloved.

It is the encounter with shunyata, however, that many people balk at in sex. Of course we do not realize that shunyata is what drives our fears. We are afraid of this, that and the other thing. Sexual experience runs the gamut from sacred to profane, landing most often in the middle between the two as a merely desperate, mechanical act. We may discover that we are stuck, lodged hard against the wall of societal injunctions, negative self-image, fear of rejection, childhood emotions of unlove, and demeaning fantasies. These obsessions have taken root in our minds, which have received far too many negative impressions from a culture that has lost its connection to the sacred.

As Westerners, we have been taught to fear and avoid entire dimensions of experience—sex, death, birth, the void, the annihilation of identifications and attachments. Because of this conditioning, practicing tantra in the form of sexual union may involve a raw confrontation with painful or wrathful aspects of our own psyches. This is one reason why the contemporary fascination with popular ideas of "tantric sex" are so ridiculously puerile and deluded. Most people believe that if they can have sex for hours at a time and practice conservation of orgasm, then they are enacting a tantric (and therefore transformational) rite; Lee has repeatedly said this is not necessarily so. In terms of sexual yoga, tantric practice is cultivated within the work of the clearing away or purification of identifications and *kleshas* (troubles, afflictions) that discourage the deity from entering the scene. It goes without saying that this is very big, long-term work.

Traditional tantra takes this principle of purification of the temple or container (the body-mind complex) very seriously. There is a tantric visualization in which, by the progressive dissolution of the five elements within the body, the practitioner's identifications and attachments are dissolved into emptiness, or the void of death, then they are re-emerged and reordered as a new, pristine body, now fit to serve as the temple, throne or *pitha* of the deity.[4] In this way, the practitioner embraces death every day, for it is said by many wise ones that we must die before we can really live.

Lee gives us a very pithy clue in his essay on sex: Pay attention to your partner. This placing of attention on the other contains secret potentials in and of itself, for within relationship slumbers the hid-

---

[4]   In classical tantric ritual, in which the goddess Shakti is awakened or invoked as kundalini, the sleeping serpent force, a purification of the five elements—earth, air, fire, water and ether—must occur at the level of each chakra as kundalini makes her ascent toward the crown of the head. If the goddess within can ascend through these psychic centers to reach union with her Lord at the crown of the body (the seventh chakra), then the practitioner experiences the bliss of union. A common mythic image that points toward this experience is Radha and Krishna together in the grove at the full moon; another well-loved image is of Shiva and Parvati in loving embrace, dancing or in sexual union.

At another level, the rite called *bhuta-shuddhi* is performed as a preparatory practice to the worship of the ista devata or chosen deity, which is so central to the tantric lifestyle. This purification and dissolution of the elements is described in the *Mahanirvana Tantra* as an internal ritual in which the yogin visualizes the dissolution of the elements, beginning with the earth, or muladhara, located at the base of the spine, which dissolves into the water element at the second chakra, which dissolves into the fire element at the navel center, dissolving further into the air element at the heart, again dissolving into the ether element at the throat, which dissolves finally into infinite consciousness at the crown center. When this process is complete, the practitioner's body-mind is considered purified. (Feuerstein, *The Yoga Tradition*, pages 475 and 476.)

den power to awaken consciousness to the process of transformation. Paying attention also has a unique, purifying action that comes into play. We are purified by attention when it is placed in a higher context, and because energy follows attention, when you pay attention to your partner, you are building force in the here and now of the present moment, where anything is possible, including breaking through blocks. Many of the blocks encountered in sex are due to prior conditioning that tells us, erroneously, what sex "should" look and feel like. Maybe we think sex should be glamorous; maybe we think that there is only passion if we are wildly expressive or out of control. All pre-conceived notions are just another prison of the mind that prevents the natural arising of the elegant body.

Bauls cultivate a natural, easy relationship to sexual experience and the flows of energy or life force in the body, in which passion and passionate desire are considered auspicious and necessary fuel for the fires of transformation. The Bauls take the *sahaja* road when it comes to the use of rigidified rituals, heavy reliance on complex mantras and other ultra-laborious or codified formalities of practice. This is not due to lack of discipline, nor is it a way of cutting corners; on the contrary, in the Baul path there are specific yogas of breath and bodily disciplines which are learned and practiced always under the auspices of the guru's guidance.

Yoga can be viewed as an art form, and as with all art forms, one gains skill, craft and technique through a learning process, but in the end it is the Muse or Mistress who brings the artist and the art to life. In exactly the same way, Bauls rely on the Divine Influence of their gurus; they trust the wisdom of the natural body and surrender to its knowledge and sovereign power over yogic techniques. The mind and all of its constructs are subsumed in the moment when all the elements and "vectors of energy," as Lee often says, come together and suddenly the divine instinct of the body takes over; mind and ego are no longer in control because control has been surrendered to God, the Universe, to Divine Will. Sexual yoga cannot be separated from the invocation of deity, and, in the process of invocation, as kundalini shakti ascends, the body is regenerated as its natural blueprint of Organic Innocence, the tacit condition of Creation. Because "the body knows," and because the body never lies or tricks us as the mind can and will do, the Primacy of Natural Ecstasy floods the body as the natural arising of the total organism, giving rise also to the revelation of yoga: the transformation of being.

The fruits of tantric practice are many. In the domain of Enlightened Duality, as practice builds momentum over the years there is a natural inclination to cultivate what the Buddhists call *bodhichitta*—loving kindness. We begin to realize, through deep union with the other, that we are connected to the entire world and the entire Universe, both seen and unseen. This profound awareness of interconnectedness within the field of Life is a unitive vision so potent that we are turned toward compassion, service and the nectar of loving regard for the other. As a quality of being, loving regard exists within an immense spectrum, from simple impersonal regard for the basic goodness of the other to worship of divinity as it is perceived in Life in a myriad of potentials. Loving regard can manifest as *sarvatmabhava* (the total love of the *gopis* for Lord Krishna, as expounded by Vallabhacharya), *sahaj samadhi* (open-eyed ecstatic union) or *mahabhakti* (great, overwhelming devotional love mood for the ista devata).

Cultivation of a natural relationship to sex and sexual yoga, practiced within the right context, also produces states that catalyze a tacit bodily knowing, which may give rise to profound feeling states, including all manner of *rasas* and *bhavas*. It is wise to contextualize these states beyond egoic identification: they arise as a result of interaction with dimensions of divinity. We cannot claim them or feel proud about them; to do so is to court spiritual pride and eventual downfall. Instead, we come to understand that one of the fruits of this practice may be the spontaneous arising of worship and adoration, which may occur randomly or when actively courted within the process of daily life.

In a theistic tradition such as that of the Bauls, adoration of the personal God, the Supreme Being, is the highest form of prayer. Adoration is a condition of being that is distinct from the state of union, in which there is no other, for in union all differences have been obliterated in the prayer's absorption into the Divine. Prayerful adoration is often a joyful, deeply internal mood of praise, which may become an inner disposition, an inherent radiance that we may or may not be consciously aware of, but that flows within the circuitry of the body and between partners. This radiance of adoration also has a circuitry that is connected to the entire pattern or multiplicity of Creation and flows outward, connecting the individual organism with Life in a reciprocal flow. Adoration may have different rasas as well; it is not confined to one mood because it partakes of Life in its full array.

Therefore, the guru's gift is an eternal marriage that expands the possibilities to Creation itself. Within this marriage, there is a love affair with the personal deity, and the deity's raiment as Mother Nature in all her glory—worship of the sun and moon and reverent gratitude for the night sky, all of which may arise as the guru's Divine Influence. It is a love affair with the Universe and its splendid sweeping process of secret becoming: from unseen cosmic array of quarks and particles to inert gases and minerals, to the secret life of crystalline structures growing under the earth; from invisible amoeba swimming in a pond to tadpoles, snails, mice, mountain lions and gazelles, trees, buds, vines, leaves and the whole cornucopia of the vegetable queendom, to the enslaved daily life of those foolish but extraordinarily beautiful creatures we so generously call "human beings."

Bauls also worship the sun and the moon as fundamental living symbols that embody the great poles of Life: purusha, the masculine sun-father, and prakriti, the feminine moon-mother, which are reflected in the human body as the *ida* (lunar) and *pingala* (solar) flows of the subtle nerve pathways. The moon rises in its myriad cycles of birth, growth and death from the fullness of radiance (*purnima*) to the emptiness of the new moon (*amavasya*). The seasons of the year also reflect these patterns of birth and death and rebirth in cycles of growth and development, or becoming. This constant demonstration of the amazing juxtaposition between impermanence and continuity communicates also the objective Realness of both nondual and dual, with its inherent potential for conscious awareness of the whole play.

The Bauls understand that human nature is most exquisite in its innate divinity: the entire universe is contained within the blueprint of the human being. It is a fact of physics that we are organically made of the stars. Human beings are a microcosm of the macrocosm, and in that sense, we contain the entire cosmos and its potential, from alpha to omega, as the Great Process of Divine Evolution.

In the love affair with Life, Great Prakriti as Mother Nature exudes the most precious fragrance in the flowering love of children in particular. In Lee's teaching, the child comes first. Parents, grandparents and significant others sacrifice themselves, foregoing self-gratification and self-reference for the welfare of the child. Hindu dharma says that the child is God, and should be served as such for the first seven years of life. This is because the child's divine innocence is still intact, and should be preserved in every possible way by loving and wise adults.

This awakened love and conscious connectedness to all of life is the source of profound heartbreak as well. At the local grocery store we see children abused, shamed, emotionally brutalized, slapped or beaten by angry, stressed-out parents and caregivers. Of course, this is only the tip of the iceberg. Children are tortured, starved to death, sold into slavery all over the world. Any individual who undertakes a serious spiritual practice in any tradition will labor under the weight of love and compassion, for we cannot avoid heartbreak at the suffering of our fellow beings, most poignantly experienced in the plight of children.

Loving and in fact revering our children comes naturally when we are living by our hearts. We can only truly love children if we also love the elderly, for they are two prime points of experience in a continuum of becoming as described in Lee's teaching, "The Divine Path of Growing Old."[5] If we love the beginning and the end of incarnation, then we love all that comes in between. Both elders and children have a relationship with shunyata, children having been recently washed in the font of forgetfulness—the shunyata of birth—and elders standing at the brink of forgetfulness—the shunyata of death.

Children live very close to the shunyata of Reality; it has not yet been conditioned out of them by preachers, politicians, schools and societal rules. The Path is the process by which we regain our childhood birthright that was stolen from most of us at such an early age—if we walk with a steady beat and persevere toward the unveiling of our original innocence. Once we are reunited with Organic Innocence, we are conscious of our inviolable roots in the unity of all, for Organic Innocence is the point of origin and connection, where we are married to all of life.

---

[5]   This essay appears in *Laughter of the Stones* by Lee Lozowick.

Being married to all of Life in a true sense is immediate, both mystical and tangible—a direct experience of union in multiplicity. Multiplicity is true; oneness is true. That these opposites co-exist in us is the grand paradox. Yogi Ramsuratkumar often fell into ecstatic bhavas in which he would exclaim, "My Father is everywhere, everything, past, present, future, far, farther, farthest, all, one! Only my Father exists. My Father alone exists!" This all-inclusive declaration is Yogi Ramsuratkumar's great assertion of Just This, which is an assertion simultaneously of both the nondual and the dual. Similarly, Lee says of his father Yogi Ramsuratkumar, "Multiplicity died in its meeting with You." Multiplicity has died, meaning there is no longer a dual state, while at the same time, a "You" (which is a "Thou") still exists, as well as one who can speak of the "You." How can such a thing be? Only by the miracle of God's Grace.

"God does not live in the sky." "There is only God." These teaching phrases from Lee means that God is everything, everywhere, tacit, innate, unborn, undying, all-pervading. This is so natural to us that we don't even realize it is the subtle background of all that we are perceiving. We remain unaware of God's pervasive presence, or even that we are experiencing shunyata and the arising of phenomena, because we tend not to put the grand terms of the Path on our experience in ordinary moments. Sometimes we are aware that a precious experience of aliveness is unfolding within us, and that this is actually a moment of fruition on the Path, but more often than not we are simply feeling relaxed or mildly elated in the experience of here and now, in which there is a natural expansion within the rasa of enjoyment. There is free sensation in the body; a no-problem breeze is blowing. Delight and gratitude are the twin children that play in Eden, the garden of divine innocence. Sometimes the mind does not engage (which is a good thing) in reflection upon that elevated state until later, when someone comments on a particular mood or rasa that was present: "That was a wonderful afternoon," or "That was a really divine mood at dinner," or, "There was such a communion among us…"

We live awash in the tidal flows of a great ocean. The classic metaphor is that when we are one with the ocean, we do not know that we are the ocean. And yet, the condition of the ocean is such that it moves, and we take form as a droplet or a current for some brief infinitude of time. Papa Ramdas once instructed his devotee, the young Ramsurat, to cultivate more of the nirguna aspect of the Divine precisely because Ramsurat was so steeped in the saguna, demonstrated in his extreme devotional bhavas and attachment to his beloved Papa Ramdas and Mataji Krishnabai. Ramdas had a profound understanding that to worship saguna without nirguna—or the opposite—resulted in a skewed and incomplete realization, which can result in what author Vijaya Fedorshak calls "the shadow on the Path." Both dimensions of realization are vital to a true, abiding, mature relationship to God: Reality as it is. For Papa Ramdas, the prime injunction to his devotees was to chant the *nama* of God, an activity that resonates with both saguna and nirguna.

In December 1953, a devotee asked Ramdas, "Should we realize the nirguna or saguna aspect of God?" Ramdas answered, "Both." The devotee then asked, "Nirguna and saguna are opposites. Are they not?" Ramdas replied:

> *No, they are like the sun and its rays. The rays are not different from the sun. Nirguna is the changeless and formless Spirit and saguna is the manifestation; they are like the sun and its rays. The nirguna is beyond the intellect to comprehend. That is why He is called achintyarupa. He is the purusha. He is also the prakriti.*

> He is *purusha* and *prakriti* together and also beyond
> both, and is called *Purushottama.*[6]

One of the most important ways that Bauls of the West approach shunyata is through the direct experience of the void as the realm in which transformational potencies are encountered. This is one of the reasons that the void is considered fertile; it carries infinite potentialities and creativity while it is also experienced as an encounter that annihilates the personality as it is. Even in very small increments, when we consciously touch the void—however briefly—we are different, even in small or invisible ways, due to its amazing transformational power.

Enlightened Duality is an ordinary term for the greatest mystery that Life holds within its immense arms. Enlightened Duality is light sparkling on the vast sea of connectedness, and if we investigate this amazing phenomena of form to the point of penetration, we will come upon shunyata, the Sanskrit word that communicates the notion of emptiness. To say that there is emptiness, or that all forms are empty, does not mean that they are dark or nihilistic. On the contrary, shunyata has been described as vast space lit by sunlight, but even this is a qualified description that does not capture its mystery. Across the face of shunyata ripples the diamond light of possibility—Creation, which is none other than *sat-chit-ananda.*

Postmodern quantum physics has a lot to say about space and emptiness. Quantum theory states that radiant energy is transmitted in the form of discrete units at the subatomic level—the most

---

[6]   Swami Satchidananda, *The Gospel of Swami Ramdas*, page 359.

infinitesimal building blocks of matter. "Discrete units" seems to echo Samkhya: the reality of discrete, individual beings (*monads*). It also sounds a lot like Ramanuja, Madhva ("Difference is real") and the many other great traditional dualists of the bhakti tradition in India. Tom Robbins, a twenty-first century visionary and grand synthesizer of information, translates quantum mechanics into exactly the teaching we are considering in this essay:

> *"It gets better," said Switters. "This is only theory, there's no empirical evidence, but the belief now is that when they crack the final nut, split the most minute particle—and we're talking about something smaller than a neutrino—what they'll find inside, at the absolute fundamental level of the universe, is an electrified vacuum, an energy field in which light and darkness intermingle. The dark is as black as a bogman's toejam, and the light is brighter than God's front teeth, and they spiral together, entwined like a couple of snakes. They coil around each other, the light and the darkness, and they absorb each other continuously, yet they never cancel each other out. You get the picture. Except there isn't any picture. It's more on the order of music. Except the ear can't hear it. So it's like feeling, emotion, some absolutely pristine feeling. It's like, uh, it's like...love."* [7]

When we have encountered a raw experience of impermanence, it will often throw us, even momentarily, into the void before we are cast back into duality in a state of bewilderment, loss and grief—or perhaps into joy, equanimity, or acceptance. Any profound shock or radical change in life circumstance precipitates intimate spiritu-

---

[7]   Tom Robbins, *Fierce Invalids Home From Hot Climates*, page 414.

al contact with shunyata, even if it is momentary, and it is in these priceless moments that we encounter the transformational power of the void. Events of all kinds precipitate a descent into the archetypal realm—even, and maybe especially, when we fall madly in love. Shunyata makes an "appearance" in our lives whenever we are in a transition from one state to another.

The deep-rooted Western fear of the void seems to stem from a fundamental misunderstanding about its true nature. We glimpse shunyata and because it is perceived as empty and unknowable, we make a leap of association and project upon it a negative voidness that is nihilistic and depressing. This cold, nihilistic view of "the dark sea of awareness" is found throughout Castaneda's work, for example—the sorcerer's path, which most would agree is nontheistic. If we look at a range of spiritual traditions, we see that when divinity is added to the total perspective, the void is perceived differently.

Some say that the void per se is not nondual union, because it is fertile or full; nor can it be called dual, because it is empty; in essence, the void is a domain of experience that is indescribable. Ancient shamanism called it "the underworld," which could only be entered by one who has been through some form of dismemberment that results in egoic and psychic death—an experience so intense that it is usually referred to in symbolic language as being flayed, drawn and quartered, or utterly destroyed.

The Sumerians of six thousand years ago referred to this underworld domain as "a bright and fruitful realm," echoing the Buddhist description of emptiness as "luminous." Although it should be noted that when Inanna, the great goddess of the planetary sphere of Venus, went to visit her sister Ereskighal, the queen of the underworld, she lost everything: her crown, her royal robes, jewelry and implements of power. She was then killed and hung on a hook on the wall to rot. This is a perfectly apt symbolic communication of what it feels like to have egoic identifications destroyed by the events of life. Many have experienced the void as hell, exactly because of the dismemberment of ego and identifications that one must go through in order to enter that domain, even if you are a goddess. From Sumeria of six thousand years ago we can make connections with contemporary physics in the writings of Tom Robbins again, on the subject of darkness, light, the void, love and hell:

> *If Domino could imagine that God occupied the fundamental subatomic particle, where did she think Satan lived? In the fundamental anti-particle? In a quarklette of dark matter? Wouldn't the presumed interweaving of light and darkness in that minutest of maws give her a clue that God and Satan might be codependent if not indivisible? The real question was where did the neutral angels reside, the ones who refused to take sides? There would be, of course, plenty of elbow room of a sort in that elementary space. Because the light waves therein would have been transformed into photons had they struck any matter, indications were that the space was infinitely empty. Which also would suggest that God and the Devil were energies in which, outflanking Einstein, mass dropped out of the equation.*[8]

As in ancient Sumeria and in other traditions, including esoteric Christianity, the fertile darkness is objectified beyond good and bad as the void, or the abyss—or the dark night which prefigures the light, or the cloud of unknowing. Any way you want to look at it, the mystery remains. Buddhism, Hinduism, Christianity and Sufism all have their own version of the void, and there are many different schools, lineages, traditions and points of view on shunyata that have been argued back and forth, some of which are explored in Appendix IV.

---

[8]   Ibid, page 418.

The mystery of shunyata deepens when we experience a loving intention behind this and all aspects of Creation, for the play of the Lord arising from the Lord's very lacuna is the ultimate mystery. We are given the most delicate, ephemeral glimpse—short-lived as it is—of an unknowable Great Being that moves across the face of a Great Nothing: the breath of God moving across the ocean of Creation, diamonds on the surface of the Deep.

Somehow, from the Baul perspective, we do not need to bend our minds around all this, although hopefully this foray into what some of the great traditions have to say about shunyata has been helpful in considering tantra, because tantric practice of any kind is not possible without an active relationship to emptiness, mystery, voidness. The Bauls call this *jayente mara*: living death. One who has already died and still lives is one who is empty, a Great Nothing—*sunya*. This is alluded to in Yogi Ramsuratkumar's statement, "Ramdas killed this beggar in 1952."

It is a miracle of Life that the "Great Nothing" of Yogi Ramsuratkumar somehow had—and still has, years after bodily death—a personal relationship with his devotees. Even though Brahman is nirguna, without attributes, somehow there is also saguna: there is sat-chit-ananda, truth, beauty and love. There are the three *gunas*. There is a triune deity: the Hindu Brahma, Vishnu, Shiva; the Christian God the Father, God the Son and the Holy Ghost (Mother); the Celtic Maiden, Mother and Crone. There is multiplicity and diversity. There is birth and death. There is creation and destruction and all that is between. There is the grace of becoming; there is compassion, love, heartbreak. All we need is to open our hearts and jump into the flow of Life to feel into the truth of this.

Why is all this splitting of philosophical hairs about shunyata important? Because seeds are planted through our sincere digging into the earth of things through the process of study. What is important is that we cultivate vulnerability, an open heart, a receptivity, an acceptance. If we are interested in alchemical transformation, which may be engaged within the perception of Reality as Enlightened Duality, then it behooves us to consider these ideas until they become true of us in the sense of *bartaman*—we have the direct experience of them.

When we feel something ineffable drawing us toward moods that may arise as love, devotion, praise, longing, adoration of the grandeur, the splendor, the magnificence of the Source of all this, then we find ourselves becoming very magnetized by the possibility of alchemical Work—which might also be called "being Woman in Life," as Lee said recently. When we are touched, even bruised, by the butterfly wings of gratitude, heartbreaking love, worship, beauty, then we are in an alchemical process. As soon as we embark upon the path of alchemy, or *rasayana*, we will begin to have a different experience of that dimension of Life known by the name of shunyata. We will come to know the void as the transformative potency that it is, even if it is experienced differently than it has been described in these pages. Shunyata is so mysterious that it cannot be pinned down by any description; nonetheless, in moments we touch its borders, stand at the portal, or step inside its domain—and in those moments, we are changed.

Returning to the insight which began this consideration, months after the day when we were driving through the mountains of Ardeche, I ran across this quote from William Blake: "Eternity is in love with the creations of time."[9] This is statement of Enlightened Duality, in which there is a deep and perhaps inexpressible kinship with the insight, "My guru has married me to the entire world in the circle of eternity." This message, which came from somewhere deep inside in the void, caused me to ask again, as I have pondered this many times: What is eternity?

Eternity, that mystery or myth that seems to defy definition at every turn, no matter how hard the philosophers try, is a concept that fits very well into the perception of Enlightened Duality. The dictionary provides several definitions of the word "eternity." 1) Time without beginning or end. 2) The state or quality of being eternal. 3a.) The timeless state following death. 3b.) The afterlife; immortality. 4) A very long or seemingly endless time. The second of these is the "definition" that is most pertinent to our exploration, although we could explore all four.

Beginning with eternity as "the state of quality of being eternal," some say that eternity is actually a condition in which there is no time—and no passing of time. In this sense, eternity is a timeless dimension, which is often attributed to Brahman, or God, as the unqualified ground of being. Eternity is not the void, nor is it nirvana or the nondual state, because when you are in eternity, you know it. That's a brave statement, as some may disagree with it, because personal experience—as objective as that experience may be—is still open to interpretation.

Like shunyata, eternity is another immense mystery whose location is now. The present moment is the only location in space and time where one can access the eternal. Being in the present moment is a matter of paying attention in a focused, laser-like way. Total attention is the payment, in fact, to get into the present moment of now—the eternal now. Lee once wrote a song about eternity in

---

9   From Steven Pressfield's book, *The War of Art*.

which he says, "Eternity is just a moment, a moment that forever exists." We cannot explain such a radical state of being, we can only experience it directly.

We may access eternity when we become Woman in Life through the placement of attention in the present moment. Eternity is a tangent point where nonduality and duality meet in awakened, conscious participation in a mystery we cannot describe. We know when we have been there, and each time we make the trip, so to speak, it seems that we have accessed profound transformational energies. What is the fastest way to get to eternity? Just like the void, we get there primarily through the experience of sex, death, birth, and secondarily through creative acts of all kinds, including prayer and adoration. If you are writing a poem or composing a song or singing the Name of God (in any myriad of ways) or painting a picture or praying or completely and totally present with a child, a dying friend, an aging parent, or in deep sexual-love communion, you can touch eternity.

Since it is impossible to describe or define the actual qualities of eternity, we turn to *sandhya bhasa,* or twilight language. Using twilight language, as William Blake did, we can say that eternity is always waiting for its lovers, who are lost in time. Eternity is longing for us, and takes us gently into Its divine caress as soon as we hone our awareness to a delicate point. Eternity may give you a kiss, sometimes one that lingers. In the in between world, the borderline realm of twilight—where tantra, or continuity, is the modus operandi—we can speak freely of eternity. We can mix up our metaphors and jump from one image to another. We can use whatever works to get the point across. What do we find when we get to eternity? The Beloved. We can say, perhaps, that eternity is the abode of the Beloved. Eternity is the Beloved's inner chamber. As soon as you try to grasp or catch the Beloved, He is gone. Disappeared into…emptiness. He is uncatchable, unknowable—a theme that Baul poets love to explore in their poetry.

Formless,
The flower floats.
But where is the plant?
And the water?
Yet still, the flower
Eternally floats
On the waves
Of life.
The bees buzzing,
Drink its honey
While Lalan,
Seeking, chasing,
Misses the flower.

Lalan

"Eternity is in love with the creations of time." The Beloved longs for us just as we long for the Beloved, for what else are we, but "the creations of time"? We are created and live within time. When we stop seeking and chasing phantoms, we come to a stillness where we may stand our ground; then we become creative forces, so that the Beloved may enjoy our creations as well—our songs, poems, dances, sculptures, paintings, our worship, our loving relationships, all of our joys and sorrows, and our moments of awakening to Life.

The thing about eternity is this: Everyone has a room in eternity. It is in the halcyon hallways of eternity that we are alone with the Beloved. In fleeting moments, we glimpse the radiant gleam of an alabaster cheek, the purple-lidded mystery of eyes that gaze into our own, a thrill of sublime happiness, the perfect, full curve of the lips, the flowing tresses. We cannot describe this experience except through poetic language because we are reduced to nothing but awe and wonder. Everything is reduced to ash but pure being and pure mood. We do not want to be anything in the face of such Perfection.

We have tasted the nectar of adoration, and the more we taste that nectar, the more we want it. We should be cautioned that developing a "taste" for adoration is a sure road—perhaps a very long one, or perhaps a very short one—toward annihilation in love, in which sooner or later the Beloved becomes all and everything. In that process the lovers of God become nothing. Great Nothings that worship, praise, adore…in the eternal forever.

So this is what we are called to?
Who are You? No one.
What is there to Realize? Nothing.
Yes, how completely perfect and how totally Mad.
Nothing to find except Nothing.
And no-one to become except no-one.
And how to be given this Gift?
We need Your Grace to have Faith,
to be Obedient, to await Surrender.
What to do about this catastrophe?
Praise Yogi Ramsuratkumar and
delight in His most awesome Beauty,
pranam at His universe-treading Feet,
bow our heads in gratitude
for the mercy of His Blessings
and Praise Him again, all over in
each and every moment.
This is lee lozowick, Father,
Your true heart-son and wild Heretic,
open-handed and free
of every attachment but You,
yet so attached to You that
this attachment is no-attachment —
it is consuming, not separate, One,

all, total, time, space, Just This.
      With each cell, in fact each atom
of this being chanting Yogi Ramsuratkumar,
            Faith, Devotion, Obedience, and Surrender Live.[10]

---

[10]   Lee Lozowick, *Gasping for Air in a Vacuum*, 2 November 1999.

Prayer and Supplication

Lee Lozowick

There is no rigid definition of prayer. Whenever we use language relative to a subject like prayer, it's always going to be somewhat inexact. There is a certain mood around the word "prayer," but almost anything could be a prayer, depending upon the context in which it is offered. So don't get stuck on the word "prayer" as if there is a specific, exact form that *is* prayer, because that's very misleading. We could even say, loosely, anything that serves Reality is prayer. Obviously, given the number of individuals there are in the world, prayer could take on almost any form or manifestation.

What's important is the mood, the aura of our prayer. When your heart is pure and your actions have integrity, and your wish is to somehow serve, then however you are trying to accomplish those things could realistically be experienced as prayer. It could be simply wishing somebody well in ordinary language, or it could take the form of a very highly ritualized practice like those found in convents and monasteries. You approach it from the perspective of a *feeling*, not an intellectual definition. So, start praying whenever you want.

It is important to make a distinction between prayer and supplication, both of which have their place and their context. My master Yogi Ramsuratkumar used the word "praise" to mean prayer—simply to praise selflessly, because you have a commitment to the radiant glory of Reality or of God. When you praise, there is no motive or wish for reciprocity; there is no question of getting anything in return. You are simply praising Truth, Reality, the Divine, because It is pure, transcendent, stainless, majestic—It is what It is.

On the other hand, supplication by definition means that you expect something to come back to you. "O Lord, bring me health. O Lord, protect my children. O Lord, I need some money." That is supplication, which is different than prayer. Supplication is not necessarily the wrong way to pray; it has its time and place, and it can be very effective. When your child is sick and you want them to get healthy, if you make a supplication and your child gets healthy—fantastic! It would really be counterproductive and immature not to make such a supplication to the Divine because you feel it's not proper or that it's not true prayer. If my child is sick, I will do whatever gets them better, even if I have to get down on my knees and supplicate all night long. We don't want to be such purists that every time we feel a supplication would be useful, we catch ourselves and say, "Oh no, I can't do this—it is not the highest teaching," because supplication has its time and place, and yet it is not prayer.

There are certain phrases used both in the East and in the West, such as the Jesus Prayer in Eastern Orthodox Christianity. There are many versions of it, but it is essentially: "Lord Jesus Christ, Son of God, have mercy on me, a poor sinner." This can be a prayer or a supplication, depending upon the context in which it is used. For most practitioners, if the practice is serious—and the practitioner can take stock of themselves with ruthless self-honesty—we start out with supplication and it becomes a prayer. The same thing is true of mantras like, "Om Nama Shivaya," or "Hare Krishna, Hare Krishna,

Krishna, Krishna, Hare Hare; Hare Rama, Hare Rama, Rama, Rama, Hare Hare." Usually when you first discover those mantras, the ego is saying, "If I'm going to spend three hours a day mumbling this mantra, I want something." It may not be something material; maybe we want some kind of realization. Even so, as long as the context is, "I'll do this as long as I get that," then it's supplication, no matter how high the goal. Even asking for God is still asking; it's not praise. But, often if we stay with the practice long enough and mature in it, it becomes prayer.

Just the vibration of "Om Nama Shivaya" can be pure, radiant praise, without any feeling of needing to receive something in return for the offering of that mantra—a principle that applies to any system of prayer, depending upon the context. Obviously, if we're on our knees in church desperately saying, "God, I need some money," it's not likely that we have the context that will turn our supplication into praise. On the other hand, if we're just intoning a verse of praise or a name of God, even if we start out supplicating, we can end up in prayer in one period of fifteen minutes.

You have probably had the experience of "being lifted up," as they might say in the Christian church. Maybe you've been in church out of some obligatory relationship to your parents or social clique, and you're just mouthing the prayer mechanically, feeling irritated and bored, and all of a sudden you find yourself lifted up in glory, feeling completely infused by the love of Jesus, or by the grace of Ramana Maharshi, or Anandamayi Ma—the kiss of the Shekkinah, or whatever your experience might be. You don't know how you got there, but you're there, and in being there you are almost impaled by the mood of prayer. The same words that you were saying mechanically and annoyingly just moments ago have become words of radiant praise! Of course, that's when the trouble can start: "Wow, mercy is really cool! Wow, I need more mercy, so I'm going to pray again." As soon as you put that kind of demand on it, it's not prayer anymore.

If you are naïve, you can say the same prayer and get very frustrated, wondering why you aren't getting the same response. If you are completely selfless in the offer of praise, you might find yourself in the end weeping with gratitude for the mercy of God.

July 2007
Hauteville, France

The Storm of Grace

M. Young

*R*eflections on Enlightened Duality go on and on, because there is "no top end," as Lee has said of the Great Process of Divine Evolution. There are infinite windows and doorways and portals into the experience of Life in its inherent realness—a reflection that was spurred on when I found myself in the guru's company in mid-November 2008 in one of the great American Sodom and Gomorrahs...Los Angeles, the City of Fallen Angels.

We left the mountains of Arizona two hours before dawn. It was *purnima*, the day each month when the full moon vigil is kept on the ashram by chanting the *nama* of Yogi Ramsuratkumar for twenty-four hours, and so the sound of soft melodic voices coming from the meditation hall lent an auspicious mood to our departure. Descending from the mountains into the valley, we entered the Sonoran desert with the full moon sailing in the west just as the sunrise began to spread its colors in flaming pink and tangerine across the dawn sky. Dark amethyst clouds scudded along the edges of this magnificent display of sheer terrestrial beauty as we traveled the crack between the worlds, zooming down the valley road through a desert landscape. Soft greens of chaparral, sage and cacti touched my senses, forming a living tapestry set against the volcanic crags of purple mountains in the surrounding distance. For two hours we drove in silence with Lee at the wheel, suspended between the interplay of rising sun and setting moon in a breathtaking theatre of solar and lunar forces.

The next day I walked on Venice Beach with two friends. The compelling cosmic dance of the day before lingered in my awareness as we entered into the unique, unrestrained liveliness of this borderline realm, where the vast continent meets the vast ocean of the Pacific. Venice Beach is an almost mythic place in American lore, a place where *prakriti* reigns in a peculiar way. Instantly we were immersed in a crazy, funky, rollicking Southern California street scene. It was the world of illusion in brilliant tones: an American bardo scene, like Las Vegas in its unreality, but at the same time it was somehow vividly real. It was a very adult kind of scene, unless you walked further out toward the beach, for there were also green grassy areas, trailing bougainvillea vines blooming in red and orange, tall graceful palm trees, landscaped trails for walking, running, skating, or bicycling. Beyond that was the sandy white beach with the surf crashing in, and an endless expanse of deep blue ocean meeting a pale blue sky.

The crowd strolled along the boardwalk mingling with hawkers, blaring music, and strung-out marginal characters selling cheap tourist junk on the pavement. Surfers, locals and counter-culture folks of all kinds were out in full array to take in the sun and surf. A guy on roller blades dressed in colorful rags and sixties garb, his massive dreadlocks piled up underneath a crocheted hat, stopped to play electric guitar licks for the youngsters walking down the street. His presence struck a chord for me. A little Jimi Hendrix, a little Bob Marley, a bit of David Bowie, he seemed to have a very big heart. A young teenage boy who stopped to listen—"Hey man, great!"—smiled and joked around with him. Later I found out that he is a rather iconic figure, a well-known and loved Venice Beach street prophet who dispenses spontaneous street wisdom here on a daily basis.

A young man with a reptile sitting in a few inches of water in a clear plastic tub yelled at us, "Hey, I've got a two-headed turtle! You *do* wanna see this!" Beach bums slept on cardboard beds on the green grass that bordered the sandy beach. A tall, powerful African American man dressed in camo army fatigues, carrying a stuffed backpack, stood in the middle of an intersection on the boardwalk asking for money. He addressed the crowd in a loud voice, as if running for office: "Help a wino get drunk! Come on, help me out. Help a wino get drunk! I'm tellin' you, it's my ambrosia—help a guy get drunk…" Bigger than life and amazingly vivid, this guy, who obviously lived on the streets, was humming with high-voltage energy. I wondered what his story was.

Venice Beach is a gaudy, multicultural, multi-racial marketplace where the sirens of desire sing their song. Food abounds in many forms: chili-cheese fries, hot dogs, hamburgers, empanadas (Mexican pies), Coca Cola, beer, wine. Easy access to marijuana, XTC, acid, psilocybin, peyote and any other hallucinogenic substance is understood—as well as harder, more deadly substances that might be desired. Beads, jewelry, shawls, shoes, macramé necklaces and bracelets, shells, imported wood carvings, cloth, bags, incense of all kinds, surf boards, beach towels, sunscreen, belts, shoes, skirts and dresses from Africa, India, Indonesia, and Bali, call to all who pass by.

Tattoo parlors, head shops and restaurants abound on one side of the walkway, while on the other side people spread out their wares: a couple making sage bundles from a pile of freshly dried wild sage; burned out druggies selling bogus variety goods; entertainers; Jamaicans selling junk; tarot readers, palm readers, psychic readers—these were the actors in this movie, animating the roles of fictional characters on a surreal movie set. There are many homeless, sleeping along the beach, carrying all their possession on their backs, with grocery carts filled with blankets, bags, clothes, most of them dirty, stained, smeared, unkempt—but free in their own way. Southern California is full of people who live on the streets.

At Venice Beach the street people and beggars pack an energetic wallop; in one way, they are reminiscent of the sadhus in the cremation grounds at Tarapith—you want to guard your energy around them, because they know how to forage on many levels. The question was, as always, how to make use of all this barely contained pandemonium and vivid eccentricity? Over the years I have traveled numerous times in my guru's company to places like Las Vegas, Disneyland, Los Angeles, and many other locations where you know you are in a strange alternate reality that is marvelously different than the one you usually inhabit. All big cities are particular bardo realms: in this I include New York City, San Francisco, London, Paris, Berlin, Dresden, Brussels, Amsterdam, Vancouver, and the big cities of India. It's good to have the capacity to walk through those realms without being attracted or repelled (for either way we are distracted, fascinated and seduced), and this of itself is one of the arts of *sadhana* involving the perception of Enlightened Duality.

As in most of these scenes, shopping is one of the attractions. I have found that, when traveling in general, shopping is one of the big seductions that can take me away from my true purpose, so that awareness becomes dulled, scattered and unclear. From there, it's likely to be downhill all the way. Of course it is possible to shop without losing my self—but it's a very fine line. It is always best to stay attentive and vigilant, because this disposition lends itself to freedom—free-floating attention, free energy, free awareness, free and genuine gesture of word and deed.

The steady presence of the Santa Ana winds, which come to Southern California every year around this time, had the temperature soaring at Venice Beach and Santa Monica, where we were spending time at a tribal arts show. Our hosts told us that these winds are called "Santa Ana" but actually the name is derived from the Spanish "Satana," because they are considered ill winds that bring an uncomfortable heat to the usually idyllic coastal weather of the Los Angeles area. I had been on the Pacific Coast many times over the years;

never had it been hot like this. Satan's Wind indeed: it was ninety-three degrees with seventeen percent humidity at the beach that day. Maybe it wasn't global warming; maybe the heat was exacerbated by all the fires burning around the L.A. area, in Sayre, Palos Verdes, on the freeway and up north in Santa Barbara. Everywhere the air was filled with heavy gray smoke and fine ashen cinders.

After our foray in Venice Beach, we drove out the Pacific Coast Highway, heading north to Topanga Canyon just along the shoreline. The golden path of the western sun shone across the ocean with a sulfuric cast. The air was thick with fumes, a combination of the usual L.A. pollution and the additional burden of smoke from the local fires. It reminded us of Bombay, or Mumbai, where the sun also sets over a western ocean in an unmitigated, hazy thick veil of pollution.

Up in Topanga Canyon where we were staying, the smell of smoke and heavy burning filled the air. The presence of the fires permeated everything. All in all, twenty thousand people had been or were in the process of being evacuated from their homes. Sitting out on the patio overlooking the canyon as twilight faded into the smoky dark of an early evening, we waited for Lee to arrive from conducting business in Santa Monica. The conversation revolved around the lineages of which we and our hosts are a part: our friends were long-time devotees of Swami Muktananda and are now disciples of Arnaud Desjardins.

They regaled us with stories of Baba Muktananda, and then the conversation turned to Yogi Ramsuratkumar: his love of chanting and dancing; the way he wanted Lee's poems sung to him in his latter years; his "Father's Work" that was so clearly demonstrated in his cigarette smoking. What was it about how Yogi Ramsuratkumar smoked that struck us so deeply? His cupped hands sheltered the cigarette, and the hidden heat of the draw, the tiny crackling embers of tobacco that combusted and transformed matter from one state to another—from solid mass to ephemeral smoke—ignited also a smoldering within the person who sat before him. The smoke wafted upward to disappear as it merged into air, and this too spoke to the deepest part of the being who sat before the Beggar King. The mystery of Yogi Ramsuratkumar spoke to the mystery within me, so that "I" could sense the prayer of that burning within. Lee once wrote:

> Tell me Devaki Ma,
>> for you of all of us must know,
> can this be true,
>> what I see before my eyes?
> I watch the smoke
>> from Bhagwan's sacred cigarettes
> as it spirals, twists and turns,
>> beautiful in the afternoon sunlight.
> I don't read Tamil or Sanskrit
>> but I would swear
> that this smoke is spelling words;
>> Father Praising God,
> telling Ramnam
>> even in this way!
> This is lee Lozowick,
>> the son of Yogi Ramsuratkumar
> offering pranams to the dirty Beggar
>> and to His Blessed Mother Devaki.

When I met Yogi Ramsuratkumar the first time, love dawned instantaneously. I had never seen anyone whose entire manifestation in life was so empowered by spontaneity, free of forethought or motivation. Many countless people had the experience, like me, of being heart-melted by his inexplicable bright fire. There was a force field that emanated from him, which influenced all around him, while at the same time there was the palpable feeling that those radiations transcended space and time to touch places, people and realms beyond the local sphere. When I focused attention on him, the moment turned to darshan: his body was revealed as a *mudra*, the atmosphere rarified into a diamond-like clarity, and I perceived the beggar in rags as deity. I became aware of my being as a part of his mandala, which radiated from a sublime dimension.

His intensity had the effect of shining an almost unbearable bright light on everything and everyone around him. The spiritual force of his presence deepened ordinary awareness into the subtle matrix of Life, causing the good and bad of the manifest world to become essential, vivid, real, and sublime in its mysterious emptiness. His every gesture was compelling, commanding and yet wholly pure, unmotivated, imbued with Grace. Perhaps it was in part this very purity and unmotivated, untarnished, childlike innocence that disarmed our defenses. Life in his company opened awareness to a multi-dimensionality that could be very disconcerting: while the inner war of the *kleshas* was never more distracting and revealed in its obsession, simultaneously we existed with Yogi Ramsuratkumar on an exquisite plane of love and bliss.

In this state, revealed and raw, the quality of life depended on where my attention was focused, and therefore it could be heaven, or it could be hell, or it could be anything inbetween. When self-reference ruled—my psychology, my neurosis—then it was hell. If the focus of attention was God-referenced, then the inner experience became ineffable, heavenly. At times when I was bound in duality, forced up against the kleshas, there before me was the undeniable truth of Yogi Ramsuratkumar—a natural human being who embodied freedom, compassion, humor, delight.

Years later I discovered that this radical experience of multidimensionality is called "coemergence," or "coemergent wisdom," in Vajrayana Buddhism. Coemergence means that the realms of samsara and nirvana are not separate and, in fact, coexist. The term coemergent wisdom describes the vivid, raw, fresh quality of *mahamudra*, or Assertion: the experience of Reality as it is. I found this Vajrayana teaching to be of tremendous value; not only did it affirm my direct experience, it provided an essential wisdom perspective that helped to integrate that experience.[1]

Whenever we were visiting Yogi Ramsuratkumar, Lee instructed us not to interject ourselves into the equation with questions and comments. He said that Yogi Ramsuratkumar, like a child, would respond to whatever was put before him, and if we were the ones "leading" the play with questions, ideas, comments and extrapolations of our own construction, then what we would receive was the machination of our own egos—not the master's spontaneous movement. In the company of Yogi Ramsuratkumar, Lee always wanted us to have whatever Yogi Ramsuratkumar would give to us. Sometimes that involved wonderful *lilas*, when his playfulness delighted us. Often it meant that we were receiving blessings at such a subtle, infinitesimal level, they could only be perceived by the soul's organ of perception in incarnation—the human body, with its mystical heart, complex nervous system and subtle correlates. This was because Yogi Ramsuratkumar could spend hours doing "nothing" but smoking and listening to the people around him chant the Name of God. During those hours when boredom, fantasy and idle distractions could reign instead of the focus of pristine attention upon a vast being who was radiating the space and its occupants with divinity, what was really going on within that "Great Nothing," Yogi Ramsuratkumar? The answer to that question was (and is) a matter of direct perception, involving the very same mystical heart, complex nervous system and subtle correlates already mentioned.

In quantum physics, briefly considered in a previous essay, physicists say that everything is in a state of flow. No one thing—like a

---

[1]   Reginald Ray, *Secret of the Vajra World*, page 286. See also Jeremy Hayward, *Warrior-King of Shambhala: Remembering Chögyam Trungpa*, pages 276–277.

particle, for example—exists at a single point; it exists or is "smeared" over a large area that is flowing. Particles respond like waves and waves respond like particles, and all of this is changed mysteriously if it is being *observed*, as if at the most infinitesimal level of creation, God responds to our attention. The bottom line is that we have the power to change things by placing our attention, and therefore, there is no such thing as a casual observer: we are responsible for everything in Creation because we are interrelated, and because of the inherent power of relationship. The greatest mysteries of Life are all about relationship—a very big scope of relationship: with the Divine, with human beings and all the vast realm of experience therein, with the animal, plant and mineral world, with earth and sky, with the primal elements of earth, air, fire and water, with moon and sun, with the solar system, the galaxy.

Clearly, the less we interfere with God's plans, the more we get Divine Intelligence guiding the show of Creation, causing all this interrelatedness to appear as the Will of God, rather than the will of humankind. This is why the teaching phrases, "Spiritual Slavery" and "Surrender to the Will of God" are in complete opposition to advanced technologies and science that relentlessly press on in pursuit of controlling life: cloning, stem cell research, nuclear power, creating black holes, interstellar travel, to name a few examples.

What if Spiritual Slavery was the context of how we made all decisions in life, for the good of Life? What might be God's response then if praise and worship were the subtle quality of our mood, the focus of our attention? Who knows what grace and benevolence would flow, or what beauty and wonder might be revealed to us? Maybe what would emerge by divine design is relationship with the personal God, the Beloved—in ways that are unimaginable, of course, but worthy of pondering, because, as we know, anything is possible.

The pathways, hallways and rooms in the mansion of objective relationship are infinite in potential, but they all have certain qualities in common. For instance, the transformational quality of relationship always carries a feel of intimacy. Intimacy occurs in the present moment and simply is not possible when the mind is distracted, pulled into the past or future. I remember our final parting with Yogi Ramsuratkumar in 2000, two months before he died. He called each of Lee's *sishyas* (students) to his private chamber in the back of the temple complex, where we received an intimate moment with him. One by one we entered the room to see the two of them waiting in an empty space—Lee kneeling at Yogi Ramsuratkumar's side. What happened for each one of us in those moments of gift and blessing was between that individual and the lineage of our gurus.

The undeniable, profound, loving regard of the master for his devotees—the Grace and Benediction of the lineage—was Yogi Ramsuratkumar's gift to us on this day of farewell. He could no longer walk, and after everyone had had *darshan*, Ma Devaki and his other attendants wheeled him to the back door of the temple in his reclining chair, where he watched us drive away, his hands raised in blessing. Words fail to describe the heart-rending of that good-bye, for the dharma says we are one, there is no separation, and yet, I knew I would never see him in that physical body again. The finality of this fact was overwhelming. The grand lila of Yogi Ramsuratkumar in this life was ending, and although he would live on in many ways—in his many devotees, and most especially in his spiritual son Lee Lozowick and in Ma Devaki, his "eternal slave"— the physical era of his divine play had come to the inexorable end that only death of the human body can render. Today, we are left with bittersweet longing—love in separation.

And so, we departed for the long journey home—by van to Chennai, then a lengthy stay in the airport before the flight that would take us halfway around the globe of our planet. At the time of this trip, I was intensely struggling with major changes that had occurred in my life in the past year. I had hoped for some absolute and permanent resolve of my psychological obstacles in Yogi Ramsuratkumar's physical company. On the way home I felt buffeted about, tossed here and there by the harsh winds of my own affliction; I was disappointed that a miracle—some kind of healing—had not occurred in me. Then I realized that something else was happening: in between these onslaughts of the mind at its worst, *bhavas* of sublime bliss played in the inner landscape. Underlying the world of appearance and form—and the worries and obsessions of the mind—was the Supreme Reality, concentrated in the being of Yogi Ramsuratkumar. My mechanical personality continued in its habitual routine while a veritable storm of bliss was going on inside, on a different level. I could perceive the coemergence of Reality as different levels of experience manifesting in me; again I had the perception that the quality of life as it unfolded from moment to moment was informed by where and how I placed my attention.

Several years later, when I was struggling again over my reactions to people and situations, I spoke with Lee. Distracted and upset, I was casting a negative light on everything. Lee listened then said, "That is ridiculous. You are in denial about your life. You are surrounded by a storm of Grace." When he said that phrase, "a storm of Grace," my mind was stopped by the truth of his words. The whole edifice of my illusions—my argument, my facts, my position—was dispelled by the upswelling memory of leaving Yogi Ramsuratkumar's company in 2000 and the tacit, subtle yet bodily perception of the storm of bliss.

After Yogi Ramsuratkumar left his body, the second volume of Lee's poems to his Master was published in 2004, which included this poem:

> The storm outside is wondrous,
>   the power of the thunder inspiring.
> Yet it is small in comparison
>   to the storm inside,
> the thunder and lightning,
>   the sound and light

of Your Name resounding
  within Your son without respite
(and how thankful he is,
  for no lessening is wanted).
Mother Nature is most impressive
  and beautiful in Her own way,
but Father Yogi Ramsuratkumar
  is awesome, unspeakable
and dazzling in His Divine Beauty.
  You must be Praised, Father,
not because You deserve it
  but because no other response
to Your Majesty fits You,
  as You are in Your Surrender
to Your Father in Heaven.
  This is lee lozowick,
Your devoted and obedient son,
  sitting happily in Your dusty Footsteps.[2]

That night in Topanga Canyon with fires burning everywhere, as we spoke of Yogi Ramsuratkumar's fire, his smoking, his Blessing Power, the Storm of Grace was brought to life in Southern California, to that mountainside patio overlooking the smoke-wreathed canyon. With his presence came a healing balm that arose mysteriously and spilled out to bless this place where people were suffering change, fear, heartbreak, loss, disorientation, confusion and many tragedies we could not know but could sense and intuit in the oncoming night.

---

[2]   Lee Lozowick, *Death of a Dishonest Man*, August 10, 1996.

Swami Nityananda, Baba Muktananda, Anandamayi Ma, Neem Karoli Baba, Swami Ramdas, Yogi Ramsuratkumar—these are some of the great saints and sages and masters who have walked among us during our epoch, who infused light into darkness and worked always for the harmonizing of the world and all sentient beings. Their presence is the tangent point of Grace and Blessing Power in the world, At times when it seems very bleak, we turn toward them and ask for help. Will we receive the Grace they offer?

What unusual creatures we are!
    We build fortresses around stones that are good
for nothing but making roads and guard and defend
    those stones almost with our lives, as if those very stones
were the treasures of God, while gold and diamonds
    lie in the dust in the streets just outside
the walls of our fortified palaces, unattended and unnoticed.
    Then we sit upon the thrones we have erected,
having long and serious conversations with our self-
    appointed ministers about how to protect
those stones and about how to most wisely .
    utilize these invaluable resources,
while right there beneath the turrets and windows,
    unused and begging to be discovered,
lies all the wealth of the ages, glistening in the sun.
    We fabricate imaginary threats to our stones
all the while ignoring the jewels crying out to us.
    You, the gem of all gems, have dramatized this
for us in Your generosity, having actually lived
    in the streets, the dust barely covering Your
sparkling glory, and having been ignored for so long
    while we played king in our illusory castles.
How patient You are, oh Regent of Hearts,
    and how it must hurt You to see Your lovers

deny You in favor of common gravel.
    lee was never interested in any of it until You
drew him away from walking through fields picking flowers
    and from playing fanciful games and pulled him to You,
revealing the pure delight of True Royalty.
    And now Your true heart-son and impatient Heretic
stands in the street beside You, covered in dust,
    singing and yelling Your Name, mad as a Fool,
articulating with great exactitude to no-one
    and everyone or anyone, the difference
between stones and precious rubies and pearls.
    And in between songs and rants, lee
falls at Your Feet, begging for Mercy and Work,
    adoring You and showering You with Praise.[3]

The next morning we woke up to a world coated with ash and cinder. The mountains were cloaked in a pall of smoke. Almost twenty years ago Lee wrote in the lyrics of a song, "L.A. is on fire, Paris is burning too," in which he alludes to the decline of modern life on many levels. L.A. is no different than anywhere we go—people are suffering. The *L.A. Times* headlines on the dining table at breakfast were all about the fire. I was shocked to hear that the fires were the work of arsons. Beside the photos of destruction, a person dislocated by the fire was quoted as saying:

> "My street—ashes. We had a view, trees,
> a yard and neighbors. We felt so safe."[4]

These statements sank into my heart. Impermanence had struck at the core of their lives, and people were in pain. The average person

---

[3]   Lee Lozowick, *Gasping for Air in a Vacuum*, January 19, 2000.

[4]   *Los Angeles Times*, November 16, 2008.

does not consider the fact that impermanence rules our world until some disaster strikes. Like the Buddha, who was devastated by the glimpse of death and decay after living a sheltered life, do we turn toward the refuge of relationship with the Divine? In such events, do we place ourselves in God's hands?

Five hundred mobile homes burned to the ground in Sylmar's Oakridge Mobile Home park while we were in L.A. These were people who, although they may have had fire insurance, had lost everything—unlike Robb Lowe, Snoop Dog and Oprah Winfrey, who were also evacuated from their posh Santa Barbara enclaves that day. The sorrow was not assuaged by the idea that everyone had been "equalized" by the primal force of fire. The fact was that the poor had been made even poorer and the rich would collect a hefty insurance check and buy an even bigger and better estate somewhere. That's the way of the world. What choice do we have but to accept, to allow compassion to come?

Many years ago, in another lifetime it seems, one afternoon I came home to find our house burned. Everything we owned was destroyed, and our cat had died from smoke inhalation. It was a huge shock; we were plunged into grief and groundlessness. Within a few days, however, I began to sense a mystery was contained within this event, for it became tangible that somehow, mysteriously, karmas had been burned away. Even so, it took months to recover fully from this event. Since then, I've had a particular empathy with those whose lives are touched by the primal force of fire. The pangs of compassion I felt for the person in the trailer court provoked a consideration of how we may live in the face of suffering within the context of the Path.

We cling to the hope that we and our loved ones will be safe precisely because human life is so temporary, so impermanent, so delicate. What does it mean to be safe? The standard English definition of the word "safe" means that we are secure or free from danger, injury, harm, evil. But what does it really mean to be safe? We know well that we cannot control life. There is nothing that can stop the inexorable force of our karmas from coming to fruition in the outer world of manifestation, relationship, and events, which may mean we will face and handle great challenges: our house burns down, a beloved child dies, a marriage ends in destruction or loss, health deteriorates or we face a diagnosis of cancer, we watch a parent suffer through a painful death, we have serious financial problems. There is a new trend in the U.S. of ordinary families, especially single mothers, losing their homes and living out of their cars. Mothers and children spend the night in their cars, and in the morning the children go to school and the mother is off to work as usual—but unlike other families, they have spent the night in a parking lot.

Sooner or later, we will feel betrayed by Life. Yogi Ramsuratkumar once said to Ma Devaki, "Devaki, this beggar will betray you." This he repeated many times; he was speaking of how the feeling of betrayal is the result of the way we view the events of Life. Sooner or later, we will all experience betrayal as our illusions and attachments are crushed by the natural flow of Life; such shocks of impermanence, in which our feeling of "safety" is shattered, will occur in our lives. There is an old folk song that says, "Hush little baby, don't you cry, you know your mamma was born to die…" We will all die. Our beautiful children and grandchildren will grow old, face many trials, wither and die. The lovely summer garden in the backyard we've worked so hard to cultivate is a brief, passing form in this world of change. Life is what it is. There is no way out but to accept that fact.

When we accept the fact of impermanence, it opens up a huge possibility. We are brought to our knees by sudden events in our lives that rip the fabric of our careful (or careless) design; we become malleable and—hopefully—receptive to Grace, because we realize that we really do not have anything else. We are humbled by impermanence because we must face up to the reality that we are not in control in any way; we live and die by Divine Providence. Cosmic forces, the agents of the Great Process of Divine Evolution, are the inexorable engines behind the movement of change. We have no choice about whether we live or die; these events of being are given to us as gift. What we do have choice about is how we will live and how we will die, and it is this realization that brings us, naturally, to the Path.

Ultimately, our cry for safety is the deep and profound longing of the heart for a sanctuary that surpasses all passing, phenomenal changes in form. To be safe and free from danger, harm or evil can only be a state that is cultivated within. To be safe is to cultivate the wisdom of the spiritual Path—our true and final sanctuary. We are safe to the degree that we have cultivated the garden of practice. That which has been gleaned through practice on the Path is our assurance that, if our house burns down, if our wife or husband dies, if we are faced with a terminal illness, if war breaks out, if natural disaster strikes, if the infrastructure of our culture falls apart and we are forced to forage for food and water—even if we win the lottery, fall in love, or inherit three million dollars and a grand estate—whatever may come our way, we know that we can face it with dignity and nobility. We know that we will do the right thing. We know that we will inhere in the *sanatana dharma*.

A few months ago Lee told his students that the most important thing for us, as practitioners in troubled times, is not to worry about where we will be or what our circumstance will be if disaster strikes, but to consider *who we will be* in the face of radical change, impermanence, suffering, apocalypse. Who will you be, and how will you serve? Will your practice see you through? In September 2008 at Ferme de Jutreau, Lee said, "We are always worried about what is going to happen. We should have a more important concern: Are we capable of meeting whatever happens with ingenuity, creativity, maturity and forbearance, and maybe even acceptance?"

Lee keeps telling us that we practice until practice becomes true of us, until we are calm in the core of our being, until we have learned to accept, and then we become transparent to the Storm of Grace that is the Path—the lineage of beggars, Swami Ramdas, Yogi Ramsuratkumar and Khepa Lee—in which we find ourselves so auspiciously situated. When we become transparent enough, through the fiery alchemy of our gestures of practice, devotion, and commitment to truth, we become Surrendered to the Will of God. It is then that we have a reliable sanctuary.

Our precarious and fragile world is crumbling around us. What tomorrow will bring is tenuous at best. Many of us feel hopeless. Everyone is worried. We are worried about the environment; we are worried about the economy; we are worried about war; we are worried about the horrendous world we have created for our children and grandchildren. We must act appropriately now, when opportunity arises in the moment, with regard to all the vital issues of our lives—but at the same time, if we are paralyzed with fear or eaten up with obsession about the horrible state of the world and the dreadful prospects for the future, we will not find the precious gift of the present moment.

Of course the state of the world weighs upon everyone. Despite the fact that, by the Grace of God, the American people elected a president with a radical agenda of change—and if he is able to implement his plans it will benefit all beings on the planet Earth—we are facing a nightmarish situation. But truly it is not a political revolution that is needed; it is a spiritual revolution. The world's problems have always demanded a spiritual solution, for only by aligning to the dharma, the cosmic law, can we manifest the Will of God in this world of form. We are called to practice in the face of hopelessness because intrinsic nobility and intrinsic dignity demand this of us; our tacit being demands this of us. "Imagine" such a world, as John Lennon sang, in which all people live in Surrender to the Will of God—which would not be a utopia, for the fundamental truth of impermanence and emptiness would continue to confront any stasis that would arise.

The uncertainty of the future is a call to practice. It is the way to prepare ourselves for whatever may come. The context of our daily lives must continue to be the spiritual Path. The forms of the Path—spiritual disciplines of all kinds, meditation, ritual, yoga—are meaningless unless they are imbued with the deeper principles of dharma, which lead us always back to the fundamental mood of Life: Assertion, Surrender to the Will of God, Spiritual Slavery. When these conditions of beingness are true of us, then life becomes a prayer, and perhaps we could say that we have realized the Path, but from the Baul perspective, this includes the entire spectrum of daily life. The Path is everything we do, every day, in every way.

Two months ago at Ferme de Jutreau, Lee said:

> *Having been pessimistic these past two years or so, one of my students heard me talking in Germany a few weeks ago about that pessimism, and she said, "When I hear what you are saying, I feel hopeless." This led me to consider that we have to practice in the face of hopelessness, because it is hopeless. If you can't practice in the face of hopelessness, you don't belong on this Earth, because it is hopeless. We go up, or we go down. The guru has to make us feel hopeless so that we are able to practice in the face of hopelessness. We have to practice in the face of hopelessness, because something in us realizes that the Path is what we have been called to ultimately.*
>
> *It's important not to associate the Path with any particular point on the Path, so we aren't shocked by events or when some important person does something unethical. When we have expectations based on our psychological script, sooner or later we will be disappointed. Some of us pass through confusion and doubt and are stronger for having gone through it. Some are spun out or off the Path, because of confusion—too bad.*

> *To me, the Path is the reason we are human beings, if we include in the Path love and joy and suffering, not just meditation. The Path is a lot more than meditation."* (September 2008)

Lee's statement, "The Path is a lot more than meditation" is a very Baul view of things. Some spiritual paths place meditation at the center of the Path; as important as meditation is, without question, it is not the only way to the goal of Surrender to the Will of God, so that we are lived by and as the Divine, which Lee calls "Spiritual Slavery." We can bury ourselves in meditation and turn away from the call to serve the totality of Life.

The vision for a world governed by universal spiritual principles, a world in which people can return to living in sacred culture, should be a possibility. The only way to move toward this is one person at a time, and yet we are all in this together. Inseparable parts of a whole, we are very likely collectively facing a cataclysm so great that we will be plunged into a radical experience of impermanence, change, the mystery of shunyata. We are in a global state of emergency and alarm. How urgent has our practice become to us? How much depends on our surrender to the Will of God? Everything.

Once again, we are back to the Path, which is the final frontier—a road, once embarked upon, that has no end but goes on forever. No matter how far we travel on that Path, our lives will include those practices with which we began so long ago: meditation, diet, exercise, Enquiry, Assertion, self-observation, the principle of "Know Thyself." No matter where the road may lead, surrender, humility, service, selflessness—these polestars of the Path never stop shining and leading us on.

At some point, the practitioner on the path actually *becomes* the Path. When one has become the Path, then the mood of practice so arduously chiseled and fired in the kiln of years of effort becomes an automatic, spontaneous indwelling. With this aim calling us onward, slowly we begin to taste what it means to be true to our own dharma. We are becoming trustworthy, so that we can rely on ourselves to respond to the circumstances of the moment in a way that serves the Great Process of Divine Evolution.

There are times when we might have a glimpse of what could be called "fruition," a term often used in Vajrayana Buddhism. These are times in which we realize the harvest of the garden in some way. Anyone who has ever gardened knows the surprise and delight in discovering the miracles of the plant world and its generosity to the human realm. It's a working metaphor: in one way or another, the results of seeds planted over many seasons of practice are harvested, and we have a moment of recognizing that practice is spontaneously arising, not as an effort of will or a willful decision to act in a certain way, but organically, holistically. This is an important point to consider and reconsider: We must allow ourselves to see the degree to which we have become transparent, the degree to which the radiance of the Divine shines through us, because if we do not, we will shut down and refuse to see that which is still opaque and darkened.

What we glimpse or see is that we are being lived by the lineage, by the Divine. Using very general terms and examples, maybe we discover that the mantra we have repeated for many years frequently arises of its own volition; maybe we find that we naturally say yes, without resistance or recoil, when we are asked to serve another in some way, even when it does not really suit our schedule; maybe we find that some interior practice has become completely natural and easeful and arises unefforted. Or perhaps we begin to notice that recoil dies away quickly, whereas before it would take hours, days, weeks or months to recover from some unpleasant experience that plugged us into our psychological script. We find that we simply forgive and forget; we have the capacity to let go and move on. We can withdraw our projections on others; we stop blaming others for our own suffering.

One of the signs that practice is taking root within us is that we are able to relax and move on to the next moment with a "draw no conclusions mind," to use another of Lee's teaching phrases. This is, in and of itself, a prime practice: to be able to simply move on when we have hit a minor or major obstacle in life. To stay open to possibility, to know that we can be different in the next moment, and the other person, situation or circumstance can be different in the next moment. That was then; this is now. Every moment is literally a new possibility; reality can arise pristine and new, fresh, moment to passing moment, without the cloying projections and expectations of a mind that is fixated on the past or the future.

Two days after we returned from Los Angeles, back at the ashram, we were in the full swing of Appearance Day, the celebration of our guru's birthday. In a talk to the sangha, he spoke about his recent trip to Los Angeles, and how members of his party had been languishing in the slow pace of the tribal arts show, where Lee had an exhibit of antique statuary. Then the news came that the famous rock group, the Eagles ("Hotel California"), were soon to arrive at the show. As soon as people thought they would see the Eagles, everyone perked up and the mood shifted right away. He commented that we should see how easily our state of mind is influenced by a factor like famous people. He continued, speaking of cultivating an inherence in Spiritual Slavery, so that we are naturally guided in life. Then he said:

> *When we thought we might get to see the famous Eagles, it shifted the mood right away. When you are*

abiding in the essential consciousness that is Spiritual Slavery, fame doesn't mean anything to you. Power doesn't mean anything to you. When we are not abiding in the essence of Spiritual Slavery, we are very easily thrown off balance. We should be noticing how easily we are knocked off course, which can be very frustrating, because we realize that our attention is constantly being drawn into areas that are irrelevant and unimportant. Something completely meaningless to our own process can change our state of mind.

To be able to maintain attention—creature attention—on the Divine all the time is impossible. We all have various strengths and weaknesses when it comes to paying attention. If you are a gymnast, a ballerina, or an artist...one lapse of attention can ruin what you are working on. You have to maintain a certain degree of attention because your work demands it. If you are a fine woodworker, working with power tools, you cannot allow a lapse of attention. If you work with a band saw or some other electric tool, you cannot have a lapse of attention, but that is creature attention. On the other hand, if you are a creative marketing person, half of your best ads come from daydreaming, whereas if you were concentrating, you'd miss it. So not having concentrated attention can be useful at times.

To maintain a certain creature attention on the Divine for periods of time is useful—maybe ten minutes a day or more, depending on your commitment to the Path. Maybe you are making super-efforts, but eventually you will get tired and your attention will waver. You may notice, after an hour, that it's exhausting to willfully focus your attention on something and keep it there. We can maintain that kind of attention for various degrees of time.

There is a way in which consciousness is paid, not by effort. We may have an acute creature attention—physical and emotional—but what we are aiming for is for attention to be paid, so that we don't have to remember to pay attention. We are Remembered in a natural way. At that level, there is an increased degree of interior relaxation, even while on the outside there are certain types of creative tension required to be alert, to maintain safety, to keep our attention on a piece of art we are creating. At the same time, interiorly there is a different degree of relaxation—which is very helpful in sex, because if you have to keep yourself there [by force of will], it takes away from mood.

To be surrendered to the mood of attention being paid, you must have a peripheral attention so that you have a sense of things that are not in your immediate flow...For example, maybe you have a kind of intuition of what to order in a restaurant and what not to order. Or, like in traffic, where you may intuitively guide yourself through a traffic situation in the way that has the least difficulty. So we want to work towards inherence in a state of Spiritual Slavery, sahaj samadhi they might say in India—open-eyed samadhi—so you are moved naturally in a way that optimizes your work, your spiritual work, your relationships, so that you don't get into relationship with people you shouldn't be in relationship with, for example. There are people who are just very unpleasant, and do you need it? If you don't need it, better to be naturally steered in some other direction, toward individuals who are more pleasant company, who are more reliable.

You don't know the extent to which you are already being moved by the Work. The stated aim of the Work

*is Surrender to the Will of God. You want to move in
the direction that you are Surrendered, so that you are
moved by the Divine from the beginning of time to the
end of time, in every single detail, by the priority of the
Work rather than the priority of your personal well-
being. We all want to be healthy and happy, and yes, we
should be—but being healthy and happy are different
than having comfort and security. Comfort and security keep us buffered and isolated from other individuals
and the world and our Work. So when you are moved by
this great force, the Great Process of Divine Evolution,
then the essential movement that takes place benefits
first the Work and secondarily you personally—that
which is discrete as an individual in this lifetime, who
is born and will die.*

Every spiritual tradition has its own way of stating the universal principles of Spiritual Slavery, Surrender to the Will of God, the
Great Process of Divine Evolution. Lee's tradition and teaching is
unabashedly theistic, and so we gratefully rely upon the Storm of
Grace in all things. The Storm of Grace is, once again, *sandhya bhasa*, pointing to the mystery of the Lord, which is not separate from
the Grace of the guru. "Yogi Ramsuratkumar, Yogi Ramsuratkumar,
Yogi Ramsuratkumar, Jaya Guru Raya. This is our mantra, this is our
praise." These are Lee's words, taken from his scripture, "108 Stanzas
to my Guru and Lord, Yogi Ramsuratkumar," to which we may add
"This is our refuge and sanctuary, our hope within hopelessness, our
joy and delight."

We continue to work toward inherence in Spiritual Slavery, or
sahaj samadhi, as Lee said, knowing that we are making daily gestures toward Grace, for this is where we find the ultimate sanctuary. We cultivate radical reliance upon the guru and the lineage, and
yet in the Baul Path there is a great deal of responsibility (and at

some point most of it, in the immediate, practical sense) squarely placed upon the shoulders of the practitioner. We endeavor to make ourselves fitting containers, willing vessels, transparent chalices into which the radiance of Grace may flow.

Swami Ramdas, the guru of Yogi Ramsuratkumar, tells us that the true devotee says: "Oh God, I remember You because You remembered me first."[5] The whole notion of Grace as an acknowledgement of our dependence upon guru and God is found throughout the realization and teaching of our lineage gurus. The words of Swami Ramdas echo Lee's teachings, demonstrating the continuity of the stream of the lineage as wisdom flows from one vessel to another. Ramdas speaks with perfect fluent ease of nondual realization from the theistic perspective of Enlightened Duality; through Grace and divine madness, Yogi Ramsuratkumar's life was sculpted as a song of realization—a great eternal poem—of these precious teachings, while his son, Lee, has articulated in fine brush strokes the same teaching, and the same spiritual way. It is a fitting close for this essay to hear more of Ramdas, excerpted from his essay, "Grace Is Ever Pouring on Us from God."

> *The way of Grace is mysterious. You struggle for it and you do not get it. Sometimes, without any struggle, you get it. Its working is governed by something beyond all laws. It is not bound by any rules, regulations or conditions. You are wonderstruck when Grace comes to apparently undeserving persons, while the so-called deserving ones are still waiting for it.*
>
> *Looked at from another angle, it must be said Grace is pouring on all alike. Some receive it and some do not. Some people open the windows of their hearts to receive*

---

5   Swami Ramdas, *The Essential Swami Ramdas*, page 53.

Grace and benefit by it while others keep them closed and so they do not get it. But even to keep the windows of the heart open, we require inner aspiration and longing which can come to us only through His grace.

Grace is ever pouring on us from God, as the sun is ever shedding light on all objects—opaque, translucent, and transparent. If Grace is all in all, and comes of its own accord, governed by no laws and conditions, what is the place of sadhana in spiritual life? Why should we perform sadhana at all? The secret is that sadhana is done to make us realize that by sadhana alone we cannot attain Him. So long as our ego-sense persists we cannot see God. When we know we are utterly helpless in spite of all our efforts to attain Him, our ego-sense is crushed and we throw ourselves at His feet.

It is difficult to know why God reveals Himself to some and plays the game of hide-and-seek with others. It is His lila. He cannot be accused of favoring some and forsaking others. Let us always remember that He ever dwells in us and that we ever dwell in Him. He who reveals Himself to us is He. He who plays hide-and-seek with us is also He. Everything is He. Guru is He, sishya is He, player is He, witness is He. There is none but He. Realize this great truth and rest happy.[6]

---

6   Swami Ramdas, *Thus Speaks Ramdas*, paragraphs 60–69.

The Natural Movement of Life

Lee Lozowick

We often find ourselves in a situation where we feel tremendously altered in a positive direction. Some people might even use the word "ecstatic" or "blissful." Sometimes the altered state is so unusual that it might be a little scary—maybe we're seeing things. When they were having the great Christian debate in the Middle Ages of how many angels would fit on the head of a pin, there were probably people who actually saw angels on the head of a pin! Visionary experiences are not uncommon, like seeing life-sized or gigantic gods and goddesses. We know from Tibetan Buddhist cosmology that some of the gods are pretty scary characters, with sharp teeth and weapons and blood dripping from their fingernails. Maybe such things worry us, or if they don't worry us, we might wonder what to do with them or how to work with them.

In general, with some rare exception, the best way to handle such experiences is to do nothing about them. Some people are naturally very visionary and have altered experiences every day, but for many of us something very dramatic happens once every couple of years. It has been my experience over the years that when these experiences arise, the best approach is to do nothing but meet the experience with a sense of respect and surrender—with a willingness to go wherever any given experience wants to take us.

If we are soft and responsive in the face of the Divine, and the Divine is alchematizing us, then any gesture of aggression—even to do something that seems positive—is actually interfering with the transformational process. For example, when Yogi Ramsuratkumar was alive and we were visiting him in India, I used to instruct my students to wait for him to make a gesture. If he made a gesture to someone, then they were to respond to the gesture, no more and no less. I would tell my students, "Don't go away, don't freak out, and don't jump on the gesture and start asking questions and raving and ranting. Simply respond to the gesture. Do not ask questions, and do not make any kind of forward gesture."

I gave that instruction because the way Yogi Ramsuratkumar worked was that he was *moved* to communicate in some way, which might have been a word, a question, to ask somebody to sing or to run an errand for him. He might ask about the weather or anything else. Yogi Ramsuratkumar was called the "Godchild of Tiruvannamalai" because he was very childlike. The slightest distraction would catch his attention, and he would follow the distraction. If he was working with someone in a particular vein and somebody else asked a question or made a noise or fell on the floor, his attention was drawn to that person. Yogi Ramsuratkumar didn't want his attention on those kinds of things; he wanted to be free to move spontaneously to make whatever gesture Father in Heaven was moving him to make. Being very childlike, when there was a distraction, he would follow the distraction.

Frequently we'd be sitting in darshan with him, and some character would walk into the hall. Once a Western couple came in, and the woman fancied herself a tantric teacher. She was dressed in brilliant yellow, and the man with her was dressed in bright red. She was very tall and dynamic with wild hair—maybe she thought she was Kali or something! She immediately captured the attention of everybody in the hall. She asked if she could sing for Yogi Ramsuratkumar. He had a number of responses to such requests, sometimes an enthusiastic "yes" and sometimes a resigned "yes" or "alright." This time it was a resigned "yes." He was handling a situation that was thrust upon him.

One of the common conversations he had with me was, "How is the weather in Arizona?" "Hot and dry," I would answer. "Oh, do you live in the desert?" I never assumed that there was some sort of secret message in those questions. I simply wanted to do the best that I could to stay with whatever was going on for him. When somebody distracted him—even when the distraction was positive—like a child, he would follow the distraction. Children are very easily distracted: "Oh look at this!" Within a fraction of a second, their attention is away from whatever you didn't want them to do and on to whatever you direct them toward. Yogi Ramsuratkumar was like that.

So, if we think that flashes in the nervous system means we have attained some realization, then we are probably fooling ourselves and will probably try to fool others. If, on the other hand, we understand that there is a vast encyclopedia of phenomena that are the sparks between the weak and temporal body and the flow of energy that is the Universe, then we might be able to make use of our experience. The process of transformation is not just energetic or subtle but an organic process in which the nervous system becomes capable of holding a greater charge of energy or spiritual force.

Often the phenomenon is purely energetic. A lot of *shaktipata* initiation is unintelligible on a logical level, but we feel tremendous flows of energy in the body. Sometimes there are feelings of ecstasy, bliss, and the mind goes away. Sometimes there are experiences that seem logical. Maybe we are hearing divine voices or the music of the angels. We might think we are advanced on the Path because we are hearing the voices of the angels—the angelic chorus—but a lot of that may be a result of our disposition and life experiences.

If we use the arising of phenomena to prove something to ourselves, we are handling it the wrong way. Transformation is not about momentary phenomena. It is about who we become after a lifetime of practice. The aim of the Path is to become a complete human being, involving relationships, the appreciation of beauty, empathy for the suffering of others. The Universe is innately intelligent and ordered, and we are at the effect, transformationally, of this intelligence and order. Even the smartest of us is not able to fit the intelligence of the Universe into our human intelligence.

Even if the flow of divine energy in our lives is not personalized—as Krishna, Shiva, Shakti, or Jesus—there is an innate intelligence and order to the flow that we could call the Great Process of Divine Evolution. I have never tried to second-guess the intelligence of that flow of energy, because it is so much greater than our human intelligence. We can never know, with our human intelligence, what this order has designed. The process of transformation that happens from birth to death is far too complex to even consider understanding it rationally. We either trust the Process, or we don't. If we trust the process and the integrity of our teacher, then whatever phenomena is created by contact with the teacher is natural, and the energy will move in an intelligent way until it has done what it has arisen to do in that period of time.

Whether it is once in a lifetime or three times a day, when an altered state arises the thought may come to mind, "How can I use this?" Particularly if it is positive and manageable, the thought may come, "What should I do? Should I push it?" It can simply be a very heady spaciousness, or intense movements of energy, visions or intense emotional states, positive or negative, arising out of nowhere.

With certain experiences, there are things you can do to intensify the experience and certain things you do minimize the intensity. Should you push it, crank it up, or should you calm it down or suppress it?

Although there are occasional exceptions, when a certain mood arises for a fraction of a second, or a day or a week or a month, the best thing to do is nothing. It could be a mood of present receptivity, when you are not obsessed with anything for a rare moment, when all your mechanical behavior has nothing to be mechanical relative to, so you have a moment of pure presence. In that moment of pure presence, something is given to you.

This vehicle we are in is very soft and easily damaged; you can just stub your toe and have a swollen toe for weeks. This vehicle is vulnerable to aches and pains and various kinds of damages small and large; it's also vulnerable to gestures of the Divine. When the Divine pours something into the vehicle, the best response is to allow the movement of energy to flow into the channels that the Divine has poured it into. Occasionally, the intensity of the experience might be more than you think you can handle, but it's also been my experience that most people don't know the extent of their capacity to handle many things—including compassion, for example.

It's very common that we believe that something is too much that isn't too much. There is such a thing as too much: I know people who triggered kundalini awakenings through forceful use of technology, and great damage was done to their nervous systems and to their brains. However, we can also damage the nervous system if we force something that is not asking to be forced but is simply asking to be allowed, to move at its own pace, in its own way. Under those circumstances, *rarely* is it too much. It may feel like too much because we are not trained to handle it, or because the amount of energy that is being channelled is uncommon. Because it is uncommon, we are completely unfamiliar with it and, being unfamiliar with it, we may feel, "This is too much. I can't take any more, I'm going to blow up or burn up my brains or my nerves are going to melt!" Or we might even think, "I'm going to go crazy," because sometimes the experience is so radically different than anything we are familiar with consciously. We might wonder, "Am I going mad? Are these visions hallucinations?" The general tendency is to do everything we can to stop or change the dynamic.

A young man recently had a kind of awakening experience. He called me and said, "I'm in the middle of this experience, and everything is the same—really the same! I could do anything and it wouldn't matter, because everything is the same, everything is one, it's all light!" He said, "I could go up to the cashier and smash their head against the wall, it wouldn't even matter! Is this crazy? Should I just do whatever I feel like doing?"

I said, "No, just sit down and be with the experience, but don't act on thoughts that pass through your mind or on feelings that arise. Just sit down and be with the experience." He followed my advice, and although he was a little wild-eyed, he was just in a certain wonderment until the mood passed. There are times in which the intensity of the experience is so great that we really don't know the extent of our responsibility. It was very good that he called me, because in that state he might have actually hurt himself or someone else or done something that nobody would have understood. Imagine going up the judge in court and saying, "You don't understand, everything was light!" The judge would say, "I hope you understand that I'm giving you ten years in prison." And yet that experience of the oneness of all things was very real to him.

This whole world—our thoughts and feelings, our ethics and social conventions—has no meaning at the ultimate level of Reality. Everything is continuously light or energy; in some systems of yoga, they say everything is sound. At a certain level the only distinctions are different levels of vibration, or a different quality of tone in the sound, or different quality of brightness or wavelengths of light. At that level, nothing really does matters; it is all the same. We do not live on that level.

There are two dimensions of experience in life: 1) that which is spontaneously given by the flow of transformational force in our life, and 2) the personal areas in which we are always having to make a decision about whether or not it is too much: relationship pressures, business pressures, money pressures, having a neighbor that is noisy and aggressive—"If I live here one more week, I'm going to shoot this bastard!" Or maybe it's the circumstances of our lives and the intensity of the alchemy, the interior phenomena that is being generated inside us.

Everybody has a different threshold, so obviously there is no hard and fast rule as to when it is too much. Most decisions get made for us by the circumstances of life, even when we think we are making a big decision. Sometimes we are very lucky: for instance, when the neighbor is a problem, the neighbor moves away. Then it is very easy and painless; nobody gets hurt, and we don't have to make heartbreaking or gut-wrenching emotional decisions. At other times we really feel, "I don't know how much of this I can take."

When is it too much? Even under those circumstances when we feel we have to make a decision, one way or the other it is usually the flow of blessings that makes the decision: it seems like the words are put in our mouths, or something catalyzes our choice one way or the other. My recommendation is to always hang in as long as you can, because when you do, it is a signal to the Divine: "You make the decision. I'm too confused, too emotional. I'm not really sure what's best." Sometimes the movement of the Divine comes through our own voice or our own firm decision one way or another. Nobody knows when enough is enough. I don't know when enough is enough, except when the Universe makes the decision, and then of course the best thing is to trust the Universe and the natural movement of Life.

So, when people come to me in the midst of some altered state, describe it, and ask, "What should I do?" the response is almost always: "Nothing. Just allow it." The Divine is always gently pushing on the gates. As soon as the gates start to open, then—whoosh!—in comes the Divine. Whatever is given is exactly, perfectly relevant to the whole complex of you as a unique individual in that time and place. When, by force of will, you try to do something with what is given—even something positive—you are essentially interrupting the natural and spontaneous flow that the Divine has poured into the container in that moment.

Freiburg, Germany
August 2007

Woman in Life

M. Young

Gurdjieff said that everyone must become a Man in the Work, and I would say that everyone has to become a Woman in Life.

Lee Lozowick
Spain, June 2008

What does it mean to become a Woman in Life? An exploration of Enlightened Duality is not complete without a further consideration of this question, which—although we have touched upon it many times in many ways—has not been tackled head on. It is a question whose answer has no finality and no end point, because Woman never stops being mysterious, and she never stops the process of becoming.

Some say that Woman is the void, in the way that Kali Ma is the void. Most certainly she is emptiness and fullness. Woman is the principle of relationship. Because Woman is Mother, she has an intimate relationship with sex and the process of birth, and therefore also with the process of death and the moment of death itself. She is the physical universe; she is all planets, all suns, all galaxies, all beings of all kinds. She is every created thing. She is interrelatedness. She is connection. She is mother, compassion and wisdom.

Woman is *rupa* and *svarupa*. She is incarnation and form. She is the Earth Mother as well as Kali, the Cosmic Mother; she is also Radha, the greatest Lover of the Lord. She is the rhythms and flows of Nature. She is beginnings and endings, for she is time and the spiral of return. Woman knows and understands that all things pass to return again, and because of this knowledge, she is ruthless in her love and she has no fear. Woman surrenders to the Great Mystery because she knows the Mystery is none other than herself. My teacher has said many times, "Woman is Life." When awakened, Woman is the Great Process of Divine Evolution. Woman awakened is the pinnacle of the "evolutionary creative Universe," to quote Lee again. Woman is enjoyment, inspiration, worship, love, adoration and praise.

Many years ago, Lee wrote this song, a paean to Woman titled, "Make A Little Room For Grace," which was recorded by his first band, liars, gods & beggars:

> She blows in off the mountain
> Like a human hurricane
> She opens all your windows
> And laughs like she's truly sane
> She's not all that attached
> To clothes or to prejudice
> You got no place to stand
> And you're so grateful for this
>
> (Chorus)
> Make a little room for grace
> She's a woman
> Make a little room for grace
> Don't you love her?

Make a little room for grace
But if you play her game
When she's had her way with you
you'll never . . . ever be the same

She would never mention
What she thinks that you should do
She lives her life too freely
To be caught in the net of you
She says she has no answers
That she don't need the weight
But then she seems so heavy
She's your crystal ball of fate

Woman is about food, sex, and money.[1] For example, one of the things Lee has said several times this summer is, "You are what you eat." In using this phrase, Lee is referring to food literally and symbolically or metaphorically—subtle impression foods and relationship foods. Food of all kinds can have many effects on the organism, which has both gross and subtle dimensions; food can be nourishing and enlivening, toxic and poisonous, or neutral but essentially of no value. As sadhana becomes the central focus of our lives, it is important to develop a natural yet finely-honed ability to make distinctions: what do we take into our systems? In this regard it is helpful to reconsider Lee's frequent advice to simplify our lives, because simplicity enhances our ability to make important distinctions in all three domains: food, sex, and money.

---

[1]   "Money, sex and food" is a teaching phrase coined by Adi Da Samraj referring to the fundamental domains of life experience in the human realm.

Lee provides many examples of simplicity and discrimination in the domain in food. At lunch one day, the ashram cook asked Lee if he would like some nori. Even though he always enjoys eating nori with quinoa if it is available, Lee answered, "I only want what I have right here in front of me. Do not go back to the kitchen to get it." On other occasions, when asked if he would like some additional food brought, he has said, "Too late. I do not want anyone to go get something else. If it's not here already, I'm not going to eat it." Much can be read in these statements. On the one hand, the guru is pointing out the need to pay attention to details. At the same time, he is demonstrating many principles: there is conservation of energy and resources; there is acceptance and living with what is; there is surrender; there is beggary. Lee has respect for Life, and there is a keen and consistent care given to conserving resources of all kinds, including personal energies.

Simultaneously, Lee has a keen appreciation for enjoyment—the sheer joy of participating in the abundance of Life. "I've always said that excess is better than renunciation," he said at breakfast one morning back in late May. His French and German students and our smattering of Americans, still jet-lagged but smiling, were sitting around the long wooden table *dans la grange* of the ashram in France, the chilly, misty weather of late May hanging heavy in the air around us. The generosity and implications of his statement were quite big, especially coming unbidden from a man who, diagnosed with a life-threatening illness last winter, is committed to an extremely austere healing program that necessitates a very particular diet adhered to impeccably and without any relief or occasional indulgence. Lee has stated unequivocally—and with ferocity and humor—that he will stay on this strict diet, "Until I am ready to die. Then, I'm going out on ice cream and everything else! For now, I still have some things to do." Lee has made a supremely adult decision, and now he simply does what is required to fulfill his intention. Everything else is in the hands of Yogi Ramsuratkumar.

During the summer Lee's students were frequently offering him foods that would seem to take the edge off the severity of his discipline. He commented dryly numerous times that in making these suggestions, people were not taking care of him but taking care of themselves. Most people's relationship to food is extremely complex, convoluted and unclear; to see the guru demonstrating such amazing discipline and clarity in relationship to food strikes a primal psychological knot for many because our relationship to food is vitally tied in with our sense of survival. Lee's magnanimity toward others—"Don't stop enjoying all kinds of foods because I can't eat them now"—is hard for some of his students to take. Perhaps if we had committed to such an austere practice, we would come up against huge conflicts of discipline. We might not have the clarity or strength of purpose to watch others eat, drink and be merry while we had to practice restraint. Never is there a whiff of judgment, recoil, or rejection coming from Lee when those around him drink coffee, eat desserts and chocolate or enjoy any other dietary indulgences. Instead, he encourages us to celebrate Life, saying, "Enjoy it as long as you can."

To say that Lee's discipline of practice is inspiring seems puerile, fatuous, in the face of the extraordinary transformation that he has gone through in a short period of time. Very few people can take a serious health crisis and run with it toward the open doors of transformation; in seeing our teacher demonstrate this, we have an enormous opportunity to be humbled, uplifted, spurred to new heights of practice and acceptance by our guru's ongoing transformation in this Great Process of Divine Evolution. He continues to reinvent himself, always through the auspices of Grace. He does this because he is relaxed and at home in the world of Woman.

The unrelenting simplicity and purity of Lee's diet matches perfectly the transparency and surrender of his inner state. Lee's natural inherence in Woman appears also in his constant reminders to live in the moment and not in the future. If someone asks Lee what the tour schedule is, or what time dinner or the gig starts the next day, he invariably says, "I don't know and I don't want to know. Just put me in the van and tell me where to drive." Further demonstrations of this come regularly: "I'll find out when I get there." And, "I don't want to know anything in advance. I want to find out when I get there." Students are always asking him, "How many people are coming to the ashram for the seminar this week?" Lee answers, "I don't know and I don't want to know. When we know, it messes with the flow. Something always goes wrong because we are thinking about it too much, dwelling on it, projecting and expecting..."

This demonstration of surrender and trust in the wisdom of Life as it unfolds is an essential quality of being Woman in Life: the Spiritual Slave. Lee is surrendered to what God will have for him in any given circumstance. Let it be. Surrender to the Will of God and trust God to provide what is needed in all the details of daily life. When Lee went to visit Yogi Ramsuratkumar in November 1993, Yogi Ramsuratkumar was giving a formal blessing to Lee and his students, who were leaving the next day. Turning to Lee, Yogi Ramsuratkumar said, "My Father blesses Lee with whatever he wants." Then he paused, chuckled and amended his statement to say, "My Father blesses Lee with whatever he needs!" When we trust the Great Process of Divine Evolution, we learn that we will be given what we need, which is sometimes different than what we think we want; although, if we are awake, we discover that what we need is exactly what we want. Woman *knows* this is the truth.

There are many ways in which I find my teacher to be an example of one who is Woman in Life in the domains of money, sex and food: for example, as an advocate for children and conscious childraising; as a champion of human potential and particularly of women in sadhana; and in his deep love for the creative process. The most significant domain in which Lee demonstrates what it means to be woman is found in his relationship with his master, Yogi Ramsuratkumar—a subject richly explored in his poetry to his master. It is there that we find everything we need to know about becoming Woman in Life, about devotion, adoration, surrender and total reliance on the guru; about Reality as it is; about transformational sadhana; about the Path and about Enlightened Duality; and most of all, about Grace.

What does it mean to be Woman in Life? Pondering the theme of this last essay today as I sat down to write, my very dear fifteen-year-old friend came to my desk. She wanted to share a poem that she had discovered. While we were spending some time together, I asked her, "What do you think it means to be Woman in Life?"

She said, "That's a really good question. I haven't thought about it before. When I think of Woman, I think of the deities in India, like Lakshmi and Parvati. I think of the look in their eyes, their stance. Their eyes are magnificent. They are so gentle, but at the same time, they are strong. It's hard to portray that. You have to have the right way of thinking to capture that."

When I asked her what qualities Woman has, she reflected for a moment before she said, "You don't have to be perfect to be Woman. She is more than that. She understands her imperfections and the imperfections of others. She is bigger than being perfect. It's a big heart. When I think of Woman, I think of Mother—the traits of the Mother."

Her words were penetrating in their direct, uncomplicated honesty. While she paused to consider further, I was thinking about how deep and insidious is the psyche's fear of imperfection, for imperfection implies vulnerability. If we are vulnerable, we can be hurt, and if we are hurt, then we can die. Woman has no fear of death because she understands process, for she is the Great Process of Divine Evolution. Because she is time, she knows that everything will work out in time.

"It's a really big question," she said. "You don't necessarily have to have children to be a Mother. Anybody can have the qualities of Mother. She is embracing. She looks beyond your flaws. She sees to the essence of things. A mother loves her child so much that she doesn't look at the flaws—she sees what is really there. If you really love a rose, you don't stare at its ragged petals, you look at the rose. If you love a painting, you don't look at all the cracks and scratches; you look at what the painting really is."

Her fresh, innocent words of compassion and insight sank in as I considered further the implications of her statement that Woman can accept imperfection. She continued, "It's like going to the Kali temple in Kolkata last year. After I came out, I just stood there and watched people coming out after seeing her. They were either ecstatic or terrified. The Indian devotees of Kali were ecstatic, but some of the Westerners had looks of terror on their faces. You know, when you see someone who really believes in their deity, the real devotees who love Kali or Jesus, you just say, 'Yes, I get it.'"

We talked about our experience of going to Kalighat and Dakshineswar and making *yatra*, or pilgrimage, there to see the Kali deities. The pilgrimage to the smashan and the temple in Tarapith— where we had the darshan of Tara Ma—was an unforgettable experience. Talking with my wise young friend, it all came rushing back.

At the end of our trip to Bengal in 2008, Lee took his large traveling group of forty-five people on pilgrimage into the rural Birbhum District to Kenduli-Joydeb and Shanti Niketan. We drove for many miles through low, flat flood plains and winter rice fields dotted with graceful green palms. Along the roadside the dusty banyan trees reigned supreme, their primal downward-growing branches spreading to form thick networks.

We drove past square, thatched-roof huts built from handmade mud bricks—the traditional dwellings of Bengal—clustered together in an organic arrangement of communal life. These were held within remnants of the original jungle, in between the vast stretches of rice paddy. Men dressed in white guided bullocks down narrow roads and across the rich alluvial dirt of cultivated fields. Children played sweetly and women tended the immaculate grounds of their domains. Here I found the symmetry and beauty of an ancient way of life, still alive despite the pollution and technological nightmares of modern India.

We were headed for Kenduli, the tiny village on the river Ajoy that is the location of the terracotta temple of famed poet Jayadeva and his consort, Padmavati, the temple dancer. Jayadeva was the twelfth century writer of the *Gita Govinda*, or *Love Song of the Dark Lord*, which, inspired by the relationship between he and Padmavati, brings to life in poetic rendering the mythical relationship between Radha and Krishna. Jayadeva is the foremost patron saint of the Bauls. The following week there would be hundreds of thousands of people gathering there to participate in the annual Joydev-Kenduli *mela*, where Bauls from all over Bengal gather to sing and dance in praise of Krishna and Kali.

The temple of Jayadeva and Padmavati was tiny but remarkable, especially in its carved outer front walls, every inch of which was filled with sculptures in terracotta from the *Ramayana* and the *Mahabharata*. Inside, a priest possessively tended two small deities, Radha and Krishna, in the tiny space. Afterward we spent the night in Shanti Niketan, where we enjoyed another *Baul gan* performed by Sudhir Das Baul and company. That night, Lee made the announcement that he wanted to go to Tarapith the next day—a three hour drive which would take us farther away from Kolkata, making the drive home about six hours. Everyone was enthusiastic, though we had no idea what was in Tarapith.

The next morning we found out. We left at eight a.m., with the haunting call of Tara Ma, the Mother Goddess, leading us on. Tara Ma is one of the ten *mahavidyas*—a group of major goddesses called the "Great Wisdoms" of Hinduism. The others are: Kali, Tripura-Sundari, Bhuvaneshvari, Chinnamasta, Bhairavi, Dhumavati, Bagalamukhi, Matangi and Kamala. Many of these goddesses are extremely fierce; some are benign and merciful. All goddesses represent aspects of Woman as the Divine Mother. Of the Indian goddesses, Lakshmi and Tripura-Sundari are the most auspicious and benign; they are described as beautiful and benevolent. However, since Lakshmi is also worshiped as the Supreme Reality, even she must have a destructive side.

Tara Ma is archetypically related with Kali; she too has an ecstatic protruding tongue, a fierce side and a merciful side. Tara Ma is the deity that presides over the *smashan* and temple of the *shakti pitha* at Tarapith, where Sati's third eye fell to earth in the ancient myth. Local lore tells us that the famous Tara mask in the temple covers an ancient stone statue of Tara, the all-merciful Mother, breast-feeding Mahadeva (Shiva), whose throat is blue from drinking poison churned from the cosmic ocean by Lord Vishnu at the time of creation. I was told that there is a midnight *puja* on full moon nights, at which the mask of Tara is removed and the devotees may receive the *darshan* of Tara and Mahadeva.[2]

Walking on foot down the narrow lane that led to the smashan and the temple, we were jostled and swept along in the flow of a crowd of pilgrims. On either side of the lane were the usual vendors of religious articles: fresh flower *malas* in red hibiscus and marigold, *rudraksh, kumkum,* crude stone sculptures of Shiva in the form of *lingams,* popular poster art of the deities, incense and puja items of all kinds. All along the way were huge vats of fried gulab jamen floating in sugary syrup. At one point I looked over my shoulder

---

[2]   Months later Nara Allsop, a student of Lee's who studied deity painting with Robert Beer and has made it his life's work to paint Hindu deities, made the pilgrimage to Tarapith and was there at midnight for the darshan of the statue. To his surprise, when the bronze mask of Tara was removed, he saw that the underlying deity was a reclining Vishnu, not Shiva. He later said that it is an occasional practice to reassign a deity, in replacement of another, in India; this is not a problem in Hindu worship practice. It is done when, for some reason, it is considered to be the deity's wish—in this case, Tara Ma—to be worshipped in this way.

to see four men moving fast, carrying a corpse wrapped in a white shroud that was now about one inch away from the back of my head. Instinct took over and I stepped to the side while they ran past me toward the smashan.

Turning to the right, we entered a narrow passageway that opened out into a small courtyard area between buildings. On the right was a banyan tree growing in a circular stone base with a Shiva shrine underneath it—a small lingam dwarfed by a large trident covered in red kumkum. The shrine was black with countless offerings of ghee and littered with flowers, incense and the general scattered debris of many offerings. Two perfect, fresh red hibiscus flowers had been placed just beneath the lingam. Immediately beyond this shrine was the place where we had to check our shoes before entering the smashan. I stood briefly at the portal looking down the stone steps that led into the cremation ground, then walked down and entered another world.

My bare feet sank into dry, deep sand as I looked out over the scene and was immediately hit with sensory impressions that came into my field of perception from all directions. Beneath the trees were many white burial shrines with sadhus encamped all around. They wore red *dhotis* and *kurtas,* rudraksh and crystal malas, shawls, head wraps over matted hair. Each shrine contained a ghee-blackened stone lingam covered with red kumkum and sometimes a human skull or thigh bones. A Bengali friend had told me that this particular cremation ground does not operate by the usual rituals and codes, which makes it an ideal place for the wilder side of *sadhana,* and indeed, the human inhabitants lived under the tall trees in this sandy, riverbank smashan as if it was a small village. Everything seemed surreal, and yet reality was pounding on the doors of my senses, pummeling me with its raw truth: It was all starkly, undeniably *empty.*

What seemed to be an invisible path in the sand led further into the smashan, snaking its way under tall trees and among the shrines and sadhus. Suddenly there were mounds of earth underfoot, about six feet long and three feet wide—fresh graves. Just then a make-shift kitchen appeared on the right under a big plastic tarp that was strung up between the trees. Men were cooking rice, vegetables, dahl in huge pots and woks and serving food on banana leaf plates to a group of about twenty-five school children who were seated on the sandy ground. This tableau appeared in sharp relief to everything that had come before, and I found it soothing for a moment.

The innocence of the children in this scene was soon to be displaced as I looked to my left and saw the first burning corpse on the high bank of the river, not thirty feet away from where the children were eating. The most visible corpse—a large man with head arched back, arms, hands and legs akimbo in rigor mortis—had been thrown on top of a very small pile of wood that was just beginning to burn. The body was naked rather than wrapped in a shroud as in other cremation grounds I had visited before. Despite the provocative confrontation with the reality of death, a feeling of vast spaciousness and quietude pervaded the burning ground. It was profoundly peaceful, and I thought: Tara Ma reigns here as the all-merciful Mother.

Walking back to the stairs at the entrance of the cremation ground, we stayed for a long time at a prominent, mausoleum-type shrine that was drawing people to linger and talk with a sadhu who seemed to be presiding there. It turned out that this was the *samadhi* shrine of Bama Khepa, the mad *avadhuta* who lived his entire life in the temple and the smashan and was a *mathri sadhaka*, a devotee of the deity, Tara Ma. Bama Khepa was known to go back and forth between devotional *bhavas* and angry, fierce states in which he would rant and accuse Tara of ruining his life. He loved hearing Baul songs and Vaishnava *kirtans*, which would send him into supreme states of consciousness. Leaving behind no teachings, he lived a completely unfettered, wild and provocative life. Today he is greatly revered by the Bauls of Bengal.

Making our way to the temple, we stopped to buy garlands of red hibiscus flowers to offer to the Mother. Stepping into her inner chamber, her darshan was a blast of heat and light, an explosion of effulgent love and joy that stormed the walls of my heart and stopped my mind. Tara Ma! I felt like a child who had come home after a very long journey to be reunited with her Mother. Ecstatic energy thrilled about and played with my awareness as I looked into Her fathomless black eyes, which stared also into mine. Her divine presence cut directly through the veils of my personality. A huge smile broke out on my face, unbidden. The thought arose: If She is what greets us at the moment of death, then all is well.

The priest said, "Nam?" I gave him my name and handed over the flower offerings. He was telling people to move on, but I could not move. The priest allowed me to stand there, looking up into Her face. Stunned and absurdly happy, I would not soon forget this, for I recognized in Tara Ma our own *ista devata*, Yogi Ramsuratkumar.

Woman is an enigma. Lee has said before that the mood of Woman is either ecstatic or sweet—ecstatic as in full of wild joy and bliss, easily falling into abandon; sweet as in the sense of divine *rasa*, bhakti, *prema* or love. Sweet has many flavors and tastes, and Tara Ma is all of these: every kind of ecstasy and all the flavors of sweet. Tara Ma is known as the all-merciful Mother, ever ready to offer blessing to her children, but, like Durga and Kali, Tara Ma's ecstasy turns toward the destruction of ego when illusions reign, while her sweetness is revealed to one who seeks transcendence and worships at her feet. As Ramprasad Sen, the great poet and lover of Mother, once wrote, there is "grace and mercy in her wild hair."

The surest way to becoming Woman is through the cultivation of bhakti—the moods of divine love as expressed in worship, praise, and adoration. There is a profound understanding in bhakti

traditions that both men and women must be Woman (often symbolized by Radha) in relationship to Krishna, the Beloved or the
Supreme Reality. In any consideration of bhakti yoga, it should be
pointed out that in practice for Bauls of the West, bhakti is tempered
and ongoingly purified with the principles of "the Work." To court
bhakti alone is not enough, Lee keeps telling us: we must cultivate
radical clarity at the same time, so that we see clearly and do not fall
into the traps of the devotional path considered in an earlier essay.

Perhaps this is why the Bauls of Bengal, who are passionate about
becoming Woman in Life, worship both Kali and Krishna. Kali and
Krishna are worshipped in two ways: as aspects of Divinity and as
Supreme Beings or Ultimate Reality. We could say that Kali is ever-
ready to slay our demons and destroy our illusions, leading to clarity, while Krishna is ever-ready to play his flute, inducing states of
transcendent love and adoration and leading us by the hand into
Vrindavan, his supreme abode.

It could also be said that worship of Kali is the ecstatic doorway
and worship of Krishna is the sweet doorway, but it is not that simple, for as Ultimate Reality, both Kali and Krishna contain the whole
and all possibility. Therefore Kali has a sweet, all-merciful and loving
side, and Krishna has a destructive, demon-killing, ferocious side.
Things are symbolically complicated by the fact that Kali is usually
depicted as standing on Shiva, and Krishna is depicted with Radha.
In fact, the complete symbol of deity for many bhakti sects is Radha-
Krishna, for it is understood that they are inseparable. It is understood that Shiva or Krishna, when they represent the Absolute, can
do nothing without Shakti or Radha—the feminine principle.

Needless to say, images of Krishna and Kali represent powerful
divine beings that will commune with you and lavish their blessings
upon you as a devotee, when they are contemplated with a vulnerable heart. Kali, Krishna, Shiva, Lakshmi, Ganesh…these divine entities are very real. In principle, whatever image or representation you
have great faith in as the Supreme Reality will transmit that Reality

to you—such is the Grace of God to grant the function of an ista devata, or chosen deity. This, of course, places the responsibility upon the practitioner or devotee. It is our heartful intention, our longing, our need and our faith that calls forth the Grace of the Lord, whether that Lord is Krishna, Jesus, Kali, Mary, Tripura-Sundari, Tara, Shiva or the guru's *nama* and rupa. When we worship Krishna as the Ultimate Reality, Krishna is That. When we worship Krishna as a symbol of the sweetness of God, Krishna is that. When we worship Krishna or Kali as the personal Beloved, the ista devata, Krishna or Kali respond in kind.

In terms of the all-important cultivation of bhakti, there is no *parampara* (lineage) or *sampradaya* (school) that has developed its ways and means of devotional practice more thoroughly than Gaudiya Vaishnavism, which began in Bengal in the sixteenth century with the visionary ecstatic saint, Sri Chaitanya Mahaprabhu (1486–1533). Chaitanya is considered to be one of the patron saints of the Bauls—and, interestingly, there are many similarities in the lives of Chaitanya and Yogi Ramsuratkumar. Chaitanya was a scholar who married a local girl and taught school. He went into a trance one day in class and shocked everyone by falling to the ground raving, shouting and rolling about until finally his body became stiff. Later his first wife died; attempting to continue with family life, he married again, but the states of divine madness continued and grew stronger, until devotees began to gather around him and he began to teach the worship of Krishna. Finally he left family life behind, took *sannyasa* vows, and headed to Puri.

In Puri, Chaitanya began a new life. He ate little and spent most of the nights in meditation. He had many unusual bodily symptoms associated with the intense states of divine madness that seized him. At these times his body became distorted, elongated or compressed.

It is said that sweat and blood oozed from his pores and he foamed at the mouth. He was lost in ecstatic trance for periods of time, while at other times he was half conscious or in a normal state.

The profound ecstasies and love-maddened, sweet bhavas of Chaitanya became famous. He often experienced himself as being in Vrindavan, where he would sing, dance, then faint in a swoon. His love was not always a peaceful one. It was a "continuous fluctuation between divine and human personalities."[3] The heritage Chaitanya left to Gaudiya Vaishnavism is one of love of Krishna, demonstrated through the practice of dancing and chanting the divine name. Followers of Chaitanya consider their path of divine love to be the epitome, the mountain peak, of Vaishnavism (devotion to Lord Vishnu). Tagore pointed out that Gaudiya Vaishnavism emphasizes *madhurya*, or the sweet love of God, which is practiced by the *bhakta* who lives for the supernal sweetness that is discovered in worshipping Radha and Krishna. A Gaudiya Vaishnava, then, is one who is surrendered to and absorbed in Radha-Krishna and also in Sri Chaitanya Mahaprabhu.[4]

In the Gaudiya Vaishnava sampradaya, there are two kinds of bhakti: *vaidhi* and *raganuga*, meaning respectively, 1) devotional practice based on the rules of conduct prescribed by the Shastras, in which the bhakta develops a very strong sense of right and wrong and remorse, and over time develops love of God; and 2) the pure, passionate, enthusiastic pursuit of the finer aspects of love in all forms, which is characterized by profound states of longing and holy yearning for the sweetness of the Lord. These two fundamental approaches can also be understood as 1) awe and reverence for the deity that focuses on the magnificence of the Divine and 2) a more

---

3   June McDaniel, *The Madness of the Saints: Ecstatic Religion in Bengal*, pages 35–36.

4   Steven J. Rosen (Satyaraja Dasa), "The Meaning of Gaudiya Vaishnavism," *Nama-rupa*, Volume 5, November 2008.

intimate mood of loving God.[5] It is said that vaidhi practitioners go to Vishnu's heaven Vaikuntha, whereas raganuga practitioners go directly to Krishna's supreme abode of Goloka Vrindavan, considered the highest dimension of the spiritual kingdom by Gaudiya Vaisnavas.[6] Raganuga is considered the higher path. Gaudiya Vaisnava practitioner Steven Rosen (Satyaraja Dasa) writes:

> *Vaidhi and Raganuga, then, are different forms of the same thing: they are both forms of sadhana, or devotional service in practice, leading to the goal of love of God, albeit manifesting in different forms of that love. This stems from their initial, fundamental difference in genesis or motivation: the Vaidhi-bhakta, or the devotee following by rules and obligations, whereas the Raganuga-bhakta, or the practitioner of the path of devotional passion, is driven by inner longing and love.[7]*

Practitioners of Gaudiya Vaishnavism worship the three deities of Vrindavan, each of which are a form of both Radha and Krishna: Sri-Sri Radha-Madana-mohana; Sri-Sri Radha-Govinda; and Sri-Sri Radha Gopinath. These three deities refer to the devotee's relationship with the Lord, the various activities that support and engender that relationship, and the perfection of that relationship. Steven Rosen further writes:

> *Gaudiya Vaishnavas perceive the culminating objective of Vedic hymns—and of all religion—as devotional service to Krsna as Madana-mohana, Govinda and Gopinath. Madana-mohana is glorified as that fea-*

---

[5]   Ibid.
[6]   Ibid.
[7]   Ibid.

ture of God that is so indescribably beautiful that he even charms the god of love; Govinda is the Lord as the pleaser of the senses….; and Gopinath gives insight into his internal divine activity, performed in the spiritual realm, as the lord of the gopis, the cowherd girls who are his greatest devotees.

These three deities are meant to represent the truth of Radha and Krsna as a whole—that the divine is both female and male, the prefect balance of lover and beloved, waiting to be reunited with one and all in a spiritual, ecstatic relationship of unending bliss.[8]

Generally speaking, practitioners may begin with the vaidhi aspects of the path and slowly, over time, grow into the raganuga, or more esoteric practice. The goal of practice is the perfection of rasa, and its practitioners are called *rasika-bhaktas*. This should sound very familiar to Lee's students, as it has some very close, if not exact, links to Baul practice. Sri Chaitanya, one of the primary patron saints of the Bauls of Bengal, was considered to have realized both Krishna and Radha as all three of these dimensions of Godhead. Because he embodied both divine masculine and divine feminine, he is depicted iconographically with golden skin—not Krishna's usual blue or Radha's typical white. Gold carries an obvious alchemical symbolism and is also the color of the sun, our living symbol of wholeness.

Because he became both Radha and Krishna, Chaitanya is a great example of one who became Woman in Life, going beyond nondual realization to embody Enlightened Duality. In Chaitanaya's teaching, there is no masculine without the feminine; they exist because of one another. It's the relationship between the two that is the pivotal, cru-

---

[8]   Ibid.

cial genius of the whole Plan—the Great Process of Divine Evolution. And without Woman awake, aware and fully participating, there will be no relationship between nonbeing and being, between Absolute and relative. There will be no Great Process of Divine Evolution.

One night in Freiburg in late August 2008, Lee was joking around with some of us over bridge. I picked up my big black travel bag and rummaged through it, which provided the catalyst for Lee's comment: "Why do all women have big black bags?" Then he predicted, "If women keep going the way they are, by the year 2030 women will have purses as big as trucks!" We all laughed heartily. Then his predictions turned serious, as he plowed ahead with, "There won't be any men left if women keep going the way they are."

I asked with a smile, still feeling good-natured about the exchange, "Are women to blame for everything?"

"Yes," Lee rebutted with certainty, "women are to blame for *everything*."

Two weeks later, back at Ferme de Jutreau in France, Lee gave several spontaneous teachings on Woman, saying that women are everything. Women are already realized; they just have to accept. Men have to work hard for realization, Lee said.

At tea on September 19, Lee brought the conversation back to this subject again, saying, "Everybody who knows what they're talking about says that women already have it—women just have to accept that they have it. It's men who have to work for it. Men get too intellectual about it, and women get too emotional about it."

Someone asked him, "So does that mean you're optimistic?"

Lee smiled and rejoined, "Yes, I'm optimistic, in a desperate kind of way."

Later that same night, as the animated conversation flowed from one subject to another, Lee answered another question.

"What is objectivity?"

"Objectivity is defined by the body, and all science is defined by the mind," Lee answered.

"Is there objectivity?" another person queried.

Lee answered, "There is subjective objectivity and there is objective objectivity. Subjective objectivity is our differences. Objective objectivity is consistency. It is not about our differences but about our sameness—our universal similarity."

These comments were germaine to the consideration of this book: Subjective objectivity, in which difference is real, and objective objectivity, in which it is all One, were a different way of describing the difference between Enlightened Duality and nonduality.

Was Lee really serious when he said that women are responsible for everything? I think the answer to that question is yes. Those of us who find ourselves in female bodies have a big responsibility to show up as Woman. How much harder will it be for those in male bodies to find their way to Woman if the females are lost? The stakes are enormous: the fate of the Earth and maybe even the solar system hang in the balance. Will we give up the drive for power in favor of love? Woman naturally knows the truth of Reality as it is, and it is her responsibility to transmit this to man. If a man becomes Woman in Life, then he too has this ability. This, I believe, is the reason why Lee said, "Yes, women are to blame for *everything*."

It is a statement that rings with the truth and actually redefines feminism. In fact, the statement, "Women are to blame for everything," can be viewed as an ultimate declaration of radical feminism: Women are to blame for everything because Woman is Everything. If we take this statement seriously, we find that anyone seeking to become Woman—male or female—must step outside the indoctrination of Western culture, where the values of the feminine are degraded and devalued. Through a return to our own Organic

Innocence, we must redefine what it means to be a woman and what it means to be Woman.

Yogi Ramsuratkumar told his devotees many times that all he wanted was praise, the implication being that praise could be the basic mood of one's life. When Woman is brought to life, praise is her natural disposition. In this context, there is very little—if any—difference between praise and prayer. In asking us to praise, Yogi Ramsuratkumar was asking us to pray in the way that is not a supplication of any kind, but a spontaneous burst of gratitude, joy and recognition. Praise places us in communion with the Divine; through praise, we become resonant with Reality as it is. It is our greatest joy and exaltation to praise and worship the Supreme Reality as Brahman, Buddha, Krishna, Jesus or Kali—the one Lord by any name we choose. As disciples and devotees of the Path, we grow into an obligation to praise and adore the Divine in form: not only as the guru and the lineage gurus, but also as one another. In this way, we take responsibility for bringing to Life the great possibility of everything and everyone around us.

When praise is the mood we choose to cultivate, praise itself will work its transformative magic within us. What would happen in our individual lives if we made the decision—above all else—to praise? To live from the basic ground of praise as an attitude toward life does not mean that we believe we are enlightened, perfected, or that we are "finished" with sadhana; nor does it mean that we put on rose-colored glasses or adopt a Pollyanna attitude of nostalgia or naiveté—far from it. To have an attitude of praise requires our commitment to be a mature human being who participates consciously in a Grand Design: the Great Process of Divine Evolution. How would our attitudes be uplifted by such a commitment? How would we be different day-to-day? How would our decisions and actions change in practical, immediate ways? How would the disposition of praise change and clarify our inner world?

In Arizona in the fall of 2008, one night in darshan Lee once again defined Enlightened Duality, then spoke about the vital necessity of maturing as human beings, if we hope to participate in the open-ended Reality of the Great Process of Divine Evolution:

> *Everything that exists is essentially and inherently Divine, and there is the Reality that different things have different value and carry different weight. If we were in Vaikuntha, maybe it wouldn't be that way—if we had no senses and no bodies and we were atmanic atoms of existence. If we weren't human beings incarnated in mortal form and there was no such thing as the three gunas and the senses and different levels of the organism and mind and ego, then everything in existence is equal; everything is the Divine, and that's it.*
>
> *If you view this Work as a progress, not a digress, then in its progress, we understand that different things carry a different weight. Given that, imagine what our lives and our practice could be if we were practicing with more maturity? It's an important distinction for us, because many of us have had the satori of "all things in Creation are essentially and inherently Divine," and that can be a heady realization. It's heady because even though occasionally that satori comes matter-of-factly—when you are walking down the street and you notice that everything is inherently Divine, and you just say, "That's interesting," and keep walking—more often that satori is associated with ecstasy, elation and euphoria. The three "E's"! Within the three "E's" there is the tendency to*

make an assumption: that you've seen Reality, and that's it, rather than, you've seen Reality and it is open-ended.

The assumption usually associated with that insight is that your life will change dramatically, now that you have seen Reality. If you don't catch me in the right moment within that satori, you'll be lucky not to be carried away with illusions; you could spend years caught up in illusions that are very difficult to disabuse you of!

A month later, Lee continued in a similar vein, emphasizing once again that although we are always receiving divine blessings, we must place the mantle of sadhana on our shoulders and take responsibility for our own process of maturation:

Yogi Ramsuratkumar has been watching over us a lot longer than we have been on the Path in this lifetime. Your mechanical habits are of no use to the evolutionary creative Universe. At this point, self-observation is a practice that none of us can afford to neglect or take lightly, because when you allow your chronic habits to interfere, it creates very big problems. If you observe yourself, you will change.

The point is to become useful to the evolutionary creative Universe. The rarity of the dispersion of esoteric practices on my part to my students is because people have not grown up. Even living in love with Life, appreciating beauty, does not replace maturity.

Praise is inherently greater than an appreciation of beauty, which is an important distinction in light of Lee's statement, "Even living in love with Life, appreciating beauty, does not replace maturity." Lee has often said that maturation on the spiritual Path is a holistic process that involves growth and integration on all levels—not just a brilliance that develops in one area. Praise opens a window in the moment through which a sublime light shines upon our beings at all levels. The pure spiritual force of praise subsumes psychological strategies, distractions and fascinations; praise brings light to darkness and transmutes toxicity.

Although praise may be deeply fulfilling to the soul, it is not satisfying in the conventional egoic sense; there is no sense of ownership or self-importance in praise. The one who praises is empty—a sunya. To praise is not to possess. Garchen Rinpoche once gave a series of talks at Lee's ashram in Arizona, in which he gave this teaching: Sometimes we are walking along and we see a beautiful flower, and immediately this feeling that we want to pick the flower comes up. From the tantric perspective there is another possibility: rather than picking the flower and making it one's own, the tender joy of experiencing the precious nature of the flower and its pristine beauty may be internally offered to the deity.

This teaching opens up a great wealth of possibility, if we have taken on a practice of "Just Praise." To choose a life of praise is a powerful way in which we become useful to the "evolutionary creative universe," which engenders a maturation process within us as human beings. We tend to define maturity by the demonstrations of what we do rather than how we are being; while it is true that maturity shows up in action, true maturity comes from within our beings. Because praise is a state of being, we do not have to wait for pujas and formal worship ceremonies to praise—there are countless praiseworthy moments that occur in our lives every day. It may be that the simple affirmation of what is good and auspicious in any given moment is the potent catalyst of a deeper alchemy within us; transformation may be hiding within the simple and humble process of finding joy and delight in the myriad arisings—of people, places and things—in the ordinary matrix of daily life.

We cultivate a relationship to the sacred nature of the world when we cultivate an inner disposition of praise. Perhaps we begin quite humbly, with praising small events: the spring garden coming back to life, the first butterfly of the season, or cherry trees in bloom; the migration of birds, the laughter of children, a friend's warm smile; a favorite song or a violin solo; a delicious meal, a brightly burning fire under stars at night; a moment of kindness and generosity shared between those who usually oppose each other. These things are praiseworthy because the myriad arisings of life are each a hologram of the whole: God is contained in every single aspect. As Parvathy Baul said in an interview, "For the Baul, the ocean of knowledge may be communicated simply by a bird singing on a branch." The moment of that satori, in which we glimpse the sanctity and one-ness of Life, is a moment in praise of Creation and its Creator. Such a moment is not the end of the spiritual journey, but the beginning of something—and we know not where it may lead. Speaking in this context, praise becomes inseparable from prayer. To praise, then, is to pray; to praise and pray is to worship.

Today is December 1, 2008, Yogi Ramsuratkumar's Jayanti Day, the day of his birth in the incarnation in which we knew him as the Beggar King of Tiruvannamalai and the spiritual father of Lee Lozowick. Every year on Lee's ashrams in Arizona, France and India, and on the Yogi Ramsuratkumar Ashram in India, this day, December 1, is celebrated with great joy by devotees and friends. It is a day set aside for praise.

Just after dusk last night, when the sky was finally dark and stellar, the brilliant lights of Venus and Jupiter shone brightly near the Moon in her beautiful crescent phase. This alignment in the evening sky was a gorgeous, auspicious sight that inspired a consideration of why our ancestors developed the science of astrology—reminders of an ancient and sacred way of life, a way of life that gave birth to the entire tradition of the *sanatana dharma*, the knowledge of *guruvada*, the wisdom of the Vedas, Upanishads, the Bhagavad Gita, the Tantras and so much more. When human beings live close to the rhythms of Earth and cosmos, without the distractions provided by electricity and computers, it becomes obvious that the events of the night sky are profoundly connected to happenings on Earth. Venus and Jupiter being two of the important benevolent planetary deities in the solar system, aligned with the moon in Capricorn, seemed to bear auspicious tidings for our invocation of Yogi Ramsuratkumar.

It has been almost eight years since Yogi Ramsuratkumar left his body behind to enter into *mahasamadhi* and move into the unseen world. Still, he is here with us. In Arizona this year, 2008, his Jayanti began with the *dhuni* fire, where everyone gathered under the stars at four a.m. Near the fire, in the chilly dark predawn, sweet coffee was served beneath the bare boles of wintry cottonwood trees. This has become a tradition that we carry on in remembrance of Yogi Ramsuratkumar, for he always served sweet milky coffee on his ashram on holy days, when the chanting and rituals would begin long before dawn. We made small offerings to the fire and sang his name, while the children played at our feet.

There is a most precious, delicate mood that happens on these mornings, long before morning twilight, when the devotees gather to pray, chant, praise, and worship. During the usual busy, hectic days of our lives, we practice giving kindness, generosity and compassion; despite our best intentions, abrasion and tensions arise. These are sometimes easily digested, sometimes not. Sometimes things stick in the craw for days, weeks, months or years. The Christians wisely teach that you must not only forgive; you must also forget, which is truly the hardest to accomplish.

Papa Ramdas, a great realizer of perfect nondual union that was demonstrated in his life as Enlightened Duality, once wrote:

For the bhakta, *God is the very embodiment of love, compassion, forgiveness, and grace. He visualizes God in the recesses of his own heart. He surrenders completely in thought, word, and deed to his Beloved, and adores Him with an unflinching devotion. By a constant meditation of the Lord, the* bhakta *imbibes into his own being the Divine attributes, ultimately reaching a status of perfect union and oneness with Him. Compassion, mercy, and love now illumine the nature and therefore all actions of the* bhakta. *He becomes the very image of God, for the impurities and weaknesses having been removed by the grace of the Lord, he stands revealed as the very sun of the Truth, radiating all around him the rays of love, kindness, and grace.*

Now the greatest virtue that shines forth in all its splendor in the bhakta *is forgiveness. As God has forgiven him, so he forgives all the world who wrong or have wronged him. He ever returns good for evil, both in thought and action. He is self-sacrificing to a degree. He is ever willing to serve and toil for others, to give them solace and relief. He loves all with an equal vision, be he friend or foe, rich or poor, good or wicked, high or low, wise or ignorant. He endures peacefully ignominy and persecution and gives himself away in every manner for the good of others. He is unassuming and humble in all he does. He recognizes God as all in all. He experiences God seated in his heart as causing, by His power, all movements in the world. He beholds and feels God's presence everywhere. Verily, he always lives and moves in God and is the very being of God.*[9]

---

[9]   Swami Ramdas, *The Essential Ramdas*, pages 6–7.

Yogi Ramsuratkumar's Jayanti is an excellent day to renew our vows to practice. It is a moment in time when we generate prayer, praise and a certain intention, when the slate is wiped clean. As with any time that we celebrate the Path and the lineage, we can use this day as an opportunity to drop held resentments that poison our inner world. We struggle with believing that we can work out our psychological knots at the level of the mind and ego, and we cannot. They will continue to haunt and plague us, to hold us back from serious work on the Path; just when we have gained momentum and we are soaring or moving purposefully forward, some element of psyche will rear its head and drag us back down into the dungeon. The only solution is to drop it altogether and shift the focus of attention to the refuge of the dharma, the guru and the sangha. On Jayanti, let us be moved to let go of whatever is between us, whatever is in the way of communion and the joy of this life together.

Hours before the first pale rays of the sun would light the eastern horizon, the holy beauty of the night sky reflected our purpose back to us. In the high desert, the night sky is resplendent, awe-inspiring, and this morning the starry heavens gleamed down upon us, the Milky Way vast and breathtaking in its transmission of endless impersonal omnipresence. The soft burning power and tenderness of the morning fire ritual revealed our intention for the day. Our personal selves would take second seat to the practitioner, and what a joy this is!

Oh Yogi Ramsuratkumar, Inspiration, Light of lights,
    may Praise of You roll from infinite lips,
may Love of You fill infinite hearts,
    may Obedience and Surrender move infinite hands
and lives and may Faith in You turn every sinner
    into a saint, all indecency into goodness,
laziness into productivity and emptiness into fullness.
    Oh Yogi Ramsuratkumar, King, Glory of Glories,

may Your Name echo in every room and chamber,
    may Your Name resound on mountain
and in valley, in jungle and desert, over sea
    and ocean, in every continent on Earth.
Oh Father of Your most Grateful and Blessed heart-son,
    may You be known in one of Your many Forms
by all those seeking solace, by the happy as well
    as sad, by those in poverty and wealth,
by the policeman, the judge, the businessman,
    the corporate president, the mechanic, the lawyer,
the scientist, the weak and the strong, the
    physician, the thief, the astrologer, the pure
and impure, the child and the adult.
    May Praise of You melt hardened hearts
and minds, may Praise of You live for all eternity,
    may Praise of You Bless every living creature,
man, animal, bird, fish, insect, plant and
    spirit, ethereal, astral, subtle and godly.
May Praise of You reach every distant star,
    infuse Heaven and Hell, make the devil dance
and keep pouring from the pen of this
    lee lozowick character, in Poetry and Prose.
May Remembrance of You, Yogi Ramsuratkumar,
    arise in every lover of God, devotee, disciple,
in the Teacher and the student, in the Master
    and slave, in the Brahmin and Sudra.
Dearest One, All, Unity Itself, Truth and Time,
    this little beggar lays his prayers and his body at Your Feet.[10]

---

[10]   Lee Lozowick, *Gasping for Air in a Vacuum*, 24 March 2000.

At four-thirty everyone went into the darshan hall to chant and circumambulate the shrine that had been created in the middle of the room with the *vigraha* of Yogi Ramsuratkumar. This vigraha is a twelve-inch-high bronze statue that was a gift from Lee to Yogi Ramsuratkumar in 1994, the year it was sculpted by one of Lee's devotees. At Lee's request, the statue was made and numerous copies were cast from the original mold. Many of Lee's students have this sculpture on shrines in their homes. One lives in each of Lee's ashrams, and one lives at Hauteville, the ashram of Arnaud Desjardins. It is a living embodiment of Yogi Ramsuratkumar—a miracle.

There is a *lila* that goes with this sculpture. When Lee gave it to Yogi Ramsuratkumar, he held it for a long time in his lap. The people who were there with Lee swore that the heart area of the statue glowed with a red light at one point while Yogi Ramsuratkumar held it. François Fronty, a student of Arnaud Desjardins and professional filmmaker, was on the trip videotaping for a film series about Lee and Yogi Ramsuratkumar. This video would be titled "Darshan" and would focus on Yogi Ramsuratkumar and Lee's relationship to his master. Lee also saw the light, and when he told the story upon returning from India, he said, "We'll see, because François was filming the whole thing." When he played the raw, unedited footage, filmed by François, we sat in the darshan hall in Arizona and watched with great anticipation to see if the "red glow" would appear. Amazingly, it was clearly visible on the video while Yogi Ramsuratkumar was holding the vigraha. The skeptics among us could barely believe their eyes but had to admit, with some wonder and awe, that this powerful demonstration of the tangible effects of Blessing Power was undeniable.

Yogi Ramsuratkumar had a way of empowering artifacts, transmuting their actual form from rupa to svarupa—especially statues, or vigrahas. There were numerous statues of his image made during his lifetime; one in particular was made to be placed at the center of the large temple on his ashram in Tiruvannamalai, where people would circumambulate it. Yogi Ramsuratkumar spent literally hundreds, if not thousands, of hours imbuing this statue with his concentrated attention and subtle influence. For a few years he sat under a palm frond hut that was built inside the temple and placed ten feet away from the statue. There he gave darshan to long lines of people, sometimes as many as two or three thousand at a time, who filed by to see him. Sitting there beside the statue to bless each one, he was linking his influence to the statue in their minds and bodies.

Now, a decade later on Yogi Ramsuratkumar's Jayanti, the Divine Influence of the lineage permeates the ashram in Arizona. For days before Jayanti the energy gathers as a buoyancy, an energetic effervescence within, a building pressure and brightness. This spiritual force gathers in power depending upon how much intention we bring to our prayer and devotional practice. *Jayanti* is a day of feasting. The principle behind such feasting is that the deity is actually the one who is enjoying the sumptuous offerings, while at the same time, the rich, overflowing goodness of the food is a symbol of the spiritual nurturance that spills from the cornucopia of blessings as we invoke Yogi Ramsuratkumar's presence and living influence among us. Throughout the day we relish the savory, spicy Indian meals that are served. Great intention for a day of worship, celebrated in classic *pushti* style—feasting, chanting, celebrating beauty and relationships—carries the potential to generate prayer, made that much more effective by the synergy of the combined energies and intention of the sangha as a whole, from Arizona to France to India.

The capacity to re-establish wholeness, connection, and communion through the power of love and compassion, is unimaginable to the egoic mind. When Woman is awake and worshipping, she carries a profound power to heal what has been ripped or shattered in the fabric of Life. Mr. E.J. Gold says that Woman is awakened when she is adored. Adoration is a very big word with many implications, one of which could be the specific, finely tuned focus of attention in praise of the object of one's attention. The chances of waking ourselves up is highly unlikely, considering that ego will do everything it can to prevent this from happening because to awaken threatens ego's survival strategy. It is important to be clear and honest with ourselves about what we are up against in this regard, for the egoic mind (and therefore the innocent flesh of the human body) suffers tremendously under the burden of the illusion of separation.

The egoic mind, identified and informed by childhood traumas (and carrying even older karmic burdens), defines everything by its extremely restricted, narrow view. Seeing through the limitations of perfectionism, judgment and separation veils the eyes of the soul like a dark caul, obscuring the light from everything in view. The wounded psyche is traumatized and cannot be still and soft long enough to realize that kindness, benevolent regard, even blessings are flowing to us all the time from others and from the Universe. Such a wounded psyche projects its suffering on the world, engendering tremendous cynicism, seeing betrayals everywhere it looks. When we hear a voice inside saying, "People cannot even be kind one hundred percent of the time, therefore how can their prayers mean anything or have any positive effect? We are really kidding ourselves," we are under illusion, and negativity has poisoned our view.

When we are suffering, held captive within a worldview that is punitive, harsh, self-hating, and self-perpetuating in its negativity, there is nothing productive or life-affirming to be found, even in spiritual life. From this perspective, it is often argued that if one is not perfect, he or she is not capable of making a difference in the world through prayer and invocation of divine moods. I must disagree wholeheartedly with this and agree with my young friend, who so wisely stated. "You don't have to be perfect to be Woman. She is more than that. She understands her imperfections and the imperfections of others. She is *bigger* than being perfect." This is the ground of compassion and loving kindness, which opens the heart into a dimension of vast possibility. It is ground that must be cultivated if we wish to become Woman in Life.

The rasika bhaktas of this path, the *sishyas* trained under Lee Lozowick, are an imperfect lot. It is true that Bauls tend to be very unruly, prone to rebellion, egotistical and carefree to a fault—that is, careless, casual and cavalier. (The "three C's" rather than the "three E's," as Lee said.) Nonetheless, it is the truth of the spiritual process and the Grace of the lineage that reveals a radical transformation, which is occurring at very deep levels—as Lee has said, "at the causal level"—in a deep-rooted and fiery sadhana, while the flawed human personality continues to be a work in progress.

We fall short of the goal, and we must keep going. We keep our aim before us no matter what, because Woman is forgiveness and she is inspiration: She inspires us, just as she forgives us our imperfections, because she understands that imperfections are a passing phenomena in a vast, ongoing process of becoming. This is practicing in the face of hopelessness.

Today I read a poem written by Lee, the last line of which is: "Faith in action, not philosophy / For action alone is our gratitude and our Prayer."[11] We cannot allow the perceived failures of ourselves or others—the flaws and imperfections of our cracked vessels—to hold us back from gestures of gratitude, praise and prayer, or "Faith in action." We carry on with our work despite the desperately wounded and depraved condition of human beings in this world, of which we are a living part, from which we cannot separate ourselves, as much as we might want to. We practice in the face of hopelessness, and we bring Woman to Life within ourselves, through surrender, forgiveness, praise, prayer, devotion, worship.

We praise and worship with flower, flame, water, rice, ghee. We worship with song and dance. We worship with the flame of love that

---

[11] Ibid, 23 November 2001, page 634.

lives within each of us. We worship through our passion for beauty; through the quality of our relationships with one another; through pleasure and enjoyment; through meditation, discipline and practice, and through austerity when it is called for. We worship through gratitude, and sometimes we worship just by putting our bodies in the space where everyone else is worshipping while we ourselves don't "feel" anything at all. This too is valuable; if we are uninspired, we lend our energies to those who are inspired—like on Jayanti, when the men and women take turns in the predawn devotions in our dancing *pradakshina* around the shrine that supports the form of our ista devata, Yogi Ramsuratkumar. The men dance together, and then the women dance together, but in this space, regardless of the outer form, there is the possibility that we can all be Woman.

To find ourselves on the Path in the company of the lineage gurus, Swami Papa Ramdas, Yogi Ramsuratkumar and Khepa Lee Lozowick, is the fruition of our karmas. We are obligated to make the most of this precious life, to see and express our gratitude through worship and adoration of God. To remind us of this fact, in his incredible mercy and compassion—out of his unique demonstration of perfect inherence in the nondual realization, expressed as the embodiment of Enlightened Duality in his most blessed life—Yogi Ramsuratkumar gave us his nama and rupa, his name and his form, to worship. If we turn toward him, he will guide us every day of our lives. He responds to the clarity we bring to devotional gestures made toward him. When we focus our attention upon the name or form of Yogi Ramsuratkumar, he responds to the spiritual charge of our love, devotion, praise, need, helplessness and commitment. Every morning that we do puja to Yogi Ramsuratkumar, we are saying, "Still here, Lord." In our turning toward God in surrender, He turns toward us.

As Papa Ramdas says, Grace is ever pouring upon us like the sun pouring light and warmth upon the Earth. Whether we will receive Grace is in our hands and not in our hands at all, for everything is in the hands of God. One who is Woman in Life lives easily and simply within this paradox. At home within *shunyata,* she is able to practice with passion and commitment toward greater transparency, luminosity, and joy so that the vessel of this life may receive the Storm of Grace, while she also understands and honors her own helplessness and need. Let this be true of us all, that we may, as Papa says, "Realize this great truth and rest happy."

Jaya Swami Papa Ramdas Maharaj Ki Jai!
Jaya Yogi Ramsuratkumar Maharaj Ki Jai!
Jaya Khepa Lee Maharaj, Ki Jai!

APPENDIX I

Spiritual Slavery

In the Hindu tradition, the living truth is known as the *sanatana dharma*; in other traditions it is known as the universal teaching, the *buddhadharma*, the perennial philosophy, or cosmic law. The word dharma, meaning "sight" or "to see"—along with many other Sanskrit words and terms—have been used in this book in order to fully capture the essence of intended meanings of spiritual realities as well as to honor the tradition which Lee Lozowick's teaching ultimately calls "home." To know that Lee's teachings of Enlightened Duality stand upon a matrix or foundation of tradition greatly enhances our understanding of Lee's spoken words. In order to more fully understand the context from which Lee speaks in the essays of this book, it is helpful to begin with an understanding of the formal teachings Lee himself has given over the past thirty-five years, which must begin with his original core teaching of Spiritual Slavery.

In 1975 Lee experienced an event of radical awakening from the ordinary state of separative, egoic perspective that characterizes the human dilemma. After five years of intense *sadhana*, Lee entered a week of retreat in which he was, to use a classic phrase, "practicing as if his hair was on fire." He has often said of this period of time that he felt he had come to a dead end on the Path. Meditation, visualization, mantra and yogas of all kinds came easily to him; metaphysical ideas and techniques had been mastered and left behind in the process of becoming a state-wide teacher of meditation and parapsychology in the Silva Method. There was nowhere left to go but to leap into a completely different domain of existence.

At the end of the retreat, Lee was repeating the mantra, "Om Sri Ram Jai Ram Jai Jai Ram," when he fell into a night of profound and deep prayer in which he asked to be taken completely by the Divine. He slept as usual but woke up the next morning a changed man. Everything was clear, pristine, tacitly obvious as the fact that, "There is only God." Everything that exists is only God; all is one, unitive, complete, perfect. We are not separate from God, nor are we separate from one another as human beings or from nature or any other aspect or appearance—subtle and gross—of the Divine, which is the entire world, universe and cosmos at all levels. We do not realize the obvious, tacit truth that "there is only God" because human beings are ensnared and blinded by the illusion of separation.

Lee woke up that morning and discovered that he was resting in a tacit Surrender to the Will of God that had transformed him into an obedient servant of a higher Will—which we might call the Divine, the Universe, the Absolute or by many other names. Lee called this state Spiritual Slavery. Lee, as a separate self, no longer had any volition of his own; somehow Lee as a separate self had ceased to exist overnight, and in his place was one who had become a slave in the most sublime sense—a slave to the Will of God. Every arising and subsiding of appearances, all of it, was now the Divine manifesting. He opened his controversial first statements of awakening, published as *Spiritual Slavery* (1975) with this comment:

> *The path of the Great Ones is not liberation, rather it is bondage. Liberation means being free. On the contrary, those who have achieved what the unillumined would call liberation are truly bound into slavery: slavery to mankind, slavery to the dumb, asleep robots that most people are; slaves to the insipient personalities, bodies,*

minds that most beings think they are. Yes, the truly Great Ones are locked into service to the world, to the "New Age."

Listen: We already are consciousness itself. We already are free. We already are happy. See, there is nothing to attain. Absolutely nothing. Hope is a big crock. Hope is a rip off. Hope deludes us into the search, into seeking. We need to realize consciousness, not attain it.[1]

He ended the same book with these words:

The traditional paths of awareness or of truth studies speak of the need to be detached. They claim that attachment to the material plane keeps one from attainment. And the more evolved spiritual teachers say even the attachment to the non-material is still attachment. They've just upgraded the act. Listen. One who is realized is totally attached. See, everyone is realized already. Everyone has as their basis of existence prior condition: God. The purpose for life is to realize you are realized. That is the payoff. One who realizes he or she is already realized becomes totally attached to Reality. You would not be if Reality did not exist. No one would be alive if Reality did not exist. Reality is God's sole and total form. Period. There would be no existence if Reality was not. I am totally attached to Reality, for without Reality I would not be. I am a slave. I am not free. I am a compulsion of Aliveness. I am happy all the time. No choices, no alternatives. Just happy, just Alive. Just This.

---

[1]   Lee Lozowick, *Spiritual Slavery*, page 5.

I am completely attached to all forms of Reality, for Reality is my creation. I am totally attached to the sole form of God. I am that form of God, which you have come here to be. The only reason you exist is to become me. I am the payoff. I am the only reason that Reality is created after the fact, after the truth of prior condition. I am the form of Reality that you exist to realize. I am the form of God that you have not yet realized you are. I am that one. Just This.[2]

These were and are hot words, as provocative and barbed for the separative ego as they have ever been when realizers of various Paths have uttered the radical truth of their realization of unity. One of the most controversial saints of Islam was al-Hallaj, who said: "I am He whom I love and He whom I love is I. We are two spirits dwelling in one body. When you see me, you see Him." His ecstatic public preaching often brought his listeners to tears. "O you [who hear me], save me from God! He has ravished me from myself, and does not restore me to myself. Alas for anyone who finds himself abandoned after such a presence, alone after such a union."[3] Al-Hallaj was both worshipped and condemned as a heretic by his peers, particularly for his well-known phrase, "I am the Truth." Eventually he was arrested, tried and executed, but his words have lived on. In the end, he said, "Forgive the people, and do not forgive me. Do with me what you will...all who have known ecstasy long for this, alone with the Alone."[4]

Many realizers have been brutally punished, even unto death by fire, crucifixion as in Jesus' example, and other inconceivable means, for speaking the simple truth of the fundamental Vedic maxim: *tat*

---

[2]   Ibid, pages 60 and 61.

[3]   al-Hallaj, *The Oxford Dictionary of World Religions*, page 45.

[4]   Ibid.

tvam asi, "You are That." This is also encapsulated in the breath practice of *hamsa* (swan), the two syllables of which refer to the ingoing (*ham*) and outgoing (*sa*) breath, as well as the ascending and descending currents of life force in the body. Georg Feuerstein writes: "[These syllables] contain a great secret, for the continuous sound of the breath conveys the message, 'I am He, I am He, I am He.'"

Going further into *Spiritual Slavery* we find in the closing paragraphs the seeds of Lee's later teachings on Enlightened Duality— "I am completely attached to all forms of Reality....I am totally attached to the sole form of God."—as well as his core teaching of Assertion: Just This. We find in Lee's teachings the whole formula of the Heart Sutra: Form is emptiness; emptiness is form. Lee's statement of nondual realization is seamlessly presented at once with the radical awakening of direct knowledge of Reality and an Enlightened Duality. Therefore, when Lee asserts "Just This," all of this—the nondual vision of unity and the awakened realness of the distinctions we see and experience now—is implicated as tacitly real and true.

This event of radical awakening from the illusion of separation catalyzed major changes in Lee's life. Within six months students began to gather around him and the Hohm Community was born with Lee as its spiritual preceptor. A year later Lee made the first of many trips to India. On this trip he met for the first time his master, Yogi Ramsuratkumar. This meeting exploded Lee's certainty that his realization had come not from a human source but "from God" as an Unknown; over the next few years it became clear to him that it was the Divine Influence and subtle Blessing Power of Yogi Ramsuratkumar that was at the source of his own awakening, and in fact, Yogi Ramsuratkumar was Lee's spiritual master. Thus began the first of many countless times when Lee would describe God as Yogi Ramsuratkumar, in exactly the way that many classical scriptural texts state: Guru is God, and should be worshiped as such. This statement is true precisely because the guru, if the guru is a true guru, has indeed realized the divinity within.

Many subsequent meetings between Lee and his master occurred from 1977 through Yogi Ramsuratkumar's *mahasamadhi* in February 2001 at age eighty-three. This relationship changed Lee's life and his teaching work to such a degree that everything prior to this event was obscured in the radiance of that relationship. In 1992 Lee had all extant copies of *Spiritual Slavery* burned in a massive bonfire on the Arizona ashram. It seemed that Lee wanted to forever dispel his early claims of autonomous enlightenment, to clear the slate in a way for the expression of his devotion and utter commitment to Yogi Ramsuratkumar that would permeate his teaching and work for the rest of his life, most poignantly and clearly expressed in his poetry to Yogi Ramsuratkumar.

The relationship with Yogi Ramsuratkumar was a profound catalyst and influence that has guided—and continues to guide—Lee's every step. The fundamental teaching of Spiritual Slavery has remained the core of Lee's teachings that have been given over the years. The statement, "There is only God," has remained a fundamental truth that reveals both the nature of reality as unitive and nondual while it also contains the theistic affirmation of God. However, as time wore on and the subtle power of Yogi Ramsuratkumar permeated every sphere of Lee's life and activity, the young American teacher began to experience radical insights and revelations into the Path that was being delivered to him by the Grace of Yogi Ramsuratkumar. As the teaching was revealed, it became very clear that Lee was not speaking of God as an idea but of God as a living, absolute Being that can be directly experienced by the complex of the human being, through the body. The truth that "There is only God" is both a statement of absolute nondual realization and a statement of an intimate relationship with the Divine within the interplay of opposites.

If this is so, and unity is the underlying fabric of all Life, then why do we need the spiritual Path? Because every human being has a divine destiny and a manifest destiny. Everyone lives out their manifest destiny, at the level of the unerring laws of cause and effect, through which our karmas become ripened over time. However, to discover and live into one's divine destiny is to live beyond the world of concrete manifestation, into the causal dimensions, where the soul is transformed or, perhaps more accurately, built. Ultimately, our purpose in being incarnated here is to surrender to and embody the Divine Will, or the Will of God. Every person has a manifest destiny, which is guided by the karmas one has accumulated—in which the law of cause and effect is the supreme force. One's manifest destiny will be fulfilled, regardless of one's state of consciousness, or degree of sleep or awakening, because the cosmos operates like a perfectly oiled machine, in a way, or the most precise time piece imaginable.

There is another possibility, however, which is that every person has a divine destiny. Divine destiny is the fulfillment of the higher law, which is Surrender and Sacrifice: Surrender to the Will of God into a state of Spiritual Slavery. The word "sacrifice" means to be made sacred. When we are sacrificed into a higher level of awareness, we begin to long for our own origins—the original self or *atman*. Whatever event may occur that breaks open our sleeping unconscious state to the degree that we glimpse a radiance, a lucidity, a sweetness—and we catch the scent of the Beloved—is the moment when we enter the Path of becoming, an unfoldment of being in which the individual *jiva*, or soul, enters consciously into the Great Process of Divine Evolution.

Many people walk the Path for a long time before they encounter their preceptor, master or guru. It is possible to accomplish many things on the Path before meeting your guru, but the presence of the guru speeds up the process significantly. And, in the end, the spiritual master is absolutely necessary, for it is by the Grace of the guru and the guru's lineage that we are ultimately and radically Surrendered at the Feet of the Divine—an event that we, as separate egoic identities, cannot accomplish for ourselves. Surrender to the Will of God is a moment of Grace, a sudden enlightenment or translation into what Yogi Ramsuratkumar called "sweet slavery," echoing Lee's original proclamation: Spiritual Slavery.

APPENDIX II

The Only Grace is Loving God

*I*n 1983 Lee entered into an unusual state or *bhava* that lasted for some months. Toward the end of that time, he wrote *The Only Grace is Loving God*, which became a testimony of his experience. Written in ecstatic twilight language, the teachings encapsulated in *The Only Grace is Loving God* do not answer the questions that the thinking mind inevitably poses; rather, it speaks to a deep longing that resides within the human spirit. Instead of answers, we are left with burning questions.

Lee's teaching "the Only Grace Is Loving God" cannot be explained. It is not a simple reiteration of a religious concept of "loving" the God of our understanding. It has nothing to do with religion, in fact. It is a radical glimpse into an absolute mystery that is supra real, the direct experience of which occurs only through Grace. Many people feel that they love God, and certainly there is love of God alive in the world today, but an important distinction must be made: Lee asserts "the only Grace is Loving God" from within the context of Enlightened Duality—the "I and Thou" relationship between human and divine.

There are distinctions that Lee has made within this teaching: We can only Love God if we have Obeyed God, and Loving God is both Gift and Whim. To Obey God is to Surrender to the Will of God in ultimate, irrevocable terms. When one has Obeyed God—in a living, abiding Surrender to the Will of God—then one may receive the Gift of Loving God. It is a Gift that is entirely Graceful: that Grace exists at all within the perfection of nondual unity—and that God may bestow the Gift of Loving God by means of Grace—is the Whim of the Supreme Being. These are extremely delicate, exquisite domains of experiential knowledge that cannot be adequately explained; they must be lived. The Gift of Loving God is the ultimate benevolence, the unimaginable auspiciousness, of the Supreme Lord.

Lee claims that "the only Grace is loving God" is not his personal experience but rather a revelation of the human possibility—a claim that is refuted by virtue of Lee's obedience and devotional love for his master, Yogi Ramsuratkumar, as *ista devata*. The ista devata is the particular form of God that delights one's heart to the extent that, through one-pointed focus of attention and adoration, the adorer experiences transcendent love of the Divine. Worship of and concentration upon an ista devata is a sublime practice employed by many yogic and tantric paths in which a particular image works like a fermenting wine in the interior life as the living form of the Divine. When the juice becomes wine, the lover then tastes the intoxication, or *rasa*, of love. To meditate with one-pointed focus of attention upon one's ista devata is to eventually become the qualities of the *devata*.

> There must be You, only You.
> No bad Poet and no other, only You.
> This is lee lozowick,
> the true heart-son of Yogi Ramsuratkumar,
> asserting Just This, the dirty Beggar's
> Indivisibility, His Totality, His Thisness.[1]

For years Lee sought his Beloved in the form of Yogi Ramsuratkumar, sending poem after poem to his master begin-

---

[1] Lee Lozowick, *Death of a Dishonest Man*, June 4, 1997.

ning in 1979. After visiting the beggar saint in 1976 and 1979, when Lee arrived in Tiruvannamalai to see his Beloved in 1986, Yogi Ramsuratkumar did not recognize Lee and sent him away, saying, "I know what you want, Lee. Go find a guru somewhere else." Lee left brokenhearted but with the certainty that Yogi Ramsuratkumar was his master, and if his master had asked him to go away, he would be obedient. Lee returned to the States, where he continued to write poems—frank confessions of the heart on fire for Yogi Ramsuratkumar—and send them to his master in India. Two years later, in 1988 Yogi Ramsuratkumar called Lee back to India. When Lee arrived in Tiruvannamalai, the beggar showered love and affection upon his Western devotee, demonstrating a loving, tender, affectionate relationship with Lee that continued until Yogi Ramsuratkumar's death in February 2001—and beyond, as Lee's poetry written since that time attests.

The *lila* of their relationship unfolded as a mutual love affair expressed year after year when they were together during Lee's annual visits to his master in Tiruvannamalai. Many of Lee's students and friends witnessed this extremely rare demonstration of relationship between guru and disciple. Their relationship endures in Lee's poetry, as the poems are alive with the transmission of Yogi Ramsuratkumar. It is in Lee's poetry, written in the classic Indian form of *ninda stuti*, or ironical praise, that we find the Assertion of Enlightened Duality, in which Lee both confesses and praises the tender heart of the true lover.

> So many say they want God,
>   they want to melt into His Oneness.
> I too once wanted such a thing
>   but no more Dear One, no more.
> I met my Darling one day.
>   He is a great Sinner and a dirty Beggar.

His beauty was so radiant and bright
    that He broke my heart and bound me to Him.
If to have perfect Union
    would be to lose this Madman
I want none of it —
    only Him and Him alone.
I am afraid You will be angry
    with Your arrogant and foolish son
but how can lee not worship his Lord?
    It is not every day one meets his Ram.[2]

Lee's poetry makes it abundantly clear, again and again, that Yogi Ramsuratkumar is the literal representative of the Supreme Reality. It is important not to be confused by the poetic metaphors herein; we are still considering Assertion, or Just This. It is the great secret of realization that nonduality and Enlightened Duality emerge simultaneously within awareness, giving rise to wisdom in the form of the ista devata. Yogi Ramsuratkumar as ista devata is Krishna, Shiva, Jesus; he is everything and a "Great Nothing," as Lee calls Yogi Ramsuratkumar in another poem.

Father, Father,
    Your son is going mad —
falling asleep at night
    muttering Your Name,
awakening in the morning,
    mind filled with pictures of You,
tears rolling from eyes,
    heart hungry
for the nectar
    of Your Glance.

---

[2]   Ibid, June 21, 1992.

> More, more, lee yells
> > into the Great Nothing
> of Your Allness,
> > Oh Slave of Your slaves.[3]

Again, the reader of this poetry should not be distracted from clarity by Lee's easy play within the domain of what appears to be the world of opposites, particularly in his devotion to Yogi Ramsuratkumar, for this is an Enlightened Duality that arises from the realization of nonduality, asserted as Just This:

> So this is what we are called to?
> > Who are You? No one.
> What is there to Realize? Nothing.
> > Yes, how completely perfect and how totally Mad.
> Nothing to find except Nothing.
> > And no-one to become except no-one.
> And how to be given this Gift?
> > We need Your Grace to have Faith,
> to be Obedient, to await Surrender.
> > What to do about this catastrophe?
> Praise Yogi Ramsuratkumar and
> > delight in His most awesome Beauty,
> pranam at His universe-treading Feet,
> > bow our heads in gratitude
> for the mercy of His Blessings
> > and Praise Him again, all over in
> each and every moment.
> > This is lee lozowick, Father,
> Your true heart-son and wild Heretic,
> > open-handed and free

---

[3]   Ibid, December 1995.

of every attachment but You,
yet so attached to You that
this attachment is no attachment —
it is consuming, not separate, One,
all, total, time, space, Just This.
With each cell, in fact each atom,
of this being chanting Yogi Ramsuratkumar,
Faith, Devotion, Obedience, and Surrender Live.[4]

Lee as "bad Poet" speaks to his father, Yogi Ramsuratkumar, as the personal God, in intimate terms: he is playful, reverent and irreverent, brash, awed, submitted, boldly in love, ruthlessly clear, serious and sober, whimsical, sweet and tender, vulnerable and madcap, arrogant and foolish (as he says), wise and profound. As a body of work (well over a thousand poems published to date), we may discover in Lee's poetry to his master every rasa or mood of true feeling that is possible in relationship, for relationship is exactly what Enlightened Duality is all about. He is completely attached, completely nonattached. He is in perfect unity with his ista devata while he simultaneously begs for separation so that he may continue to worship and praise his Beloved.

When we approach the mystery of the Beloved by any name or in any form, we are entering the domain in which symbolic language becomes necessary. Because of this, the most potent and effective declarations of loving God (which may actually communicate the mood or transmit the state of loving God) are found in poetry: the poems of Rumi, Hafiz, Kabir, Ramprasad Sen, Mirabai and Andal, to name a few. Poetry is a fantastic medium from which the secrets of Enlightened Duality may speak to the heart in *sandhya bhasa*, or twilight language. When the poet's words become arrows of truth, when

---

[4]   Lee Lozowick, *Gasping for Air in a Vacuum*, 2 November 1999.

the poet becomes the true messenger of truth, beauty, and love, in the process he refines, articulates and embodies these exalted qualities in all forms. The poet is the harbinger of unity and diversity, of Assertion and of Reality as it is; of oneness and of love in longing, or *viraha*. The poet becomes the messenger of Grace.

APPENDIX III

Guruvada

The advent of the guru is a wonder of Creation. The guru is mother, father, sister, brother, child, lover, friend, master, slave and beloved. The guru is *nirguna* and *saguna*, unlimited and unbounded, unborn and undying, and within that circle of all that is, the guru is the very self of the devotee. Once we have received the guru's *darshan*, it is always true of us. Even if a moment of darshan fades into the background when the egoic mind reinstates its supremacy, it is imprinted at a cellular level, and the body both knows and remembers having seen. The doctrine of *guruvada*, or the necessity for—and complete reliance upon—the preceptor, is central to Baul sadhana.

> *The whole field of Indian philosophy and religion is characterized by a unanimous emphasis on the Guruvada, or the doctrine of the preceptor....All the systems of Indian philosophy and religion are mystic, for according to all the systems, truth always transcends intellectual apprehension or discursive speculation—it is to be intuited within, through the help of the preceptor, who has already realized it. Truth is transmitted from the preceptor to the disciple just as light from one lamp to the other. The only way of knowing the truth is, therefore, to seek the grace of the Guru....It is believed*

that the true preceptor in his nondual state identifies himself with the disciple and performs from within the disciple all that is necessary for the latter's spiritual uplift. The true disciple becomes an instrument in the hands of the true preceptor. It is for this reason that in Indian religions the Guru is held in the highest esteem. Sometimes the Guru is a substitute even for God, or at least God is to be realized through the medium of the person of the guru, who stands as the living proof for the existence of God. [1]

As in all tantric paths, Baul sadhana places the guru in a vital role; ultimately, very little is possible without the guru, and many of the esoteric practices of tantra are so powerful to the nervous system that, without wise guidance, they can cause severe burnout, spiritual emergencies, physical or nervous breakdown or psychosis. Therefore, the guru's help and guidance is critical at every juncture along the way. At some point we realize that we would be in deep trouble—lost and adrift on the tide, pulled hither and yon with no way to steer a course—without the intervention of the guru in our lives.

Therefore *sadhaka* and *sadhika* enjoy the nectar of devotional love, the many rasas of mood and cultivate radical reliance upon the guru as the divine mirror, the one who transmits Ultimate Reality, the guide and context of Life. The guru is the dispenser of Grace; the guru is the one who passes on the flame, the *jyoti*, or light, of awakened consciousness. For Bauls, the guru may also be the Man of the Heart, the *ista devata*, the doorway to the Beloved and the Beloved Himself or Herself. Because the guru has sacrificed his individuality in order to assume this function of giver of Grace, when the devotee or disciple realizes the magnitude of the guru's sacrifice, he or she is stricken with an exquisite obligation born of gratitude and love.

---

[1]   Das Gupta, *Obscure Religious Cults,* pages 87 and 88.

APPENDIX IV

Shunyata

The concept of *shunyata* is given a central place in Buddhist teachings and is therefore particularly well-developed in the *buddhadharma*. Shunyata refers to the void—emptiness—but various schools of Buddhism do not agree completely on the subtle inflections of its meaning, but let us begin with a very minimalist sketch of the three vehicles of Tibetan Buddhism.

A long-time disciple of Chögyam Trungpa Rinpoche and professor at Naropa Institute, Dr. Reginald Ray carefully and clearly lays out in *Secret of the Vajra World* the progression of the three *yanas* (vehicles) of Buddhism: Hinayana, Mahayana and Vajrayana. Each yana rests upon the foundation of those preceding it. The practitioner begins with Hinayana, in which he or she takes refuge in the Buddha, dharma and sangha, enters the Path and begins an arduous process of training in meditation, mindfulness, ethics and wisdom.[1] Generally speaking, the Hinayana practitioner has embraced the four noble truths of the Buddha and the eight-fold path; the goal of this practice is the liberation of the individual from maya, or illusion.

Dr. Ray states that after the first turning of the wheel, which elucidates the Hinayana teachings, the Buddha's teaching evolved further in his efforts to provide help to those who were attempting to follow

---

[1] Reginald Ray, *Secret of the Vajra World,* page 67.

his way, so at Vulture Peak Mountain he gave the crucial Mahayana teachings which are defined by the concepts of shunyata and buddha-nature. In Mahayana, called "the great vehicle," the practitioner moves beyond concern for his or her own liberation by taking the vow of the bodhisattva to liberate all sentient beings; the practice involves meditation but also engages the six *paramitas* or "transcendent actions"—selfless activities dedicated to cultivating *bodhichitta* (loving kindness), compassion and wisdom (*karuna* and *prajna*).[2]

The third vehicle of Buddhism, Vajrayana, is the tantric or fast path, in which the practitioner intends to attain enlightenment, liberation, *moksha* in one lifetime—namely, this current one. Vajrayana Buddhism, the tantric vehicle of Buddhism, with which Baul practice has the most resonance, rests upon the teachings or "views" provided by Hinayana and Mahayana. Therefore, Mahayana teachings on emptiness, or shunyata, inform every aspect of Vajrayana practice; even the deities visualized as *yidams* (*ista devatas*) in tantric ritual, as found in Vajrayana, are considered empty and beyond thought or qualities.[3]

Dr. Ray writes further of shunyata: "These teachings are understood to have been given in a second and third turning of the wheel of dharma emphasizing, respectively, the vacant and the present qualities of shunyata." [4, 5] It is wise to take note of the important

---

2   Ibid, page 67.

3   Ibid, page 92.

4   Ibid, pages 80 and 81.

5   When Buddhists refer to the turning of the wheel of the teaching, they are speaking of the *dharma-chakra*, which is the symbol used in Buddhism to represent the eight-fold path of the Buddha (the wheel has eight spokes), but it also refers to the three cycles of the Buddha's teachings. The doctrines that the Buddha taught in his first sermon at Sarnath centered on the four noble truths; this was the first turning of the wheel of dharma. The second turning of the wheel came with the doctrines of *prajnaparamita*, which focused on the teaching of shunyata or emptiness and prajna and comprised the Mahayana path. The third turning of the wheel delineated the Buddha's intention for his teachings. (John Powers, *A Concise Encyclopaedia of Buddhism*, pages 67 and 68.)

language used here: the *vacant* and the *present* qualities of shunya- ta. Of course, when one speaks of qualities at all, we really are not speaking of union with the Absolute, because in perfect union with the Absolute there are no qualities, indicating that shunyata is not a nondual state. The Vedas tell us that perfect union is *nirguna*— Brahman without attributes. If you are in union, then you are not there to speak of an experience of a dimension that is both vacant and present. But then, to apply Hindu philosophy to Buddhist phi- losophy is rather like comparing apples and oranges when it comes to theism and nontheism, even though these two great religions have a profound resonances in many ways.

Writing about the Heart Sutra, the formula of which is "Form is emptiness; emptiness is also form," Dr. Ray states:

> *The Heart Sutra is saying, in essence, "'What form real- ly is, is actually empty of whatever it is we may think of when we say "form." ' There is no substantial or defini- tive thing as "form" .... The text continues, "Emptiness is also form." This is to say that emptiness, the absence of objectifiability, is encountered within, in the very midst of our experience of what we think of as form.... It is saying, 'If you are looking for emptiness, this ulti- mate, where will you find it? You will find it nowhere else but only as form."*[6]

Beatrice Lane Suzuki wrote in her classic book, *Mahayana Buddhism*, that the void, or emptiness, is one of the most misunder- stood principles of Mahayana.

> *It is the most daring declaration to state that all particu- lar objects which we see about us, including ourselves, are*

---

[6]   Ibid, page 93.

void, of Void, from Void, with Void, and in Void. They stand in every possible prepositional relationship to Void. When Void is understood in the sense of emptiness and made to stand in contrast to fullness or substantiality the gravest fault is committed. Against this the Mahayanists had constantly to fight, because our ordinary way of thinking is to divide, to polarize, to set one thing or idea against another....It is for this reason extremely difficult to make Western readers realize what void means in its Buddhist sense, for they have never come across this way of seeing things in their history of thought. So let us repeat once more that Void is not to be confused with nothingness, contentlessness, mere negation of existence.[7]

Clearly any purely intellectual consideration of emptiness is ridiculous, since, as Suzuki goes on to explain, the void is so mysterious that it can only be apprehended intuitively by prajna, or transcendental wisdom (knowledge). Once prajna has been awakened within, she asserts, "you will know instantly what void is, and.... you will never be dispossessed of what you have taken hold."[8] Prajna is so far beyond the constructs of mind that we cannot think of shunyata in any terms that are familiar to us. Prajna is what Bauls call *bartaman*: the radical direct knowledge of Reality. According to Mahayana, there are two kinds of prajna: radical knowledge itself and knowledge in relationship to knowing. Suzuki continues:

In a similar manner, the Mahayana speaks of Suchness as having two aspects. It will be better to say that our intellect compels us to put this qualification on suchness or void. The first is unchangeable suchness or void

---

[7]   Beatrice Suzuki, *Mahayana Buddhism*, pages 44 and 45.

[8]   Ibid, page 45.

in itself, and the second is conditionable suchness or
no-Void.[9]

As already pointed out, the teachings on shunyata are very subtle in Mahayana Buddhism, and its exact nature is open to ongoing
debate. One source says there are up to *twenty kinds* of emptiness
recognized in Buddhism, including the emptiness of emptiness.[10]
Ultimately, the Buddhist view of shunyata is one of luminosity and
bliss. But it seems the point of departure between the Buddhist view
and the Baul view is that Buddhism tells us there is no *atman*, no
self, no *svabhaba* (own-being), no God, and no relationship between
individual being and God—whereas relationship with a personal
Beloved implies tacit beingness.

It is important to acknowledge this fundamental difference between
Mahayana and Vajrayana teachings and Baul perspectives because
religious scholars are convinced that the eclectic, open-minded and
free-spirited historic Bauls of Bengal, who embraced whatever they
found useful in other traditions, were closely linked historically with
not only Vaishnava Sahajiyas but also Buddhist Sahajiyas. Over the
centuries, Bauls freely shared ideas, spiritual practices, art, lifestyles
and even consorts or partners with both Sahajiya groups and with the
radical Sufis of their place and time. Contemporary Bauls continue
on in this spirit; it is not unusual for a Hindu Baul to be partnered
or playing music with a Sufi Baul (Aul). However, among the Bauls
of Bengal I have met and known, there has not been any evidence

---

9   Ibid, page 45.
10   John Bowker et al. *The Oxford Dictionary of World Religions.* page 929 and 930.

of overt Buddhist teaching and practice in a strict or concrete sense. On the contrary, Bauls are decidedly Hindu, with close ties to the Sufis, although clearly the universal truths of Buddhism, particularly Mahayana and Vajrayana, resonate well with the Baul way of life.

The Bauls are more typically aligned with Hindu Samkhya philosophy, which postulates a plural Reality in which there are countless spiritual *monads* (transcendental selves) having an existence within *purusha* and *prakriti*. According to this ontology: "On the one side are the countless mutable and unconscious forms of Nature (prakriti), and on the other side are the innumerable transcendental Selves (purusha), which are pure Consciousness, omnipresent and eternal."[11] The Bauls call their gurus *sunya*, an appellation that describes their fundamental emptiness and luminosity, indicating also that shunyata exists within the human being; likewise, Lee calls Yogi Ramsuratkumar a "Great Nothing" in one of his poems. The guru as *sunyam* has realized the nirguna dimension of the Absolute, while at the same time, the guru is adept in his or her inherence in *sahaja samadhi*, which automatically postulates the *saguna* dimension and a positive void that is rich and potentized.

In the actual living of all this, Bauls generally skip over all the postulating and wordplay and go straightaway to the direct experience of the miracle of existence as the grace and gift of the Supreme Being. Bauls are implicitly aware that there is a reciprocal ongoing process between Creator and Creation that may be consciously lived, while the void is an objective dimension of existence within the individual being. When we practice Assertion, or Just This, the void is included in that Assertion of what is, as it is.

---

[11]   Georg Feuerstein, *The Yoga Tradition*, page 101.

Hinduism is far too ancient, vast and complex to adequately represent in a few paragraphs. In fact, the term "Hinduism" is considered a misnomer, because it comes from a Persian word that means those who come from the Indus Valley.[12] Rather, Hinduism is an immense, honeycombed beehive of transcendental wisdom that takes form in myriad spiritual ways and means, cults, sects, schools, *sampradayas* (spiritual clans), *paramparas* (lineages) and so on and on. Chosen deities of all kinds abound because theism is alive and well in the great sects of Hinduism—Vaisnavas, Shaivaites, Shaktas, Nath Siddhas, Bauls, Sahajiyas, Pushti Marga, Gaudiya Vaishnavas and many others—which are the result of thousands of years of wisdom passed down from generation to generation. Most Indian Hindu practitioners of these great traditions are fluid and conversant in the languages of *advaita* and *dvaita*, bhakti and *jnana*, Vedic rites, all the great Indian spiritual literature and epics. All this and more is inherited knowledge that lives at a cellular level in those who are born in Mother Bharat.[13]

Emptiness or void is not foreign in any way to the Hindu tradition. The term shunyata originates from the Sanskrit word, sunyam, which means "nought" or zero and points toward Brahman without attributes. The fluid and profound Sanskrit language, in which the Vedas and the Upanishads were written, ties all this together. Most would agree that the ancient Vedas are at the foundation of this creative proliferation of transcendental wisdom. Hinduism is a holistic mandala that defies rational understanding, but when it comes to the transmission of radical, paradoxical experiences of the Divine, Hinduism is unsurpassed. The sanctity and transcendent power of the Sanskrit language alone gives Hinduism an enormous edge in terms of transmitting the truth through the written word in sacred texts of all kinds.

---

12 *The Oxford Dictionary of World Religions*, page 431.
13 An ancient name for the subcontinent of India.

A few thousand years after the *rishis* revealed the wisdom of the Vedas, the Upanishads came as enlightened commentaries on those ancient revelations. The Upanishads deals with concepts of advaita (nonduality, unity), *aditi* (unboundedness) and *amrita* (immortality), and which also clearly embrace the ideas of dvaita (duality), *dita* (the bound) and *mriti* (death). In the Upanishads we find the wisdom that Life contains both absolute and relative, and both aspects are inextricably linked; the Infinite contains within it the finite, and the finite contains within it the Infinite.[14]

The Vedas and Upanishads are the foundation upon which insights and revelations of later teachings and movements were built: tantra, Vedanta, Samkhya, Patanjali's *Yoga Sutras*, the much revered *Bhagavad Gita* and all the vast plethora of wisdom and traditional paths that make up what we call "Hinduism" today. There is a beautiful and profound knowledge of the holistic nature of all things that is found in the ancient teachings of Hinduism. There is a Sanskrit word that communicates a radical understanding of wholeness and completeness: *purna*. In the Upanishads, written in *sandhya bhasa*, we are given:

> *Om*
> *purnam adah*
> *purnam idam*
> *purnat purnam udacyate*
> *purnasya purnam adaya purnam evavashishyate*
>
> *Om. That is the whole. This is the whole. From wholeness emerges wholeness. Wholeness coming from wholeness, wholeness remains.*[15]

---

[14]   *The Upanishads*, translated by Shearer and Russell, page 8.

[15]   Ibid, page 10.

This understanding of wholeness or holism is so intact that devotees of Kali and Krishna—of many different tantric sects, including the Bauls—have a tacit understanding that their ista devata is a Cosmic Whole that is all-inclusive of both nirguna and saguna. Krishna and Kali are examples of those deities who are both ista devata, or personal Beloved, and Cosmic Absolutes. Both Krishna and Kali embody many wondrous, graceful and fierce attributes and also symbolize the void aspect of Reality, as seen in their dark color. In them we find love, compassion, mercy, grace, creation and destruction, ferocity—including a passionate propensity for demon-slaying and general warrior-like behavior—as well as salvation, beauty, splendor, mystery, eroticism, fertility and voidness. For the devotee of Kali or Krishna, all this is accepted as aspects of an integrated whole.

Carl Jung called this instinct for wholeness or completeness, found within the human being, the archetype of the self. From the Hindu point of view, the goal of life is to realize experientially Brahman, Purusha, Godhead or Self. Most Hindus find no problem whatsoever with the interplay between the relative and the Absolute and everything in between, including the concept of emptiness. They do not seem to linger upon this idea of sunya, for it is part of a comprehensive, all-embracing whole. Instead, it seems that the Hindu way is to symbolize the void in the imagery of their deities. For example, when a deity is depicted with black or dark blue skin, this is an indication of their ultimate cosmic nature: the void of deep space. Kali's black skin automatically communicates the void aspect of her attributes. The severed heads worn as a necklace around the goddess's lovely neck tells us that She will severe all attachments, identifications and illusions, leaving nothing but the Divine Mother Herself, who out of infinite love for Her creation will bestow the gift of true being as an aspect of Her own Self. Some goddesses are depicted as the night sky because the night sky shows us the truth of Reality: there is the blue black of vast space, within which the diamond fire of the stars—suns of wholeness—radiate their light.

Dark as night, Kali is shunyata, the terrifying nature of the void, the fecund emptiness that contains and gives rise to the brilliant, scintillating array of Creation. Beautiful and terrible beyond compare, ruler of time and space, she is beauty, grace and mercy; she is the compassionate Mother who will cut off the head of ego. Kali is the force of transformation within that moves the seed to burst with its own growing life, destroying the old form so that the new may emerge. She is the one who stands at the doorway of birth, who receives her child in her arms again at death—"the mother and child reunion," as Paul Simon wrote.

> *At the heart of this phenomenal world,*
> *within all its changing forms,*
> *dwells the unchanging Lord.*

> *He who sees everything as nothing but the Self,*
> *and the Self in everything he sees,*
> *Such a seer withdraws from nothing.*
> *For the enlightened, all that exists is nothing but the Self,*
> *So how could any suffering or delusion continue*
> *for those who know this Oneness?*

> *He who pervades all is radiant,*
> *unbounded and untainted,*
> *invulnerable and pure.*
> *He is the knower, the one Mind,*
> *omnipresent and self-sufficient.*
> *He has harmonized diversity throughout eternal time.*

In these lines from the Isha Upanishad we are given very early teachings on the essence of what would later be termed "tantra," which could be reiterated in this way: There is only God. When we realize that the manifest world holistically contains the all-pervasive, all-inclusive Supreme Reality, we would be wise not to reject or discriminate against any aspects of life. We do not need to live in a cave to realize this Supreme Reality, or practice extremes of asceticism, deny pleasure and enjoyment of all that is so generously given in this realm of the relative. If we keep our eyes upon the Lord, then all experiences, when they are accepted fully and with faith, lead to the discovery that there is no separation and no conflict between diversity and eternity—and we will come to know the inner harmony of that realization.

All-inclusive means exactly that: The Supreme Reality also contains the void. In the same way, the void is part of this as a realm of natural experience. Perhaps we could also say, then, that the void is part of Creation, because if it was not, we would not be able to apprehend it—to touch it and live to share our experience, because we would have disappeared into union, Oneness, Allness.

APPENDIX V

Madanagopala

The Red Krishna

Description of the Cover Art
by Nara Allsop

The form of Krishna known as Madanagopala is to be found in the sculptural programme of several Vaishnava temples of the Vijayayanagara era (fourteenth to eighteenth century) in southern India and, in particular, Tamil Nadu.

Madana is sweet enchantment, the seducer of the mind, and Gopala is the youthful herder of cows. In this form, Krishna has absorbed and subsumed the qualities of the god of love and sexual passion, Manmatha or Kama. The heats of lust and infatuation have been transformed into the rich *rasa* of transcendental love. Madanagopala sweetly sings and plays His flute, calling all to approach this exalted disposition—entering His world of luscious, enlightened duality where manifest form is the scintillating vibration of His eternal love play.

Madanagopala may be ten- or eight-armed and is depicted standing or seated upon a hexagon. As well as His flute, He carries various implements. Starting at the deity's top right is the solar discus or chakra, the elephant goad/hook (*ankusa*) and then the flower arrow. From the top left, he holds the sacred conch (*sankha*), the three corded noose (*pasa*), and the sugarcane bow (*ikshukodanda*). The flower bow and arrow are both implements normally carried by Kama and his consort Rati, the goddess of pleasurable sensual enjoyment. Here, however, they are depicted as devotees of the Lord and they offer a garland of wild flowers from all seasons (*vanamala*). The single arrow held by Madanagopala is representative of Kama's five powerful arrows of desire, each arrow representing a unique aspect of passion: excitement (*unmadana*), heat (*tapana*), drying up (*sosana*), paralyzing of normal bodily functions (*stambhana*) and full infatuation (*sammohana*).

The god of sensual love, Kama, is known by various epithets—Manmatha, Kandarpa, Madana, and Mara. Here He is shown on Krishna's right. He holds aloft his standard—the makara banner from which Kama gets the additional name of Makaradhvaja, meaning that his flag is marked with the makara. It is symbolic of potent creation and fertility. Kama's skin colour (*nupura*) is red, though variant forms are green or golden yellow. His father is Dharma Prajapati. The most famous mythological episode involving Kama is his having been burnt to ashes by Siva, whose meditation Kama had sought to disturb. Kama went on to be reborn as Krishna's son, Pradyumna. He has two consorts, Priti (delight) and Rati (pleasure).

Rati is depicted on Madanagopala's left. She is the daughter of Daksa Prajapati and her presence is likened to the youthful unfoldment of Vasant (spring) and with it, the longing in all nature for procreation. She is exceedingly attractive and well versed in seductive arts. Her hair is piled up into an elaborate ornamental knot (*kesabandha*), secured with a golden band decorated with fresh spring leaves and flowers. These impressive south Indian coiffures are to be seen on the figures of queens, princesses and high-ranking temple patrons.

As a pair, Kama and Rati are carved on pillars leading to the garbha griha. Their animal vehicles (*vahanas*), the goose, swan or parrot, are interchangeable. Lovely forms can be seen in the seventeenth century marriage hall (*kalyana mandapa*) in Kanchipuram's Varadaraja temple. Outstanding even in the superlative world of Vijayanagara sculptural art are the splendid examples in Sri Villiputtar's Andal temple complex. Here Rati sits astride a goose, admiring her own reflection in a mirror held aloft in her left hand, while the right holds a kohl stick.

Seated in the center at the bottom of the painting is Vishnu's chief vahana, Garuda. He is shown as per his description in the *Vishnu-dharmottara*, with a body the color of an emerald, fierce bulging eyes and an eagle beak. There are many variant forms of Garuda—in North India one does not tend to see Garuda associated with Krishna, however, in the south, it is more frequent. In Vaishnava temples, Garuda is installed in a small shrine facing the *garba griha* (home of the main deity), or on a high pillar within the temple compound, or just outside the main entrance, as in Puri's celebrated Jagganath temple.

Forming a canopy over Madanagopala's head is the lush foliage of a Kalpakataru or wish-fulfilling tree. The tree boasts many types of flowers and fruits and is perpetually in bloom. It is a feature of the god's celestial realms. Nestled within its foliage are several *kili* (parrots) and a *mayil* (peacock). Krishna cherishes both types of bird and is said to have several as pets. Midway to Madanagopala's right is his favorite tree, the *kadamba*. It bears small, globular orange/yellow flowers with a beautiful perfume. In season, the flowers are much favoured for use as garlands. Growing at the Lord's feet are a profusion of flowering sacred *tulasi*, a plant considered an incarnated goddess. Tulasi leaves are used as offerings to all Vaishnava deities and its wood is favoured for use in malas for mantra sadhana.

The two brown decorative panels at the sides of the arch display *kinnaras*. The term kinnara translates as something like 'what are these?' as they are a bizarre and beautiful composite of various creatures, animal, human and divine. They are usually shown playing musical instruments—especially, the *veena*. Kinnaras have intoxicating siren-like voices, but are auspicious in nature and loving by disposition. They are often carved in light relief on temple pillars.

Lastly, within the orange border are two decorated friezes of the Vaishnava sectarian marking or Namam. The Namam is worn on the forehead and is typically of two forms (of course, there are variants). The form depicted on the upper strip is the Vadagalai which is U-shaped. The one on the lower strip is the Tengalai which is Y or V shaped. The central stripe between the U or V is known as the Tiruchurnam and is traditionally made of a lime and saffron mix or red ocher. The meaning of the Tiruchurnam is the same as that of the bindu: the wholeness of divinity and the point of utmost potency from which all manifests. The wearing of the Namam is a highly important preparation for all kinds of ritual action or worship within the Vaishnava fold and is considered to be sanctifying for both the wearer and observer.

Nara Allsop
January, 2009

Glossary

SANSKRIT

Advaita: Nonduality. The state in which all distinctions of object and subject, perceiver and perceived are experienced as illusions due to ignorance (*avidya*).

Amavasya: The new moon.

Ananda: Bliss.

Anandalahari: A handmade, one-stringed instrument played by the Bauls of Bengal.

Anuman: Secondhand knowledge, gleaned through scripture, ritual, or the rules of behavior, prescribed injunctions of orthodox religion. Bauls call this "gossip" and "hearsay."

Aropa: The principle of the inherence of the divine within the human being; the tacit attribute of divinity within the individual.

Bartaman: Direct, personal experience of Reality as it is or any aspect of Reality. Direct apprehension and experience of the Divine.

Baul: From the Sanskrit word *vatula*, meaning "wind" or "mad."

Bauls: A five-hundred-year old loosely affiliated group of wandering minstrels of Bengal; tantrikas who engage a sadhana of yoga of breath and sex to discover the "man of the heart" and realize the relationship with the personal deity, usually symbolized by Krishna. Their way of life, cosmic view and teachings are encoded in their song and dance; performing music and dance and begging is a sacred way of life for the Bauls.

Baul-gan: Singing of traditional Baul songs.

Bhava: A strong divine mood.

Darshan: True seeing; receiving the sight of the guru.

Dharma: Cosmic order and law that informs all levels of existence with alignment to Divine Will. *Sanatana dharma* is the principle concern of Hindu teachings and is defined as eternal law.

Drala: From the Shambhala teachings of Chögyam Trungpa Rinpoche, the dralas are the living patterns of energy—the primordial wisdom of this world, or of Nature—having the capacity to inform human awareness and to actually serve as a bridge between the concrete and abstract worlds. The drala principle is known in all traditions, often as gods and goddesses, nature spirits, fairies, elemental energies etc.

Dvaita: The Hindu philosophy which posits that distinctions have a reality of their own, and that the subject-object relationship of "I—Thou" between a worshipper and God persists even after final union or merging in the state of unity.

Gita: Song.

Gunas: The three cosmic forces that inform all processes of evolutionary life or manifestation at all levels, as expounded in Samkhya philosophy. The *gunas* of Samkhya philosophy are: *Sattvas*, or equilibrium and harmony; *Rajas*, or passion and activity; and *Tamas*, or inertia. See also Samkhya.

Kundalini: Also Kundalini Shakti. The primal creative life force called the "serpent power" that sleeps at the base of the spine until awakened to ascend through subtle psychic channels to the top of the head, awakening and empowering the system of the seven chakras along the way.

Maha: Great.

Manipura: The jewel city, referring to the third chakra or psychic center, located at the navel in the body.

Mantra: A sacred phrase or name of God repeated as a practice, or focus of attention, to invoke the presence of the Divine.

Manur manush: A Bengali Baul term which is translated as "the Man of the Heart," referring to the realization of the unitive, nondual self as doorway to the Beloved.

Mudra: Sacred gesture. Gesture, posture or position of body or hands that invoke primordial truth.

Nama: Name—often used to refer to the Name of God.

Nirguna: Without attributes or qualities; nondual.

Parampara: Spiritual lineage.

Purnima: The day of the full moon. From the Sanskrit word *purna*, meaning complete or full.

Rasa: Juice, taste, flavor; mood.

Rasayana: The path of alchemy in tantric sadhana.

Rupa: Form.

Sadhana: Spiritual discipline; work on self.

Sadhaka: Spiritual practitioner, especially of the tantric path; *sadhika* (fem.).

Sadhu: One who has renounced worldly life in every way and has taken vows to pursue spiritual aims solely.

Saguna: With attributes or the qualities of the three *gunas*: for example, the Divine experienced with the qualities of mercy, love, wrath or ferocity.

Sahaj: Inborn, the natural condition. Natural, innate, easy.

Sahajiya: One who follows the sahaj path, usually going against orthodox religious injunctions, caste restrictions and Vedic rules in favor of a direct, personal experience of the Divine, usually through the auspices of Grace.

Sahaj manush: (The "natural man.") A tenet of Baul sadhana referring to the human being who is spontaneously within the realization of Reality as it is.

Sahaj samadhi: Open-eyed ecstasy in union with the Divine, while fully aware and functional within the perspective of Enlightened Duality. *Sahaj samadhi* is that state of unitive consciousness or oneness with the Divine that is sometimes called "open-eyed ecstasy," in which the individual person remains fully functional in an easy and natural way. Lee Lozowick once said of *sahaj samadhi*: "There is nirvakalpa samadhi [in which one experiences the ecstasy of union but is absorbed in bliss], but the more mature form of samadhi is sahaja samadhi—'what is, is.' The ultimate fruit of devotion is sahaja samadhi, so that we are in communion with the Divine to such a degree that our being is permeated, and we don't have to be anything other than what we are." HSM Study Manual IV, page 374.

Sahaja: Natural, easy, innate.

Samkhya: One of the six classical schools of Hindu philosophy, founded by Kapila in the sixth century BCE, which assumes a dualistic system of *purusha* (spirit) and *prakriti* (matter or Nature), which have opposite yet complementary characteristics and are the origination of the universe. In Samkhya, *purusha* is originally manifold while *prakriti* is one. *Purusha* exists as countless spiritual monads or selves that will seek evolution through *prakriti*. Matter is characterized by the three *gunas*: sattva (harmony, lightness), *rajas* (passion) and *tamas* (darkness, inertia) which are originally in equilibrium, but as evolution begins under the influence of spirit, an interplay of these three forces moves the evolutionary process. In the ultimate stage of evolution, the spirit or monad has realized *kaivalya*, or aloneness, and in this is fully satisfied.

Sampradaya: The spiritual clan or school that practices according to the preceptor or visionary guru.

Sarvatmabhava: The absorption in "total love" for Lord Krishna, according to the Bhagavata Purana and Vallabhacharya's commentaries on the Love Games of Lord Krishna.

Satsang: The gathering of disciples or devotees for communal worship or consideration of dharma.

Shaktipata: Literally, "descent of power," referring to the process of tantric initiation.

Shunyata: Emptiness; the void.

Soma: A name of the moon in Hindu mythology; also a fermented plant liquid described in the Vedas and used in sacrificial rites. The word soma is often used now to imply a nectar that is intoxicating in the spiritual sense.

Sunya: Zero; empty; void.

Svarupa: The divine form which exists a priori for every created aspect of manifestation.

Triveni: Mythical place where the three divine rivers converge: The Ganges, Yamuna and Saraswati, as a metaphor for the meeting place of the three psychic channels, *ida* (lunar), *pingala* (solar), and *sushumna*, in the human body (the head).

Vigraha: A divine image that has been spiritual empowered.

Viraha: Love in separation, which produces a particular bittersweet rasa or mood due to the state of longing.

ENGLISH

Assertion: The tacit, conscious affirmation of Reality as it is in the moment; what is here and now, inclusive of nonduality and Enlightened Duality. The phrase that characterizes Assertion is: Just This.

Beggary: The expression of Spiritual Slavery which is demonstrated in a relationship of simplicity, receptivity and gratitude to Life or Grace, in which accepting whatever Life has to give is the guiding principle of daily activity. Beggary assumes the exact conservation and care of resources in every domain; money, sex and food, literally and symbolically speaking.

Divine Alchemy: The process of radical spiritual transformation which occurs within the body, is inclusive of all levels of being, and is catalyzed by the guru's transmission of Reality or Grace.

Enlightened Duality: The perception of Reality as it is.

Enquiry: Use of the phrase "Who am I kidding" to penetrate the veils of illusion, or the fundamental illusion of separation, in which we operate as beings that are separate from the Divine, until through that Enquiry the practitioner penetrates the knot of separation to see Reality as it is.

Heart Breath: One of the three core practices of the Hohm Sahaj Mandir; instruction is received by oral transmission.

Organic Innocence: The underlying ground of being of all Creation; the unconditioned, pure, basic ground of all manifestation, both gross and subtle. The human body is both the access point to and exists as Organic Innocence, therefore an important subsidiary understanding of Organic Innocence is embodied in the teaching, "The body knows." Organic Innocence, similar to "basic goodness" as taught by Chögyam Trungpa Rinpoche, is the unconditioned ground out of which arises the possibility that we may act in a way that is aligned with the highest good for all.

Primacy of Natural Ecstasy: The mood or *rasa* of existence, Creation, or Organic Innocence.

Bibliography

Ambalal, Amit. *Krishna as Shrinathji: Rajasthani Paintings from Nathdvara*. New York: Mapin International Inc., 1987.

Armstrong, Jeffrey. "Difference is Real." *Hinduism Today*, June, July, August, Summer 2008, 39–53.

Baul, Parvathy. *Song of the Great Soul*. Kerala, South India: Ekatara Baul Sangeetha Kalari, 2005.

"Blind Devotion." Lyrics by Lee Lozowick, composed by Ed Flaherty, recorded by Shri on *Good Thing*.

Bowker, John, editor. *The Oxford Dictionary of World Religions*. New York: Oxford University Press, 1997.

Castaneda, Carlos. *The Teachings of Don Juan: A Yaqui Way of Knowledge*. Berkeley and Los Angeles: University of California Press, 1969.

"Course of Action." Lyrics by Lee Lozowick, composed by Ed Flaherty, recorded by Shri on *Shrison in Hell*.

Das Gupta, Ph.D., Shashibhusan. *Obscure Religious Cults*. Calcutta, India: Firma K.L. Mukhopadhyay Publishers, 1969.

Ma Devaki. *Saranagatham*. Yogi Ramsuratkumar Trust, Tiruvannamalai, Tamil Nadu, January, 2009.

EnlightenNext. "Spore—Playing God with Evolution." December 2008, 24.

Feuerstein, Georg. *The Yoga Tradition*. Prescott, AZ: Hohm Press, 2001.

Gurdjieff, G.I. *Life is only real then, when "I am."* Great Britain: Routledge & Kegan Paul, 1981.

Hayward, Jeremy. *Warrior-King of Shambhala*. Boston: Wisdom Publications, 2008.

Hixon, Lex. *Great Swan: Meetings with Ramakrishna*. Boston: Shambhala, 1992.

Los Angeles Times, November 16, 2008.

Lozowick, Lee. *Death of a Dishonest Man: Poems and Prayers to Yogi Ramsuratkumar*. Prescott, AZ: Hohm Press, 1998.

———. *Feast or Famine—Teachings on Mind and Emotions*. Prescott, AZ: Hohm Press, 2008.

———. *Gasping for Air in a Vacuum: Poems and Prayers to Yogi Ramsuratkumar*. Prescott, AZ: Hohm Press, 2004.

———. *Laughter of the Stones*. Prescott Valley, AZ: Hohm Press, 1979.

———. *Living God Blues*. Prescott Valley, AZ, 1984.

———. *The Only Grace is Loving God*. Prescott Valley, AZ: Hohm Press, 1982.

———. *Spiritual Slavery*. Mt. Tabor, NJ: Hohm Press, 1975.

Majumdar, A.K. *Bhakti Renaissance*. Bombay: Bharatiya Vidya Bhavan, 1965.

McDaniel, June. *The Madness of the Saints: Ecstatic Religion in Bengal*. Chicago: University of Chicago Press, 1989.

Powers, John. *A Concise Encyclopaedia of Buddhism*. Boston: Oneworld Publications, 2000.

Pressfield, Steven. *The War of Art*. New York: Grand Central Publishing, 2003.

Sri Ramananda. *Tripura Rahasya: The Secret of the Supreme Goddess.* Translated by Swami Sri Ramananda Saraswathi. Bloomington, IN: World Wisdom, 2003.

Rajneesh, Bhagwan Shri. *The Beloved, Volume I.* pages 282 and 285.

Ramdas, Swami. *The Divine Life.* Kanhangad, India: Ramnagar, Anandashram, 1945.

———. *Thus Speaks Ramdas,* Kanhangad, India: Anandashram, 4th edition, 1969.

———. *The Essential Ramdas,* Delhi: World Wisdom, 2005.

Ray, Reginald. *Secret of the Vajra World,* Boston: Shambhala, 2002.

Rigopoulos, Antonio. *Dattatreya: The Immortal Guru, Yogin and Avatara,* New York: State University of New York Press, 1998.

Robbins, Tom. *Fierce Invalids Home From Hot Climates,* New York: Bantam Dell, 2001.

———. *Wild Ducks Flying Backward: The Short Writing of Tom Robbins,* New York: Bantam Dell, 2005.

Rosen, Steven J. (Satyaraja Dasa). "The Meaning of Gaudiya Vaishnavism." *Namarupa,* Volume 5, November 2008.

Satchidananda, Swami. *The Gospel of Swami Papa Ramdas,* Kerala, India: Anandashram, 1990.

Suzuki, Beatrice. *Mahayana Buddhism,* New York: The MacMillan Company, 1972.

Svoboda, Robert. "Robert Beer Interview." *Namarupa.* Volume 03, September 2008, 5.

———. "Tantric Prospectives." *Namarupa.* Volume 01, July 2008, 6.

"Take Me Away." Lozowick and Durham, *Tongue of Poison, Soul of Love,* 2008.

"To Me." Lyrics by Lee Lozowick, composed by Denise Allen-Incao and Everett Jaime, recorded by Denise Allen on *Not Just Another Diva.*

Tyborg, Judith. *The Language of the Gods*, Los Angeles, CA: East-West Cultural Center, 1976.

The Upanishads. Translated by Shearer and Russell. London: Mandala/Univin, 1989.

Books by Lee Lozowick

Spiritual Slavery (1975)

Beyond Release (1975)

Laughter of the Stones (1977)

In the Fire (1978)

The Cheating Buddha (1980)

Acting God (1980)

The Book of Unenlightenment/The Yoga of Enlightenment (1980)

The Only Grace is Loving God (1982)

Living God Blues (1984)

Poems of a Broken Heart (1993)

Derisive Laughter (1993)

Poems of a Broken Heart, Part II (1995)

The Alchemy of Love and Sex (1996)

The Alchemy of Transformation (1996)

Conscious Parenting (1997)

Death of a Dishonest Man: Poems and Prayers to Yogi Ramsuratkumar (1998)

Gasping for Air in a Vacuum: Poems and Prayers to Yogi Ramsuratkumar (2004)

108 Poèmes et Prières à Yogi Ramsuratkumar (In French and English, 2005)

Getting Real (2007)

Feast or Famine: Teachings on Mind and Emotion (2008)

JOURNALS

The Eccentricities, Idiosyncrasies and Sacred Utterances Of A Western Baul (1993)

In The Style Of The Eccentricities, Idiosyncrasies, And Sacred Utterances Of A Western Baul (1993)

In The Mood Of "In The Style Of The Eccentricities, Idiosyncrasies, and Sacred Utterances Of A Western Baul" (1994)

Cranky Rants and Bitter Wisdom from One Considered Wise in Some Quarters (2002)

The Little Book of Lies and Other Myths (2006)

A Small Collection of Feuilletons by One of the Rasnochintsy (2008)

"A Tale Told by an Idiot, Full of Sound And Fury, Signifying…" Something Far Too Important To Be Disregarded (In Spite of Shameful Syntax, Misspellings and Sentences Almost As Long as the Mississippi River) (2009)

AVAILABLE ONLY IN FRENCH

Oui, et Alors? (La Table Ronde, 2001)

L'Alchimie du Réel (Les Editions du Relié, 1993, out of print)

108 Poèmes et Prières à Yogi Ramsuratkumar (In French and English, 2005)

Courage D-eduquer (Editions du Relié, 2005, out of print)

Conseil D'un Ami Spirituel (A.L.T.E.S.S., 1998)

Eloge de la Folle Sagesse (Editions du Relié, 2003)

Nessayez Pas Vivez (La Table Ronde, 1999)

Le Petit Livre Des Ados (A.L.T.E.S.S., 1997)

Le Petit Livre Des Amante (A.L.T.E.S.S., 1997)

Le Petit Livre Dos Femmes I (A.L.T.E.S.S., 1996)

Le Petit Livre Dos Femmes II (A.L.T.E.S.S., 1997)

Le Petit Livre Dos Hommes (A.L.T.E.S.S., 1997)

L'Alchimie de L'Amour et de La Sexualité (Editions du Relié, Poche, 2006)

Books by M. Young

As It Is—A Year on the Road with a Tantric Teacher (2000)

Yogi Ramsuratkumar—Under the Punnai Tree (2003)

Agony & Alchemy: Sacred Art and Tattoos (2005)

Caught in the Beloved's Petticoats (2006)

Other Books About Yogi Ramsuratkumar

Only God: A Biography of Yogi Ramsuratkumar (2004), by Regina Sara Ryan.

A Man and His Master (2003), by Mani and S. Lhaksam.

Father & Son (2009), by Vijaya Fedorshak.